Imagining Internationalism in American and British Labor, 1939–49

THE WORKING CLASS IN AMERICAN HISTORY

A list of books in the series appears at the end of this book.

Imagining Internationalism

IN AMERICAN AND BRITISH LABOR, 1939–49

Victor Silverman

University of Illinois Press
Urbana and Chicago

Manufactured in the United States of America

This book is printed on acid-free paper.

Library of Congress Cataloging-in-Publication Data
Silverman, Victor, 1957–
Imagining internationalism in American and British labor, 1939–49 / Victor Silverman.
p. cm. — (The working class in American history)
Includes bibliographical references and index.
ISBN 0-252-02490-7 (acid-free paper)
ISBN 0-252-06805-X (pbk. : acid-free paper)
1. Trade-unions—Great Britain—Political activity—History.
2. Trade-unions—United States—Political activity—History.
3. Trade-unions and communism—Great Britain—History.
4. Trade-unions and communism—United States—History.
5. International labor activities—History. I. Title. II. Series.
HD6667.S56 2000
322'.2'0941—dc21 98-58097
CIP

1 2 3 4 5 C P 5 4 3 2 1

To Lorraine

Contents

Abbreviations ix

Preface xi

Acknowlegments xiii

Introduction: The Transformation of Labor Internationalism 1

PART 1: Ideas and Realities in the International Labor Community 17

1. Communists, Socialists, and Liberals in International Labor 21
2. Chinese Sailors, Exile Unions, and the Limits of Practical Internationalism 36

PART 2: The British 47

3. "Castles of Dreams": British Workers and the World 49
4. "What We Want We Shan't Get": The Decline of Internationalism 66
5. "Hoodwinking Ourselves": British Unions and the Politics of Internationalism 85
6. "A Grave and Conscious Moral Force": The TUC and the End of Alliance 100

PART 3: The Americans 115

7. "A House Divided against Itself": American Workers and the World 117
8. Americanism and Internationalism 127

9. "A Positively Mystical Vision": The CIO and the Politics of Internationalism 144

10. "Neither Stalin nor Standard Oil": The Search for a CIO Identity 165

Conclusion: Cynicism and Universalism—The World the Workers Lost 183

Appendix 195

Notes 201

Bibliography 265

Index 285

Abbreviations

ACTU	Association of Catholic Trade Unionists (USA)
AFL	American Federation of Labor (U.S.)
ALCIA	American Labor Conference on International Affairs
ASC	Anglo-Soviet Trade Union Committee
ASW	Amalgamated Society of Woodworkers, TUC
AUCCTU	All-Union Central Council of Soviet Trade Unions
BDDFP	Belgian, Danish, Dutch, French, Polish Seafarers Federation
CIO	Congress of Industrial Organizations (U.S.)
CGT	Confédération Générale du Travail (France)
CGT-FO	Confédération Générale du Travail–Force Ouvrière (France)
CGTU	Confédération Générale du Travail Unitaire (France)
Comintern	Communist International
CSF	Centre Syndical Français en Grande Bretagne
CSU	Chinese Seamen's Union (Hong Kong and Great Britain)
CTAL	Confederación de Trabajadores de América Latina
CTM	Confederación de Trabajadores de México
ECOSOC	Economic and Social Council (UN)
EITUC	Emergency International Trade Union Council
ERP-TUAC	European Recovery Program [Marshall Plan]–Trade Union Advisory Committee
HMG	His Majesty's Government

ICFTU	International Confederation of Free Trade Unions
IFTU	International Federation of Trade Unions
ILH	Division of International Labor, Social, and Health Affairs (U.S. Department of State)
ILGWU	International Ladies' Garment Workers' Union—AFL
IMMOA	International Mercantile Marine Officers' Association
ITS	International Trade Secretariats
ITF	International Transport Workers' Federation
MCS	Marine Cooks and Stewards Union—CIO
NMU	National Maritime Union—CIO
NLRA	National Labor Relations Act
NLRB	National Labor Relations Board
NUPE	National Union of Public Employees, TUC
NUTGW	National Union of Tailoring and Garment Workers, TUC
NUGMW	National Union of General and Municipal Workers, TUC
NUS	National Union of Seamen, TUC
OSS	Office of Strategic Services (U.S.)
RILU	Red International of Labor Unions, Profintern
SWOC	Steel Workers Organizing Committee—CIO
TGWU	Transport and General Workers' Union, TUC
TUC	Trades Union Congress (U.K.)
TWU	Transport Workers' Union of America—CIO
UAW	United Automobile Workers of America—CIO
UE	United Electrical, Radio, and Machine Workers of America—CIO
UGS	Union of Greek Seamen in Great Britain
UGT	Unión General de Trabajadores de España (exile Spanish union)
UMW	United Mine Workers (U.S.)
UN	United Nations
USWA	United Steel Workers of America—CIO
WFTU	World Federation of Trade Unions
WTUC	World Trade Union Conference

Preface

This project, like so many other histories, is as much an effort at autobiography as it is a dispassionate intellectual exercise. Originally, I came to study international labor in midcentury because I sought to understand the roots of anticommunism in the American labor movement. The crisis of American labor in the late forties and early fifties and the destruction of American communism had touched my family and my family's close friends deeply. Many were Communist union activists, and I grew up almost instinctively hating such nefarious figures as Walter Reuther, James Carey, and Joe Curran.

As I traced the tangled and ugly history of factionalism in the union movement (an ugliness for which the objects of my childhood hatred were not solely responsible), I realized that domestic politics could not be easily separated from those of other countries. In the process of uncovering the international component of the destruction of the American Communist Party, I also discovered, to my surprise, that the Communists' erstwhile enemies shared many of their opponents' ideas about the world. The expansive nature of the broad American left in the thirties and forties shocked me, for the received knowledge—both personal and academic—had suggested that the divisions between Communists and other leftists were deep and ideologically profound. The impact of the cold war and the bitter factional fights of the late forties had almost completely obscured the points of consensus that had actually bound the left together for nearly two decades. Both Communists and liberals had sought in the later years to emphasize points of conflict and sources of division.

As a scholar working in the late 1980s and 1990s, I found my work still touched by emotions of forty or so years earlier. This was brought home to me after a friend read a chapter in draft form and commented that in his family (he is the son of a lifelong Socialist), Walter Reuther was practically a saint and the Socialists the only real left—an assertion unimaginable in my neighborhood. It struck me then how much I was fighting my parents' fights. More important for my analysis of the history of world labor, I realized the need to reexamine and revise my own conceptions of what the left was and of what it meant to be a trade unionist in the twentieth century.

As I worked out this revision, a similar problem became apparent: the nature of idealism. Another friend, a diplomatic historian, questioned my chapter titles, maintaining that my emphasis on the idealism and visionary side of labor internationalism undercut my argument that such internationalism was a practical and realistic goal articulated by hard-nosed political types. I had indeed set out to demonstrate that the idea of uniting workers across national boundaries in order to change radically the basis of the international order was, in the context of the midforties, quite reasonable (if ill fated). Yet I found that the division between realists and idealists, between the hard-nosed and the soft, existed only in the minds of people trying to figure out why the hopes they had once held were so soundly dashed. In the midforties it was quite realistic to be idealistic. In fact, the division was entirely arbitrary, imposed as result of debates of international relations theorists. Like my assumptions about the fundamental nature of the conflict between Communists and non-Communists, my acceptance of the division between realism and idealism was a legacy of the era I studied.

These two small discoveries underscore the intellectual benefits to be gained from reconsidering the 1940s with the hypothesis that the cold war was not an inevitable event. This work was, of course, influenced by the collapse of the Soviet Union and the end of the cold war, which demonstrated that many of the most basic intellectual categories accepted by Communists and anti-Communists alike were actually assumptions informed by the painful experiences of the cold war. The vast changes in world politics in the last fifteen years have deeply affected the way people consider their past, allowing us to grasp many things that once seemed incomprehensible or stupid. This book is, in many ways, a product of its times.

Acknowledgments

This project has been long in coming. It would have taken far longer if not for the help of many people and organizations. Grants from Pomona College, the Fulbright Commission, the University of California at Berkeley, the Benjoya-Minor Fund, and the Kaiser Foundation made the research and writing of this book easier, if not very lucrative. Several unions kindly granted me permission to use their archives: the Transport and General Workers' Union, the Amalgamated Clothing and Textile Workers Union, and the Trades Union Congress.

A great many archivists and librarians were a help to me, but some went out of their way to be of assistance: Richard Storey and Alistair Tough of the Modern Records Centre, University of Warwick, Coventry, U.K.; Richard Boyden and Tab Lewis of the National Archives and Records Service, Washington, D.C.; Ilona Einowski of the California State Data Library; Dorothy Sheridan of the Mass-Observation Archive, University of Sussex, Brighton, U.K.; Rosemary Stones of the Trades Union Congress Registry, London; Pat Clark of the U.S. Department of Labor, Washington, D.C.; and Lawrence Holly of the National Storage Center, Suitland, Md.

My biggest intellectual debt is certainly to the people who supervised the dissertation that led to this book: Diane Shaver Clemens, Thomas Laqueur, Michael Rogin, and David Brody. Diane Clemens, especially, was more than an adviser; she became a good friend.

Many other people helped me with close readings, helpful suggestions, or good drinks. In Britain: Arthur Marsh, Victoria Ryan, Tony Lane, Ken Lunn, Nick Tiratsoo, Alan Ware, Jim Obelkevich, Tony Mason, Anthony Adamthwaite, Anthony Carew, Richard Hyman, James Hinton, Rachel Peckham, Hannah Peckham, Pam Payne. In the United States: Alan Lawrence, Ronnie Lipshutz, Dave Fogelsong, Dave McFadden, Robby Cohen, Steve Leikin, Pink Cloud,

Susan Stryker, Nancy Quam-Wickham, Jeff Quam-Wickham, Larry Glickman, Betty Desants, Peter Hoffenberg, Jim Gregory, Randy Baker, Richard Allen, John Windmuller, Russ Moses, Michael Micklin, Maura O'Connor, Laura Tabili, Hans Rindisbacher, Nelson Lichtenstein, and Laurie Glover. The staff of the University of Illinois Press, especially Richard L. Wentworth and Theresa L. Sears, my copy editor, Polly Kummel, and my indexer, Ty Koontz, skillfully shepherded this book to publication.

My family put up nobly with this project. I could not have done it without them.

Imagining Internationalism in American and British Labor, 1939–49

Introduction: The Transformation of Labor Internationalism

Out of the enormous horrors of World War II came a hope for the creation of a peaceful and just world order. For a short time in the mid-1940s this dream seemed on the verge of realization as the nations of the earth, after vanquishing the threat of fascism, attempted to create new structures of international relations. The World Federation of Trade Unions (hereafter WFTU, or World Federation), which united unionists of almost all political loyalties from around the globe, figured prominently in this attempt. The feeling that the world was about to embark on a new era unlike any other was quite powerful. Yet below this hope lay the discordant fear that the international unity forged in the struggle against the Axis might be transitory, that the world would still be subject to the same forces that gave rise to the war in the first place. With high hopes and unvoiced misgivings people around the world joined in the process of creating the postwar order. Within a few years, however, increasing East-West tension gave birth to a bipolar world system utterly unlike that desired by the visionaries of the midforties. The rise and fall of this dream among trade unionists is the subject of this work.

The creation of the World Federation in 1945 formed part of optimistic plans for what could be termed the bureaucracy of peace, institutions that would regularize and contain global conflict. "We have never had such an organisation before as the World Federation of Trade Unions," Sir Walter Citrine, head of the British Trades Union Congress (TUC), observed enthusiastically in 1946. "We have never had anything like it."[1] The World Federation sought to ensure that the unions participated fully in the reordering of the world after the war. Its founding conferences "are supremely significant in their vivid demonstration that labor can submerge all national, racial, and ideological differences in the higher interest of the common cause which unites all freedom loving people," Sidney

Hillman, a leader of the Congress of Industrial Organizations (CIO), told President Harry Truman in 1945.[2] The process of planning for the postwar world had begun in 1943, once the tide of the war had clearly shifted in the Allies' favor.[3] Trade unionists in Britain, the United States, and, indeed, around the globe worked for a national and international transformation that would eliminate the causes of war by making workers, through their representatives—the unions—central forces in the new institutions governing international affairs. The "UN could not be a success," Walter Citrine predicted, "without the support of the people. . . . If [the] WFTU pulled out, [the] UN would collapse."[4] The central purpose of the World Federation was to democratize the emerging international system.

However, the World Federation could not fulfill its purpose. After 1946, which was the clear beginning of the diplomatic cold war, cooperation between Communist and non-Communist unions became increasingly difficult. In 1947–48 the Marshall Plan focused the struggle for Europe not only on the need for economic reconstruction but also on the need to win over the vast majority of European people. Likewise, Communist policy, in the words of one Soviet trade unionist, centered on "the apple of their eye, the unity of the international working class."[5] In the charged atmosphere of the late forties, working-class politics became too important, in the eyes of national policy-making elites, to be left to workers. Active intervention by the State Department and the British Foreign Office, along with agitation by anti-Communist strategists in the American Federation of Labor (AFL), brought divisions in the World Federation to the fore. The organization split in 1949, with the American, British, and Dutch members forming the rival International Confederation of Free Trade Unions (hereafter ICFTU, or International Confederation). Labor's attempt to weld "one voice for sixty millions," as Hillman had earlier described it, ended in failure.[6]

The World Federation's collapse fit an old pattern. The history of labor internationalism is a history of failure, of dreams disappointed, ideals compromised, and institutions corrupted. The International Workingmen's Association (IWA), founded in 1864 by Karl Marx, anarchists such as Mikhail Bakunin, Mutualist followers of Pierre-Joseph Proudhoun, and more practical trade unionists, remained a talking shop. The larger and longer lived International Federation of Trade Unions (hereafter IFTU, or International Federation) (1901–45) barely survived the nationalist passions of World War I. Its most notable success was an international coal boycott during the 1926 British general strike. During the twenties and thirties the International Federation faced intense and bitter competition from the Communist-run Red International of Labor Unions (RILU, or Profintern). The World Federation, on which this work focuses, superseded both the RILU and the International Federation. It brought together Communists, Socialists, and liberals from every corner of the globe but fell victim to the cold war four years after it was founded. The International Confederation, which arose in competition to the World Federation in 1949, foundered for decades on disputes about the rights of colonized peoples and the power of the United States.

Yet there is more to this story than the tragic inability of workers to move beyond the boundaries imposed by their national or power bloc identities. Rather, unionists' faltering and intermittent internationalism marks a significant attempt to transform world politics in the twentieth century. The unionists are not significant for what they accomplished but for what they thought, dreamed, and believed.

This work explores the thinking of labor internationalists in a crucial decade during which it seemed more likely than ever that workers could influence world politics. However, it is more than simply a record of what a variety of people believed. Instead, it illustrates the complexity of British and American working-class thought in interaction with the sometimes promising, sometimes troubling realities of international affairs. Thus it focuses on ideas in relation to the creation and collapse of the central institution of world labor in the 1940s: the World Federation. What emerges is a portrait of the ways basic working-class perceptions of the world, as well as responses to discrete political problems, refracted workers' positions in the larger world.

Yet even a cursory reading of the history of labor internationalism in the forties, reveals a remarkably contradictory set of ideas. Union leaders and rank-and-file opinion changed rapidly. Disputes abounded. Although most British and American unionists said at the time that they shared in the internationalist vision of the mid-1940s, many later claimed they had actually never believed in the possibilities of coexisting with the Soviet Union, creating effective world organizations, or integrating colonized people into the system. The difficult theoretical problem underlying this work is establishing whom we should believe and when we should believe them.

The issue of whether people *truly* believed what they expressed is a difficult one. It involves more than the complex methodological problem involved in expectations and power dynamics in interviewing or other public statements. I consider in the conclusion the problem of the relationship between belief and ideology, between hegemonic conceptions and self-awareness. Critical to understanding the role of internationalist thought in the politics of the forties is an exploration of this theoretical issue because of the plethora of contradictory ideas expressed at the time and recalled later. Ideas interacted on a very basic level with the enormous possibilities of the historical moment.

What Happened

Ideas did not exist in a vacuum; rather, they motivated people who operated within a real and powerful play of institutional forces. The outline of the World Federation's institutional history is simple (though it requires a substantial number of acronyms!). The organization originated in the Anglo-Soviet Trade Union Committee formed by the All-Union Central Council of Soviet Trade Unions (AUCCTU) and the British TUC in 1941 to foster cooperation and solidarity during the war. Subsequent attempts to expand the committee to replicate the war's Grand Alliance of the United States, Britain, and the Soviet Union by including the AFL and the CIO foundered on the former's refusal to work with the Soviets or the CIO. Pressed by the world crisis and popular sentiment to institutionalize the amity engendered by the alliance, the TUC hosted the World Trade Union Conference in early 1945. The TUC—not the already existing International Federation—organized the conference because the International Federation excluded the Soviets and the CIO. The AFL leadership maintained its earlier resistance and refused to participate. Dozens of other union centers (national umbrella organizations) did attend the conference and agreed to found the World Federation. Negotiations for the constitution of the World Federation continued through the spring and summer of 1945, culminating in the founding conference of the World Federation in Paris that October. The World Federation set itself the tasks of aiding the reconstruction of trade unions in Europe and in less industrialized countries, influencing the United Nations (UN), and absorbing the independent International Trade Secretariats (ITS), organizations of unions in particular industries. Although the World Federation did aid a number of new unions, its leaders failed to convince the Trade Secretariats to affiliate, leaving organized world labor still divided. World political leaders rebuffed the international's attempt to gain power at the UN. Worse, unions from the imperial powers resisted the World Federation's involvement in their territories. In 1946–47 tensions between Communists and non-Communists increasingly limited the federation's actions. Finally, in 1948–49 Western unions demanded that the World Federation endorse the Marshall Plan. The Soviet representatives predictably resisted, advocating neutrality. The Western unions took this as an opportunity to withdraw to form the rival International Federation in 1949.

Labor and the World System

Although the unions' mission to transform world politics ultimately failed when the World Federation split in 1949, the brief history of the united federation nevertheless provides a new way to view the Grand Alliance and the onset of the cold war. By looking at the sources and effects of U.S. and British union involvement in global affairs, it is possible to conceptualize international relations as something greater than the doings of diplomats, however important those may be. In this way the diplomatic level becomes one of a myriad of spheres that collectively constitute global events. With this perspective, familiar occurrences take on new meanings and new dates appear in the historical chronology. For instance, in the experience of millions of trade unionists in dozens of countries the cold war began only in late 1948, rather than somewhere between mid-1945 and late 1946, as placed by most diplomatic historians. In a deeper way this perspective rewrites individual countries' social and political history, revealing their profound connection to global events; that is, it shows how national history was really international.

The high tide of labor and the left around the world in the midforties clearly reflects the global character of domestic events. The idea of labor internationalism was reborn in several nations at the same time. By examining the global side of worker and trade union experience, it is possible to see workers not as part of an "exceptional" national unit but as one subgroup that participated in a worldwide process of international relations. Although it sometimes makes sense to talk of "many exceptionalisms," as comparative scholars now do, it is also useful to view national experience as part of a common global history.[7]

However, the plans of the trade unionists for incorporating themselves in the mechanisms governing the emerging world order signaled a new direction for world labor. Previously, the dominant thinking within the unions had been opposed to the operations of the diplomatic process in theory, if not in practice. With the exception of the AFL, trade union ideology for seventy years had assumed that the unions, working with their associated labor or Socialist parties, would oppose the machinations of diplomats and statesmen. During what E. J. Hobsbawm calls "the classical age of working-class internationalism," the labor movements conceived of themselves as the building blocks of an alternative, more pacific system.[8] Of course, agreeing on such principles in the abstract was much easier than putting them into practice. The most notable failure of the international movement was the inability of the Second Socialist International and its syndical associate, the International Federation, to maintain their internationalistic antiwar program in the face of the nationalist upsurge of World War I.[9] By the midforties, however, trade unionists had for the most part accepted that they could not soon expect to replace the diplomatic system. Rather, they envisioned a corporative world—one ruled by global institutions that would represent all elements of society.

As labor revised its ambitions, the multilevel nature of international affairs became more apparent to those at the top of the pyramid of world power. Although the nation-state remained the essential intellectual and practical component of world politics, transnational institutions, principles, and relations took on increasing importance, forcing a reconceptualization of the nature of world affairs. Diplomacy, conceived of as the process that adjusted relations between nations, appeared unable to handle adequately the dangerous complexity of the midtwentieth century. Further, the traditional system had been based almost entirely on European power and European conflicts and alliances. It proved difficult, and eventually impossible, to integrate non-European peoples into this system, both because of cultural differences and because of challenges to European power such as those made by the Japanese.[10] The desperate need for new forms and methods of international relations was apparent to anyone who reflected on the disastrous results of the diplomacy of the 1930s.[11] The world experienced economic disaster and world war because of an ineffective world organization, the League of Nations, and the ineptitude of diplomats.

The attempt to create a new labor international and to integrate it in world institutions came at just the right moment. Long-term changes in international relations such as the globalization of trade, production, and investment, along with the recent worldwide conflagrations, had generated a new consensus among midcentury elites that was confirmed by the necessity of achieving an alliance with the USSR to fight the Axis powers. The changing role of the USSR was crucial to the unions' project. Now that the Soviet Union was an ally of the two great capitalist powers, Communists around the world attempted to re-create the Popular Front with non-Communist opponents of the Germans, Italians, and Japanese. In the United States and Britain this meant that the Communists became loyal supporters of the government and worked hard to ensure industrial peace. Thus the political preconditions for a united world labor movement were met after the Germans invaded the USSR in the summer of 1941. Nevertheless, although the unions could overcome their internecine hatreds, they could not necessarily translate this unity into world power. But they did have the key to world order: the enormous and growing political strength of the Popular Front throughout the world in the midforties.

The contrast between the united World Federation in 1945–48 and the WFTU-ICFTU split in 1948–50 reveals a gap of ideology, political circumstance, and trade union philosophy. It also shows labor's relationship to the world system of the time, a world system that changed drastically in those years. Moreover, the disintegration of a single unifying institution into two competing organizations was an important sign of the division of the world into competing spheres.

Between 1943 and 1947 the contours of a new state system based on the cooperation of the major capitalist and Communist powers began to emerge from the ravages of war. From 1947 onward, however, the more familiar and unhappy cold war superseded this potentially more peaceful set of relations. The transition between the two was a wrenching experience for hundreds of millions people around the world and constitutes one of the main formative international experiences of the twentieth century.

The world economy in the 1940s, on the other hand, although closely connected to the state system, especially in the cold war, did not see wrenching dislocations—aside from, and this is a big qualification, the German and Japanese attempts to create realms centered on themselves. During the period from 1943 to 1947 the main point of conflict was between the United States and the old imperial powers regarding U.S. domination of the world economy. This included conflicts involving how colonial economies would be integrated in a U.S.-centered postwar order. The position of the USSR in this system, interestingly enough, was quite ambiguous. By 1948 the ambiguity was resolved with the Marshall Plan's exclusion of the USSR from the Western economies. The USSR, in turn, tightened its grip on Eastern Europe in order to create an autarkic realm independent of the larger world. (Socialism in one region, it could be called).

Workers' places in these two systems differed drastically. The system of the mid-1940s emphasized incorporation of labor in international and national institutions, whereas the ideologically charged cold war system demanded labor's loyalty to pro- or anti-Communist camps. Despite these differences, however, workers and unions faced a common challenge throughout the 1940s: how to respond to and influence the vast changes underway in their world.

What the leaders, the rank-and-file, and even the public responded to in the mid-1940s was the structure of power in the world. They understood that the alliance had created the basis for a new world order and that the problem of how to bring that system to reality was the great challenge of their time. Only by looking at the broader ideas and consciousness of workers and their leaders, and at how they attempted to put these conceptions into reality, can we see their relations to the great forces of the age.

Other People's Ideas

Unfortunately, scholars have not generally recognized these connections. One problem with earlier treatments of union internationalism is that such works remained concerned with refighting the issue of communism and anticommunism. Of course, this conflict was an essential element of the political history of the twentieth century. Nevertheless, the focus on issues of right and wrong, of assigning blame for the disastrous battles between Communists and their opponents within and without the trade union movement, prevents a clear view of critical aspects of the era. For instance, Denis McShane's recent treatment of metal workers' involvement in the World Federation almost single-mindedly emphasizes Communist versus anti-Communist conflict and so misses an opportunity to explore the common meanings expressed in the labor movement in the mid-1940s.[12] As a result of this focus, previous works have concentrated on the breakup of the World Federation and the seemingly unavoidable conflict between Communist and anti-Communist union leaders in the late forties. The earlier period remains largely unexplored.

Most treatments of labor internationalism in the forties have underestimated both the appeal of labor participation as an independent force in world affairs and the widespread compulsion to overcome party conflict. The story of the trade unions' foreign policy is not solely, as some scholars would have it, the almost inevitable development of close and supportive relations between labor and government that resulted in labor's slavish devotion to the needs of the state.[13] Nor was the World Federation merely a temporary aberration, an organization "based upon a passing situation, misunderstanding and errors of judgment," as Adolf Sturmthal described it.[14] These analyses, which search for the loyalty of the unions to the government and focus on the split in the World Federation at the very outset of the organization, read the history of the cold war backward and lend the developments of the late forties and fifties an air of inevitability. In reality, years after the diplomats had given up on East-West cooperation, many loyal union leaders in the United States and Great Britain found themselves opposing the cold war programs of their governments and remaining true to the ideals of mid-decade. Although the focus of recent scholarship has shifted from the battles within the institutions to the efforts to rebuild the European labor movement after the war, the literature remains tied to the teleological framework established by earlier works.[15]

This study is different because it takes seriously the attempt to create a world organization and to transform the nature of international affairs. It consequently explores the ideas and relationships that made the World Federation possible. Thus the emphasis shifts from the 1947–50 period, when the pressures of the cold war made the internationalist project seem a naive delusion, to the 1941–46 period, when the abilities of labor seemed almost limitless. It treats the institutional history as secondary, though not unimportant, because many able studies have documented the formal history of the international labor movement.[16] Most important, without this study it is difficult to understand the dynamics of world labor, or indeed the tragic effect of the cold war in general, because the late forties and early fifties can be distinguished as a time when the ideas, relationships, and hopes built up during the war unraveled.

Given the constraints of time and research funding, this work explores in detail only two union movements comprising the World Federation: the TUC in Britain and the CIO in the United States. It touches to a lesser degree on Soviet trade unions and even more lightly on those of Poland, China, France, Italy, Germany, Korea, Japan, Mexico, Palestine, Lebanon, French and British Africa, and India. Obviously, it is impossible to give all these organizations and the people they represent the study they deserve in even a very long book. But the British and U.S. unions provide an excellent starting point, if only because of their central roles in these events. Moreover, the British and American labor movements are close enough in conception, structure, and relations to the state to provide a reasonable comparison.

Union Politics/World Politics

The belief that unions could play a universalistic role may now seem naive, but in the 1940s unionists could make this claim quite credibly. The war had transformed the political face of Europe and Asia. Social Democrats and Communists were the most powerful political forces from Great Britain to Japan; unions more often than not provided their parties' backbone. The Office of Strategic Services reported in 1945: "As a result of their direct participation in politics, many European trade unions find themselves either forming part of their national government or occupying the role of opposition to which political reins soon might fall. In either case labor has a political as well as a class responsibility. . . . Within many countries the political roots of labor are striking deeper."[17] Further strengthening the unionists' claim to power and universality was the special role of the working class in the war and the ensuing peace, as Philip Murray, president of the CIO, explained in 1945. "The workers and the common people of the United Nations are the principal architects of the military victory we are winning," he said. ". . . Labor unions reflect and express the viewpoints of the common people. . . . A peace to be enduring must be based not only upon agreements among governments but upon the friendship, understanding and common effort of the great mass of their people."[18] International relations in the 1940s, the unionists learned, were far more complex and involved many more groups and levels of society than traditional diplomatic history has considered. The very importance of the unions, however, proved to be the downfall of the new union international, because the world of labor became one of the main battlegrounds of the cold war.

"If labor in the U.S. cannot get along with labor in the USSR," James Carey said of the breakup of the World Federation, "the U.S. and the USSR cannot possibly get along."[19] Carey's warning points to the broadest conclusion of this work: the seemingly distinct spheres of diplomacy and labor were actually closely connected. The problem of how to work with Communists—which for more than twenty years had been the most difficult challenge for middle-of-the-road and right-wing labor leaders—became in the midforties the most serious problem facing Western elites. "The lasting peace—for which the people of the World now yearn," Murray advised UN delegates in 1945, "will not be realized unless such unity continues based upon the military power and political solidarity of the United States, Great Britain and the Soviet Union."[20] The collapse of the World Federation naturally held ominous implications for world politics. Walt W. Rostow, then an adviser to the Economic Cooperation Agency of the Marshall Plan, worried "over the parallels that will be drawn for the UN and other organizations on the 'possibility of working with the Russians.'"[21]

Simultaneously, first- and second-world diplomats and trade unionists alike faced the newly assertive people of the third world.[22] Like their pin-striped brethren, the blue-collar leaders elevated some less industrialized countries to big power status. U.S. representatives, for instance, pressed China on an unwilling Britain and USSR, both in the World Federation and in the United Nations. The battles between and among colonial and metropolitan unions in Palestine, Cyprus, Persia, French Africa, Hong Kong, and India presented one of the greatest challenges to the World Federation. As Ken Hill of the Jamaica Trades Union Council warned his colleagues, if the international labor movement did not act on issues involving third-world countries, it "would . . . leave the world to be betrayed into another war within the next or the present generation."[23] The unique alliance between Communist and non-Communist northern countries allowed a remarkable degree of cooperation, especially between Americans and Soviets who found common ground in opposing the imperial system. However, the need to work with Danish, Belgian, French, and especially British trade unions, which were committed to their countries' imperial policies, forced compromise-minded northern anti-imperialists to shortchange their colonized brothers and sisters.[24]

◆ ◆ ◆

Although the World Federation approved a variety of politically popular resolutions that opposed imperialism and racism and supported the regional organization of unions in southern countries, it actually had little effect. The problem lay in the power of the unions in metropolitan countries—the TUC and the French Confédération Générale du Travail (CGT), for example, refused to allow substantial interference. For instance, the World Federation refused to permit Viet Minh–led unions from Indochina to affiliate, because the CGT claimed it already represented them.[25] Further complicating the general issue, the Americans and Soviets who found common ground in opposing the colonial system did not trust each other enough to cooperate positively in Africa, Latin America, or Asia. Nevertheless, the World Federation had a few successes. It proved most effective in publicizing the third world's problems and mobilizing affiliates and international opinion to help the new unions. For example, it helped Gambian unions win higher wages for colonial employees in 1946.[26] The World Federation also could confer legitimacy on a union center by allowing its affiliation. In 1946 its executive bureau established a colonial department and gave it the money to help poor unions and put pressure on the United Nations Trusteeship Council to support trade union rights in areas under its jurisdiction. Yet the conflicts between the Communists and non-Communists, colonial and noncolonial powers, made the World Federation ineffective.

The difficulties posed by decolonization, like the challenges of cooperation by Communists and non-Communists, revealed key dynamics of the emerging structures of world power and politics. The cold war created a bipolar system that forced most conflicts in the world, including colonial ones, into Communist or anti-Communist terms through economic, military, and ideological means. But before this happened, a rather different system had begun to emerge. Although the new world order of 1943–47 never fully developed, its form was readily apparent in the formal structure of the United Nations. The great powers of world, through their control of the Security Council, would benevolently dominate the world to prevent atavistic challenges to peace such as that posed by fascism. Democracy in the new system would be ensured through the General Assembly. The opposition of General Assembly democracy and Security Council power reflected the implicit divisions of the new system—the coalition of the Grand Alliance versus the mass of the world's nations. Aware of this problem, the unions created the World Federation on a more formally democratic basis, limiting the power of the largest trade union centers. Nevertheless, to function effectively, the World Federation, like the UN, required consensus among the powers in its executive bureau.

The new international union organization was premised on three realities of the new world system that most deeply affected the unions: the alliance of Communists and non-Communists against fascism, the leadership of the industrialized countries over the developing world, and the growth of union power in the world economy. First and foremost, the trade union movements of the Allied countries, which had been split in regard to communism, now found themselves powerful and united in opposition to the fascists. The Western alliance with the USSR healed the main split in international labor as antifascists of all political stripes worked together. The World Federation also tapped into the growing nationalist movements of the colonized and southern countries and consequently became a forum, however ineffectual, for working-class anti-imperialism. Finally, a widespread desire for cooperative reconstruction and peaceful international relations after the horrors of war inspired demands for mass participation in world politics. Popular diplomacy and mass mobilization during World War II had legitimized and stimulated the involvement of working people (or, rather, the representatives of their organizations) in diplomacy. British and U.S. workers' involvement in and reaction to these three currents largely determined the role they played in world labor in midcentury.

The relationship of national and labor diplomacy was more complex than this summary reflects because the two spheres were not merely mirrors. Labor's foreign policy grew from a variety of sources that cannot easily be simplified. The international labor movement had its own history and was subject to political and social forces distinct from those that dominated international affairs as whole. Domestic political concerns and popular sentiments created the urgency behind U.S. and British labor internationalism. Union leaders had to respond to diverse political and social pressures, including popular attitudes toward the USSR and toward foreign issues in general; threats from anti-union forces in society at large that sought to reverse labor's wartime gains; government pressure to serve as instruments of national policy; the threat of schisms from leftists and Communists within unions; and, of course, their own ambitions. Working-class thought about international issues reflected and expressed people's experiences at work and in their unions, their communities, and their political organizations. On the one hand, labor leaders appealed to a well-developed ideology of organized labor, responded to rank-and-file concerns, and grappled with factional conflicts. On the other hand, their actions necessarily depended on labor's relationship to various government agencies and the political system as a whole.

The unions joined in international affairs for more than domestic reasons, however. They also expressed the needs and traditions of labor movements the world over. The unions inherited and followed a long tradition of labor internationalism, which critiqued nationalism and stressed the common experience of all workers. Marx and Engels's dictum that "the working men have no country" resonated deeply with one part of the unionists' experience.[27] Throughout the

150 years of modern trade unionism, workers' organizations had repeatedly come together to explore and build on their common experiences as wage earners and unionists, experiences that cut across national lines. This transcendence of nationality, of course, abstracted a few elements of workers' lives and so underestimated the importance of the cultural, racial, and political nation to workers and their organizations.[28] Each universal workers organization, from Marx's own International Workingmen's Association to the World Federation, failed in the end to overcome the penetration of national interests in class concerns.

Yet to read the history of international labor and the World Federation as the story of an inevitable, if tragic demise is to miss half the tale. The internationalistic impulse was real and compelling; given the right circumstances—in this case the Grand Alliance—it could be extremely powerful. The intense pressures of the war reawakened the labor movement's universalism, which had been wrecked by twenty-five years of international crisis and sectarian hatred. Earlier international trade union organizations had disintegrated because of the support most Socialists had given their nations in World War I and, subsequently, because of the split between Communist and Socialist unions in the 1920s. The Popular Front began the process of healing these divisions, though the German-Soviet Nonaggression Pact and the Russo-Finnish War reopened the ideological divide. The formation of the World Federation marked a high point of the world working-class movement. Unlike the First World War, World War II drew Socialists and eventually Communists together in the fight against fascism, curing for a brief time the divisions in world labor. Their failure to transform the world system convinced many on the left that the working class would not be the sole motor of social change. The World Federation was, in a way, the last chance for a worldwide social transformation created by the working class.[29]

The unions projected a new world in which labor would be an intrinsic part of world government. By joining together the trade unions of the victorious powers of World War II, the World Federation looked to a world run by cooperation between nations and by incorporation of diverse voices in policy making. The World Federation's adherents stressed cooperation of the contending nations because Western unionists saw themselves as better able to understand and deal with the Soviets than the foreign offices of their own governments. They emphasized incorporation, because the conception of world government expressed in the World Federation integrated working people's organizations in decision-making processes while it simultaneously delegitimized capitalist power. The role of Mexican union leader Vincente Lombardo Toledano in organizing and promoting the World Federation reveals much about the organization's direction. The kind of corporate state that Lombardo Toledano and his Mexican allies were creating in their country, a system in which powerful labor leaders were an intrinsic part of the ruling party, stood as a common goal of union leaders throughout the world.[30]

Contradictorily, one weakness of U.S. and British commitment to world labor was that the unions' leaders also adhered to a version of nineteenth-century liberalism that rejected state interference in the unions' actions. Corporatist relations, either with their own governments or with a prospective world government, threatened this ideal of independent labor power. Thus a tension existed within the union leaders' approach to international—and national—incorporation, which the members of the World Federation never completely resolved.

The political structure of the World Federation, a coalition of diverse ideological groups, and the federation's attempts to restructure in its own image the labor movements of European and colonized countries also expressed a consensus of international labor. The World Federation's tolerant premises embraced every variety of trade union, from the state-controlled Soviet organizations, which were instruments of government power rather than representatives of workers' interests, to the militantly independent Australian unions, the corporatist Mexican confederation, and every variety in between. More than anything else, the World Federation epitomized the rapprochement of political parties and trade union types. Although both the British and U.S. union centers believed their style of unionism to be the best type of organization, during the World Federation period they and the federation's other constituents sponsored a form of unionism that was based on the Resistance coalitions that came to power in Europe immediately after the war.[31] British and U.S. leaders accepted the World Federation's model as an intrinsic element of their global ambitions. In Italy, Germany, Japan, France, Czechoslovakia, Poland, Iran, and Korea the World Federation championed labor organizations that included representatives of all political parties in their leadership. U.S. and British unions did not formally recognize political parties in their internal structure but accepted the temporary necessity of integrating politics in the new or rebuilt unions. In helping to rebuild the unions of the war-torn countries, Michael Ross, CIO international representative, explained to an official of the Office of the Military Governor of the United States for Germany that "the CIO is prejudiced in favor of a structure which would closely resemble that of the CIO itself."[32] This self-importance, however, contradicted the consensus of the World Federation that the new unions should explicitly encompass political parties. So, rather than contradict the World Federation's policy, the CIO decided against promoting its brand of unionism. For a time, cooperation outweighed replication. This new union structure was more than political expediency for the unions. Rather, the structure was a model for the world they sought to create, a world that united all peoples who had fought against the fascists.

The world the unionists hoped to build can best be understood through the eyes of union leaders and workers themselves. The body of this work examines the sources of U.S. and British labor internationalism in the 1940s. Part 1 examines the background and ideology of international labor as a whole. Parts 2 and 3 explore, respectively, the British and U.S. experiences of internationalism at midcentury. With the sources of labor internationalism established, the conclusion explores the implications of the course of union internationalism for the larger world.

Part 1

Ideas and Realities in the International Labor Community

"The trade unions of the world," Sir Walter Citrine exclaimed without exaggeration in 1945, are "now confronted with one of the most serious problems ever to be considered in their history."[1] The new realities of the world, the veteran British union official argued to an international group of union leaders, required the creation of a truly inclusive international trade union movement.

This new movement, however, did not spring fully formed from Citrine's head. Rather, it built on the existing international trade union movement, one that had bitter and deep divisions along ideological, national, and racial lines. The movement had to adapt to an enormously complex set of problems, ranging from the intellectual and political challenge of including Communists and non-Communists in the same organization to effectively integrating workers from less industrialized countries in a union structure dominated by Europeans. A remarkably diverse group of people thrown together in the cauldron of wartime Britain—exiled European Socialist union leaders; American, British, and Russian officials; Asian, African, and European sailors; refugee blue-collar workers and schoolteachers—grappled with these problems and created the contours of world labor.

This section illustrates how exceptional leaders and average workers grappled with the intense divisions and enormous possibilities inherent in international trade unionism. Chapter 1 recapitulates the institutional and ideological evolution of the big international federations that dominated thinking about the world labor. Chapter 2 examines attempts by unions of European exiles and Asian workers in wartime Britain to fight for bread-and-butter goals—representation with employers and better wages and working conditions, as well as higher levels of dignity and respect on and off the job. By illustrating these contrasting institutional and working-class histories, the stories of day-to-day union struggles and of intense ideological and bureaucratic battles, Part 1 sketches the significant poles of the international labor movement at midcentury.

International labor in the forties, as a movement, had three main components. The first part was made up of the formal internationals: the International Federation of Trade Unions, which was a federation of national federations founded in 1901 and dissolved in favor of the World Federaton of Trade Unions in 1945; the World Federation itself; the International Trade Secretariats, which were associations of national unions in a particular trade such as the International Transport Workers' Federation (ITF), which was associated with the International Federation; and the small internationals of Christian unions. Second were the various constituents of the internationals—the national centers, such as the American Federation of Labor or Britain's Trades Union Congress, and national unions in various trades, such as the National Union of Seamen in Britain, which belonged to the ITF. Finally, from a variety of nations came a unique group of workers who were internationalists, not via their membership in a particular organization or belief in an internationalist ideology but because they had been thrown together by the war. Together the three components formed the community of international labor.

It is useful to conceptualize the international labor movement as a community, for the internationalists grappled with a number of identity-related problems. They had to decide who would and would not be in their community. They had to agree on and defend a set of unifying ideas in a dramatically changing environment. In short, they had to decide the rules and composition of their movement and figure out how it fit into the larger world.

For rank-and-file union members, internationalism meant a vague broad set of ideas. Only occasionally did international cooperation become practical union activity. For trade union leaders, in contrast, internationalism meant world organizations, the play of competing ideologies—and the chance to travel to interesting places overseas.

The realm of international labor was for the most part a world of bureaucrats and politicians. Strikingly, in contrast to the revolutionary manifestos that heralded the founding of the First International in the nineteenth century, the plans for the creation of the World Federation in the 1940s flowed from committees in the form of thorough, reasoned, methodical—in a word, *bureaucratized*—reports. Although they make for dull reading, these works, such as the International Federation's 1944 *Project for the Reconstruction of the International Trade Union Movement,* reveal much about the nature of world institutions and the people who sought to create them.[2] They were careful seasoned operatives, with long and sometimes bitter experiences of revolutionary enthusiasm. They sought a stable practical internationalism.

Walter Schevenels, general secretary of the International Federation, is an excellent example of the talented politician-bureaucrat at the top of the international labor hierarchy. Fluent in four languages, he had two years of college education. As with many union leaders, he came from the ranks of the skilled trades and from a strong union family. His grandfather, Denis Schevenels, had been one of the early members of the Belgian section of the First International. His father, Jules, helped found the Belgian Metalworkers Federation. The younger Schevenels, born in 1894, had been a tool-and-die maker for six years before becoming secretary of the Antwerp branch of the Belgian Metalworkers Federation in 1921 when he was twenty-seven—the same position held earlier by his father. Walter Schevenels's career from then on was as a union official as well as an officer of the Belgian Social Democratic Party. He was elected assistant general secretary of the International Federation in 1929 and general secretary in 1930. He moved to Amsterdam, then headquarters of the International Federation, and relocated with the organization to Berlin in 1931. In 1933 the organization fled to Paris. He arrived in London in 1940—again fleeing the Nazis—bringing with him his wife, what he could of his staff, and the IFTU's records. In 1945 he presided over the dissolution of the International Federation and its absorption into the

World Federation. In a sense, his story encapsulates the story of the international movement.

The Soviets resented Schevenels's service to the Socialist-led International Federation and denied him the general secretaryship of the World Federation. He nonetheless worked hard as assistant general secretary to make the Grand Alliance–influenced institution a success despite its painfully diverse group of unions. With the schism in the World Federation in 1949, he seemed the logical choice for the highest post in the new anti-Communist International Confederation of Free Trade Unions. Yet his attempt to make the World Federation a success, despite his strongly expressed misgivings, worked against him. The rabidly anti-Communist leadership of the American Federation of Labor viewed him as tainted by his contact with Communists. Instead, he became assistant general secretary for Europe, a position over which the AFL had less influence. He stayed as head of the European Regional Organization of the International Confederation until his death in 1966. Throughout his long career he remained committed to moderate Socialist principles and, with the exception of the midforties, uninterested in forming a coalition with the Communists.

As head of the International Federation during the war, Schevenels stood at the center of the international labor community. Deeply involved in the movement-in-exile in Britain, he played a role in everything from writing the constitution for the World Federation to representing French shipwrights unfairly dismissed from their jobs. His style and ideology and his personal and political predicament as an exile and in dealing with Soviets and other Communists or with workers from the third world represented the movement as a whole.

1

Communists, Socialists, and Liberals in International Labor

Understanding what the world labor movement became requires understanding what the movement had been. The World Federation grew from the international labor community of the interwar period. It inherited many of the people, structures, goals—and conflicts—of the old movement, which had centered on the International Federation of Trade Unions and, for a time, the Red International of Labor Unions (RILU). However, like many inheritances, probate was difficult and confused. The international union movement, institutionalized in the International Federation, had been devastated by the rise of fascism and the onset of war. Their movement in tatters, the union internationalists needed to reevaluate some of their most basic assumptions. The difficult intellectual and political process that led the Western trade unions to accept the Soviets as partners in a world organization can be grasped only in the context of the intense conflict of the Social Democrats and liberals with the Communists before 1941.

Free Trade Unionism Before the World Federation

However transitory the World Federation was as a united organization, its creation resolved one of the most profound conflicts in international union history—albeit for only a few short years. The predominant ideology in the International Federation before the war had been in favor of social democracy and a worker-centered world order similar to that proposed by the World Federation. Although the International Federation had sought to aid the development of trade unions around the world, its European orientation led it to neglect the plight of colonized workers. Moreover, the leaders focused substantial energies on defining and defending their movement against the Communists. Indeed, the most difficult problems faced by the IFTU involved its relationship with the RILU and the

Soviet trade unions. Because the Soviet trade unions and the other members of the RILU were certainly committed to similar goals—a Socialist world, workers' power, the defeat of fascism—and shared roots with the Social Democrats, the conflict raised vexing questions of identity. It was the fight over communism, more than any other single factor, that forced the International Federation's leadership to decide the nature of the movement.

The institutional history of the International Federation illustrates the intellectual impact of communism. The pre–World War I International Federation had been dominated by moderate trade unionists, most of them Socialists from a tremendous variety of factions. The organization that formally became the IFTU in 1913 had been founded in 1901 as an international secretariat that presided over regular conventions of European and, after 1910, U.S. trade union federations. The early moderates, recognizing the ideological diversity of the union movement, insisted on a narrow conception of the role of the organization. It was to be "scrupulously careful to avoid having anything to do with political questions."[1] They declined a call by representatives of the then-syndicalist French Confédération Générale du Travail (CGT) to discuss antimilitarism and consider a general strike. They also affirmed that they would have nothing to do with "all theoretical questions and such as relate to the theoretical tendencies and tactics of the Trade Union movement in any particular country."[2]

The First World War and postwar revolutionary upheaval transformed the International Federation. In 1919 the trade unions' leaders refounded the IFTU, which had lapsed during the war. The reborn organization abandoned its apolitical stance; its 1920 conference rang with revolutionary phrases. Instead of avoiding political questions, the postwar International Federation unanimously approved resolutions calling for socialization of the means of production, opposition to the white counterrevolutions and an end to the isolation of Russia. The American Federation of Labor (AFL) under the anti-Socialist leadership of Samuel Gompers refused to participate because, as Edo Fimmen of the Netherlands, secretary of the International Federation, put it, "The IFTU was too revolutionary for the Americans."[3]

Despite American perceptions, the International Federation had long been a supporter of a relatively liberal economic order. Although the organization promoted international institutions that would—with labor participation, of course—regulate the world economy, it also opposed protective tariffs and other nationalistic economic policies. Instead, as the IFTU General Council resolved in 1929, "the working class has no reason to oppose" the concentration of world capital and changes in industrial production. Rather, "the unions would combat with determination and uniform lines the obvious penchant of the bosses to benefit solely from the advances which flow to humanity from the rationalization of production."[4]

The International Federation may have been too revolutionary for the AFL, but it was far too moderate for the Bolsheviks. The Bolshevik Third International organized a counterfederation in 1920, which formally became the RILU in 1921. The RILU attacked the International Federation as a "Yellow International" of "Social Patriots" who were incapable of "securing . . . the victory of the proletarian masses in all countries."[5] The Communist rhetoric and political challenge forced IFTU leaders to define the meaning and character of their movement in a variety of articles, editorials, proposals, and programs. However, attempts to define the unifying ideas of trade unions and their internationalism led to substantial disagreements.

The Communists' attack forced the International Federation to reaffirm its belief in socialism and at the same time to define clearly its commitment to free trade unionism—an idea that became the central tenet of the movement. As with the principle of democratic socialism articulated by such thinkers as Karl Kautsky, labor unity and power could come about only if unions freely chose it.[6] In 1920 delegates to the first IFTU convention after the war assured "the central affiliates of their autonomy and freedom of action" and forbade "any obedience on their part to any resolutions from outside bodies."[7] If this wasn't clear enough, the International Federation declared that "to govern a country and to claim to direct the workers' International are two things different and irreconcilable; . . . it is inadmissible that the chiefs of a government, even communist, should be at the same time the chiefs of the workers' International."[8] This fundamentally liberal idea of a separation between labor and government formed the ideological difference between the International Federation's affiliates and their RILU antagonists. This idea evolved into the concept of free trade unionism, perhaps the essential way non-Communist international labor defined legitimacy.

The midtwenties saw attempts to ease relations with the Soviets. Yet despite substantial working-class sympathy for the Russian Revolution, attempts to work with the new Soviet trade unions were intensely frustrating, according to the leadership of the British Trades Union Congress (TUC) and the International Federation. The Soviets, the RILU, and the Comintern, for their part, condemned the Social Democrats, especially the Germans, after they opposed the failed revolution of 1923 as "a wing of fascism."[9] The International Federation, under British pressure, did agree in 1925 to allow the All-Union Council of Soviet Trade Unions (AUCCTU) to affiliate, but the Soviets responded that they wanted instead to have a world labor congress of all unions "which recognize the principle of class war." Because this meant superseding the International Federation, the leadership refused.[10] The same issue arose during World War II with a different outcome.

The unhappy relationship of the International Federation and the Soviet trade unions is part of the larger story of the internecine warfare on the left during the interwar years. Following a policy of "boring from within" (though reading bland summaries like this one, it might be considered boring from without as well), U.S. and European Communists fought serious internal battles with non-Communists. These battles led to the formation of separate Communist organizations, or at least organized factions, within the unions in the early twenties. The Amalgamated Clothing Workers, under Sidney Hillman and others, fought a protracted and bitter battle with Communist factions at this time. In France and Czechoslovakia the Communists led breakaway groups of unions in 1921–22. In 1921 the Communist-led unions formed the RILU. During its approximately twelve years of life the RILU claimed more than 17 million members in fifty countries, 10 million of whom were in the USSR. The Chinese were the second largest group, the French breakaway Confédération Générale du Travail Unitaire (CGTU) the third.[11] In contrast, the International Federation had 13 million members in 1929 in twenty-eight countries, all but five of which were in Europe. (The exceptions were Canada, Argentina, Palestine, South Africa, and Southwest Africa).[12]

With the shift in the Communist Party line of the third period in the late 1920s—when the Comintern predicted imminent world revolution—Communists gave up their boring and formed even more independent trade unions. They often had remarkable successes in areas abandoned by the mainstream unions such as the fields of California. The American Communists formed the Trade Union Unity League from the Trade Union Education League to counter the AFL. In Europe similar conflicts and the inability of the trade unions to deal with the protracted economic crisis gave rise to more internal opposition organizations and full-blown splits. The National Minority movement in Britain and the Revolutionary Trade Union Opposition (Revolutionäre Gewerskschaftsopposition) in Germany in the late 1920s sought to create, at least in their institutional rather than popular forms, a power base for Communists within the union movement.

However, with the collapse of the Weimar Republic and the growing aggressiveness of fascism, Socialists and Communists once more tried to find common ground. The growth of the Popular Front—one of the most significant political developments of the 1930s—met with mixed success. Certainly the political parties and the trade unions were able to work together in remarkable ways. Nowhere was the unification more effective than in France, where a general strike by the CGT and CGTU in February 1934 marshalled the strength of the left against fascist and royalist groups and led to the unification of the Communist and Socialist union confederations in 1936.

Despite a renewed willingness to work with Communists in the midthirties, the leaders of the International Federation maintained that their organization should not concede to Soviet or RILU demands for fusion because, as French Socialist Leon Jouhaux argued without irony, the IFTU "has always acted for the unity of the workers of the world."[13] The International Federation benefited immensely from the Popular Front. The memberships of the federation's constituents grew dramatically from pre-Front lows—although other factors, such as an increase in employment stemming from the easing of the depression, played a major role. By 1939 the International Federation was composed of union centers representing more than 20 million workers from twenty-three countries, an increase of 7 million in ten years, despite the loss of the German, Czechoslovak, Spanish, South African, and Southwest African unions. In contrast, by 1935 the RILU was a shell with all but 500,000 of its members Soviet.[14] The Soviets and Communists acceded to demands for unity and allowed the RILU to collapse.

Nevertheless, between 1936 and 1939 attempts again spearheaded by the British to bring the Communist-led unions into the fold failed. The process broke down because of the resistance of many unionists to revising their ideas about the proper relations of unions to outside forces.[15] The British suggested that the AUCCTU join the International Federation. The Soviet unions agreed to join in 1937 but demanded substantial changes in the International Federation's structure, including the appointment of three presidents, one of whom would have to be a Soviet. They also wanted guarantees that "the millions of francs which would be paid by the Soviet Trade Unions would not be used for propaganda against the USSR and the Soviet Trade Union Movement."[16] In other words, they wanted an organization friendly and responsive to their needs.

An alarmed AFL reaffiliated with the International Federation in 1937 partly to signal a commitment to Europe by some internationalist-minded union leaders such as David Dubinsky and Matthew Woll. They also worried about the possibility of legitimizing the Soviets—and, not coincidentally, the Congress of Industrial Organizations (CIO)—if they became members of the IFTU. William Green, president of the AFL, responded to the British proposal: "This council of trade unions of the Soviet government of Russia does not represent a free democratic trade union movement, functioning free from government domination and control. In this respect we cannot distinguish any difference between the Central Council of Trade Unions of the Soviet Government of Russia and the Nazi- and Fascist-controlled labor front movements of Germany and Italy." Admission of AUCCTU, Green continued, would cause "disunity, internal strife, and perhaps the ultimate destruction of the International Federation of Trade Unions."[17] The International Federation's leaders agreed and refused to change the structure to admit the Russians. AFL opposition and the rapidly deepening European crisis foreclosed expansion of international labor.

With the advent of the German-Soviet Nonaggression Pact and World War II, any hope for further cooperation disappeared. The remaining affiliates of the International Federation disappeared in occupied Europe, though a few leaders and workers managed to flee into exile or to construct limited underground organizations. The Popular Front in the United States and Britain disintegrated as the Communists, foolishly following the tactical dictates of Soviet foreign policy, abandoned their alliance. This low point of international labor, however, rapidly gave way to an entirely new and intellectually challenging situation when the German army invaded the Soviet Union in 1941.

The Western trade unions needed to immediately reconsider their relationship to their Soviet counterparts in order to show, at the least, solidarity with those fighting the common enemy. This was not an easy process because the Soviets were hardly a perfect ally. Few could simply forget the bitter recriminations of the twenties, the purge trials of the 1930s, the Nazi-Soviet pact, and the murder by the Soviets of Polish Socialists Victor Alter and Henryk Ehrlich.[18] The debate about bringing the Soviets into the labor community was particularly intense because the International Federation had defined itself against the Communists. The very idea of what was and was not a legitimate trade union had emerged as a response to the Communists' challenge. The process of intellectual revision proved dramatic.

A year after the German invasion of the Soviet Union, the leaders of the International Federation were still unsure how to deal with Soviet trade unions. A committee of the Emergency International Trade Union Council (EITUC), which operated in place of the International Federation's regular executive during the war, concluded that it should strive for "the widest possible international trade Union unity after the war" and create a world federation.[19] Yet the EITUC remained divided about whether it could trust the Soviets to behave.

The change in attitude by the International Federation's leaders became apparent as they began to talk about postwar plans. Walter Schevenels, the uncredited author of the EITUC's elaborate proposal, *Project for the Reconstruction of the International Trade Union Movement,* recognized the failings of the prewar International Federation: "Trade union conceptions, national traditions, and political conditions were so different in various parts of the world that many countries, mostly extra-European, remained outside the IFTU."[20] Further weakening worldwide unity was that the IFTU had prevented the affiliation of two centers from one country. Thus the CIO could not affiliate because the AFL was already a part of the organization. The *Project* proposed a world federation that would redress this problem.[21] The expansive impulse overcame the narrowness of the prewar assumptions of the movement, and in April 1943 the EITUC acceded to the principle of an "all-in Federation."[22] Walter Citrine, head of the British TUC, explained: "True trade unions must be asked to come in."[23]

Schevenels and Citrine did not arrive at their acceptance of the AUCCTU easily. Citrine, who was quite strongly anti-Communist, recognized labor's predicament in the changed world situation. At one of the last significant International Federation meetings in the fall of 1945, he described the problem the movement had faced a few years earlier: "There are two possible attitudes for the Western democratic movements in view of the profound differences of trade union conceptions existing between them and Soviet Russia, that is—isolation or collaboration. . . . The most efficient way to conciliate those varying points of view is collaboration."[24]

In February 1945 Schevenels summed up the new attitude in writing about the London World Trade Union Conference (WTUC), which included the Soviets, International Federation members, the CIO, and even Christian trade unions. "For the first time in the history of the Trade Union Movement," Schevenels happily proclaimed, the WTUC "brought together delegates from organisations whose aims, methods and conceptions in trade unionism during the last 25 years could not have been more different." Schevenels found the conference participants "sincerely animated by a spirit of collaboration." For him "this display of good will and sincere desire for understanding . . . was actually the most positive and tangible result" of the WTUC.[25]

The optimism of the midforties appeared well grounded, even though problems with the Soviets were there from the beginning of the World Federation. However, these initial conflicts, involving, for example, the voting method the new federation would use, could usually be overcome. Certainly, as Denis McShane and Anthony Carew argue, the unions in the USSR were quite different from those without state control.[26] Nevertheless, in some ways it was easier for Socialists to cooperate with the Communists than with liberals because Communists and Socialists shared some common ground and intellectual heritage.

Nevertheless, the leaders maintained substantial skepticism. Citrine and Schevenels still worked to prevent the Soviets from gaining too much power during the 1945 world conference in London. They excluded trade unions from ex-enemy countries and "recently artificially created Trade Union Movements" from Eastern Europe, Italy, and Iran that the Soviets supported. Citrine and

Schevenels argued that the exclusions were necessary in order to build "a sound and solid foundation" and to "preserve for the near future the true spirit of international and democratic trade unionism."[27]

The Soviet unionists' long memories of the bitter conflicts of the prewar era and the vituperative style they brought to bear against any opposition could be quite trying. For instance, in the spring of 1945 in discussions about the structure of the new world federation, Schevenels and other non-Communists opposed Soviet proposals that decisions of the World Federation be binding on its constituent federations. This was a dramatic departure from International Federation practice and would have made the World Federation, according to Soviet leader Vasili Tarasov, "a powerful and effective organisation."[28] According to Schevenels, however, the new organization "should maintain the autonomy of the National Centers." Moreover, he and Citrine felt strongly that the organization needed to "focus on syndical objectives." The Russians, the Confederación de Trabajadores de América Latina (CTAL), and other defenders of a centralized federation, the Belgian claimed, wanted a "recreation of the Red International of Labor, an organization whose main principal was revolutionary and political agitation."[29]

Had this proposal passed, it is unlikely the TUC, the CIO, or the other Western organizations would have been able to participate in the new international organization because it went against their deeply held principles of voluntarism. In a series of tense meetings in the spring and summer of 1945, Schevenels made the International Federation case against binding decisions. The Soviets replied that the IFTU was "effete" and "bankrupt." The Soviet attitude dismayed Schevenels: "After all the efforts, the appeals and the mutual assurances of good will in order to attain that desired trade union unity[,] it has an ominous effect upon those who believe in the spirit of rapprochement to see the communist supporters of world unity display their bad faith."[30] The voluntarist principle prevailed in the end.

The issue of voluntarism in the World Federation, however, crystallized the differing conceptions of trade unionism. The Soviets, following Trotsky (though not acknowledging it, of course), believed that trade unions should be transmission belts of the Communist Party. This unifying, controlling impulse made a central powerful World Federation appear to be logical, indeed essential, if the WFTU were to be part of a workers' movement.

Later in the World Federation's existence the question of voluntarism reappeared when the International Trade Secretariats resisted subordination to the federation. officials of the trade secretariats resisted incorporation, McShane argues, because of their dislike of Communists.[31] Yet independence mattered the most intellectually, and it was expressed in terms of anti-Communist conflict. This was demonstrated in 1943–44—before the problem of working with the Soviets was on the table—by the resistance of J. H. Oldenbroek of the International Transport Workers' Federation and other ITS leaders to Schevenels's proposal that their organizations be subordinated to a proposed postwar International Federation.[32]

To the Western leaders, centralized power contradicted the basic principles of their movement and their power over their separate organizations. Yet the ideas that defined the movement underwent a startling evolution in response to the Soviets and the changing world system.

The Transformation of Free Trade Unionism in the World Federation

The defining ideas of the international labor movement revolved around the concept of free trade unionism—a concept diametrically opposed to the Leninist principle of centralization and control. Free trade unionism, however, was not a fixed idea. The evolution of this ideology reflected the unions' attempts to harmonize their organization with the changing world system.

U.S., British, and other internationalists believed that bonafide unions, truly representative of the workers in each country, could express best the common aspirations of working people the world over. A free or bonafide trade union, by the original definition, was not controlled by any outside group, political party, church, business, or government.

Predictably, then, a central problem for the unionists in creating their organizations was to determine which organizations were legitimate and which were not—a problem that inevitably involved party considerations. The intellectual tool they used was the idea of bonafide unionism, an idea loaded with meanings and susceptible to use by almost anyone. Fortunately for the unionists' sense of consistency, the definitions often overlooked the intimate relations between the TUC and the Labour Party or the German Allgemeiner Deutscher Gewerkschaftsbund and the Social-Democratic Party. In creating the World Federation, non-Communist union leaders had to abandon long-accepted definitions of what made a bonafide labor organization. Far from remaining the property of anti-Communist business unionists, the idea of free trade unionism became essential to the common language of British, U.S., and Soviet unionists in midcentury.

In the Nazi-Soviet pact years, free trade unionism assumed a new, more aggressive and more overtly political meaning as unionists mobilized for the war. Feeling betrayed by the Soviets and their supporters, non-Communist union leaders came to equate communism and fascism as the twin totalitarianisms, both equally outside the pale of legitimacy. Confessional unions also remained suspect because of the Catholic Church's sympathy with fascist parties.

The classic definition of free trade unionism, articulated best by the AFL, however, ignored a substantial change among many labor leaders about what they believed a free union actually was. The idea did not simply return to its pre–Popular Front meaning. Rather, it came to embrace any organization involved in the fight against fascism or against outside aggression. This change proved crucial because it allowed for the rapid acceptance of the Soviet and other Communist unions once the USSR joined the Allies in 1941.

Because the fight against the Germans and the Japanese was being waged by the free nations of the world, opposition to the Axis made one free. Any union, including the USSR's AUCCTU, that participated in the good fight became by definition a fighter for freedom. But how could this antifascist conception be joined to earlier ideas of independence from government control, a quality the Soviet unions most decidedly lacked? The leaders of the AFL never doubted the answer. Their commitment to anticommunism precluded any expansion of the world of legitimate labor. But for union leaders more desperately in need of allies, such as those in Britain, or those with more tolerant political inclinations, such as those in the CIO, the problem could have become embarrassing. However, for the CIO and the TUC, the need for cooperation overrode consistency in ideology.

In 1941 the British and the Soviets re-created their joint committee of the 1920s, the Anglo-Soviet Trade Union Committee (ASC), based on their common resistance to the Germans, which they now defined as free trade unionism. "I knew there were theoretical differences about the relations of the unions to the State and the exact measure of independence which the Soviet trade unions had to the Communist Party and the Communist International," Citrine told members of Parliament in 1942, "but it seemed to me all those were transcended by the fact that we were both in the war together."[33] Citrine and his colleagues avoided confronting the Soviet unions' lack of independence by either ignoring it or defining it away. Schevenels denied that the International Federation's leaders broke longstanding policy to not deal with the Soviet unions by working within the World Federation; he even maintained that the International Federation had never excluded AUCCTU for political or ideological reasons. He claimed that "the IFTU has never barred the Soviet Trade Unions from affiliation on the ground that they are not free and independent. . . . The IFTU invited the Soviet TUs to affiliate without any conditions" in 1920, 1925, 1936. Some union centers may have argued that the Soviets should not be admitted because they were not free, he conceded, "but they were not supported by the majority of the IFTU." In fact, this is a disingenuous argument, for the majority turned down Soviet affiliation without openly addressing the issue of free unionism and Communist power that lay at the heart of their refusal.[34] Nevertheless, Schevenels's revisionist history illuminates his intellectual evolution.

Some pro-Soviet thinkers made the radical argument that because the USSR had a different political and economic system than the United States and Great Britain, it could not be expected to have the same type of labor organizations. Others, such as Allan Haywood, the CIO's director of organization, argued that at the very least "the difference between the American and Soviet governmental systems cannot hamper unification of the trade unions of both countries."[35] Similarly, the CIO's second in command, James Carey, explained the ground rules of his organization's cooperation with the Soviets: "We have some reservation about how free the labor movement is in the Soviet Union, but we are not going to impose our ideas on them, nor they on us."[36] Pressed by reporters about state control of AUCCTU, the Clothing Workers' Sidney Hillman replied, "The internal affairs of the Soviet Union are their concern not ours."[37]

When the British extended invitations to the unions of the world to come to the World Trade Union Conference in London in 1945, the meeting that led directly to the formation of the WFTU, they expressed the expansiveness of the new form of free trade unionism. They invited labor from all countries at war with the Axis powers. Even neutral countries' unions could participate, albeit in only part of the conference.[38] In the first two years after the war an international labor consensus on the proper nature of trade unionism guided the World Federation's action in helping to rebuild or create unions around the world. Although tensions between Communists, Social Democrats, liberals, and Christians affected the functioning of the new organizations and caused conflicts within the World Federation itself, the wartime definition of free unionism, and the coalition of Soviet, U.S., British, and Resistance groups that it represented, still provided a common ground and the potential for future cooperation. In providing support, encouragement, and advice to unions attempting to rebuild themselves in the wreckage of Europe and Asia, the World Federation's partisans promoted a form of unionism that united antifascist trade unionists of all parties, much like the Resistance coalitions that led many European governments immediately after the defeat of the Italians and Germans. Rather than exclude parties, as prescribed by free trade union principles, the Resistance coalition unions mandated representation in union government for each antifascist party.[39] Hillman explained: "We can not permit old factional quarrels to stand in the way. To do that would be to repeat the fatal errors of the thirties, to betray the trust which had been reposed in us and again to reap the awful penalty which history visits upon those who disregard her lessons."[40]

The AFL leadership refused to accept this expansion of the labor community. Indeed, when the International Federation proposed to expand the organization after the war by including the Soviets, "only the delegate of the AFL [Robert Watt] strongly opposed the possibility of admitting the Soviet Unions."[41] Watt's aggressive attack on the Soviets surprised even as hardened an anti-Communist as J. H. Oldenbroek of the International Transport Workers. Oldenbroek, who later was the AFL's choice to lead the International Confederation of Free Trade Unions (ICFTU) argued with Watt: "If we discuss old differences, [we] will never achieve [labor unity] . . . but sometime or other we had to forget all [the old grievances against the Soviets] as we have to forget wars in order to achieve something better."[42]

The AFL leaders were not convinced by the Europeans' logic. The AFL's Executive Council refused the TUC's invitation to participate in the London conference of 1945 because both the CIO and the AUCCTU would be there: "The proposed representation at the conference invites discord and division rather than harmony and unity. The delegations from some nations invited can not truly represent free and democratic labor because no free and democratic union movement now exists in those countries."[43]

This conflict led to a serious split, because the Europeans had changed their views of how to deal with the USSR. "On this side of the Atlantic," Schevenels told the AFL's Green, "all trade union leaders feel very, very strongly it is imperative to clear up in one way or another the relations between the Russian workers and us." The veteran Belgian was "not sure that the American comrades fully realise what moral and psychological effect the role played by the Soviet Russia has had upon the great masses of the European people, including the British." He conceded that "problem[s] of whether and how far Trade Unions are or are not under the control of governments is no doubt of fundamental importance for the future of our international movement." Yet he thought the issue could be dealt with later. For now, "to settle our relationship with the Russian workers is still more urgent."[44]

Basing their opposition on a strongly liberal voluntarist tradition, the AFL leadership championed a vision of a pure "free trade unionism."[45] The AFL affirmed the idea of unions as entities almost completely independent of political parties and government. The principle of unionism, Green wrote in October 1944 after the TUC decided to go ahead with the all-inclusive World Trade Union Conference, had at its core "collective action by those concerned to promote their work interests and to protect themselves against injustice." Nevertheless, unions must be voluntary organizations. The contrast between free unions and those "under an authoritarian government" was that workers could choose whether to join. As important was that the unions themselves were free of government or political party control. This last aspect of free trade unionism, the AFL argued, made Communist trade unions unqualified for membership in the international union movement.[46]

The AFL's intransigent anti–Communist Party stance must have made its Social-Democratic friends in Europe wince. Green argued in the AFL *Federationist* in 1944 that "an alliance between unions and political parties is dangerous at any time because it facilitates political control over unions." Although phrased as a criticism of the Nazi Labor Fronts, Green's warning could certainly apply in principle to the relationship of the TUC to the Labour Party. The TUC and its constituents held substantial formal power within Labour at the party's annual conference, in its ruling body (the National Council of Labour), and through directly supported members of Parliament. Although the TUC had been deeply imbued with liberal ideas in the nineteenth century, it had, by its commitment to the Labour Party, substantially changed its view on the relationship of state to labor and of party to union.[47] A "free labor movement," Green emphasized, "must be free from alliance with political parties which seek control of political office."[48]

The application of the ideology of free trade unionism meant exclusion of the Soviet Union from the halls of world institutions. U.S. internationalist David Dubinsky's International Ladies Garment Workers (ILGWU) made this explicit in 1944 as the unions grappled with reviving the International Federation: "We are not setting up blueprints for the labor organizations of any country, in Europe or elsewhere. . . . But we insist on certain basic principles that must be common to all trade unions, and one of these principles is freedom of action and freedom from state domination. Such basic freedoms the Russian unions still do not possess."[49] As Anthony Carew points out, for the AFL leadership under the influence of Jay Lovestone, the former Communist Party head and then professional anti-Communist, anticommunism was "the overriding purpose of 'free' trade union organisation."[50]

The International Federation leaders did agree that free trade unions were a critical basis for democracy. They argued in the case of Germany, for instance, that "the creation of a trustworthy trade union movement should be considered one of the vital pre-conditions for building up a genuine democratic regime."[51] Even so, the Europeans' commitment seemed questionable to the ideologues of the AFL.

The AFL leaders objected to the decision by the International Federation's General Council to disband in favor of the World Federation and replace the organization with a trust to administer its remaining funds. Even though Green, president of the AFL, was elected a trustee, the AFL refused to participate. In 1944 it began to create its own institutions, notably the Free Trade Union Committee run by Lovestone and another veteran anti-Communist, Irving Brown, with a proposed budget of $1 million, to fight the World Federation and perceived Communist influence around the world.[52] The Europeans, in turn, refused to bow to AFL demands for an emergency conference of the International Federation in the summer of 1945.[53] Instead, the International Federation's Executive Council organized a September meeting with the International Trade Secretariats, to which the AFL did not send a delegate. The Americans had pushed themselves out of the community of international labor.

With the increasing success of the Communist left throughout the world and the consequent deterioration of East-West relations, the wartime coalition of Eastern and Western unions fell apart. The Christian unions pulled out early and resisted aligning with secular groups for years to come.[54] Beginning in the winter of 1947, tensions within the World Federation increased and the consensual operations of the organization began to break down.

Although most unionists continued to express confidence in the basic assumptions of the World Federation into 1948, changed circumstances both in international affairs and in national politics rendered their basic ideas increasingly anachronistic. Although the unions originally saw the World Federation as a transcendent force able to unite the disparate nations, conflicts involving political and labor reordering in Germany, Japan, Greece, Mexico, Poland, and Czechoslovakia, along with domestic political pressures, forced most unions to act in line with their national or party affiliation.

More than any other single issue, the proposed European Recovery Program, or Marshall Plan, pitted non-Communists against Communists and divided world labor. Non-Communist unions, including the TUC and CIO, worked outside the World Federation to support the Marshall Plan. The conflict intensified to the point that cooperation on the basis of the now-ancient Resistance coalition could no longer be imagined. Rather, the CIO and the TUC, with the coordination of the U.S. State Department and the British Foreign Office, orchestrated a walkout from the WFTU. The former World Federation members now claimed they were the true free trade unions, because they (supposedly) did not take orders from governments. In 1949 they founded, along with the formerly isolated AFL, the International Confederation of Free Trade Unions, an organization devoted to supporting "with all their strength the efforts of the peoples suffering under police state rule . . . to free themselves from totalitarian oppression."[55] CIO leader Walter Reuther explained the new position of international labor not as choosing between "Stalin and Standard Oil" but rather as following "down the broad democratic middle where people fight for both bread and freedom."[56] More succinctly, venerable French Socialist leader Leon Jouhaux proposed that "we have to be watchdogs of the Marshall Plan."[57] The dreams of world labor became one of the great casualties of the cold war as the unions once again took sides in the battle over communism. The ideology of free trade unionism now meant what the AFL had wanted it to mean all along: anticommunism. Reuther, Jouhaux, and others on the left were not able to preserve the elements critical of the capitalist West in the intellectual mix.

The fate of Schevenels in the ICFTU illustrates well the transition from the expansive thinking of the mid-1940s to the growing influence of the AFL. By 1949 the Belgian was one of most experienced and competent labor bureaucrats in the world. He had served nineteen years as general secretary of the International Federation and four years as assistant general secretary of the World Federation. He had been the obvious choice for general secretary of the World Federation, but Soviet resentment of the IFTU had doomed his candidacy. In a painful irony five years later the AFL blocked Schevenels's nomination as general secretary of the ICFTU and viciously attacked him as a tool of the Communists. Lovestone, Brown, and the AFL's Executive Council no doubt recalled Schevenels's advocacy of cooperation with the Soviets, his willingness to dissolve the International Federation, and his effective service in the World Federation. The TUC leaders, however, recognized his predicament and ensured his appointment as secretary of the ICFTU European division, over which the AFL had relatively little influence.

In contrast, the experience of the International Transport Workers' Oldenbroek proved more positive. Oldenbroek had led the anti-Communist International Trade Secretariats in their opposition to being included in the new World Federation. Despite a briefly held belief in including the Soviets, he ensured that the Trade Secretariats remained independent and outside the WFTU. The Transport Workers' leader crowned his efforts when he became the AFL's choice to be general secretary of the ICFTU.[58]

2

Chinese Sailors, Exile Unions, and the Limits of Practical Internationalism

The vast carnage of the Second World War created the opportunity for an enormous experiment in practical trade union internationalism. These experiences, as much as the conventions and debates of the leadership, reveal the nature of labor internationalism. The war forced millions of people to become refugees, hundreds of thousands of whom found sanctuary under the protection of Great Britain. Many were workers, largely sailors. Groups of these workers created unions that cooperated across national lines with other exile groups and with the British trade unions, even creating a multinational federation. This practical experience, however, exposed the limitations of the labor internationalists.

The Loneliness of the Exile Unions

Refugee trade union leaders moved quickly on arriving in Britain to form exile union groups. Austrians, Germans, Belgians, Czechoslovaks, French, Poles, and Spaniards built organizations with varying degrees of success. They existed under the umbrella of the International Federation, receiving from it more than £1100 (U.S.$4,400) per year.[1]

In contrast to the almost millennial rhetoric and invocations of the manifestos at big conferences, the day-to-day work of the trade unions was rather mundane. They concentrated on jurisdictional issues, helping sort out which workers belonged to which unions; lobbied for incremental changes in working conditions; channeled money to needy organizations; offered centralized information about foreign labor; certified the legitimacy of new unions; and offered dramatic propaganda appeals to workers in occupied Europe.

Exile unions on shore failed to establish a strong syndical presence. Rather, the small numbers of rank-and-file workers and the resistance of British unions and employers severely curtailed their power. The exile unions worked more naturally in the fertile and complicated environment of exile politics. Refugee leaders sought to take care of the needs of the few rank-and-file workers they represented while remaining deeply involved in the maneuvering of exile governments and parties.[2]

Typical among the foreign unions was the Centre Syndical Français en Grande Bretagne (CSF) formed in 1940 of French workers in Britain, Cameroon, and the French merchant marine. The center joined workers together "to maintain the traditions of the French labor movement persecuted by the Germans and Vichy."[3] It inherited the politics and traditions of the Confédération Générale du Travail (CGT). Although Leon Jouhaux, the veteran Socialist and CGT leader was jailed by Vichy, other leaders fled as the repression mounted. René Rous, head of the center, remained in contact with the underground labor movement.[4] Most were Socialists yet supported the French colonial system and advocated the complete unity of all French—read *imperial*—territory.[5]

The exile union organizations had dual purposes, which reflected their political and economic situation. The center, an organization of "French workers who have escaped Hitler's yoke," described its two essential goals as "to defend in accord with the British trade unions the material and moral interest of its members" and "to aid with all means at its disposal the liberation of France and the victory of free peoples over Hitlerism and Fascism."[6] As a political organization, the leadership believed that avoiding Communist contagion was critical. The British Trades Union Congress and the International Federation, which aided the exiles, helped ensure that Communists did not gain influence.[7] Schevenels and, through him, Citrine also tried to keep abreast of union activists' attempts to maintain some sort of organization in Vichy France.[8]

The CSF, the International Federation, and the other refugee organizations were very dependent on the British TUC and its constituents. The exile unions had offices in Transport House, the TUC headquarters, received substantial funds from it, and, perhaps most important, relied on it to mediate with British employers and the government. This cooperation had its downside as well, as the range of freedom for the unions was limited and the TUC unions were quite jealous of their jurisdictions. The British unions were often of little use when employers discriminated against French workers.

A typical case of the failings of the British-French relationship came about when two French shipwrights, Suzanne and Los Rios, appealed the denial of supplemental wages by their employer, the Chelsea Yacht and Boat Company, a shipyard on the Thames in London. The workers appealed to the CSF which appealed to the International Federation, which appealed to the TUC. The yard owner refused to pay the French workers a wage supplement he paid to English shipwrights because of what he claimed to be slowness and inferior craftsmanship. The employer claimed that he could get the same work done "with three English workers in place of six French workers." The TUC's response when the center complained was that only the appropriate union, in this case the Shipconstructors' and Shipwrights' Association, could negotiate with employers. With little resistance from that association, the company eventually fired the French workers, claiming they did not have the proper training for skilled shipwrighting.[9] The level of bureaucratization, confused jurisdictions, and antiforeign feeling limited the integration of the exile workers on shore.

Other unions made membership difficult for refugee workers, demanding substantial fees in full. For instance, "the attitude of the Electrical Trades Union toward foreign trade union groups," complained Schevenels, "makes it difficult for them to organize their nationals."[10] An exception was the industrial National Union of General and Municipal Workers (NUGMW), which signed an early agreement to represent foreign workers through their exile organizations and cooperated well with the French center, among others.[11]

The center concentrated on political and propaganda activities, which was far easier than organizing workers and, to the political activists at the center of the exile organizations, more compelling. It tried to maintain solidarity and spirit among its members and friends. The leadership sponsored a demonstration on August 9, 1942, that marked the 150th anniversary year of the writing of the *Marseillaise* "to show the complete solidarity between the free nationals fighting for freedom and social justice with the unreserved support of international labor." They invited General Charles de Gaulle, U.S. Ambassador John Winant, Soviet Ambassador Ivan Maisky, Schevenels of the International Federation, TUC head Walter Citrine, and Ernest Bevin, the Labour minister and union leader.[12] They organized similar activities in 1943, holding small rallies and fund-raising events in Liverpool, Warrington—the location of a relatively large concentration of French machinists—and London. A Liverpool rally organized by the union of French merchant sailors raised £45 (U.S.$180) to help colleagues in France.[13] Schevenels also organized a number of meetings and rallies "to tighten the bonds between the foreign union militants" and their British colleagues.[14]

The French center did try to assert control over the only large group of French workers available: the sailors. However, weak organization and the complexity of organizing at sea limited its success. The center represented approximately three hundred French sailors in the middle of 1941. By the end of the year their membership had doubled. Yet there were a total of two thousand French merchant seamen. As René Rous confessed, "The solution to this problem of recruiting [the unorganized] has not yet been found."[15] Complicating the CSF's drive, the International Transport Workers' Federation claimed jurisdiction and rebuffed aggressive organizing moves by the center.[16]

The CSF in the end could only engage in limited activities. Rous issued proclamations, appealed to TUC affiliates on behalf of aggrieved French workers, and represented the few workers he could, notably teachers at the Lycée Français at Penrith and machinists in a plant in Warrington.[17] A small organization, with its strongest shop on land a group of French teachers, the center represented fewer than fifteen hundred workers in 1941.[18]

The CSF proved typical of the other foreign trade union groups. None had substantial membership. All the exile groups together represented fewer than eight thousand workers in 1943, with the Belgians, the single largest organization, more than half of the total.[19] As with the French, sailors comprised the largest trade among the exiles. Schevenels conceded, "The increase in membership has been much slower than the available number of compatriots now employed in Great Britain suggest." He attributed the problem to the nature of the exile workforce, "the overwhelming majority of [whom] are racial or political refugees of the middle-class."[20]

In the end the most important achievement of the foreign unions in Britain was their relationship to the European underground and their support for union reconstruction after the war. The International Federation funneled thousands of pounds to underground organizations whenever possible.[21] Schevenels cooperated actively with the U.S. and British secret services during the war and with the occupation authorities afterward. He provided them, for instance, with the names of "suitable advisors" among "Austrian friends" and promised lists of Resistance fighters after liberation.[22]

Postwar problems caused by the growing Communist–anti-Communist conflict in Europe forced the International Federation and its allies to intervene in a number of exile union conflicts. For instance, in 1945 the problem of whether to support the Soviet-backed government in Lublin, Poland, split the Polish seamen despite efforts by the International Federation, the International Transport Workers, and British unions to keep the sailors firmly in the London government's camp. After the union's executive board voted in favor of Lublin, the pro-London members organized the election of a new president, who promptly and unconstitutionally suspended the pro-Lublin executive and appointed his own loyalists. But his moves did not solve the union's problems. Many, probably the majority, of the crews of the exile government's ships failed to heed London's call to remain in exile and sailed for home.[23]

Schevenels conceived of his and the international movement's role in rebuilding continental unions as one of trying to help them "find the road back to political common sense, rehabilitation and practical trade union work."[24] With the liberation of Germany and the imminent demise of the International Federation, Schevenels recommended the exile union organizations close up shop.[25] Yet as late as January 1948 the IFTU board of trustees, which administered the moribund organization's International Solidarity Fund, continued payments to the German Trade Union Office in London. The purpose of the payments in this period, of course, was to bolster anti-Communists rather than antifascists. It helped support the trade unions of the CGT–Force Ouvrière, which broke off from the Communist-led CGT in late 1947. It also provided 10,000 French francs per month to Karl Peyer, an exiled Hungarian Socialist.[26]

Limited numbers, a sometimes confusing and inhospitable environment, and the inability to overcome national lines even in exceptional circumstances prevented the refugee unions from fulfilling their promise. More holding actions for exile union leaders than real syndical organizations, the refugee unions revealed significant limitations to international cooperation. Other exile organizations, those of the sailors, however, had greater success—though the maritime unions too reveal the limits of internationalism.

The Brotherhood of the Oceans

In contrast to the French center and the other refugee federations, the sailors created a substantial, powerful multinational organization. Charles Jarman, general secretary of the British National Union of Seamen (NUS), and J. H. Oldenbroek of the International Transport Workers, along with a number of seafarers' leaders, deserve substantial credit for this achievement. They recognized the necessity for international and interethnic cooperation and worked hard to make it a reality. The sailors' success also came from their large numbers and economic and military importance. A substantial coalition of nationalities coalesced around common wage and working condition demands. Yet several groups, which I discuss shortly, were excluded. Their fate, as much as the success of the coalition, mark the compass of sailors' internationalism.

Because their ships were at sea when their countries were overrun, sailors formed the largest and most varied group of refugee workers. The Norwegian Seafarers Union; the Belgian, Danish, Dutch, French, Polish Seafarers Federation (BDDFP); and the Chinese Seamen's Union (CSU) organized and protected exile sailors. These trade unions functioned semiautonomously, with the significant exception of the Chinese. German and Japanese aggression forced thousands of sailors to take refuge under British protection and, in exchange, to serve British shipping needs.[27] In some cases, they sailed under the British flag and were subject to British rules; others shipped out under their own flags and national regulations.[28] Nonetheless, those under British flags remained under their original ownership (if the owners remained in occupied countries, charges were paid into escrow accounts) or passed into the control of the exile governments in London. The number of foreigners sailing under British flags of convenience during the war was enormous. More than half the Norwegian merchant fleet, almost two hundred ships totaling more than one million dry-weight tons and employing 30,000 sailors, asked for and received British protection when the Nazis seized control of Norway.[29] At least another 60,000 sailors came from occupied Europe, India, Africa, and Asia.[30] At their most numerous in 1944, foreign ships accounted for more than one third of the total British fleet of twenty-one million tons.[31]

Paradoxically, unity among the Europeans grew from Norwegian independence. The Norwegians never participated in actions with the Allies. Led by their exiled officials, Konrad Nordahl and Thor Sonsteby, the Norwegians parlayed a semi-independent position into real material benefits, gaining wages and conditions second only to those of U.S. sailors. Several reasons account for Norwegian success: they began the war with better conditions than their fellows; they worked the largest single fleet after the British and Americans; and their membership was more militant than most others. Infighting among the seafarers' representatives caused hard feelings, which reinforced the Norwegians' independence. At one meeting Oldenbroek of the International Transport Workers castigated the Norwegians for backing a group of sailors who had tied up ships in the Red Sea in mid-1940, arguing that no Allied sailors should get better wages than the British. George Hillman of the Transport and General Workers' Union agreed, stressing that "it is a question of loyalty." The Norwegians disagreed strongly, and the meeting ended, as the minutes taker put it, "on an acrimonious note."[32] The resentment engendered by this 1940–41 wage competition poisoned future relations between the Norwegians and their fellows and prevented complete unanimity from developing.

The other sailors envied Norwegian success and pressed their leaders for improvements in conditions and wages. The leader of the Belgian Seamen described the process as akin to "secret diplomacy." The International Transport Workers' Seamen's Section organized a number of meetings in 1941–42 to put together a unified international wage policy. Arguing for unified wage negotiations, the Belgian leader described the current process: "We are now running in a vicious circle. In the name of equality the Dutch seamen are putting forward a claim for equality with the Norwegians. The Belgians then follow suit. After that, the Norwegians, seeing that there is a possibility of advancement, put in new claims, and the movement starts over again. Comparisons with America put an additional impetus into the matter. In this matter the rules of caution have not been observed."[33] Most of the sailors' leaders agreed to cooperate, but the British minister of war transport, Lord Leathers, opposed a uniform wage scale, mainly because of the cost.[34]

International cooperation and amalgamation was the logical solution to the problems facing merchant sailors in the Second World War. Jarman, leader of the British merchant mariners, explained, "If there is one good thing this war has done it was [the] bringing together of the seafarers organizations of the whole free world."[35] The first step taken by the seafarers' unions was to create a new organization, the BDDFP, which united the exile sailors.

Despite high hopes for the BDDFP, government intransigence limited its effect. Joint negotiations held by the BDDFP, the British sailors, the International Mercantile Marine Officers' Association (IMMOA), the shipowners, and the government failed in the fall of 1942. Exhibiting a previously unknown concern for trade union independence, Leathers, a Conservative, told the seafarers' representatives that a unified agreement would "tend to reduce the value or significance of the different national organizations."[36] Unwilling to accept Leathers's fatuous concern for national autonomy, the unions appealed to Philip Noel-Baker, the Labour parliamentary secretary of the ministry. But the government was unified; Noel-Baker restated Leathers's argument almost verbatim.[37] Government recognition of the sailors' unity was not to be. Nonetheless, by coordinating their wage demands, the European sailors achieved practical equalization by the end of the war, even though they never caught up to the Americans. Merchant sailors from the third world remained far behind the Europeans.[38]

In contrast to the limited success of the BDDFP, opportunities for helping sailors laboring in the worst conditions slipped by the unions. Chinese, Arab, Indian, and African seamen were kept out of the BDDFP on the basis of race. There were exceptions, such as Arabs who shipped out of South Shields—they received British union wages and respect from union sailors.[39] Fears of communism, moreover, reinforced orientalist assumptions about nonwhite unionists by the seafarers' international leadership and prevented solidarity.

Neglected by their union brothers, Chinese sailors organized themselves into a union, the Chinese Seamen's Union, in Great Britain. This effort at self-improvement failed. The collapse of the CSU not only left Chinese sailors on British ships worse off after the war but also painfully illustrated the limits of trade union internationalism.

Chinese sailors, many of whom were British citizens, had long labored under conditions far worse than that of their European coworkers. They earned less money and worked the most dangerous and dirty jobs. Often restricted from leaving ships in port, they obtained the security of a hiring pool only in 1944, two years after the white sailors.[40] The Chinese quickly came to resent their substandard conditions and the growing disparity with British sailors in wages, conditions, and respect. Racism in Britain pushed the Chinese sailors to the breaking point. As one man expressed it:

> Years ago, I feeled the leeches of the Capitalists of the foreigner, how did they press and squeeze us for more than a century. Though even at the present time when we passing by the street they give us a strange sight, it means they leer us. I am telling you the truth, I can't bear any more. So I anxious the great revolution will come. This latency will burst one day like an active volcano. Then and ever they [buried] under the ground. There comes the real Paradise all peoples, or may I say human beings are happy, lovely and no body would be able to see man eats man.[41]

After years of ill treatment, the East Asian sailors turned to the Hong Kong–based CSU in 1940, in their attempt to build an autonomous union. The union's center shifted to England with the Japanese conquest one year later. Although the organization suffered from accusations of Communist infiltration and, somehow at the same time, domination by the Nationalist Chinese government, it articulated its demands in normal trade union terms:

> There are rumours that a section of Chinese seamen in Liverpool are looking to their own pleasure only, are remaining on shore for long periods and are reluctant to resume duty. This (alone) is not to be wondered at. The most lamentable aspect is the gambling, the whoring, and the inevitable rows. . . . This Association hopes, therefore, that the British Government and the Shipping Companies will adopt appropriate measures to assist the progressive seamen in stopping these malpractices, so that we may be able to fulfill our duty of opposing aggression.[42]

Conditions and wages for Chinese citizens were governed by the Anglo-Chinese Agreement of 1940. Having their employment terms dictated by a government agreement was, aside from racism, the main issue for the men and should have been a clarion call to the Western unions, steeped as they were in their ideology of free trade unionism. But the Chinese sailors' hopes for aid from the NUS, the International Transport Workers, and the British and Chinese governments were misplaced.

The bulk of the Chinese seafarers in Britain sailed out of Liverpool. The Chinese government sought to maintain control over their organization and attempted to force the CSU to move its headquarters to London. In the end the Chinese government won, but only after British authorities deported a group of strikers and the NUS and International Transport Workers maneuvered the Chinese union into a subordinate position.

The organization's real heart and muscle lay in the organized sailors of Liverpool, who initiated the CSU in 1940 with a strike demanding that their war risk bonus be increased to the level of white Britons'. The NUS and the ITF quickly became involved in the dispute, as much to prevent the Communist Party from gaining support as to help the sailors. The strike leaders denied they were reds, though they did receive some help from a local Communist support committee and some of the strikers undoubtedly had Communist sympathies. Yet the leadership was decidedly uncommunistic.[43]

Despite their belief in bread and butter unionism, the Chinese could not expect their struggles to receive unqualified support from the British and European sailors. Oldenbroek believed that the Chinese had some potential as unionists but worried that they did not yet act like proper union members. "It is highly desirable," he told T. W. Chen, leader of the Chinese union, in 1941, "to bring Chinese trade union practice into line with our own."[44] What this meant in practice, however, was bringing the union under the control of the British sailors and International Transport Workers to prevent Communists from gaining too much ground.

In 1942 the Chinese sailors struck Anglo-Saxon Petroleum, a major employer of Chinese on its dirty and dangerous oil tankers. The company eventually agreed to recognize the CSU—but only on the condition that the union's officers be approved by the International Transport Workers. The company further refused to negotiate wages or hiring practices with the union at any time, maintaining that these should be decided only by the British and Chinese governments.[45] The strikers had little choice but to agree: most were being held in detention, and many activists had been deported and drafted. After two years the strikers, along with hundreds of Chinese deserters, were sent to India to be drafted in the revealingly named Operation Bilge. The program ran into stiff opposition from General Joseph W. Stilwell, who worried about the effect of unwilling conscripts on his troops' morale. As a result, hundreds of deportees remained in Bombay for the duration of the war. The program ended with the war.[46]

The International Transport Workers jumped at the chance offered by the company to take the Chinese union under its wing in receivership. The Chinese sailors had a small piece of revenge though: at the first opportunity after the strike they elected two officers who had been convicted of desertion. This proved a serious action, for it ended their official relationship with the ITF.[47] The Ministry of War Transport then empowered Jarman of the NUS to decide when the Chinese organization became bonafide—a certification that he refused ever to make because the union, under Chinese law, had to be under the formal control of the Chinese embassy.[48] Attempts by the militant Chinese sailors in Liverpool to assert their independence ended in a Catch 22: they could not act independently because they could not form a bonafide union, and they could not be a bonafide union because they could not act independently.

The irony of the situation was that the Chinese sailors were indeed seeking the "free" status that the NUS and the ITF touted so highly. The Chinese merchant mariners sought independence from government control; they hoped also to make their own agreements with employers without becoming a company union. Problems arose, at least in terms of their relationship with other union organizations, because the British and European union leaders could not accept that the Chinese would refuse British tutelage. What the British sought, complained T. W. Chen, was "interference in the affairs of the Chinese union."[49] Wong Kwok Hong, another CSU activist, explained that Chinese militance arose from frustration. "Chinese seamen very often experience disdainful treatment," he told the ITF in late 1942, "which leads to violent reactions on their side. Knowing, or believing, that talking is no use, they down tools [go out on strike]."[50] The International Transport Workers and the British sailors proved unable and apparently unwilling to address the source of the Chinese grievances. To the contrary, Jarman warned the Chinese leaders to control their men or else: "If the Chinese Seamen's Union is unable to fulfill its task . . . then matters will have to be thought over with a view to replacing the Chinese seamen with more reliable men."[51] International solidarity proved unable to overcome long-held prejudice.

Limits of Internationalism

Internationalism in theory is an elegant democratic idea, based on the common experiences of working people around the world. It is possible to imagine internationalism as manifesting the most egalitarian instincts of labor. Yet such internationalism has more often than not been simply imagination. The success of the coalition of European sailors shows the hopeful possibilities of internationalism. Their failure to bring in the better-paid Norwegians and the worse-off Chinese reflects the stark limitations that racism, national identity, and economic competition imposed, even in a moment of history most favorable to international cooperation. Similarly, the weakness of the French center, although partly a reflection of the small numbers of French workers in Great Britain, was also the result of the unwillingness of British unions to either admit French workers as equals or cooperate fully with the French center.

Union leaders and workers expressed the meaning of labor internationalism through both their formal discussions and in the way they built their organizations. Predictably, this meaning was contradictory. Able to unite—at times—across national lines, the refugee sailors and the exile unions nevertheless could not overcome deeply held prejudices and powerful national interests. Similarly, the union leadership fought about who could and could not be included in the movement. For the international labor community as a whole, then, the crucial problems became the processes revolving around self-definition: finding unity and creating division, seeking universality and discovering particularity. Moreover, why the ideas of free trade unionism evolved and why the sailors and other exiles attempted to work together had as much to do with the alliances and exigencies of World War II as they did with the common principles and experiences of the workers of the world. Internationalism, and the world of international labor it expressed, resulted from the colliding impulses and needs of thousands of people.

Although the perspective from the center of international trade unionism tells much about what the movement was and wanted to be, the ferment proved particularly intense at the national level. A closer look at the United States and Britain reveals how and why the British and the Americans, especially in the CIO, fit their internationalism to their hopeful and threatening times.

Part 2

The British

Revealing a keen understanding of the predicament of the Trades Union Congress (TUC), Paul Tofahrn, assistant general secretary of the International Transport Workers' Federation, wrote in 1945: "It will certainly be difficult for the TUC to eliminate the national and imperial interests of Great Britain from all thinking about the problems of war, peace and social progress. But it is absolutely necessary, and not impossible."[1] The TUC's foreign policy, in fact, oscillated between the necessity, as Tofahrn put it, of embracing the perspective of international labor and the contrasting compulsion to defend the country's perceived national interest. This oscillation reflected the political imperatives and ideological understanding of the unions' top leaders.[2] Forced to follow the beliefs of the vast majority of British trade unionists, the unions' leaders promoted the integration of the Soviet Union and other antifascist forces into a cooperative, bureaucratized world system. But also like their supporters, the TUC leadership had profound misgivings about the role of colonized people and others from less industrialized countries, including the Irish, in the new world order. Although these popular ideas informed trade union policy, the relationship of the leaders to the government and to the rank-and-file determined how the unions acted on their constituents' beliefs. Most trade union leaders felt strong misgivings about the role of the USSR, in contradiction of their movement's dominant thinking and their own policy.

Nevertheless, between 1941 and 1947 they overcame these doubts, in part because support of the Soviet Union was the stated government policy but mostly because the popularity of the USSR among trade unionists limited their options. After the German invasion of the Soviet Union, British trade union leaders willingly cooperated with Soviet unions and tried to convince the anti-Communist American Federation of Labor to join in as well. Still, the British union leaders were only partly enthusiastic about this cooperation, which led to the calling of the World Trade Union Conference in the winter of 1945 and the founding of the World Federation that fall. The TUC's leaders placed themselves in a paradoxical position. They believed in Britain's role as a great imperial power that was confronting a dangerous European continent while preserving the British Empire.[3] Contradictorily, the union leaders supported the construction of a world system that proposed the elimination of imperial power and toleration of Soviet preeminence on the Continent. The election of the Labour government in the summer of 1945 and the appointment of trade unionist Ernest Bevin to the post of foreign minister, however, did not ease the TUC's problems.

Understanding why the foreign policy of the British labor movement moved in two directions at once requires an examination of the thinking of the rank-and-file and of the relations of union leadership to the membership and to the government. Further complicating the story, the factional conflict between right and left Labourites and Communists within the TUC played a major role at critical junctures. Chapters 3 and 4 explore the paradoxical nature of British working-class thought. Chapter 5 contemplates the complexity and antinomies of TUC policy and traces the sources of that policy. Chapter 6 sketches conflict and cooperation between the government and the TUC at the dawn of the cold war. It also offers a case study of the National Union of Seamen to highlight the evolution and ideology of international policy. Part 2 ends with consideration of the nature of British anticommunism and the intellectual crisis of the British unions' foreign policy.

3

"Castles of Dreams": British Workers and the World

Less than a year after World War II began in Europe, woodworker L. S. Grindon wrote an insightful assessment of plans for world organization:

> From the working-man's point of view, not that anyone bothers about what the working-man thinks, except perhaps his wife, the present situation of international affairs is detached and incomprehensible; it does not belong to him and he wonders why, particularly as patriotism is evidently expected to spring spontaneously from him. . . . Prophets of better times, leaders of ideologies, democratic wizards of finance, have each their turn in creating new hopes . . . and soon our beautiful castles of dreams come crumbling down, and history repeats itself leaving the working man out in the cold again.[1]

Grindon aptly summed up the experience of British workers at midcentury. In contrast to the Americans, British workers had a decidedly class-based world view. Benefiting from an imperial economy, native British workers considered themselves superior to foreigners, colonials, and immigrants. Yet they also experienced real class oppression and hardship, especially as Britain's dominance of the world economy declined. Further, the terrible price in human lives exacted by the United Kingdom's involvement in Europe's wars impressed on Britons the importance of reorienting the way nations interacted. They perceived the postwar world in class terms, believing the USSR was a pro–working-class force in global politics. Yet, as their position as a subordinate class within a weakening but still formidable world power suggests, working people experienced deeply contradictory impulses. The potentials of the wartime alliance allowed a synthesis of these impulses and made pursuit of a new world order plausible. The crises of the cold war, however, exposed the hidden fault lines of universalist thinking—nationalism, racism, and self-interest—that eventually shattered the wartime dreams of world order.

The power of these widely held working-class ideas forced British trade union leaders to join a system of international organization that they did not wholly believe in. However, after the Labour Party, the leadership of the TUC, and, significantly, Ernest Bevin, the trade union leader who was then foreign minister, decided to go along with the reordering of world politics by the United States in the cold war, British workers needed to choose between their dreams of democracy abroad and their plans for it at home.[2] The effort to grasp the meanings of the new international order brought home to the British working class the dire consequences the cold war had for its political position. This realization—that the world system dreamed of in the midforties might threaten both the Labour government that working-class people had long awaited and their own well-being—severely weakened left-leaning working-class internationalism and reduced participation in politics in general. A crisis of popular thought in the late forties, brought on by the conflict between optimistic dreams and political realities, enabled union leaders to act in accord with the government and their own convictions by taking sides in the cold war. Working-class interest in foreign affairs decreased.

Like the government, the trade unions for the most part abandoned their pro-Sovietism, and many, if not the majority of workers, assented to the anti-Soviet internationalism of their leaders. Orthodox explanations of this evolution stress popular disgust at Soviet repressiveness in Eastern Europe as well as newfound affection for the United States (or at least its money).[3] Recently, Peter Weiler, following Gabriel Kolko, has suggested "that the new cold war consensus was also created by the propaganda activities of the Labour leadership and the United States."[4] Although these arguments together explain much about the development of the cold war, both misunderstand and undervalue the development of working-class thinking. They make the simple and almost predictable mistake of not considering how working-class thinking evolved, or even what working people actually believed. That many working people's ideas about world politics changed between 1939 and 1949 is incontrovertible. Simply recognizing this fact, however, does not explain it. Moreover, not all British workers wholeheartedly supported the cold war; even at moments of crisis, such as the first months of the Korean War, the majority believed accommodation could be achieved with the USSR.[5] It is easy enough to prove that Labour leaders attempted to reorient working-class thinking about world politics, but it is much more difficult to explain how and why thinking about international issues actually changed.[6]

Understanding the thinking of the working class requires the use of sources different from those that most scholars have consulted for studying the international labor movement. Complicating the choice of sources was the frequent difficulty of winnowing out expressions that came from relatively unrepresentative people, such as Communists or other party activists. Particularly helpful were in-depth qualitative surveys that offer an excellent sense of how people thought.[7] At the time, Mass-Observation in Britain, the Survey Research Center at the University of Michigan, and the Office of War Information in the Washington, D.C., were the most notable practitioners of this form of sociological research.[8] Their findings complemented the results of quantitative opinion polls and form the basis of the findings presented here. I use anecdotal evidence from letters, diaries, newspapers reports, and so on where they illustrate these findings.

One of the most remarkable aspects of British—and American—working-class thought about the issues of internationalism is that it remained relatively constant through war and cold war. Middle-class opinion in both countries was much more volatile, following closely the ups and downs of government and political party positions.[9] In this respect, trade union leaders were far more similar to the middle class than to the rank-and-file. They let the party line (whether Communist, Labour, or Democratic) influence their ideas quite strongly. As one study concluded of the rapid endorsement of the cold war by the middle class in the United States, the ideas of middle-income people are "more subject to change as the tenor of world affairs shifts."[10] Average workers, in contrast, maintained the same core of ideas through the major political changes of the forties, through the Nazi-Soviet pact period, the Grand Alliance, and the opening years of the cold war.

The reasons for this constancy are not clear; the evidence does not offer any obvious answers. Some sociologists at the time attributed it to a lack of education and consequent inability to follow events and adjust to changing circumstances.[11] A more plausible explanation is that middle-class people identified closely with either a state or party.[12] Workers, in contrast, were more alienated from and cynical about the workings of power politics and therefore were less likely to quickly follow a government or party line. This chapter explores the sources and meanings of British working-class internationalist thought in order to explain the changing roles that workers' ideas played in world politics before the cold war. The next chapter continues the story through the postwar years.

Nationalism and Internationalism

The sources of internationalism *and* nationalism lie not only in the experiences of war, the manipulation by elites, and the conflict of East and West but also within working-class thought. This thinking reflected and expressed people's experiences at work, in their unions, in their communities, and in their political organizations.

Although British workers tended to be highly class conscious, James Cronin points out that "the working class that came to be represented by the Labour Party in 1945–51 was . . . a mature social formation, and the party, with its cautious demeanour and pragmatic outlook, was its thoroughly apposite political vehicle."[13] Working-class consciousness in Britain was decidedly unrevolutionary and had been since the failure of the Chartists a century earlier. Working people, with notable exceptions, did not believe in direct syndicalist action as a political method or as a political value. Rather, bureaucratized organizations and representative democracy appeared to be appropriate means and ends for social change. The majority of British workers supported the Labour Party and more than 40 percent of the workforce was unionized in 1950.[14] Forty-five percent of the British people as a whole defined themselves as members of the working class in 1949.[15] This powerful yet cautious class awareness suffused workers' ideas about international affairs.

British workers lived not only in a consciously class-divided society but in one that was undergoing the wrenching strains of decline from its place at the center of the world economy during the nineteenth century. Workers' response to the decline, however, was not revolutionary upheaval. The 1920s, for instance, had not been a time of prosperity or industrial peace for Britain's working class but nonetheless had a moderating effect on the unions. As an indirect response to the ravages of the Great Depression, which had arguably begun in 1921, the general strike of 1926 received overwhelming support from British workers and represented the high tide of a syndicalist urge that had become powerful during World War I. Remarkably, the strike was largely nonviolent. TUC leaders struggled to ensure it remained a peaceful nonrevolutionary action. Its aftermath, and the rise of Ernest Bevin, Walter Citrine, and other moderates to power, ensured that the trade unions would not become instruments of revolutionary struggle. Rather, they committed themselves to a combination of political reform through the Labour Party and industrial compromise by independent trade unions and employers on a semicorporatist basis.

The moderation of the unions reflected a cautious group of workers who lived within narrow social constraints. British workers before the war rarely traveled, had low levels of car ownership compared with U.S. workers, and had little experience of other parts of the country—let alone the world—except on occasional trips to the seaside for holidays. Their orientation was local, toward their communities, which were, on the whole, homogeneous and clearly distinct from those of their better-off countrymen. Exceptions were the port neighborhoods, where sailors from all the nations of the world rubbed shoulders in a diverse maritime community. The other main group with foreign experience before the war was veterans, whose experiences in France and Belgium provided them with at least a modicum of familiarity with people from other countries. An even smaller group of working-class soldiers served in Britain's colonies. In a few urban neighborhoods immigrant Eastern European Jews and Irish added a measure of diversity, but they often were ghettoized. In relation to foreign affairs and social change British working-class life before the war can be summarized as resolutely local and in many ways parochial. The relationship to the "pink areas on the map" that denoted British territories or Commonwealth lands, or to the wider nonpink world, was quite minimal and distant. A Cockney truck driver in China during the war explained that "having learned very little about China at school, I suppose I can't be blamed for thinking . . . that Chinamen were like the characters I had seen in the pantomime Aladdin."[16]

World War II and the subsequent collapse of the British Empire had a great effect on people's consciousness as the British were forced once again to deal with the world beyond their neighborhoods and beyond the English Channel. The challenge of dealing with others faced even children evacuated during the war. Patricia Yu Lin found that the experience of evacuation increased tolerance among working-class children.[17] One daughter of a railway worker described her world view as a child: "I knew there were other types of people in the world but I hadn't come across them."[18]

Soldiers, sailors, nurses, and others returning from abroad in 1945 and 1946 came home to a country in much better condition than most of the places they had left. Yet the country's prospects were far from bright, even with the triumph of Labour and its ambitious program of nationalization and social reform. It seems unlikely that Labour would have won in 1945 had the British not been desperate for some sort of solution to what seemed like the never-ending crisis of their society. The nation was nearly bankrupt, with a serious monetary crisis, the specter of return to the painful unemployment of the interwar years, a further erosion of British industrial strength, and bombed neighborhoods and city centers. Although Britons felt good about their stand against the Germans and Japanese, about "standing alone" in 1940–41, theirs was still a nation of fixed social lines, insecurity, poverty, and limited options for the masses; at the same time, strong living traditions of solidarity and working-class identity supported lively working-class cultures at work and at home.

More critical was that the terrible price in human lives exacted by the United Kingdom's involvement in Europe's wars impressed on Britons the importance of reorienting the way nations interacted. The idea of including the USSR and peoples from the colonies and third-world countries in a system of worldwide bureaucracy seemed a natural and realistic solution to the world's problems. As their position as a subordinate class within a weakening but still formidable world power suggests, working people experienced deeply contradictory impulses.

"The very word foreign," Walter Citrine wrote in 1942, "has lost much of its meaning as breathlessly we listen for news from wherever the fight is thickest."[19] A large portion of the working class followed international relations closely—especially during the war when international relations were a matter of life and death. World events entered into the way working people conceptualized proper trade union behavior and structure, and, in turn, they could understand international relations from the point of view of trade union principles. The war and the seemingly remote realm of international diplomacy had direct influences on the political opinions and expectations of the British working class. Some learned internationalism in difficult circumstances. J. H. Witte, a working-class soldier, spent years in a German prisoner of war camp in which the Czech, Russian, French, and British inmates learned to help each other out despite language barriers and desperate circumstances.[20]

A collapsing of national and class concerns reflected the way working people perceived themselves in the world. The commonly expressed idea of a "New World" implied not only international reorganization but also a reordering of domestic class relations, workplace relations, and internal union operations. Industrial unionism, one railway worker argued in 1942, provided the best model for world politics: "Take a look at Europe to-day and you will see the dire results of the pre-war craft mentality in the foreign policy of nations. Poland refusing the aid of the Red Army, Belgium regarding the extension of the Maginot Line to the coast as [an] unfriendly act, are but two crying examples. . . . No, the 'non' and the craft unionist are as different as the bow and arrow is to the rifle, but the modern need is for the dive bomber of unity."[21] According to one catering employee, who saw interdependence in broad terms, a closed shop was needed because "people can not isolate themselves and live alone to-day." Referring to his union's upcoming conference, this caterer predicted, "A new world is dawning, and the items on the agenda will be freely and openly discussed and decisions arrived at by delegates."[22] World affairs were domestic affairs—and and vice versa.

The natural wartime concern with foreign affairs reinforced a critical theme of trade union and Labour thinking about international affairs: a distrust of self-centered nationalism and a belief in international solidarity. The breakdown in world order in the 1930s confirmed the belief that international relations needed to be reordered to avoid future wars. Britain, as an imperial power and one of the USSR's chief prewar antagonists, had to accept radically different techniques and goals in its foreign policy. In this evolution of traditional Socialist internationalism, Britain would have to participate in the bureaucratization and containment of conflict. Many people agreed with the intentions but probably doubted the realism of a group of Llanelly trade unionists during 1944 who called, "in the interest of civilisation and humanity," for the "abolition of national boundaries."[23] Although it tried to domesticate its radicalism, the Communist Party of Great Britain and its supporters were the most consistently (if this adverb can actually be used for them) internationalist group.[24] Nonetheless, it is surprising how much support existed in varying degrees for the radical sentiments expressed by carpenter D. Sherif in June 1939: "Workers have no country."[25] As in the case of corporatism in economic issues, however, the ideal of international organization turned out to be neither attainable nor totally desirable.[26] Working people adhered to Labour in part because they saw it as an alternative to the aggressive nationalism common among Conservatives that they believed was a cause of war.

Labour's internationalistic impulse dissuaded nationalistic workers from joining, even if they might share other concerns. For instance, G. A. W. Tomlinson, a Nottinghamshire coal miner and son of a lifelong Socialist, recalled that his conversion to conservatism began at a Labour meeting at the local movie theater when the speaker turned to internationalism:

> Then, nearing the end of this speech he [the speaker] said (and I shall never forget the effect of his words on me): "What is this England that you are supposed to love? It is only a tiny portion of the earth's surface. Why should you be expected to love it, or be prepared to die for it any more than you would for Russia, China, or Greenland?"
>
> I was thunderstruck. "Because it is England!" I yelled out in fury. . . . Didn't they know that most of the happiness that ever I had came from this love of England that they spoke so contemptuously about? Did they think that they would ever convince the farmers of England that they ought not to love the land they tilled?
>
> The socialists, I decided were a lot of mugs. I didn't want anything to do with them and I went home and told my father so.[27]

A chief element of the Conservatives' appeal was their consistent rejection of internationalism and a constant promotion of the theme of patriotism. Although Labour did not challenge the most sacred elements of patriotic thought, the monarchy and the church, it nevertheless expressed strong internationalistic ideas that were missing in conservatism.[28] Few workers came to the same conclusions as Tomlinson. Most tried to balance their sympathy for the Soviet Union, their resentment of their nation's class structure, and their feelings of patriotism. Labourism—before Bevin's triumphant domination of foreign policy—included a commitment to Socialist internationalism and anti-imperialism.[29]

In the end the war was the greatest reason for the upsurge in internationalism. Sailor Patrick Fyrth remarked on the political transformation of his fellow seamen: "The interest in the post war world surprised me, because I didn't know many of them were interested in politics. . . . We were of course just entering the phase where in every camp and every ship a tidal wave of indignation arose, from which sprang the determination that the post war world would be nothing like the past, and which led to the labour victory in 1945. That night off Cape Bon I think most were agreed that those of us who survived would make sure there would be changes."[30]

Workers and the Workers' State

The USSR occupied a special position with the rank-and-file of the Labour Party and the trade unions, as well as the working class in general. Not only did the Soviets to be appear a model for domestic social change but their apparent exclusion from Machiavellian world politics confirmed their position as representatives of a better form of international relations. From the first years of the Bolshevik Revolution, the USSR had been immensely popular among British workers. During the 1930s the consensus of Labour and trade union opinion had supported the Popular Front and opposed the Munich settlement. The Nazi-Soviet pact and the subsequent invasion of Finland upset many believers in the Soviet Union's positive world role but still did not eliminate basic sympathy with the USSR.[31]

The Winter War of 1939–40 between Finland and the USSR divided the left with explosive debate in newspapers and branch rooms as the British cabinet considered the merits of intervening in support of the Finns. In a rehearsal for government and official Labour policy during the cold war, Labour's right wing mounted a high-powered, pro-Finnish propaganda campaign.[32] The TUC and the Labour Party sent delegations to Finland, released and distributed books, pamphlets, and newsreels decrying, in Bevin's words, "the terrible spectacle of a great power like Russia, calling itself a Socialist state, crushing Finland, a situation which can not be defended."[33] The cynical L. S. Grindon, a carpenter, believed the Russians were "turning violently imperialistic, rabidly patriotic and generally deteriorating into the worst form of international bogy."[34]

But many other non-Communists sought to understand, and often to justify, the Soviet action. Bryn Roberts of the National Union of Public Employees urged his fellow trade unionists to "view the Finnish issue in proper perspective" and equated the occupation of Finland with British control of Malta and Gibraltar.[35] The social research organization Mass-Observation consistently found that working people would not believe the USSR was in the wrong or might even become an enemy of Britain. Even at this low moment of Soviet popularity, many people shared the optimism of one man, who affirmed in 1939: "You never know with Russia; she's a dark horse. I still believe she'll come in our side."[36] Although orthodox elite opinion doubted the effectiveness of the Red Army, especially after the purges of top-ranking officers in the late 1930s, and the relatively poor showing in the war against the Finns, respect for Russian achievements and power led many people to hope for an eventual alliance with the USSR. Most tellingly, a sixty-year-old woman prayed while bombs fell on London: "I hope to god they come in our side."[37] Mass-Observation concluded in a 1943 study: "Throughout recent years ordinary people have preserved considerable respect for and have shown considerable skepticism about published news and views derogatory to her [the USSR's] strength and system. . . . There has been a consistent and deep underlying feeling that Russia represents the interests of the ordinary person, that it is a country where people are happy and have a say in the things their government does."[38]

Scholars have often confused middle-class opinion about the USSR with that of the whole of British society. According to this view, the invasion of the Soviet Union caused an about-face in popular perceptions. For the middle and upper classes the Grand Alliance did lead to a temporary reversal of anti-Soviet belief. Among working people, in contrast, the Grand Alliance confirmed the confidence in Soviet beneficence that workers had repressed during the German-Soviet alliance. Even recent analyses have collapsed popular beliefs into those expressed by the top leadership of the Labour Party or the trade union movement.[39] Although a substantial overlap certainly existed, views expressed by trade union leaders, and their actions, did not always have widespread support. As Chapters 5 and 6 demonstrate, the motivation of the leadership included considerations of power and political compromise that did not usually enter into more popular approaches to foreign policy. For many in the middle and upper classes it is nonetheless true that the alliance and the tremendous sacrifices of the Soviet people and Red Army gave rise to a new respect for the Communist state and its leadership. "The past with all its crimes, its follies, and its tragedies, flashes away," Winston Churchill affirmed in an emotional radio speech on June 22, 1941. Avoiding an endorsement of atheistic communism, the prime minister sanctified this ideological revision as support for Russian soldiers who were "guarding their homes where their mothers and wives pray."[40] Similarly, Citrine claimed to be moved by the "immeasurable possibilities [which] unfolded themselves in my own mind as I listened on that Sunday morning to the broadcast announcement of the Nazi invasion of Soviet Russia."[41]

In contrast to the calculated response of anti-Communist leaders, popular reactions were overwhelmingly enthusiastic. Few events involving foreign lands have affected the British people as deeply as the Nazi invasion of the USSR. Beyond providing relief at finally having a powerful ally on the Continent, the entrance of the Soviet Union into the war sparked an excited reevaluation of world politics among British workers. The alliance of the USSR and Great Britain, which was formalized in the Anglo-Russian treaty of May 1942, provided a means for reconciling conflicting impulses in working-class thought and promised an opportunity to make long-held dreams of worldwide social transformation a reality.[42] Arguing for an intriguing blend of nationalism and internationalism, railwayman B. Read expressed some of the feelings of 1941:

> When that [victory] day arrives, beside the Union Jack—saved from coronation day—that will hang out of my bedroom window will be the Red Flag. If the latter can not be had for love or money, then I will borrow one from a signal cabin and get the wife to sew the jolly old hammer and sickle on it. Before the Soviets signed the non-aggression pact I was inclined to communism. To-day I declare myself a Communist, with the exception, love of King and country. Long live the King, Churchill, Stalin, and Roosevelt![43]

Read's apparently contradictory combination of king, country, and international communism was not exceptional. To Conservatives, the Anglo-Soviet alliance was a matter of necessity, but to most trade unionists, Labourites, and other leftists it contained potential for changing the world. By 1945 the power of Anglo-Soviet unity and the upsurge in working-class internationalism appeared so overwhelming that it was inconceivable to most people that there would be no attempt, at the very least, to radically reconstruct the global order.

Citrine was quick "to envisage some of the political and ideological problems which were bound to arise as a consequence of the new alignment of social forces which Hitler's action would bring about."[44] Government ministers and trade union leaders scrambled to ensure that the Communist Party of Great Britain did not gain too much from the "new alignment of social forces," as Citrine put it. Official policy attempted, perhaps hopelessly, to "combat such anti-Soviet feeling in Britain as might jeopardize the execution of the policy defined by the Prime Minister" and at the same time to "prevent initiative from falling into the hands of the Communist Party."[45]

The efforts to limit the growth of the Communist Party were only partly effective—party membership surged to sixty-four thousand in 1942 from a low of twelve thousand during the first half of 1941. Communists naturally rose to the fore in pro-Soviet organizing.[46] Seventy-thousand people jammed Trafalgar Square on July 26, 1942, in what was then one of the largest demonstrations in British history, to voice demands orchestrated by the Communist Party for a second front in Europe.[47] Even at government- and TUC-sponsored events, class resentment articulated in pro-Soviet terms could not be contained. Perhaps most expressive were the number of voices raised in singing the *Internationale* as opposed to *God Save the King*. In London at a celebration for the first anniversary of the British-Soviet alliance, for instance, a staff member of Mass-Observation who was present estimated that 95 percent of the people sang the Communist song whereas only 75 percent sang their national anthem.[48] Recognizing the subversive power of the *Internationale*, the BBC did not play the song until forced to do so by public outcry.[49]

Official efforts to control popular opinion about the USSR were most successful when they guided people to activities acceptable both to the government and their own inclinations. Government-, church-, and TUC-sponsored rallies and meetings were the most visibly successful efforts to co-opt enthusiasm for the Red Army. Donations for relief to the USSR, though less apparent, were equally important. The National Council of Labour's Help for Russia Fund, which the TUC General Council ensured was free of Communist infiltration, raised almost £1 million (U.S.$4 million) from September 1941 to December 1945.[50] Although more than half the donations were made in the first two years of its operation, British workers and their organizations continued to donate throughout the war, giving a total of more than £200,000 (U.S.$800,000) in 1944 and 1945, well after the worst crisis was over.[51]

Although the alliance period did not transform the Communist Party into a truly mass party, popular support for the idea of communism did grow. In part, this resulted from the inability of the Labour Party and of government policy to distinguish between the Soviet Union and its organized British acolytes. To most working-class people—and a good many from the upper and middle classes as well—the distinction between supporting communism abroad and seeking it at home was not so clear. Some critics found that the Labour and TUC leadership demonstrated the same sort of ideological flexibility for which they condemned the Communists. "As one who has never been a member of the Communist Party or attended their meetings or bought their papers," wrote railwayman H. W. Franklin in the fall of 1941, "I wish to protest against these political and trade union leaders being so childish and petty. Inconsistency, it seems, is only the name to charge other people with; their own changes of policy they call statesmanship."[52] The Labourites' approach to the problem was to claim that Labour had the best method of achieving socialism in Great Britain, whereas the Communist Party was better suited to Russian conditions. Both parties sought the same goal, socialism, because, as Citrine declared, "the great social and economic achievements of the past twenty years in Russia, were founded on the right principles of collective ownership and control."[53] The right opposed yet supported communism. Although Citrine denied that the "British Trades Union Congress was behaving with fatuous inconsistency" in lauding the Soviet Union while refusing to have anything to do with the British Communists, this policy did raise questions about the leaders' sincerity.[54]

Working people saw a connection between the Soviet system and that nation's ability to resist the Nazi onslaught. A railway union official organizing in Cumberland and Westmoreland met a woodman in Long Martin who "regaled us with the wonders of communistic enterprise in Russia. . . . That woodman appreciated the fact that those soldiers with a cause in front of them had belied all those tales about a decrepit army—they were selling their blood in the cause of a new civilisation. How ignorant are the denizens of Mayfair proved, when men with common sense begin to talk."[55] The woodman and his friends were not alone. The sentiments of one sixty-five-year-old skilled worker show the failure of the government's strategy: "I'm not much interested in politics, but all I can say is that the system that has done so much for Russia is worthy of a trial, it cannot make a bigger mess of things than our political parties."[56]

The Soviet system was a model for what many British people hoped to achieve in their own country—even if they did not see the Communist Party as the proper vehicle for their movement. Another young working man echoed the idea that because the class problems that plagued Britain had been eliminated in the Soviet Union, that country was more efficient and powerful: "I like the system—the workers are better looked after. . . . Well, they're all workers—you may think it's funny of me but I've studied the ants and the bees and I think the Russian system is like their's—they get rid of the drones."[57] In this light, Communist repression served a positive purpose, according to railwayman Read: "That cute silent man in the Kremlin has his secret police—the OGPU—for a good purpose to purge the country of its aristocracy and its Nazis."[58]

Many supporters of the USSR envied Soviet workers' apparent ability to combine patriotic feeling with the defense of socialism. The appeal of the paradoxical trio, king, country, and communism, grew from the desire for a nation truly worthy of enormous sacrifice. A 1943 survey by the Ministry of Information found increased interest in the Soviet system among workers "who are impressed to see the Russians 'so ready to fight and die for it,' imbued with the spirit of patriotism, not money-making."[59] "I've the highest admiration for them," one young working man told Mass-Observation. "During the last war they were under a monarchy with precious little to fight for. This time things are different. They are fighting for their country; the Russia they've created themselves."[60]

Support for Russia had its most concrete effect in the workplace, where class conflict continued despite the wartime crisis. Reports abound of worker apathy, intermittent production, and absenteeism—not to mention more dramatic actions such as wildcat strikes and slowdowns.[61] The most dramatic incident was the engineering apprentices' strike of 1944, but numerous other strikes took place or were barely avoided by action of shop stewards, union officials, or government.[62] Although Ernest Bevin, as minister of labor in the coalition government, successfully maintained traditional forms of labor-management relations, he nonetheless promoted a corporatist direction of labor and the labor market through such means as the Essential Work Order and the use of repressive measures such as Regulation 1AA, which forbade strikes.[63] Despite government efforts to increase production and repress conflict, industrial difficulties continued.

Yet for most workers, including many who continued to resist employers' power in industry and transportation, the cause of the Soviet Union had an almost magical effect. By the summer of 1941 normal propaganda efforts to increase production appeared to be faltering, but workers increased the output of armament plants by 20 percent during the last week of September 1941, after the government pledged that the entire week's production would be shipped to Russia.[64] Often the only effective stimulus to increased output was an appeal for production for the USSR. One study by the Ministry of Information of a Clydeside munitions factory found little patriotic feeling among the six thousand women and five thousand men employed there in 1941. Morale was low and absenteeism on the increase, as was resentment against management for production bottlenecks and material shortages. The women workers' attitudes especially disturbed the investigator: "On the whole their work seemed to be regarded as a personal rather than a national effort, and a backache, an ailing child, or a cross husband are thought to be just as important as they are under peace-time conditions." One issue, however, could rouse these disenchanted workers to forget the hard conditions of their work and their lives. "Almost the only enthusiasm for the war effort" came after the Ministry of Information showed the propaganda films, *Soviet Women* and *Salute to the Soviet.*[65]

Typically, miners went their own way. The Ministry of Information's Scottish regional intelligence officer put it rather patronizingly:

> Some of those who are most vociferous in their demands for a second front, for collaboration with Russia, and for increased production, are chronic absentees because of their disinclination to pay income tax. The contradiction between their

beliefs and practices does not seem to have dawned on them. In all districts the miners are suspicious of the official Labour Party. In general they are unable to agree that disputes should be settled without strikes. The Labour Party and the Trades Unions appear to them to be "organs of the government."[66]

The miners were able to combine their localism, based on a strong sense of community and antagonism to the mine owners and the state, with a radical internationalism because their ideas of the USSR were as much the result of their wishes for British society as they were a product of deep understanding of the Soviet system.

The excitement and satisfaction of helping the Red Army and the Russian people did not lose effect as the war dragged on. Across the country, workers cheered references to Russia or the Red Army in factory morale-boosting speeches. All through 1942 and 1943 the Ministry of Information recorded "a steady demand for further information about Russian methods and Russian life." A study of the East Anglia region in 1942 found that "talks on Russia still appear to be a major incentive to an increase in production."[67] Repeated Ministry of Information surveys found deep and continuing support for and interest in the Soviet Union.[68]

Similar sentiment brought large numbers of demonstrators to numerous rallies in favor of opening a second front to aid the Soviets. Of course, not all were so enthusiastic. One poet put his reaction into verse:

Let's have less nonsense from the friends of Joe,
We laud, we love him; but the nonsense—no.
In 1940, when we bore the brunt
We could have done with a Second Front.[69]

Nothing expressed better the feelings of working people toward the USSR than the reception given to touring delegations of Soviet trade unionists. An initial delegation of high-ranking trade unionists arrived in the winter of 1942 and received a tremendous greeting. Later delegations did not receive the same overwhelming reception as that given during the crisis, but the Soviets were nonetheless very popular as speakers and celebrities. Similarly, Britons who traveled to the Soviet Union became on their return much sought-after speakers. John Potts, former president of the National Union of Railywaymen, parlayed his Soviet experiences into a part-time career. Citrine was perhaps the most notable travel publicist. He wrote a series of articles on his 1941 journey to Russia that was first published in the *Daily Herald* in London and then as a popular book.[70]

The first delegation of Soviet trade unionists to visit the United Kingdom arrived in late January 1942. After a brief stay in London, the delegates embarked on a whirlwind tour of factories and industrial towns. The rousing reception given them revealed two aspects of British working-class social and political thought. The first, of course, was enthusiasm for things Russian; the second, a deep ambiguity about the role of women in the war effort and their role in the economy in general. The trade union delegations brought out this ambiguity because so many of the Soviet trade unionists were women and because they pressed for increased employment of women in the British economy.

The Soviets visited dozens of factories and mines, almost uniformly receiving a warm greeting. In the North Midlands a regional intelligence officer for the Ministry of Information accompanied some delegates as they moved rapidly through Nottinghamshire, Derbyshire, and Lincolnshire: "The reception given the delegates by workers left no doubt about their enthusiasm, they were proud to be watched at work and very proud when given the opportunity to shake hands and there was much surreptitious wiping of hands in hopeful anticipation. A number of shops organized a cheer of welcome when the delegation appeared or broke into the 'Internationale' or rattled their tools. It appears the Russians heard 'Hip, Hip, Hooray!' for the first time, an expression that intrigued them."[71] A. R. Rollin, a Russian-born official of the National Union of Tailors and Garment Workers, acted as a translator for the delegates who visited Yorkshire and joined the Soviet unionists as they journeyed more than a mile underground in one of England's deepest mines. The workers in this Castleford pit reacted with enthusiasm, Rollin recounted:

> The atmosphere was warm, the miners were only dressed in shorts and their bodies covered with coal dust. But they cheered wildly in acknowledgement of the greeting from their Russian comrades conveyed to them by the delegation and the latter's appeal for increased production to defeat the common enemy. . . . The foreman who guided us said that the delegation's visit was the best thing that had happened since the war and that it was the first time in his forty years experience that he heard cheering miners down in the pit.[72]

In contrast to the cold war image of the gray apparatchiki, the Soviet delegates, especially the women, enjoyed a surprising amount of individual celebrity during their visits. Even though she spoke only in Russian at the London Empress Hall meeting, the dynamic trade unionist Klavdia Nikolayeva was able to rouse the audience from the slumbers induced by her superior's long dull speech. A large crowd of autograph hunters pressed against the stage while she spoke and had to be pushed back by guards.[73] The delegate's popularity led several civil servants to worry about the potential disruption caused by her "fiery propaganda oration" favoring equal pay for equal work for women.[74]

The civil servants were right to worry because the government had struck an uneasy balance between respecting traditional roles for women and encouraging their entrance into industry.[75] The Soviet women both aided and threatened this balance. On the surface the Russians' statements were usually nothing to which the government or the trade unions could object. In fact, they helped legitimize and promote the entrance of women into industrial labor—a goal the government and the unions obviously supported. Stressing the need for improved daycare facilities, the Soviet delegates praised plants that employed large numbers of women and criticized those where few women worked.

But the Soviets went too far in advocating the dangerous idea of equal pay, a concept opposed by the craft unions. Moreover, the Russian women's style, the radical egalitarian ethic, and the female aggressiveness they preached and personified challenged assumptions about women's proper role and demeanor. One strong orator, Anastasia Malkova, inspired a reporter to speculate on the Soviet women's femininity: "If she is typical of the Russian women whose part in the country's struggles we have heard so much about, then they must indeed be a sturdy and virile part of womankind."[76] Although the women's comments were usually taken in a positive way, misgivings were never far from the surface. After all, virility was not a notable female virtue. British women themselves displayed insecurity about the Soviets. In the North Midlands, for instance, a Ministry of Information officer "noticed that the women workers were more tentative in their response than the men, but some individual women came forward to express their personal admiration and gratitude."[77] Young women workers especially liked the famous sniper Lieutenant Lyudmilla Pavilchenka who toured England in late 1942. Older workers in the south, however, thought her personality "quite alien to our womanhood."[78]

Britons who visited Russia, such as M. W. Irwin, who sailed in the Murmansk-Archangel convey in the spring of 1942, were impressed by the bravery and strength of female workers. Irwin particularly noticed the one woman docker who helped unload a thirty-eight-ton tank in the middle of an air raid: "She was rugged and tough and her weatherbeaten features gave some idea of the hard existence she had led; her hands were massive and she showed no fear."[79]

In contrast, the leader of the first delegation to England, Nicolai Shvernik, achieved a less troublesome form of popularity. He dressed, to the surprise of the *Manchester Evening News,* "like a typical Lancashire business man in his blue melton overcoat, fawn coloured shirt and tie and Anthony Eden hat." Despite his un-Bolshevik dress, Shvernik aroused more excitement than the restrained British foreign minister could. After Shvernik's speech at a munitions plant, one woman climbed on the stage, "clung to his neck, kissed him on the forehead, and then shouted 'Come on, Girls, Let's all kiss him.'" Moments later, "scores of elderly grey haired women jumped on to the platform and struggled to kiss" Shvernik. Management convinced the women to get back to their seats, and in what may have been an attempt to cool their ardor, they all sang the *Internationale.*[80]

On a much larger scale the Soviet delegates received rousing welcomes at several major meetings and conferences around the country. At the biggest gathering, a meeting at London's Albert Hall in mid-January 1942, a staffer from Mass-Observation could not contain his feelings: "A great roar heralded the entrance of the Russian and English delegates. The 'Internationale' was struck, and with a great cheer thousand upon thousand Englishmen sang as they never sang before. There was spirit, real spirit. Union of the forces of democracy against fascism! At last we had what we had so long waited for!"[81]

Later delegations did not receive the same celebrity treatment, although the visitors remained popular throughout the war. A delegation of young Soviet workers and soldiers received a warm greeting at the end of 1942. In the Midlands, workers banged their tools on their workbenches in a noisy welcome, and in Manchester they mobbed the visitors. "The workers have got so blase over distinguished visitors that even the king wouldn't raise a cheer," commented an impressed aircraft factory manager, "but the Russians did."[82] Beginning in 1943, the All-Union Central Council of Soviet Trade Unions sent delegates to the annual Trades Union Congress. Other delegations toured the country in 1943 and 1944, visiting war factories and mines. In one case, two delegates were the first women to visit the coal face in St. Helens since the exclusion of women from the mines in the 1840s.[83]

World War II transformed British working-class thought about the world. It promoted dramatically increased awareness of and concern with foreign relations. A vague sympathy for the Soviet "experiment" grew into tremendous enthusiasm for cooperation in reordering the world. Yet the ideas of the British were by no means simple. Rather, they reflected the complexity of their position in the world and the multiple pressures of global politics. The end of the war brought a profound shift in those pressures. What happened to the working class in the early cold war could not have been easily predicted from what had gone before.

4

"What We Want We Shan't Get": The Decline of Internationalism

Anticipating the collapse of wartime dreams even before the defeat of the Germans, one working man worried that "for what we want we shan't get, I can tell you that, we shan't get what we are fighting for."[1] This man proved prescient, though he was relatively unusual in his pessimism in mid-1945. The process of confronting this disappointment occupied most workers' thoughts about international affairs after the war.

The cold war transformed the way British workers thought about the world. Yet this change did not mean that most workers abandoned their midforties vision in favor of the anti-Communist internationalism promoted by the Labour government after its victory in the summer 1945 elections. Rather, the cold war caused a fracturing of working-class thinking, a dissolution of the consensus about the USSR, Europe, and the third world. This process proved difficult and contradictory while revealing the intense interaction of racial, national, and class ideas that made up working-class consciousness in the 1940s.

Working-class internationalism was a highly ambiguous phenomenon. It expressed elements of tolerance and intolerance, paternalism and brotherhood, expansiveness and small-mindedness, all mediated by British experience and the underlying consensus of Labour politics. Support for the Soviet Union developed from an idealization of the Soviet state—working-class people projected onto the Russian screen the resolution of their domestic class conflicts. Support—and opposition—to the reordering of Europe and the decolonization of the empires grew from similar sources. When these concepts clashed with difficult realities, such as the Soviet occupations, the assertiveness of colonized peoples, social conflict with Polish refugees, or the pronouncements of Labour leaders, the ensuing intellectual crisis eviscerated working-class internationalist thought.

Workers and the Cold War

The persistence of support for the Soviet Union into the late 1940s is an unexplored factor of the development of the cold war. Envy and admiration of the Soviet system were not turned easily into endorsement of Anglo-American foreign policy. British workers tended to disbelieve even the Labour government's stance when it became critical of the USSR. Ernest Bevin himself had to at least verbally commit himself to seeking better relations with the USSR even though he had long feared the Russians as dangerously aggressive.[2]

Even before the end of the war Britons worried that the postwar world might be dangerously divided. Workers feared that the Soviet Union would be pushed out of the alliance and refused to believe that the Soviets might do anything wrong in Eastern Europe. Perhaps as a result of second front propaganda, working people thought their country was not doing enough to help the Red Army. Mass-Observation conducted a number of interviews in the spring of 1943, the majority critical of Anglo-American policy. A forty-year-old man remarked presciently: "We call them allies in name only, I don't think we're cooperating with them. We make no attempt to see their point of view. Even before the war there were numerous ways of cooperating with them. I think we're making a big mistake, and after the war there'll be trouble in front of us. We're making a bitter enemy of Russia."[3] In the months leading up to the Teheran conference of November 1943, the Ministry of Information found "increasing awareness of the possibility of post-war difficulties in the international sphere, and a growing fear that 'the end of war will not mean an end of strife.'" Most commonly, pro-Soviet workers worried that "[we] may not be as eager to be friendly with Russia as we might." The Ministry of Information also discovered worries that the United States might dominate Britain in an anti-USSR entente after the war, but the first face-to-face meeting of Churchill, Stalin, and Roosevelt in Iran subdued these fears and increased optimism that perhaps strife would end after all.[4]

As the war drew to a close, working-class anxiety about tensions among the Allies continued despite rising spirits. Beneath the relief at the end of the war lay fears about the shape of the postwar world and the relationship among the three Allies. The Labour government's assumed sympathy for the USSR failed to quiet these fears. "I think that there shall be a war because the secret of the Atom Bomb was not shared amongst the allies, and the Russians will do their best to make a better bomb," a middle-aged working-class woman predicted in October 1945. "I don't want another war," she added, "[but] there's not much chance of all of us working together."[5] Fear of war continued to mount through 1946.

Nor was the founding of the United Nations reassuring. As the weakness of the UN became apparent, people became more pessimistic about the possibilities of peace. In February 1946, 45 percent of those polled in a London working-class district thought another war in Europe was likely within twenty-five years. By June that percentage had risen to 70 percent.[6] Although war fears eased with the passing of the Iran crisis, continuing conflict about Germany and the coalition governments of Eastern Europe undoubtedly fueled anxiety.

Despite the worries, workers continued to absolve the USSR of blame for the developing cold war. "There is a clear class difference," Mass-Observation found, "a low position on the social scale correlating as might be expected with a more favourable attitude to Russia." One working woman explained her ideas: "I feel we should make Russia our best friend. She's done so much to help us through this trouble and deserves to be trusted more."[7]

Although there was substantial discomfort as West-East relations worsened and reports of Soviet brutality appeared, the majority did not become strongly anti-Soviet. "I've been in favour of them myself," a thirty-five-year-old man affirmed, "but what you hear from the boys when they come home—well it's an eye opener. It's very serious, but you have to hope for the best."[8] Some working-class opinion was undoubtedly influenced by direct experiences in the occupation of Germany. Truck driver Victor Blackburn wrote his family that the brutality and arrogance of Russian soldiers in occupied Germany convinced him that "they must be classed as bad as the people who ran the Concentration Camps." He was convinced that "before very long we shall be falling out with them."[9]

Yet, a survey in London in March 1947 found more working people unfavorably disposed toward the Americans than the Soviets. A young worker's comments in mid-1947 were typical: "Time will show exactly what is going on in Russia. I think things are all right, but you get such completely opposite stories. I have not made up my mind about it." A forty-year-old skilled worker ruminated, "Well, I don't know, she may be a friend, or she may not."[10] British workers became confused and worried but did not turn against the Soviets. By the fall of 1947 a plurality of working-class respondents expressed unfavorable opinions of the USSR. Yet these working people tended not to be openly hostile. Their replies, as social scientists Tom Harrisson and H. D. Wilcock put it, "take on a plaintive rather than positively hostile note."[11]

The bipolarity of the cold war forged a link between attitudes toward the United States and the USSR. Distrust of the United States and positive views of the Soviet Union, as Leon D. Epstein puts it, "were really opposite sides of the same intellectual coin."[12] Despite a common heritage and gratitude for aid during and after the war, Britons of all classes distrusted and feared the United States. In part this feeling grew from resentment at being displaced as the foremost world power by a greedy competitor and by Britain's subsequent dependence on U.S. financing and arms. For working people the United States had the additional fault of representing unabashed capitalism. Nonetheless, the working class was less consistently anti-American than the middle classes in 1947, according to one Mass-Observation survey.[13] The broader middle-class dislike of the United States can be explained by a higher level of nationalistic resentment at displacement by the United States.

By the midtwentieth century, economic inequities in the United States, exacerbated by the effects of the depression, had undercut the U.S. image as a land of opportunity. Further, the international role of the United States came to be seen as a major prop of an unfair and dangerous world system. On the eve of the Japanese attack on Pearl Harbor, one young working-class man put it rather strongly: "I don't think America is a really democratic country. You see they've got the capitalist system."[14] Among working people only 18 percent considered the United States the "land of promise," as the British Institute of Public Opinion put it.[15] Although by 1943 Americans were more popular than they had been before they actively joined the war, when compared with the other Allies they nonetheless ranked above only the Poles.[16] Even the U.S. declaration of war aroused nowhere near the level of intellectual ferment or popular excitement that the Nazi invasion of the USSR had aroused.[17] American involvement in the war did eventually win over many British hearts, and the level of approval slowly climbed to a high of 58 percent in 1945. However, it quickly dropped after the war. In March 1946, while the United States temporized on a loan to bail out the failing British economy, only 22 percent of Britons overall expressed approval "about the Americans."[18]

Distrust and dislike of the United States followed moral and political patterns, some of which had become in evident in friction with U.S. soldiers stationed in Britain.[19] Many more Labour voters disapproved of U.S. behavior than did Conservatives.[20] The behavior of the United States, both domestically and abroad, offended many working people's sense of justice and proper social behavior. One middle-aged Cockney put it this way in late 1945: "I've only got one opinion: unfortunately I can't get a passport—but there's only two countries worth living in the world today—Russia and New Zealand. If I could get a passport I'd go to Russia tomorrow. Russia and New Zealand are the only place in the world where there's men. England, France, America—they're all degenerate."[21] Even Walter Citrine found many characteristics of the United States difficult to accept. On an official TUC visit to the States in 1943, Citrine found it odd that "there is no appearance of the sabbath." The rough culture of the New York working class also disturbed the straight-laced trade union leader. After witnessing a drunken brawl he wrote, "No one bothered about anything or anybody except themselves. Civilisation. Democracy. The basic qualities upon which statesmen have to build the new social order. Not very promising at first sight."[22] Other trade union leaders on visits to the United States seemed impressed—and a bit disturbed—by the comparatively huge salaries of U.S. trade union leaders and their opulent union headquarters.[23] In contrast, despite their political differences, Citrine found the Soviets' style in trade unionism, like the headquarters of the All-Union Central Council of Soviet Trade Unions, "solid but not ornate."[24] American culture, like American politics and international behavior, could be both attractive and repellent.

The conflicting forces of U.S. and Soviet culture, politics, and power pushed many working people to seek an alternative basis for Britain's revised world status. The idea of Great Britain's balancing the Soviets and Americans and becoming the basis of a "Third Force," as it was described by the Labour left in the 1950s, grew from distrust of the United States, an uneasiness about confronting the Soviet Union, and a submerged longing for a restoration of Britain's role as a world power. W. H. Stokes, a district organizer for the Amalgamated Engineering Union who was very active in fighting Communists within his organization, outlined a vision of his nation's world role in a speech in 1947. He argued that Britain should avoid attacking either the United States or the Soviet Union: "The obvious danger at present seems to be the conflict between the USSR and her associates and the USA and her associates. Britain can play a deciding part in this conflict by steadily refusing to become an associate of either."[25]

John Benstead, general secretary of the left-leaning railway union, wrote a revealing essay about foreign policy in June 1946. Although a Labour left-winger, he argued for support of Bevin's foreign policy, refusing to accept that Bevin, in alliance with the United States, might be leading the country into further confrontation with the Soviets. Benstead supported a continued alliance with the USSR and feared U.S. policy but at the same time felt disturbed both by Bevin's anticommunism and by Soviet truculence. In international affairs he found "a mixture of power politics and opposing ideologies is producing a kind of 'devil's brew' which is bemusing the common people in every country." Yet because they want only peace and coexistence, the working class should back the foreign minister: "Bevin is carrying a heavy load, and it is imperative that we should support his efforts for peace and open diplomacy, whilst discouraging any tendency which might be construed as encouraging American-British capitalism against the Soviet Union. His efforts to promote democratic liberty against totalitarianism of any kind must command the support of all liberal minds, using the phrase 'liberal' in its broadest sense."[26] Benstead's quandary reflected the left's predicament in the cold war.

Articulating a popular inclination against falling into the U.S. orbit, Labour leftists argued for a middle position between the blocs, not necessarily endorsing Soviet policy but certainly not approving confrontation in Eastern Europe. In their calling for a Third Force in world politics, Labour leftists sought to unify the social democratic forces of Europe to present an alternative to Soviet and American power. Yet, as Henry Pelling points out, by the end of the 1940s the collapse of the Resistance coalitions in Europe, the positive effect of U.S. financial assistance, and the apparent reflection of social democratic policies in the liberalism of Truman's Fair Deal undercut the appeal of the Third Force among party intellectuals and activists.[27] The Keep Left group of members of Parliament that emerged in the late forties proved unable to keep the Labour Party on the left. Ironically, the ideal of European unity became a Conservative doctrine in which a united Europe would oppose Russian expansionism and create a new era of European world preeminence.[28]

The Polish Problem

The collapse of the wartime vision (which followed the partial reversal of attitudes toward the United States and the USSR) was a critical element of the transition to cold war consciousness. However, the sources of this difficult change involved more than Anglo-Soviet-American relations. Deeply believed hierarchies of race and nationality proved intrinsic to what the British viewed as possible in the postwar world.

Racial or ethnic ideas played a crucial role in attitudes toward the Polish-Soviet conflict, which, along with the future of Germany, lay at the heart of the friction between East and West in the mid-1940s. Many workers supported the USSR in its conflict with the Poles, in contrast to the policy of the British government. As with their views of the United States, however, the British based their ideas not only on pro-Russian sentiments but also on a dislike of the Polish people—a reaction that grew from more than political concerns. Disregard for Polish anti-Sovietism arose from prejudice against the Poles themselves, as well as from a Socialist internationalism that was especially sensitive to Soviet interests. Dislike of Polish exiles and immigrants in Great Britain increased workers' distrust of Polish nationalism and reinforced British workers' willingness to trust the USSR's intentions and policies. Xenophobia supported leftist internationalism.[29]

British attitudes toward the Poles became apparent during the war. Although Polish pilots had won friends by serving bravely in the Battle of Britain, their fighting was not enough to overcome British xenophobia. Workers in Scotland and the North Midlands "accept the Russian point of view" about the breaking of relations with the Polish government, the Ministry of Information reported in 1943.[30] After the Russo-Polish break, Mass-Observation found in a small street survey that while 43 percent were favorably disposed toward the Polish people, only 20 percent approved of the Polish government. A mere 3 percent blamed the Soviets for the break, but 56 percent blamed the Poles.[31] Other Mass-Observation surveys reinforced these results.[32] Underscoring their trust in the Soviets, many did not believe the recently publicized revelation of the massacre of Polish soldiers by the Soviets in the Katyn Forest.[33]

Conflict about the resettlement in Britain of members of the Polish Armed Forces under General Wladyslaw Anders increased resentment and ambiguity about Polish-Soviet frictions and undergirded many working people's distrust of Polish anti-Communists. The Polish forces arrived in Britain in two waves. The first came with the exile government in 1940 and were stationed in Scotland. The second and larger group actually comprised two parts. In the volatile weeks after the Nazi invasion of the USSR, the Polish government-in-exile achieved a signal agreement with the Soviets, the Sikorsky-Maysky Accord of 1941. In addition to invalidating the Soviet-German agreements of 1939, this pact called for the establishment of a Polish army on Soviet soil. The Russians released thousands of Poles from prison camps and allowed exiles living in the Soviet Union to join the army. Many, if not most, of this group, which eventually joined the British army in Egypt, came from eastern Poland and were strongly anti-Russian. The second group of the second wave were prisoners of war and escapees from German-occupied Poland.[34] By 1945, 228,000 men were serving in the Polish forces under British control and an additional 30,000 civilians lived in British Africa and in Britain itself. More than 100,000 Poles decided to return to their native land after the war, leaving approximately 140,000 ex-soldiers and civilians in Britain. According to Jerzy Zubrzycki, most of those who returned were from western Poland and had been prisoners of the Germans or had been forced laborers or soldiers for them. Those who remained tended to be residents of areas of Poland absorbed by the USSR or guests of Soviet relocation camps. The Polish immigrants to Great Britain were highly nationalistic, though they divided into two broad political groupings: conservative royalists and Social Democrats.[35] Their anti-Soviet feelings, however reasonable, did not receive a favorable hearing among British workers.

The exile army stationed in Lanarkshire, Scotland, became at times the object of popular resentment. Although at first the Scots were hospitable, intergroup feelings soon took a turn for the worse. According to the Ministry of Information, by November 1943 Scottish resentment of the Poles was growing, though not always for the most serious of reasons. Housewives, for instance, complained they could not get their clothes dry cleaned because the Poles' uniforms took priority. More seriously, many Scottish workers, known for their pro-Soviet feelings, took an immediate dislike to the Poles. The exiles were outspoken in their criticism of the Soviet Union and in their anger at the possibility that the USSR might retain the Polish territory it seized in 1939.[36] Some Scottish unionists may also have heard of the importation of Polish strikebreakers in late nineteenth-century Lanarkshire.[37] The problem of Catholicism further exacerbated intercultural conflict in a region long known for its intolerance of Irish Catholics. A number of Scots were rumored to have accused the Poles of being "Papist Spies." In England as well, intolerance reared its head when Londoners spat on Polish soldiers in uniform.[38]

By the time the British government recognized the Polish Communist government in 1945, popular attitudes had hardened against the exiles. The state had nevertheless committed itself to support the exiles' cause, and even Labour ministers felt obligated to help the Poles adjust to British life. The Labour government organized the Polish Resettlement Corps to help this process, and almost all the remaining Polish soldiers mustered out of their units into the corps.

The prospect that the Poles might stay in the United Kingdom, despite their commitment to return to an anti-Communist Poland, aroused a groundswell of resentment and intolerance. The integration of this largely Catholic, anti-Soviet group into British society would not be an easy one. Communist Party members in the trade unions organized popular resentment against the Poles into a rearguard effort to force them to return to their country and to deny them work if they stayed.[39] Although the TUC's General Council agreed to the creation of the Polish corps and to the introduction of groups of Poles into industry—so long as this was done in consultation with the appropriate trade unions—opposition mounted. The General Council's stance provoked a storm of opposition at the 1946 Trades Union Congress meeting, but the opponents of the policy were not able to overcome the big general unions' support for the government.[40]

Despite their defeat at the meeting, the anti-Polish groups expressed widespread feelings. Reflecting the strength of the Communists, the extent of distrust of foreigners, fears of economic competition, as well as popular support for the Soviet position, many trade unions actively opposed the employment of the Poles. In several cases workers walked off the job when Poles were employed. Employers soon learned that employing mixed groups of Polish and British workers was nearly impossible. Instead, they employed Poles in single nationality groups within mixed factories or job sites—a technique that employers also used with racial minorities.[41] Many TUC-affiliated unions reacted to internal pressures and banned the Poles from membership. Even those unions that accepted Poles for membership urged their repatriation. Although the issue appears to have been spearheaded by the Communist Party, the Communists' position had widespread support, especially in traditional northwestern and Scottish locales of long-standing anti-Catholic animosity.[42] The Transport and General Workers' Union (TGWU) and the National Union of General and Municipal Workers accepted Polish members but consigned them to separate Polish branches. The TGWU organizers assumed that the Poles would not permanently reside in Britain and hoped for their early return to a non-Communist Poland.[43]

In response to public sentiment the government equivocated. While actually supporting the idea of the Polish Resettlement Corps, Foreign Secretary Ernest Bevin appeared sensitive to the leftist charge that the exiles were mostly fascist and should return home. Bevin sent a letter to every member of the corps in 1946, urging the Poles to go back to Poland.[44] He also rejected Churchill's suggestion that the Poles be used as part of the occupying forces in Germany because Bevin feared they would, in Allan Bullock's words, "increase the outcry against a 'Fascist' army" and undercut any chances at a political solution in Europe.[45] On the whole, government policy toward Poland and the exiles seems contradictory. The British recognized the new Polish regime while supporting the activities of the Polish exile community. This two-track policy led many exiles to feel "let down by the British."[46]

Despite the opposition, in many instances Poles successfully integrated into workplaces and often proved loyal union members. Not all impressions of the Poles were bad; many Britons recalled the bravery of the Polish pilots who fought in the 1940 Battle of Britain. The Ministry of Information found that residents of East Riding were pleased by the polite Polish soldiers stationed in their area.[47] Some unions bowed to government pressure and expressed a more tolerant policy. The National Union of Miners, the National Union of Agricultural Workers, and the immigrant-based National Union of Tailoring and Garment Workers worked out agreements to admit Poles to membership and employment in their respective industries.[48] In one union, the Amalgamated Union of Foundry Workers, grassroots pressures forced the executive council to back down from its original no-Poles policy. After a time the Poles mixed in well in some of the mining communities.[49] Tough Bermondsley dockers revealed a humanitarian side when their families adopted orphaned Polish children and their branch of the TGWU admitted Polish members.[50]

On the whole the Polish experience in Britain was a difficult one. Many native workers expressed fears that the exiles might become economic competitors, and it often took years for interethnic conflict to be overcome. For their part, most of the immigrants considered their stay in Britain temporary, an idea that undoubtedly lessened their interest in assimilation. As would any immigrant group facing rejection, they created their own communities based on their churches and political organizations in the hope of finding some protection from their hostile alien environment. Internationalism, the Poles learned, did not mean tolerance, and it apparently applied only to people far away. "For in no country," one Pole sadly explained, "is the word foreign so offensively pronounced."[51]

An Imperial Race

The world the British sought to remake included more than Europe and the United States: the leadership and the workers they represented had to come to grips with non-European people. Like the attitudes toward Continentals and North Americans, working-class thought about peoples from colonized and less industrialized countries revealed a mix of ideas based on prejudice, experience, and self-interest.[52] The main themes are the contradictory ones of class or even simple human solidarity on one side and paternalism, intolerance, and economic competition on the other. The way the British thought about minorities at home and foreigners abroad formed critical parameters for what they believed was possible in the world.

Of course, most people in Great Britain in the 1940s, except those living in dock areas, had no interactions of any sort with people of color. At most only 100,000 people of African or Asian origin lived in Great Britain as late as 1951.[53] Kenneth Lunn argues that Britain's current negative pattern of race relations was set by the interactions of the native and immigrant populations in the century before mass migration began in the 1950s. Although the origins of these relationships do lie in this period, it was not inevitable that the experience of West Indian, African, and Asian immigrants would be so difficult. The small numbers of people of color in the 1940s allowed race relations to take on quite varied patterns. Not all early immigrants met uniformly hostile or isolating experiences. This is not to argue, of course, that their experience was easy. Rather, the newness of the situation allowed the growth of a variety of living and working arrangements. It took time for structures of segregation and racism to develop.

Black-white relations, as with native-immigrant relations in general, had a long history in port towns but were new phenomena for most British workers.[54] Although the overall trend was toward segregation and prejudice, instances of tolerance were not uncommon, founded in both Socialist ideology and simple human solidarity. Michael Banton, for instance, found that in the leftist dockland

Borough of Stepney, London, some white residents refused to call their West Indian neighbors "coloured." Instead, they were "working-class people like ourselves."[55]

The unpredictability of British reactions made the lives of immigrants insecure. Confined to ghettos, at first in port towns and later in the Midlands and northwest, Africans, West Indians, and Asians found it difficult to obtain skilled jobs and tolerant neighbors. On occasion they did, and because most of the immigrants were men, many had relationships with or married white women. Their lovers and wives, rather than the immigrants, bore the brunt of racial intolerance, because the natives apparently expected the immigrants to seek white wives. Ostracized by their families, their children taken from them by the authorities, white wives and girlfriends essentially became black—that is, they lived in the ghettos and joined in immigrant culture.[56]

Although they traditionally were sailors living in port town ghettos, hundreds of West Indians labored in the Midlands and northwestern factories during the war. The majority of these men were skilled workers. Their reception at Royal Ordinance factories and other war plants revealed the emerging pattern of discriminatory race relations but on occasion also demonstrated that integration could occur and that racial ideas were still in flux. Although they joined the workforce in some Midlands factories without any reported incidents, the story was different in the northwest. At a De Havilland plant the workers threatened a walkout if the West Indians were employed. In order to forestall a strike the Ministry of Labour had to reassure the English workers that West Indians would not be promoted over them. The Shell Company tried to fire its West Indian employees because "fellow workers object to the Jamaican's personal habits."[57] Trade unions also put up resistance to the employment of the immigrants and visitors by refusing to admit to membership journey-level workers who lacked proof, as most did, of proper apprenticeship.[58]

The case of British Honduran lumberjacks in Scotland illuminates the range of reactions and the contradictory impulses of the British people. The government brought in Honduran workers, along with Australians and New Zealanders, to help alleviate labor shortages in the Scottish forests during the war. The Hondurans living in camps near the towns of Dun, Kirkpatrick Fleming, and East Lothian got on quite well with the local communities. But they did prove difficult to manage for the Ministry of Supply, which ran the camps, because of the Hondurans' leisurely work pace and their refusal to recognize the authority of the camp management after working hours. The most serious problem, in addition to the workers' resistance to camp discipline, according to the government investigator who studied the camps in the winter of 1942, was the mutual interest of local women and the lumberjacks. At least fourteen locals married lumber workers, relationships that disturbed some area residents and camp management. But many other local people enjoyed the company of the lumbermen in their homes, community centers, pubs, and churches.[59] They did not immediately reject or segregate the black workers, even though many had misgivings about the legitimacy of interracial sex.

In areas with larger foreign and immigrant populations, most notably seaports such as Glasgow, Liverpool, and Cardiff, race relations during the war assumed a more familiar form. Bowing to local pressure, the shipowners in Glasgow maintained for the war their long-standing policy of not permitting any Chinese or West Indian sailors to remain in port. Local custom restricted Indian seamen to the worst hotels and lodging houses while ashore. They were also often denied adequate medical care.[60] European sailors found themselves better looked after. In Liverpool the European sailors' unions ensured that shipboard conditions were acceptable, helped coordinate housing and medical care, and spurred the construction of nationality-based hostels. In contrast, conditions for African and Chinese sailors were deplorable. African sailors lived in a cramped hostel without food services or heating. Conditions for Chinese sailors deteriorated rapidly after the destruction of Liverpool's Chinatown in the Blitz. They too lived in a crowded filthy hostel lacking even a bath. A proposal to build a large inter-Allied hostel after the German bombs had destroyed much of the housing in the harbor area met with little support because the European sailors felt "such nations as the Chinese do not mix."[61] Mass-Observation found that white Britons were bothered that nonwhite sailors had relatively large sums of money at their disposal while in port.[62] Even after the war the Glasgow local of the National Union of Seamen reaffirmed its opposition to the hiring of Indians or Arabs, even if they were British citizens.[63]

Lunn has made clear that a "hierarchy of races" affected how people reacted to new immigrant groups, to domestic economic or socially oriented ethnic conflicts, and to international events and causes.[64] Britons treated black immigrants and sailors much better than they treated Asians and somewhat better than they treated Arabs. Indians appeared more acceptable and more known to the British than most other immigrants, even if religious intolerance was common.[65] Still, the treatment meted out to non-Europeans was worse than that given to Europeans. These were not hard-and-fast hierarchies and often depended on local circumstances. For instance, sailor Patrick Fyrth recalled that his fellow sailors preferred working with British-Arab fire fighters from the Tyneside rather than with Irish because the British-Arabs "at least caused no drink problem."[66] Constraints on the employment of non-Europeans and on their integration in Britain were more severe than for Europeans, although for black and Asian British citizens the situation was definitely easier than for noncitizens.

The Irish occupied a peculiar position in the ethnic hierarchy through the war. Thirty thousand Irish were recruited to help solve labor shortages in Britain, bringing anti-Irish sentiments to the surface.[67] One woman, the wife of a shop steward at a Spitfire factory, condemned the Irish workers in a language remarkably similar to criticism of the African and Asian sailors: "The Irish labourers employed at the Royal Ordinance Factory make the night hideous with their drunken songs. Their wages are enormous. . . . All this is public money and probably represents the lives of good men. People whose sons, young apprentice territorials, who volunteered in 1939, are in the Middle East, feel very strongly about Irish Labourers being allowed to stay at home and waste such huge sums of money."[68] One Midlands factory manager explained that he had the same difficulties with Anglo-Irish integration in his plant as he did with black-white relations.[69] Indeed, long-held English attitudes toward the Irish probably provided the pattern for the way they related to people of color.[70]

Although the Irish and the Poles eventually assimilated more easily than people of color, their experiences paralleled those of the racial minorities and exposed the underside of British working-class internationalism: unexamined prejudices, paternalism, and xenophobia. A group of working-class soldiers interviewed by Kenneth Little expressed succinctly the hollow aspect of internationalism. The soldiers told Little that they favored racial equality. Yet when he asked them if that meant they would follow a black officer, one soldier replied plainly that it would be unlikely because they had "refused to obey even a white French officer."[71] (This may be an unfair comparison because anti-French feelings had a long history in Britain. Would they have obeyed a white American rather than a Frenchman?) One sailor, for instance, recalled hearing more nasty comments about the French than the Germans in 1939.[72]

Anticolonialism, like racial attitudes, actually grew out of real ignorance of foreign affairs and thus depended more on domestic experiences and impressions based on analogy than on direct understanding. In this light, attitudes toward Europeans and third worlders resembled pro-Soviet thinking because all were based on projections of internal concerns. Few Britons of any class were concerned with the conditions of the people ruled by England. As Little put it, "It is safe to conclude that most English people's conception of 'the Colonies' is an extremely hazy one."[73] Even among more highly educated groups, Little found an astounding ignorance. School textbooks barely mentioned the colonies.[74] Those works that did predictably described the colonies in paternalistic and racist terms, as did most popular literature. The empire simply shed glory on Britain.[75]

Foreign experience did not necessarily breed open-mindedness. One laborer told Little that he had learned from his brother in the military in Egypt that Egyptians were "wogs" and that Indians should "be classed as 'niggers.'"[76] Working-class racism could be seen in the behavior of British troops abroad. Louis Challoner, a middle-class artilleryman stationed in Egypt during the war, sniffed at the "ordinary soldier" who "seeks out a restaurant where 'English cooking' is advertised and stuffs himself with eggs and chips all the while insulting in a loud voice the entire population of the rest of the world for their habit of eating food different from that to which they have become accustomed."[77]

Colonized people did not encourage such ignorance: one purpose of the nationalist agitation in India was to arouse the mass of British opinion. Indian self-rule became a critical issue during the war because of the repression of nationalists by the colonial government. British working people were able to see the justice in Indian demands. According to a BBC listener survey of 433 people conducted in September 1941, a majority of working people felt that Indian self-rule would help the war effort and should be granted quickly. Middle-class respondents, in contrast, tended to be more willing to maintain the status quo. Working people also felt that Indian policy was inconsistent with the government's professed war aims.[78] Hugh Wilson, a working-class soldier stationed in India during the war, was typically appalled, despite his dislike of the subcontinent, "by the way the natives of India were kept under by our British Army of Occupation . . . with a rod of iron."[79] Still, middle- and working-class respondents to a BBC listener survey agreed that "the Indian question can be safely left to the government."[80]

For many in Labour leadership, however, their administration of the empire was not just acceptable but necessary. They assumed that the success of the trade union movement depended on Britain's imperial status. As several scholars have pointed out, the stated commitment of the working class and Labour to Indian independence was shot through with paternalism and racist assumptions.[81] The TUC involved itself in colonial affairs in a number of ways. Citrine was deeply involved in containing the radicalism of Caribbean union leaders after the Trinidad general strike of 1937.[82] The TUC's Colonial Advisory Committee lobbied on behalf of moderate colonial unions and sponsored a survey of territories in the 1930s. The committee proposed a uniform trade union structure for the colonial unions and more beneficent colonial administration but, revealingly, did not offer independence as a solution to the workers' lack of power.[83]

Union leaders often spoke of defense of the empire as defense of Britain, a concept more to be expected among Conservatives. In 1941 Harry J. Edwards, chairman of the TGWU Executive Council, typically warned: "The issue is clear before us. Germany has declared her intention to smash the British Empire and secure world domination. We know precisely what that means. It would mean the destruction of all our institutions—the Trade Union and Co-operative Movements and every agency designed to secure the economic freedom of the workers with the complete subjection of the conquered people."[84] Colonizers become the colonized in Edwards's nightmare, a vision that highlights the importance of empire to ambitious Labour leaders. Bevin accurately viewed the empire as "essential to our survival as a great power."[85] In its early months the new Labour government pushed for control of former Italian possessions in Africa and for other additions to Britain's holdings. It seems obvious "that the imperial role came naturally to the Labour leaders," as Kenneth Morgan puts it.[86] Minister of Labour Bevin privately tried to convince the government to offer qualified independence as a morale booster.[87] Yet the unions as a whole endorsed the official Labour Party position that, although the Indians had legitimate grievances and the government should end its repression of democratic nationalists, the Indians themselves should refrain from agitation while the war continued.[88]

Nonetheless, the idea of empire had always been troublesome for Labour and became increasingly difficult for Labourites to maintain as the war drew to a close. The imprisonment of Jawaharlal Nehru, Mahatma Gandhi, and other Indian National Congress leaders from 1943 to 1945 raised strong doubts about imperial policy. In 1945 the right-wing TGWU put itself on record as favoring immediate self-rule and the freeing of all "democratic prisoners."[89] Within other trade unions right-wing members developed a distaste for empire as the British government continued to repress the nationalist movement in India.[90] Despite the wartime emergency, some right-wing voices called for independence in 1944.[91]

The principle of self-determination appealed to many people, but, as with the ideal of equality, this principle lost its luster when confronted with reality. The loss of great power status and the self-assertion of third-world nationalists threatened British notions of superiority. After the war many trade unionists supported the government's efforts to satisfy Indian demands for independence but were also ambiguous about the prospects for the success of the new nations. H. L. Bullock, a member of the TUC General Council and head of the General and Municipal Workers, expressed union opinions after a visit to India in 1948. He reported that the poverty and illiteracy of so many people in India convinced him that in the new nation "democracy is virtually impossible."[92]

Democracy and Bureaucracy

A combination of ignorance, underlying bias, and trust in the good intentions of leadership in regard to the third-world countries encouraged working people to give those in authority a wide latitude for pursuing policy. Even in respect to Soviet policy, most workers accepted that authority had to be delegated to their leaders, whether in government or in trade unions. This passivity may seem surprising because British workers were known for their willingness to strike in the postwar era. There was, nonetheless, a disjuncture between issues of international affairs and issues involving shop-floor conflict or economic necessity. Militance coexisted—uneasily, to be sure—with a powerful belief in Labourism, a vision of politics in which average people would be involved through their leaders or organizations in a bureaucratized democracy.

Labour voters, according to Mass-Observation, were far less nationalistic than Conservatives in 1946. Sixty percent believed their country should abide by a UN decision, even if it overrode British government policy.[93] Similarly, through 1946 at least, working people supported international control of nuclear weapons and independent police power for the United Nations.[94]

Like the soldiers who said they believed in ideals of equality but would not have obeyed a black officer, these replies may have shown a social acceptance of the principle of internationalism that hid an underlying distrust of the concept. Still, even accepting that these figures might be overstated, a majority of Labour voters expressed a willingness to subordinate national interest to world interest in 1946. These are significant facts in themselves, but, combined with the consistent evidence about working-class Labourite attitudes throughout the preceding decade, they demonstrate a high degree of underlying internationalist sentiment that was brought out by the opportunities promised by the end of the war and the rapprochement of the United States, Britain, and the Soviet Union. British working-class internationalism accepted the principle of that a hierarchical bureaucratized structure was the key to world peace, even if this may have reduced British national power.[95] These expressions should not be dismissed as epiphenomena. Rather, they form part of a system of beliefs that related quite clearly to the position of workers in postwar Britain.

The use of a bureaucratic and hierarchical state to meliorate the human condition was not only a Fabian middle-class dogma but also an intrinsic element of working-class thought. That Labourism as an all-encompassing solution to human ills did not succeed does not disprove the hold such thinking had on working-class minds. It may be that Labourism, by its very assumptions about electoral politics and bureaucratic solutions, contributed to the powerlessness of the working class and foreclosed the possibility of truly far-reaching social change in Britain and so contradicted its very purposes. Yet this intrinsic weakness, or self-contradiction, if you will, of Labourism was apparent only to a minority. Rather, working-class Britons looked to increasing social organization and therefore to world organization as an intrinsic part of their effort to improve their lives.

Workers' willingness to sacrifice power to their political party and national or world government did not lead to the social transformation they hoped for national and world affairs. Instead, working people experienced serious disappointment as their leadership in the trade unions and the Labour Party succumbed to the demands of power and abandoned long-held Socialist principles or programs. In part this frustration also developed from the realization that the traditionally accepted solutions to class problems, such as nationalization and stop-gap measures like wages policy, did not actually transform their daily experience. The disillusionment with Labour during the 1945–51 period was surely great.[96]

Many antiauthoritarian workers openly critiqued the bureaucratism of working-class socialism. This diverse group of people included Communists, anarchists, and Social Democrats, but all shared a perception that, at the very least, workers should not delegate too much authority. One antiauthoritarian columnist for the *Railway Review* put it this way: "I fear that the majority of members are content to allow control from the top instead of insisting that the policy should be moulded by the rank and file. . . . There are far too many who have come to regard the union as something abstract rather than as a body which by the effort of every member, should be a virile force to combat the many impositions with which we are burdened."[97] A shop steward who was a member of the Communist Party also warned of the need for workers to actually exercise power if they were to achieve a different sort of world order after the war: "Only if we take a positive attitude towards unity as something [for which] we are personally responsible, not some vague 'they' in Whitehall. We must realise that they in Whitehall are responsible to us, and can be made to respect our needs and wishes."[98] A similar idea was the belief that working people could prevent a future war by refusing to fight. As one Labourite expressed it: "I don't think ordinary people want war, and if we refused to fight there wouldn't *be* war. But the working classes of *every* country would have to agree to that" (emphasis in original).[99] Localism and other forms of particularist identity contributed to this form of resistance.

Militantly democratic solutions, however, remained minority dogma. The majority of workers did not abandon their political parties. Voter turnout increased in the 1950 and 1951 general elections. Labour's vote total actually grew from 47.8 percent to 48.8 percent from 1945 to 1951, and the total number of Labour voters increased by 1.9 million.[100] Only the peculiarities of the British electoral system gave the Conservatives the government in 1951, even though Labour received a 230,000-vote plurality. More telling at this high point of the cold war was that the Communist vote declined by only 10 percent from 1945 to

1950.[101] These figures hardly show that Labour, the Communist Party, or the left in general had lost their working-class constituency at this point. Between 1945 and 1951 Labour retained its seats in industrial areas, and the bulk of its losses came from middle-class constituencies in the south of England and marginal seats in Lancashire.[102] The results underscore the continuity of Labour support and the weakness of the coalition between the left-leaning majority of the working class and the reformist parts of the middle class that brought it to power in 1945.[103]

While working people may have voted Labour, such a vote does not reflect political passion. Indeed, many working people felt anxious, worried, and disappointed about international affairs but nonetheless voted Labour. Despite the Labour government's policy of rearmament (paid for with a tax increase), opposition to the USSR, and participation in the North Atlantic Treaty Organization, working-class voters believed that the Conservatives would be worse. Yet the decided contradictions between the impulses of the Labour electorate and the policies of the government surely had a deep impact. Mass-Observation found a fear that international relations would return to the conflicts and divisions of 1939, concluding: "There is apathy about, certainly, but it is not the apathy of non-interest. Predominantly it is the apathy of frustration."[104] By 1949 such feelings were undoubtedly increasing. Tom Harrisson found a rise in outlandish beliefs such as astrology, or the common belief that atomic weapons had caused the severe weather of the winter of 1946–47. Harrisson also found, as have scholars examining the culture of the 1950s, much more participation in sports, gambling, and drinking. The level of overall interest in international affairs declined rapidly after the war, Harrisson maintained, and is overstated by opinion polls: "A skilled listener-in might go for days through Britain without hearing a single mention of U.N., U.S.A., U.S.S.R., India, Atomic Bomb, or Science."[105]

Events in Eastern Europe undoubtedly increased support for anticommunism among the working class and for the TUC's attempt to revive restrictions on Communists developed in the twenties and thirties. A typical negative reaction appeared among the woodworkers in 1948 when several branches of their union sent resolutions to the executive council that warned of the dangerous implications of the Czech coup for British trade unions and demanded that the council pledge that "if any drift towards Communism should appear in our organization to fight it with all their might and squash it."[106] Yet anticommunism failed to develop a mass working-class base or inspire tremendous passion among trade unionists or the working class at large. There is little evidence in the form of branch resolutions or letters that reflect a large degree of popular outrage comparable, say, to the outpouring of feeling about the British role in Greece.[107] In March 1948 one housewife, who also supported the Marshall Plan, expressed a common assessment of the Czech coup to Mass-Observation: "It seems the Communists have taken over. The majority of them must be Communists there or they wouldn't have taken over."[108]

Anti-Soviet feeling (which was a different thing than anticommunism, as the TUC leadership discovered to its benefit during the war) attracted only a minority of working people in Britain. This does not mean that workers and especially trade unionists unquestioningly endorsed Soviet foreign or domestic policy. Rather, working-class Britons believed or at least wished that the amicable big power relations of the Grand Alliance period would form the basis for a cooperative system of international relations. In general, they opposed bloc politics because they thought such a system would lead to war. Anglo-Soviet conflict after the war proved very disturbing, for it was hard to believe that a Labour government would fight against the workers' state. As one man assessed East-West relations in 1945: "The likes of you and me can not do much, but I do think that it will be a lot better now we have got a Labour government. I reckon if we had one back in 1935, there would have been no war."[109] Although the conflict over communism did not inspire mass emotions, it did have strong effects in the late forties.

Britons were willing to believe that they had a special role in the world and that they could influence the course of events in European and third-world countries. Yet the underlying distrust of people of color and foreigners in general, and the growing minority opposed to the USSR's brutality in Eastern Europe, weakened the commitment to internationalism. When the working-class leadership switched its line after the breakdown of the Grand Alliance and the confrontations of 1946–47, British workers, except for a minority of Communists and other radicals, were unwilling to oppose their leaders on foreign policy.

During the 1940s the combination of forces and ideas that encouraged thinking about a new international order and the social transformation of Britain itself proved inherently unstable. Instead, the dreams of the midforties evaporated in a wave of cynicism and disappointment. The reversal in working-class thinking about world affairs turned out to be a painful and drawn-out process. The British people did support the cold war but unwillingly, with many exceptions, and certainly without the messianic enthusiasm for anticommunism that gripped the United States. The change is perhaps best summed up in this account of a Labour Party meeting in a small town in the early fifties, when the agenda turned to the colonies:

> "I've a letter here about British Guiana," the secretary said, "it's a bit of a long letter. Does anyone want me to read it?"
>
> "Don't bother," one of the ladies cried out, "we've enough trouble in Ashton."
>
> The letter was accordingly left unread.[110]

5

"Hoodwinking Ourselves": British Unions and the Politics of Internationalism

In the 1930s and 1940s the British trade union movement and the broader-based Labour Party were deeply divided. Unlike their North American counterparts, almost all British trade unions remained within a single organization, the Trades Union Congress. In contrast to the CIO, which achieved a political consensus through an uneasy coalition of liberals, Socialists, and Communists, or the AFL, which based its unity on anticommunism and craft unionism, the TUC could not easily attain political or industrial agreement among its constituents. This essential conflict occurred because of the congress's all-encompassing nature; even though almost all British trade unionists were ultimately committed to socialism, it was terribly difficult to get the unionists, who ranged from former Liberals to dogmatic Communists, to agree on foreign policy issues. Because of this internal division the decision to participate in the World Federation was the result of a thorny political confrontation within the TUC, whereas in the CIO the choice was made almost as a matter of course.

From the failure of the general strike of 1926 to the relative security of the 1940s, a group of right-wing unionists controlled the TUC, their power underwritten by the enormous Transport and General Workers' Union (TGWU) and the National Union of General and Municipal Workers. Of course, the characterization "right wing" must be perceived in the context of British Labour: the right shared with the left an expressed belief in a state-based socialism. The right was less inclined to embrace militant union action than the left and vehemently opposed insurgent movements within unions. The right pioneered corporatist approaches to industrial conflict in the twenties.[1] The left, especially the Communists, often subsumed the party line to union principles, so left-right conflicts were not always about union tactics. Political issues remained close to the surface. The right's power had been confirmed by the failure of the confrontational militance of such unions as the miners and the railwaymen in the general strike. With the defeat of 1926 and the fracturing of the left into Labour and Communist camps, the threat of the militants receded, but another danger took its place. More than anything else, the right was defined by a vehement opposition to allowing the Communist Party a strong open role in the labor movement.[2] Two men played central parts in leading the triumphant right-wing forces in the years after the general strike, and the same two men ruled Labour and TUC foreign policy in the forties: Ernest Bevin and Sir Walter Citrine.

Citrine, the TUC general secretary from 1925 to 1946, was a former member of the Electrical Trade Union, which ironically came under Communist control during Citrine's tenure at the TUC.[3] A consummate parliamentarian, Citrine controlled the TUC's bureaucracy and coordinated the actions of the congress's right-wing unions to ensure hotheads never again dominated the union movement. Described by the U.S. embassy's labor attaché as "one of the most skillful debaters in Britain," Citrine relied on "the cogency of his argument, the clear organization of his material, and a sharp sarcasm to win support."[4]

Bevin, one of the most important figures in twentieth-century British history, more than made up for Citrine's lack of charisma. A burly teamster who enjoyed a good drink and a joke, Bevin's personality contrasted sharply with Citrine's almost puritan countenance. Bevin had been the prime organizer of the enormous TGWU. Despite their personal differences, the two men agreed on the best program for the unions' industrial and political policies. They opposed militant actions, fought the Communists, and promoted labor-management cooperation mediated by state power. Ultimately committed to a policy of nationalizing industry, they nonetheless were fearful of the state's power if it threatened union independence. Bevin, like Citrine, had close relations with the leaders of the AFL, based on the fact "that to our own cause in the labour world and to the world outlook, we have had a similar vision," as the teamster told Matthew Woll.[5]

The left in the TUC consisted of a shifting coalition of Communists, left-wing Labourites, members of the Independent Labour Party, and assorted smaller groups, along with a sizable portion of less ideological militants from some industrial groups, notably the miners. The Communist Party made several unsuccessful attempts in the twenties and thirties to gain control of the labor movement, most famously through the National Minority Movement of 1929–31 during the Communists' aggressive "Third Period."[6] A combination of TUC repression of the Communists and co-optation of leftist ideas, particularly support of the USSR, had limited the Communist Party's gains to just a few unions, although in some industries, such as engineering, the Communists gained popularity as shop-floor militants. Nevertheless, except during periods of reduced Communist militance, such as in the Nazi-Soviet pact years, the Communist

Party and its leftist allies posed a continued threat to return the TUC, if not to militant confrontational working-class politics, at least to practices and ideas far from what the leadership considered politically safe. Exacerbating the Communist danger, the left wing of the Labour Party was in general willing to work with the Communists, especially in championing the USSR.[7]

The Dilemma of Labor Foreign Policy

After refusing to load ships to supply the Polish invasion of the Soviet Union in 1920, and failing in the general strike of 1926, trade unions avoided direct action in opposition to the government.[8] When British union leaders opposed their government during the 1930s, they did so within the established political framework in concert with the Labour Party. The TUC leadership, like that of the Labour Party, came to accept traditional British national interests, generously interpreted, as complementary to the goals of their socialism. In colonial affairs especially, where a lack of rank-and-file consensus—or even interest—allowed the leadership a great degree of latitude, the TUC worked closely with the Colonial Office to ensure the development of "responsible," that is, non-nationalistic reformist trade unions in British possessions.[9] Bevin and Citrine guided the TUC to a policy of moderate internationalism, for instance, during the Spanish Civil War, a policy that at times proved quite ineffective because of their fear of supporting Communists abroad and of contradicting perceived British national interests.[10]

In one area of foreign relations, however, the unions and the Labour Party differed substantially from the government. Revolted by the horrors of collectivization and the purge trials in the Soviet Union, the dominant group in the trade unions, led by Bevin and Citrine, opposed the Popular Front and worked hard to keep the Communists out of the Labour Party. But they could not take an actively anti-Soviet position during the thirties because of the USSR's continuing popularity among the rank-and-file. The TUC thus took quite a different view of the USSR than did Neville Chamberlain's government and in 1938 urged Britain and France to join with the Soviets in opposing the Germans.[11]

Bevin and Citrine's willingness to cooperate with the USSR while opposing coalition with the Communists revealed the twisted path these union leaders had to follow to combine their mistrust of Soviet foreign policy and dislike of communism with the sympathy for the Socialist experiment that they shared (or claimed to share) with the rank-and-file of the labor movement. Bevin expressed their sentiments well at the TGWU conference of 1935: "By God, I wish Russia could have seen that if she had never supported the Communist Party in England but allowed the British trade union movement to help Russia she would have been in a much better position today."[12] But the Soviets had not followed that path, and the trade union leaders felt threatened by the Soviets' staunchest supporters in Britain and worried by Soviet policy abroad.

The failure of British and French initiatives of the late 1930s to satisfy German ambitions at the expense of Central Europe, and the weakness of Anglo-French attempts to expand their alliance to include the Soviet Union, predictably led to substantial resentment of the government. To the left, Conservative prime minister Chamberlain's policy only confirmed the need to draw the Soviets into an alliance. The dominant rightists in Labour shared many of the left's doubts about British policy and had approved of the USSR's joining the League of Nations in 1934. But such agreement in the end did not translate into support for an Anglo-Soviet alliance. The British leaders felt especially betrayed by the signing of the Nazi-Soviet pact in 1939. Citrine reportedly told Anthony Eden afterward that "were he given the choice between life under Nazi or Soviet rule he would be in doubt as to which to choose."[13] On the eve of the war both dimensions of Soviet foreign policy—its use of the Comintern and its embrace of realpolitik in the Nazi-Soviet pact—had soured the atmosphere of British labor politics and encouraged the full expression of the right-wing leadership's anticommunism.

During the Soviet invasion of Finland in the winter of 1939–40, the TUC General Council brushed aside the hesitancy of many trade unionists and rushed to propagandize in favor of the beleaguered Finns. The TUC and the Labour Party produced films and books, conducted speaking tours, and sponsored resolutions in an effort to generate an upsurge in anti-Soviet feeling. Pronouncing the "dictatorship in Russia as severe and as cruel as anything that has happened in Germany," Citrine attempted to finish off labor's infatuation with the Soviet "experiment."[14] Similar outrage greeted the Soviet seizure of the sections of Poland given it under the secret protocols of the Nazi-Soviet pact. Although many working-class people felt increasingly worried about the USSR's policy, the TUC failed to sway their basic sympathy with the USSR: significant opposition arose among intellectuals and leaders, not among the rank-and-file.

When the Germans invaded the USSR in the summer of 1941, the TUC leadership—especially Citrine—found it hard to immediately reorient as required by the changed strategic situation and Britain's new alliance. Citrine at first avoided revising his ideas. On July 7, almost three weeks after the beginning of the invasion, he insisted to Duff Cooper, then minister of information: "I honestly believe that Russia is not fighting for any principle which we might cherish. She might conceivably stop fighting at the moment it suits her, irrespective of what happens to Great Britain. To suggest [as Churchill had] that we are fighting for the same purpose seems to me to be hoodwinking ourselves."[15] At that time Citrine affirmed his refusal to propagandize in favor of the Soviet struggle. But he soon overcame his misgivings and reoriented the TUC's Soviet policy to bring it into line with the government's. The TUC, capitalizing on the labor tradition of pro-Sovietism, easily moved to the forefront of the remarkable outburst of enthusiasm that accompanied the alliance.

Between 1941 and 1946 the government could not effectively oppose efforts to create close ties between Britain and the USSR, such as those constructed by the World Federation of Trade Unions, despite the misgivings government officials might have had about such enterprises or about the TUC's ability to extricate itself from such relations in the likely event that the wartime rapprochement soured. Even though the government, and Bevin in particular, opposed the calling of the World Trade Union Conference (WTUC) and the participation of the TUC in the World Federation from the outset, they could not do so openly because of their official commitment to the policy of alliance. Nor did behind-the-scenes pressure work on the all-important issue of Communist participation in world organizations, not only because the British officially accepted the principle of Soviet participation in a postwar world organization at the 1943 Moscow conference of foreign ministers and the 1944 Dumbarton Oaks conference but also because the TUC resisted government influence for its own reasons. The TUC erred, from the government's perspective, in taking official policy too literally and creating international structures that required permanent cooperation with the Communists in order to succeed. Yet the government's hands were tied by its public position, thereby creating room for the TUC to act independently in response to the sentiments of the main body of trade unionists, that is, in accord with the political needs of the TUC leadership.

Faced with a potential combination of militant rank-and-filers, left-wing Labourites, and Communists, the union leaders could not risk contradicting popular enthusiasm for the USSR. Further strengthening the TUC's unwillingness to act as an outlet for the Foreign Office's anti-Soviet policy was a personal conflict between Bevin and Citrine that made the latter unwilling to accept any form of direction from his former colleague. As a final prop of TUC independence, the union leaders had grave misgivings about how far corporatist relations should go. They worried—not because they doubted the ultimate importance of such relations but because they constantly looked over their shoulders at a rank-and-file that feared excessive cooperation with government.

Unlike the rank-and-file, trade union leaders were unable to follow a consistent path in world politics. Their attempt to attain personal goals, those of their organizations, and those of their nation produced an erratic overall policy. The TUC leadership and that of individual unions appeared at one moment to be opposing the dictates of government and at another to be obeying them, moving first with the flow of popular sentiment, then seeking to transform it. At the root of this inconsistency lay the union leaders' political circumstances. They had to remain in control of their organizations by responding to their memberships' sentiments even as they battled dangerous militant and Communist tendencies. Internationalism directly benefited the unions in the mid-1940s, but as the British joined in the cold war in late 1946 and 1947, this policy came to threaten the unions' power. The conjunction of events that allowed the expression of global ambitions also revealed the profound misgivings many union leaders had about international activity even while all endorsed its necessity.

Sources of Trade Union Internationalism

Remarking on the need for flexibility in obtaining the best for the labor movement, Citrine once sarcastically told Paul Tofahrn of the International Transport Workers: "There is such a thing as principles in this life."[16] Citrine, with great skill, did pursue his basic principles: protecting and building the TUC's power and the strength of Labour's right wing. The realm of international labor offered obvious benefits to Citrine. The TUC embrace of the USSR provided more than prestige; it also fulfilled political imperatives of the leadership as a whole. Participation with the Soviets and Americans in reordering world labor satisfied the union leaders' urge for power over world affairs and over what they believed to be the sources of war. The true nature and goals of the USSR—a source of intense fascination as well as dread before and after the alliance period—proved relatively unproblematic at the time because of a real Soviet willingness to respect British government and trade union interests on the one hand, and, on the other, a revision of TUC thinking about the Soviet threat.

Citrine succeeded in occupying a position unsurpassed by any other trade unionist in the world. While Bevin certainly exercised more power as minister of labor and then foreign secretary, Citrine had perhaps an equal claim to eminence as general secretary of the TUC, president of the International Federation, and then president of the World Federation of Trade Unions. By his own account, Citrine served on about thirty public bodies during the war.[17] Bevin complained to Hugh Dalton in 1944 that Citrine "is always trying to be a super Foreign Secretary and is always flying about, to Washington, Moscow, etc."[18] Dalton, then head of the Board of Trade, commented in his diary in 1942 that foreign policy "now is [Citrine's] great prestige preoccupation."[19] Others noticed Citrine's changed demeanor in the war. An anonymous union leader told the U.S. labor attaché in London in 1944 that he did not "know what's come over Citrine in the last year or so." The union leader worried that "his [Citrine's] vanity is getting the better of him." Worse: "He is beginning to think of himself as a crusader. . . . He is a big man—there is no one in the movement except Bevin who can match him—but he is getting a bit careless."[20] Similarly, the AFL's Matthew Woll worried that "Citrine was playing with fire. . . . He aspired to world labour leadership."[21]

Bevin had long disliked Citrine, whose sense of propriety irritated the gregarious Bevin.[22] Citrine's restrained style concealed an effective organizer and a skilled political manipulator who, his victims were quick to realize, could be "acid in his opposition" when the need arose.[23] Before Bevin entered the government, their difficulties appeared to be based on a clash of personal styles. But as is often the case, the personal blended with the political once Bevin took office as minister of labor.

The central problem between them grew from disputes involving the proper relation of the trade unions to the government. During the war Bevin sought to establish increased government control over labor markets as well as wages, contract negotiations, and other aspects of the world of labor normally excluded from state domination by the nature of British labor relations.[24] It would have been relatively easy for Citrine to resist the intrusion of a Tory minister of labor. But Bevin was a union man who had helped build the country's largest union, the TGWU, and, along with Citrine, had rescued the TUC from more militant confrontational leaders after the 1926 general strike. Bevin's semicorporatist approach to labor relations could not be so easily opposed.

Although Bevin claimed that the government's labor policies were based on the principle of "voluntaryism," the British equivalent of free trade unionism, it is clear that he attempted to establish greater government control over labor—in the national interest.[25] The trade unions, however, did not readily concede their power.[26] Citrine eagerly entered into battle with his colleague to defend the unions' independence from government control. He did so not because he was ideologically opposed to corporatism (quite the contrary, he was a long-time adherent of such policies). Rather, he and other leaders sensitive to rank-and-file sentiment realized their membership would not allow them to give up traditional trade union independence—even for a national emergency. Bevin's claim of acting in line with the principle of voluntaryism was a partial response to such feelings. Corporatism also threatened the TUC leaders' own power, for it was certainly possible that the state would return to its traditional role as the guarantor of business's prerogatives. After the war the difficulties of state-union relations became more acute as the Labour government sought continued sacrifices from the trade unions in exchange for the nationalization program and for economic survival. Citrine's personal conflicts with Bevin lent fire to his opposition to government policies. Trade union internationalism proved a useful weapon in his battle to prevent further government encroachment in union territory and to upstage Bevin.

By the fall of 1941 Bevin and Citrine's relations had so deteriorated that Clement Attlee had to intervene to get them even to talk to each other.[27] Friction between the government and the TUC reached this intensity after Bevin proposed increased conscription of skilled workers and the drafting of women as part of new efforts to increase the size of the military without affecting production. Conflicts continued through the war. In 1943, for instance, Bevin and other Labour ministers disappointed the trade unions by refusing to support repeal of the Trade Disputes Act of 1927, which had curtailed union rights in the wake of the 1926 general strike. Citrine took Bevin's position as a betrayal, warning that "our loyalty has been very badly strained and we are not prepared indefinitely to support this manifest injustice."[28]

Citrine reversed his opposition to Anglo-Soviet cooperation shortly after the government's 1941 proposal for "direction" of labor, a program of extensive government control over workers and the labor market. Although there is no clear evidence that he reversed himself in response to the conflict with Bevin over labor policy (and was probably equally or more worried about the popularity of Communists), Citrine was undoubtedly looking for a means to increase his own stature and to demonstrate that the unions were patriotic yet independent. In the midst of a tremendous military and political crisis in the fall of 1941, British and Soviet union leaders agreed to form the Anglo-Soviet Trade Union Committee (ASC). Both groups of unionists were unsure what would come of their first collaboration since the 1920s, but both hoped the committee would answer pressing domestic and diplomatic needs. In founding the committee the Soviets and the British agreed that their common task was to stimulate increased production to more effectively fight Hitler. The ASC set its specific goals as combating German propaganda, increasing the knowledge of workers about their new allies, and speeding the production of armaments.[29]

However, the basis of Anglo-Soviet trade union cooperation during the war grew from more than a simple concern for increasing production. To Citrine, like most TUC leaders, the context in which production was increased mattered as much as the actual increase. Although the war effort might have benefited, the unionists would have done real damage had they achieved their production goals at the expense of their own or their organizations' power. For the right-wing Labourites who dominated the TUC General Council, concern for the war effort had to be balanced with the political reactions among militants to excessive cooperation with government. Union leaders also had to be wary of a government that threatened to trample on union prerogatives. The logic of government policy promised to extend controls over labor to the point where union power would be severely eclipsed—if the trade unions were not effective in their corporate duty of maintaining discipline in the workforce. The Communists and other leftists threatened—on the basis of the upsurge in support for the USSR and their domination of the shop floor in key industries—to supplant the traditional union structure in the plants and the branch meeting rooms, then to displace the right at the pinnacle of the union hierarchy. Still, the left may not have been as dangerous as it seemed. The Communist Party line at the time made the Communists more willing to give in to pressure for sacrifices in working conditions and for higher levels of production than their more conservative opponents, thus undercutting the Communists' appeal among the rank-and-file.[30]

In turning to Anglo-Soviet cooperation, Citrine sought to find and legitimize new methods of increasing production for the war effort without sacrificing union power. He sought this particular combination because he was caught in the bind of having to help the national effort even as he defended the particularist interests of the unions. "In all these matters," the General Council reported to the congress's 1941 meeting, they "kept in view the absolute necessity for assisting the prosecution of the war in every possible way, while at the same time preserving the maximum amount of self-government for industry."[31] The problem for the TUC in the summer of 1941 was how to balance the government's demands for increased production with the unions' needs to maintain and increase their power. Citrine explained the predicament to his Russian colleagues in Moscow in the fall of 1941:

> It is highly important to the Trade Union Movement that the conditions of life of its people should not be interfered with more than is necessary during a period of war. . . . We demanded that the people should be consulted at every stage. . . . We have always, as a Trade Union Movement, while working in conjunction with the Labour Party, insisted on keeping our absolute independence. Therefore, although the Labour Party has ministers in the Government, and my own colleague Ernest Bevin is a member of the cabinet, we still demand that we shall be consulted by the Government no matter what phase of policy is concerned. Our position therefore is that we are giving steady general support to the Government, but we are keeping a watchful eye on the Government to make sure that nothing is done under the guise of war to weaken our position as a Trade Union Movement.[32]

Once Citrine and his comrades overcame their anti-Communist thinking, the invasion of the Soviet Union provided a seemingly brilliant solution to the problem of maintaining control of the unions in the face of the internal and external threats. International cooperation proved a gold mine by co-opting popular enthusiasm for the Red Army and the USSR in order to disarm opposition to changes in labor practices and legitimize increased exploitation of labor. Identification of the TUC with the cause of the USSR and a concomitant reorientation of international politics undercut the Communist Party's power, which could have later aided a left-wing rebellion in union ranks in favor of a new order for the union, nation, and world.

The case of the Amalgamated Society of Woodworkers (ASW) illustrates well the problems faced by middle-of-the-road union leaders in containing frustrated rank-and-filers and reinvigorated leftists. As in the TUC, the leadership of the Woodworkers used internationalism as an easy means of co-optation and to demonstrate the union's commitment to Socialist principles. During the war Frank Wolstencroft, a General Council member and companion to Citrine on the Anglo-Soviet committee, faced an enormous revolt in his normally staid union. Communists and other leftists posed only a minor threat by themselves, but when they joined with the militant wage-conscious members in this craft union, they were able to overwhelm the elected leadership.

Concessions to the government, whether it be of Labour or a coalition, proved the most unpopular policies of the Woodworkers' leaders. Indeed, the ASW had to pull out of the National Federation of Building Trade Operatives in 1941 when that organization accepted government-mandated piecework in an industry traditionally run on a straight hourly wage.[33] But the government forced the Woodworkers to back down—indeed, the union had little choice because the Essential Work Order for the construction industry specifically mandated "payment by result."[34] The decision infuriated members, but the union's Executive Council demonstrated its mastery of the union apparatus, keeping the lid on the insurgency through a combination of compromise and control. A vote of members in the fall of 1943 revealed that 80 percent opposed payment by result and wished to refuse its introduction. Perturbed but not at a loss for what to do, the Executive Council maintained that "the whole position requires serious reconsideration" and called for another vote.[35] The outcry against piecework and against the Executive Council's disregard for democratic procedure continued to rise through 1944. The Woodworkers were also incensed about dilution, the introduction of less skilled, unapprenticed workers (often women) in their trade. Insurgents demanded the holding of an annual delegate conference, believing that such a conference would effectively democratize the union and act as a check on the leadership's compromises.

The Woodworkers' Executive Council refused to concede the legitimacy of rank-and-file anger. Attributing the uproar to Communist disruption, it attempted to stamp out the movement. The executive maintained that "inspired resolutions"—resolutions from dozens of branches, all bearing the same or similar language and by implication organized by the Communist Party—could not be considered legitimate protests. By collapsing the Communist threat to their power with that of a more general rank-and-file movement opposed to piecework and dilution, the ASW leaders underlined the interconnection of the dangers of militancy and communism. They directed the editor of the union's *Monthly Journal* not to print such resolutions, in a vain attempt to stem the rising tide of insurgency.[36] Eventually, the leadership had to concede the force of the opposition's numbers. After postponing a decision for two years, the leaders agreed in late 1945 to put the idea of an annual conference to a vote. The conference was overwhelmingly approved in early 1946. The members did have the last laugh—they rejected a request to raise the salaries of the union's officers. The threat of the Communists was minor in itself. But if the Communists had mobilized the substantial rank-and-file sentiment against corporatist labor control, limited wage increases, and dilution, they would have been a powerful force indeed. Instead, the leaders were able, because of the unresponsive structure of the union and their combination of repressive and co-optative responses, to remain in control.

Despite the insurgency, the Woodworkers' leaders did not attempt to eliminate the Communist presence from the union. They used a combination of repressive measures, which outlawed fractions (organized factions usually led by Communists), the distribution of Communist literature, and so on, all of which were within the moderate range of the TUC's anti-Communist measures.[37] But the leadership of the Woodworkers never forbade Communists to seek union office or prevented them from attending conventions, as happened in the TGWU. Rather, the Woodworkers' leadership tried to co-opt a key element of potential Communist power: support for the USSR. In the midst of the crisis Wolstencroft, the ASW general secretary, a member of the TUC General Council, and close associate of Citrine's, traveled to the USSR for the first meetings of the Anglo-Soviet committee. He paid particular attention while there to the "progressive piece work system" and relayed his impressions that Soviet success depended on the "splendid results" of the Russians' system of labor control and direction.[38]

The TUC General Council initiated the effort to create the Anglo-Soviet committee as part of its continuing efforts to control the left. The entrance of the USSR into the war shifted the political terrain of the TUC as the Red Army reinforced the left in labor. At first, the dominant right and middle were able to keep support for the Soviet Union from turning into growing leftist strength, but suppressing the left-wing upsurge proved increasingly difficult. By 1943 even the TWGU wanted the withdrawal of Circular 16 of 1934,[39] which prevented Communists from serving on TUC district councils, if only to forestall a full-blown revolt of those sympathetic to the Communists.[40] The shift of the TGWU forced the withdrawal of the "black" circular at the 1943 meeting of the TUC.[41] Although the General Council had to accede to the force of rank-and-file feeling and withdraw the circular, it managed to beat back repeated attempts to align the TUC with the left of the Labour Party, which favored the affiliation of the Communist Party.

The Joys of Cooperation

The opportunity that the German invasion of the USSR offered the left most likely convinced Citrine finally to reverse his opposition to Anglo-Soviet collaboration. Indeed, J. H. Potts, the left-leaning president of the railway union, deserves the credit for spurring the creation of the Anglo-Soviet committee. He was the first to raise the cry for formal cooperation with the Soviet trade unions, even before Citrine refused Duff Cooper's invitation to promote the cause of Britain's new ally.[42] The general secretary had to develop an effective strategy for countering the growing power of the Communist Party and its sympathizers in the unions, in the TUC, and in the Labour Party, if not on the shop floor.

The establishment of the Anglo-Soviet committee gave the government and the TUC an excuse to deny union leftists access to the USSR, as they did to Potts and to members of the Communist-led Fire Brigades' Union who had sought trips to the USSR in the early fall of 1941.[43] Rather than make explicit their opposition to independent leftist contacts with the Soviets, the TUC's leaders echoed the government argument that a trip would be too difficult because of "all the transport difficulties involved."[44] In reality, Citrine believed that "it [was] reasonable that Trade Unions should confine themselves to the contacts made by" the Anglo-Soviet committee.[45] The Russian cause had excited the British workers "into a high state of almost unreasoning admiration . . . [one] was tempted to say hysteria," Citrine informed the unimpressed executive board of the American Federation of Labor in 1942. If the TUC had not created the ASC, the miners, railwaymen, and engineers would have, he explained.[46] The Anglo-Soviet committee proved an effective preemption of uncontrollable independent contacts with the Soviets and so closed what might otherwise have been a natural path to increased power for the left.

The Soviets, desperate for the widest support possible and facing unprecedented labor upheavals at home, were more than willing to cooperate with the TUC General Council in shutting the leftists out of the ASC. At the very first meeting of the committee, held in Moscow in the fall of 1941 as German troops threatened the city, the British delegates complained of the activities of the Communist Party of Great Britain. They stressed to the Soviets the need for their participation in counteracting the effects of the Communist Party, though Citrine did apologize for bringing the issue up "because I know the difficult position you are in on this question."[47] Citrine invited the Soviets to visit Britain as "our guests" but asked that they not speak "under the auspices of any other body—political bodies etc," clearly intending that the Soviets avoid contacts with the British Communists or any other suspect group. The representatives from the All-Union Central Council of Soviet Trade Unions (AUCCTU) readily agreed.[48] They kept the promise during the life of the committee, contradicting the principles of international Communist solidarity.

The ASC also underscored the unionists' image of themselves as crucial to the diplomatic process. Citrine told the Soviets that he had originally hoped the committee meeting would coincide with the Moscow conference of September 1941, which arranged for U.S. and British aid to the USSR. "I did not mean to be part of that conference," Citrine told Nicolai Shvernik, his AUCCTU counterpart, at their first face-to-face meeting, "but we would have been meeting as a Trade Union Body in this part of the City and the Government Missions would have been meeting elsewhere."[49] This would have allowed coordination between the two bodies and not coincidentally underlines the equation Citrine made of government and trade union diplomacy.

The early good relations on the committee did not easily survive the vicissitudes of the Soviet-British relationship. Conflict about diplomatic issues soon clouded the areas of agreement, such as promoting mutual goodwill and stimulating production. Citrine later claimed that international trade union cooperation could succeed only if it dealt with strictly economic concerns and avoided any political considerations. "We are trade unions not political bodies," he emphasized.[50] Yet the coming together of the British and Soviet trade unions in 1941 was explicitly political.[51] It provided direct political benefits to each group and underlined the importance of their organizations. Citrine and his fellows saw their collaboration with the AUCCTU in clearly political terms, and in private meetings they were more than willing to reassure the Soviets of their commitment to deal with the difficult issues of their relationship: "On any political question, the T.U.C. would have no hesitation in forming and expressing a judgement," he informed the Soviets in 1943.[52] The distinction between economic issues and political ones was, in practice, irrelevant.

The only serious conflict that arose during the active life of the Anglo-Soviet committee did involve a political issue. In 1943 the Soviets demanded that the TUC endorse the immediate opening of a second front in Europe. The TUC men, for their part, resisted the demands for the second front as inappropriate to their role and, moreover, in conflict with their government's policy. "It was," Citrine explained, "a matter for expert military knowledge," not a political issue on which they could make a pronouncement.[53] The Soviets, despite the unmistakable desperation of their pleas, touched a very sensitive chord in the TUC leaders at the meeting for, as AUCCTU chief delegate Shvernik responded, the second front most certainly "was a political matter."[54] It proved a particularly delicate problem for the TUC leaders because Labour's left wing had been working with the Communist Party in Britain to mobilize support on this immensely popular issue. This situation only strengthened the leadership's resolve not to give the Communists and their allies a moral victory by criticizing the British and U.S. governments for avoiding a second front.

The TUC's domestic concerns, however, endangered their relations with the Soviets. Unwilling to give up, AUCCTU sent a fraternal delegation headed by Shvernik to the 1943 TUC conference at which the Soviet delegates pressed their requests that the congress endorse a second front. The TUC General Council once again rebuffed them and pressed forward with an ambiguous resolution after a behind-the-scenes fight. Ominously for the council, the pro–second front dispute became embroiled in TUC factionalism, with members of Labour's left wing, like Bryn Roberts of the National Union of Public Employees, leading the fight in favor of the Soviet position.[55] Sir Frederick Leggett, Bevin's assistant at the Ministry of Labour, worried that the conflict might doom Anglo-Soviet trade union cooperation and "the Russian trade union movement may again become the center of one international organisation and the British, American, and Scandinavian trade unions uneasy partners in another."[56] The Soviets, for their part, "were very miserable about the way things had worked out between them and the TUC" and worried that Citrine may not have been as sympathetic to their needs as they had first thought, according to H. P. Smollet of the Ministry of Information, who spoke with the delegation's secretary, Mikhail Falin.[57] The TUC seemed to be on the brink of a serious split with AUCCTU—talks to expand the Anglo-Soviet committee to include U.S. trade unions had stalled over CIO participation, and the TUC General Council was strongly resistant to any more compromises with the Soviets that might empower the left. Christopher F. A. Warner, head of the Northern Department at the Foreign Office, remarked that the Soviets ironically "found they got on much better in diplomatic and official circles" than with labor.[58]

But the left inadvertently came to the rescue of the General Council. Bryn Roberts did not intend to help the General Council find a way out of its political predicament when he initiated the call for a World Trade Union Conference at the 1943 Trades Union Congress. Rather, Roberts hoped to force the TUC

General Council to abandon its acceptance of the AFL's intransigent anticommunism (the General Council had formalized its tolerance of the Americans' anticommunism in forming the AFL-TUC committee in 1942). The formal joint participation of the CIO and AUCCTU, Roberts reasoned, was necessary to successful international cooperation.

More than international cooperation was at stake, however, for Roberts sought to embarrass the TUC General Council while advancing his claim to a role in the international arena. Roberts had made international affairs his specialty after traveling as a fraternal delegate to the AFL convention and as an unofficial visitor to the CIO in 1942. (The TUC did not have fraternal relations with the CIO until after the war.) After writing and actively promoting a book on the history of the AFL-CIO split, Roberts had taken on the task of organizing support in the TUC for an all-inclusive international organization.[59] Using the Public Employees' newspaper as a forum, Roberts underscored the importance of a united world labor movement: "It is, we believe, nothing short of a tragedy that no effective collaboration has yet been established between the British TU movement and that of America and Soviet Russia."[60]

But Roberts was an outsider, excluded from the General Council because of his union's continual jurisdictional conflicts with the powerful National Union of General and Municipal Workers and the Transport and General Workers.[61] Compounding his problems, Roberts, although apparently not a Communist, was on the left of the Labour Party and a close friend of Aneurin Bevan, also a Welshman and a leader of the left in the Labour Party. A proponent of industrial unionism, Roberts identified with the CIO leaders and, like them, was excluded from the pinnacles of international power. Unfortunately for Roberts's ambitions, where the CIO succeeded, he did not; the CIO's inclusion did not end his exclusion. The danger that Roberts and his allies, such as Jack Tanner, the left-leaning president of the Amalgamated Engineers' Union, would seize the international agenda was what ultimately brought about a change in the General Council's thinking. The TUC gave in to the leftists' agitation and agreed to call a World Trade Union Conference of all union centers in countries fighting the Axis. Against the better judgment of its leaders in and out of government, the TUC placed itself at the center of the movement for a new world order.

6

"A Grave and Conscious Moral Force": The TUC and the End of Alliance

Politicians and diplomats often say one thing and believe another. Certainly this was the case with Ernest Bevin, the British minister of labor and trade union leader, when he addressed delegates from more than sixty countries at the World Trade Union Conference in London on February 9, 1945: "I know of no Movement which has greater possibilities of bringing moral force to bear upon the observance of international law and conduct—a grave and conscious moral force, than this trade union movement." Bevin claimed he wanted to develop "the spirit of international solidarity" in order to transcend "narrow prejudices of national conceptions."[1] Yet Bevin had opposed the convening of the WTUC and adamantly disagreed with its premises of East-West unity. The dissonance between the ideas expressed by Bevin and his behind-the-scenes positions reflected the powerful and contradictory pressures forming the ideas of foreign relations held by British union leaders.

What had at first appeared to be a tactical alliance of the United States, Great Britain, and the Soviet Union to meet the German onslaught quickly became an essential component of international politics. Ironically, the TUC's leaders found themselves championing a situation in which they had little faith. As the war drew to a close, and considerations of European reconstruction raised fears of Soviet power and Communist ambitions in Europe and the Middle East, doubts grew within the government and among the dominant union leaders about whether British and Soviet interests could remain in harmony. Moreover, Britain's leaders worried that the nation's economic problems and imperial crises would undercut their country's postwar position as a world power. They were faced with an overwhelming need to cut back their global commitments while simultaneously protecting what remained. Given their loyal service during the war, it would have been predictable for the TUC to follow the changing policy of the government. But this was not to be—at least not immediately. In the odd circumstances of the mid-1940s extricating the TUC from its entangling alliance with Soviet unions proved quite difficult.

The TUC leaders found they could not rush to the defense of traditional British national and imperial interests if these contradicted Socialist thinking and popular sentiment. In contrast, Bevin, who as foreign minister was freer of the constraints imposed by the union membership, actively expressed his support for traditional British foreign policy. In his initial cabinet post as minister of labor, Bevin, according to U.S. ambassador Averell Harriman, had "never really risen above labor union politics."[2] When Bevin assumed his post at the Foreign Office, however, he was a man of "sound ideas," as the aristocratic Sir Alexander Cadogan, permanent undersecretary of state, discovered to his pleasure.[3] In other words, a Labour man, despite the traditions of the movement, could be a defender of British power—although Bevin did promote the democratization of diplomatic staffs and the independence of India.[4] Nonetheless, such sound ideas were not necessarily the ones we associate with the cold war, as Anthony Adamthwaite points out, though they did include a distinct wariness of Soviet goals and methods.[5] The extent of popular support for the USSR in Britain restrained right-wing Labour leaders well into the 1940s and forced them to give at least the impression that they sought rapprochement with the USSR.[6] Once in power, Labour did not entirely reject its earlier ideology, but neither did it jettison the core of long-standing British policy.[7] For those sections of Labour outside of government, however, the situation was different. Between 1944 and 1947, in fact, the TUC found itself in a degree of opposition to the government not seen since the mid-1920s—a position made all the more surprising because of the friction that arose after 1945 between Bevin and the organization he had helped to guide. Despite their common assessment of the USSR, Bevin and the union leadership fought about the unionists' efforts to construct a world order based on the assumptions of the Grand Alliance. The TUC believed in defending British interests in the third world but not as clearly in industrialized nations. In effect, the TUC and the government fought over the role of the USSR in the postwar world.

The temporary oppositional role of the TUC arose in part because of contradictions within British policy toward the USSR, the colonies, and the United States. Especially in relation to the USSR, the British government found itself caught between public endorsement of the alliance on one side and the Foreign Office's fears of Soviet ambitions in Europe and the Middle East on the other.

The TUC and the Foreign Office

In convening its world conference, the TUC plunged headlong into some difficult and, at the time, uncertain areas of British foreign policy: the reconstruction of Europe, plans for postwar relations with the USSR, and policy toward former enemies and neutral states. Although TUC leaders may have wanted to maintain pacific relations with their government, their effort to forestall a left-wing rebellion and to maintain some sort of relationship with the Soviet unions led them into conflict nonetheless. The response to the left pushed the TUC onto a path that led eventually to participation in the World Federation of Trade Unions (WFTU), a path that, once taken, appeared increasingly dangerous to defenders of the perceived British national interest. International labor cooperation awakened issues of nationalism, imperialism, and communism that many, especially those in the British government, would rather have left undisturbed. The government opposed the world conference, and subsequently the World Federation, most likely because of misgivings about relations with the Soviets and the developing conflict with Communists in Europe. But because the government still was openly committed to cooperation with the Soviets, it could not very well prevent the TUC from following its lead.

The world conference raised serious misgivings within the state. The Security Executive, a committee chaired by the home secretary, found that the conference would be too much of a risk and opposed its being held in Britain.[8] The Foreign Office also thought it a bad idea.[9] More serious from a union standpoint, Bevin worried that the Soviets would gain too much power from the inevitable result of the conference—the founding of a new world organization. The world conference, Bevin complained, was a "tragic mistake."[10] But it appears that he did not believe it tragic enough to force another confrontation with Walter Citrine and so raised no substantive objections. The minister of labor decided to keep his ministry at a safe distance from the conference and advised the Foreign Office to do the same.[11] Bevin wanted to make sure the British government did not "give Sir Walter Citrine any excuse for suggesting that there had been any official interference."[12] Government intervention would be counterproductive, Bevin reasoned, for "if we intervene an element of martyrdom will be introduced and a situation created which would be exactly what the promoter [i.e., the USSR] desires."[13] If the government stayed in the background, the "world conference will prove its own weakness and the ill-considered basis upon which it is being organized."[14] Operation Overlord, the long-awaited invasion of France in 1944, which was scheduled to occur during the world conference, did, however, interfere with the TUC's plans. The TUC postponed the conference until 1945 at the government's behest, but Bevin's hope for an early collapse of the alliance-inspired global labor organization proved premature.

Despite Bevin's advice that the government stay out of the way of the TUC, inviting trade unions from so many countries was bound to raise problems. In an attempt to avoid such conflicts Citrine consulted regularly with the Foreign Office, mostly to find information on the bonafides of various organizations. The Foreign Office, in keeping with official policy, was loath to get involved in deciding which organizations were legitimate trade unions and decided that "we do not want to answer these questions if we can help it."[15] Despite this decision, some issues were too important for the Foreign Office to keep its resolution. Citrine proved willing to incorporate its concerns in his policy. For instance, the Foreign Office strenuously objected to inviting the exiled Spanish Socialist Indalecio Prieto of the Unión General de Trabajadores, a former minister of defense in the republican government, because the invitation would endanger the Foreign Office policy of supporting the "moderate alternative" in Spain.[16] The Foreign Office denied visas to Prieto and his colleague Belarminon Tomas, though the British government, after TUC protests, finally allowed other Spanish union delegates to attend.[17]

The Foreign Office also got its way by convincing the TUC to invite only representatives of trade unions connected to the Polish government-in-exile in London and exclude those allied with the Soviet-backed Lublin government. Foreign Secretary Anthony Eden warned Citrine that inviting the Lublin Poles would aggravate the "ill feelings which already existed." Eden did not, however, explain how excluding the Communists would improve matters.[18] Underlining the TUC's commitment not to defy government policy in crucial areas, Ernest Bell, the TUC's international secretary, reassured the Foreign Office that "the Lublin Poles would not be invited by the TUC unless [the British government] recognized Lublin."[19] Where the issue was important enough, as in Poland, the British government broke its policy and worked closely with the TUC to establish limits on the unions' activities. But these limitations had more the character of damage control operations than attempts to alter the TUC's basic course.

The TUC's attempt to carry out the wishes of the Foreign Office by excluding the Lublin Poles backfired, underscoring the TUC's conflicting imperatives. The Soviets had already complained strongly about the TUC's support of anti-Communist Poles. One Soviet union official, Vassili Kuznetsov, voiced his comrades' resentment that several TUC General Council members were "adherents and protectors of the Polish reactionaries."[20] Before the world conference, the British refused to invite a representative of the newly formed Central Council of Trade Unions in Poland, a decision to which the Soviets grudgingly acceded.[21] But at the conference itself the Polish issue would not go away. The Lublin council sent a protest that "a great injustice would be done" if it were excluded and requested the right to send a representative.[22] The majority on the conference's standing orders committee agreed to the request after a dramatic last-minute appeal by a member of the Polish Seamen's Union in Great Britain, which had just declared its loyalty to the Lublin government.[23] Apparently unaware of the TUC line, British delegate Frank Wolstencroft, a staunch General Council moderate, supported the Communists' request. Citrine reacted angrily, and Wolstencroft stormed out of the conference.[24] With Wolstencroft out of the picture, the British delegates objected strongly. Since the Communists were unwilling to cause a split on this issue, the TUC got its way.[25]

Third-world delegates to the WTUC also caused problems for the TUC, even though the British were able to prevent the attendance of some unions presumed to be Communist fronts, such as those of Iran and northern (Communist-controlled) China.[26] Other delegates, such as Ken Hill of Jamaica and Wallace Johnson of Sierra Leone, had been arrested by British colonial authorities for union and nationalist activities during the war.[27] At the conference, delegates from British colonies formed the only open opposition. The Nigerian delegate T. A. Bankole asked the conference to endorse the setting of a time limit on the liberation of colonial possessions. His request received backing from only five union centers.[28] Similarly, the delegate of the Palestinian Arab Workers' Society, J. Asfour, tried to convince the delegates not to support a national home for the Jews in Palestine but met with little support. Only six organizations, all from British dominions or colonies, supported Asfour's suggestion that aid be given to Jews in Europe but not in Palestine.[29] Although the Foreign Office feared Communist activity in the colonial world, the Soviet, European, and American unions at the world conference expressed a broad consensus about what Russian delegate S. V. Zakharov called the "big, important, and difficult colonial problems."[30] The Communist delegates voted consistently with the non-Communists on what have come to be called north-south issues.

The TUC leaders for the most part felt extremely competent in overseeing the affairs of unions in the colonies and other less industrialized nations. As in popular attitudes toward race, the British-Irish relationship provided the model. Several TUC affiliates had large Irish memberships dating from the period of the unions' expansion when the whole of Ireland was an English colony.[31] Despite (or because of) this substantial presence, the TUC affiliates resisted Irish demands for increased autonomy. In 1945 the Amalgamated Society of Woodworkers, under challenge from its Irish members, upheld its long-standing policy of requiring non-Irish to attend the Irish Trades Union Congress. The Woodworkers also pushed the British TUC to convene a conference on the problems of British trade unions with Irish members.[32] But as anti-British sentiment grew in the Irish TUC, a group of Ireland-based unions withdrew and formed the Congress of Irish Unions. The TUC unions with Irish members held the conference suggested by the Woodworkers in the spring of 1946. But the conference deadlocked when the Irish representatives demanded greater autonomy and threatened to join the Congress of Irish Unions if they were not satisfied. In the end the British unions refused to set a standard policy for dealing with Irish organizations and left Irish policy up to the individual unions.[33]

For the time being, the Foreign Office had little to fear on Germany from the reborn international trade union movement. The TUC's plans for the future of Germany reflected both the consensus of labor opinion and stated government policy.[34] Wary of the dangers of complete dismemberment of Germany, the TUC nevertheless approved of substantial border changes. Many unionists demanded severe punishment for all the German people, departing from the intellectual left's analysis that the German people were at heart Social Democratic and had been misled and dominated by a Junker-militarist class. Charles Jarman of the National Union of Seamen led the most anti-German group in the TUC, calling for brutal reprisals against the Germans because "the mentality of the German nation is such that it is only amenable to such treatment."[35] Into the postwar period the sailors' union pressed for the most stringent denazification programs and opposed the admission of German unions to the International Transport Workers unless they had actively participated in Resistance activities.[36]

However, Jarman was in the minority. Occupation policy, John Benstead of the railway union argued, should not create a "submerged slave state."[37] Following this idea, the TUC presented the world conference with the draft of what became its "Declaration on the Peace Settlement." The draft supported any Allied agreements on Germany that emphasized the need to denazify the country. However, it added the demand that the unions participate in running the occupation. Citrine repeatedly argued that the unions should support reasonable reparations and the use of German labor to rebuild the devastated countries of Europe, providing the unions supervised the work so that it would not "degenerate into slave labor."[38]

The world conference proved an enormous success, leading to a far broader organization than had ever been attempted by world labor. Citrine, however, had grave misgivings about how much power to allow the new institution. Indeed, his position, that the international union movement should reconstruct slowly, was swept aside by the Soviets, the CIO, and their allies at the world conference.[39] Instead, the conference agreed to rapidly form the World Federation. During the spring and summer of 1945 delegates wrote a constitution and in the fall convened the founding conference of the World Federation. Despite his misgivings, Citrine stayed at the center of the World Federation as president. His commitment to the federation's mid-1940s-style principles of cooperation (however half-hearted) soon led to increased conflict with the government.

Friction developed between the TUC and the government about trade union involvement in the government of Germany. Efforts to press World Federation participation in Allied Control Commission affairs or in zonal administration met with strong resistance. Even arranging a World Federation tour of the British zone was difficult. Although analysts from the Foreign Office and Ministry of Labour believed that Citrine would try to counteract baleful Communist influence, they decided "it would be undesirable if the WFTU, . . . under Russian influence . . . set up in our Zone satellite unions of the kind the Russians have set up in the countries they have occupied."[40] The Foreign Office misled Citrine, claiming that Bevin favored the visit but that the other powers objected.[41] World Federation activity would interfere with the creation of "Bona Fide Trade Unions," Godfrey Ince of the Ministry of Labour warned the British representative on the Control Commission for Germany and Austria, and is in conflict "with our conception of the proper development of trade unionism in Germany."[42] The Foreign Office and the Ministry of Labour tried to deny the World Federation access to Germany entirely but in the end relented, allowing delegations to tour.[43] Active participation by the World Federation was still viewed like the plague, however, because the World Federation advocated unions that would span all four occupation zones. The French and Soviets advocated a four-zone union organization, but the British and Americans opposed such an idea in fear of Communist influence.[44]

The World Federation achieved unanimity because of a real agreement among the biggest union organizations and a widespread willingness to compromise. As conflict increased between Communist and anti-Communist forces in Europe and as the third-world countries became a battleground for the contending powers and ideologies, such unanimity became harder to achieve, to put it mildly. But the Foreign Office consensus early on anticipated conflict with the Communists, making the government wary of the world conference and the new organization that grew out of it. The TUC was willing to take such fears into account and tried to ensure that the WTUC and the World Federation did not harm British interests. Horst Lademacher and his colleagues have effectively detailed the attempts by Citrine and the TUC to limit World Federation involvement in third-world affairs.[45] Similarly, Peter Weiler has shown how Citrine tried, and failed, to prevent the WFTU from founding a colonial department.[46]

Willingness to accommodate the Foreign office's concerns, however, did not reflect a concomitant willingness to concede basic international interests of the TUC. Bringing together unionists from all over the world under the TUC's leadership was central to Citrine's vision of the role of trade unions in world politics. If he could compromise with the Foreign Office about matters of great concern to it without sacrificing too much, all the better. Nonetheless, he was not willing to blindly follow the government's dictates if this meant compromising his vision or his power. He demanded to be included in diplomacy but only on terms of strength.

The friction regarding Germany was a specific instance of a general problem. Serious conflict also developed over the TUC's attempt to carry out the international labor dream of participating on an equal basis with government in formal world politics. The coalition government locked the TUC out of the first United Nations conference in San Francisco in the spring of 1945, much to Citrine's consternation.[47] When he learned that the CIO and the AFL had been officially represented in the U.S. delegation at San Francisco, Citrine was furious. The TUC leader also "strongly protested" the World Federation's exclusion from the UN conference and even threatened to have the issue raised in the House of Commons. When the government rose to the challenge, he backed down. Relations between the British government and the union leadership remained tense for the remainder of the coalition's time in office.[48] The TUC's commitment to building an effective world labor organization ran into direct conflict with the government's attempt to forge a world order that contained the Communist threat.

The situation should have taken a turn for the better after Labour took over the British government in the summer of 1945, but Citrine and his fellow TUC leaders were soon disappointed by their comrades on international issues. Things seemed to be going the TUC's way after the new government reversed the policy of its predecessor and allowed the TUC and the employers' organization, the Confederation of British Industries, to join the British delegation to the first session of the UN General Assembly in London in the early winter of 1946. Yet this change did not satisfy the General Council. First, it was clearly a sop thrown to the TUC to preclude its pressing the government further on admitting the World Federation to the UN's Economic and Social Council (ECOSOC). Adding insult to injury, the TUC delegates were consistently, though politely, ignored at the UN.

Not realizing just how shut out from foreign policy deliberations they were, the delegates to the second part of the first session, held in New York late in 1946, decided on their own to attend the morning meeting of the government delegation. Bevin discreetly told the delegates, H. L. Bullock of the General and Municipal Workers and Will Lawther of the Miners, both reliable General Council moderates, that they were not welcome. "We were not drawn into real consultation on any of the questions under discussion in the various committees," they complained.[49]

Bullock and Lawther's experiences at Lake Success came at a low point in relations between the General Council and the cabinet, brought on by what may have been Bevin and Citrine's stormiest conflict since their 1941 battle about direction of labor. In 1945 and 1946 Citrine and Bevin clashed repeatedly about the relationship of the TUC and the World Federation to the UN. In the winter of 1946 Bevin convinced the cabinet that the World Federation should not hold a voting or otherwise special position on the ECOSOC—delivering the new federation its first major defeat.[50] Only Soviet Foreign Minister Vyacheslav Molotov favored the WFTU, leading a group of woodworkers to comment sarcastically, "If the British trade unionist is to rely on the USSR to state his case in the United Nations Organization it is only fair that the USSR should have a share of the political levy paid by that trade unionist."[51]

The British government's decision incensed Citrine and the General Council because they generally believed the World Federation, as the unified voice of the world's unions, had a right to participate on terms different from other nongovernmental organizations'. The General Council sent a deputation, headed by Citrine, to protest the decision. The deputation voiced its complaint in terms to be expected more from Labour's leftists than from mainstays of the right wing of the party. The trade unionists of the world, Citrine admonished the prime minister and Bevin, felt "very serious disappointment with the British Labour Government. . . . It seemed to be bent upon following the government of the United States of America." The power conflicts between Britain, the United States, and the USSR "were allowed to interfere with the decision that we think should have been come to," Citrine complained. The foreign minister replied heatedly: "What I do not want—and I want to be quite frank about it—what I do not want is to be put in a position [that] as an old trade unionist I am going to have the Russians using the Trade Unions in order to make it appear that I am against the Trade Unions."[52] The meeting ended on a strained note. Although the TUC could not budge the government, it continued to demand change nonetheless—that is, until Citrine resigned as general secretary of the TUC in the fall of 1946.

Citrine's successors, Vincent Tewson, who become general secretary of the TUC, and Arthur Deakin, who took over as president of the World Federation, immediately changed the tenor of relations with government. They forged a closer relationship with the Foreign Office and worked strenuously to counteract Soviet influence in the World Federation and Communist activity in the unions. Fighting the Russians proved difficult, however, because both government and labor had to live with the heritage of the Grand Alliance, that is, the legitimacy of Soviet and Communist participation in world affairs. Arthur Deakin, general secretary of the TGWU and a Bevin protégé, had to back away from Citrine's aggressive pursuit of World Federation goals. Among Deakin's first acts as World Federation president was a denial (false) that the TUC delegation had supported a WFTU protest of the British government's refusal to support "direct access" to ECOSOC.[53] The close relations ranged from such simple acts as regular consultation with embassy staff and prepublication discussion of World Federation reports to such difficult jobs as attempts to delegitimize Communist forces in Germany, Greece, and Persia.[54]

Despite the TUC's embrace of cold war diplomacy, it could not abandon its role as defender of the workers' interests, even while its leaders yearned for more developed corporatist relations. The parallels between the unions' domestic and foreign relationships to government are striking. In 1947 George Woodcock, assistant general secretary of the TUC, responded to the problems created by the unions' role in a socialized economy: "We do not propose to become the British equivalent of the Nazi 'Labour Front' and we do not intend trade union representatives to become so closely identified with management that the workman is unable to tell the one from the other. As I see it the very essence of Trade Unionism in Great Britain is independence both from the state and the employers."[55]

By 1946 Citrine had parlayed the importance of the labor movement in national affairs into a position of power in the realm of foreign relations. This does not mean the TUC fought consistently against British foreign policy; to the contrary, as the problem of invitations to the world conference had shown, the TUC did its best to respect government interest. Nevertheless, it was the TUC's qualified independence, institutionalized in its role in the World Federation, that allowed the organizations to avoid making an immediate response to the new anti-Soviet foreign policy promoted by Bevin, the Foreign Office, and the Americans in 1946 and 1947. Once Citrine stepped down from his posts in the TUC and World Federation, first to join the National Coal Board and then to take the chairmanship of the British Electricity Authority, the government moved to steer union foreign policy nearer to its own. As Weiler demonstrates, the Foreign Office took a greater interest in labor affairs and actively influenced the conduct of the unions' foreign policy once Citrine was out of the picture.[56]

Yet the outbreak of the cold war did not compel a uniform response from the trade union leaders. Each union's internal structure and the balance of political forces within the organizations combined with the underlying pro-Sovietism outlined in Chapters 3 and 4 to prevent a full-blown heresy hunt from developing in the British trade unions. Even in less democratic unions where the leadership had effective control of organizational policies, such as the National Union of Seamen (NUS) and the Woodworkers' union, the leadership was unable to inspire mass fear. Rather, the leadership's effective control forced opposition into prepolitical forms. The only outlet was explosive rank-and-file movements, such as the 1947 Merseyside rank-and-file movement in the seamen's union or the 1949 London dock strike in the TGWU.[57]

Sailors' Internationalism

The sailors provide an excellent case study of the dynamics of internationalism in the rest of the labor movement. Even though the National Union of Seamen was one of the smallest and the least democratic organizations in the TUC, its members experienced the same conflicts and fears and its leadership took part in the same evolution of international affairs as the larger, more democratic organizations. Indeed, sailors exhibited a typical combination of international pressures, internal opposition, and leadership ideology and manipulation. Although the seamen's organization had for many years been in the forefront of international organizing, the experience of the war, changes in the workforce, and the imperatives of international competition pressed the leaders of the merchantmen to take an even more active role.

The mortal peril of merchant sailors brought great urgency to the union's international policy. The war thrust the British merchant mariners into the thick of battle, taking a terrible toll on the lives of sailors and on their ships. During the course of the war Britain lost more than sixteen hundred ships.[58] These losses meant real tragedy for the sailors: more than thirty-two thousand died in enemy action in the six years of the war, 2 to 9 percent of all sailors.[59] Whatever the exact percentage, the mortality rate was stunning. The seamen's losses totaled more than 12 percent of all civilian deaths in the war.

Further contributing to the seamen's internationalism was their leaders' need to forestall Communist growth in the midst of internal union conflict. The seamen's union was a decidedly top-down organization, designed by its founder, J. Havelock Wilson, to keep rowdy sailors from active participation in their union. Wilson and the other early leaders believed that the rank-and-file was too disorderly, if left to its own, to maintain a functioning union. Charles Jarman inherited a strong administrative organization when he took over as acting secretary from Wilson's successor, W. R. L. Spence, in 1942. Regional officers were dependent on national support. Local officials often held branch meetings when militant crews were at sea.[60] Although this high level of control was effective during the 1920s and 1930s, the war changed the internal composition of the union and fostered increased militance. Most often, the members expressed frustration in individualistic ways such as pilfering, desertion, drunkenness, and other destructive behavior. But by the end of the war rank-and-file movements had begun a challenge to the established leadership, a struggle that continued into the 1970s when a reformist slate of officers finally won control of the union.[61]

During the war, conflict with the rank-and-file remained under control. But immediately afterward, rank-and-file and Communist agitation began in earnest. Building on ideas circulated by Communist seafarers in 1944, militants began to push for increased democracy in the National Union of Seamen.[62] In the summer of 1945 the Scottish branches demanded the establishment of ships' committees, that is, the creation of shipboard groups to handle grievances.[63] The ships' committees were part of the transformation of British industrial relations that saw more and more power taken by shop-floor bargaining, with national agreements becoming largely a framework for negotiation. At the time, however, few sectors of the economy had organized forms of worker control. The leadership, maintaining that the committees would disrupt the union's work, organized the defeat of the Scottish proposals.[64] Like international organization, internal activity had to be tightly controlled by the leadership to prevent disorder and to avoid Communist control.

But much more than the political beliefs of the Communists worried the union's hierarchy. What was most disturbing to the union's officers was the challenge to the organization's power structure and the union's basic assumptions about the role of the rank-and-file. Jarman warned his readers in the *Seaman* in 1944: "Everything in trade union life that Communism has touched has been badly damaged."[65] As conflict with the Communists in the international movement increased in 1946 and 1947, Jarman came to believe that the Communists' actions threatened not only the structure of world labor but the stability of his organization. Communists were articulating the rank-and-file sentiments that endangered the bureaucracy of the union.

The suppressed conflict with the rank-and-file of the mid-1940s burst into full-blown rebellion with the Merseyside rank-and-file movement that led to a series of wildcat strikes. The movement demanded shipboard bargaining and greater local autonomy, confirming the danger of Communist-inspired internationalism to leaders of the NUS. The London Rank and File Committee, which supported the Merseyside strikers, wrote: "To our transatlantic brothers, the Canadian and American Seamen whose support both morally and financially during our struggle and since has proved to the world that we who live upon the sea have one language and one Nationality[:] the Brotherhood of the Oceans, a living witness to the world's quarrelling politicians that men can live in harmony and jump to each other's assistance in times of stress without thought of country, frontier or flag to make them pause."[66]

The sailors' leaders spent an increasing portion of their time in the late forties fighting the dangerous combination of rank-and-file anger and Communist organization in their union. But like many other unions in the TUC, the NUS did not change the constitutional basis of the union to exclude Communists from membership. Although Jarman's successor, Tom Yates, wholeheartedly supported the TUC's anti-Communist drive, the union's leadership did not encourage wholesale purges of the left in the late forties. In response to Communist-led Merseyside wildcatters, delegates to the 1949 union conference (a group controlled by the hierarchy) voted to take immediate disciplinary action against any illegal ship tie-ups, but they turned down an opportunity to ban Communists as members or officers. Several speakers stressed there would be no witch hunt.[67]

It is ironic, given Jarman's antipathy to Communists, that he so willingly endorsed the World Federation. Yet he felt that if the TUC and other anti-Communist institutions could maintain their power base, the Communists would be unable to wreck the movement. Further, the survival of an international movement would obviously be dependent, he claimed, on "unity, solidarity, and mutual forbearance in the pursuit of the common good."[68] In other words, a world labor movement could work if the Communists were on their best behavior.

Jarman's plans for a postwar international organization reflected the union hierarchy's assumptions about the limitations of participatory democracy and the need for strong bureaucratic control. He opposed the free market in shipping, stressing that the industry needed a formal international organization because "the interest of British seamen can not be safeguarded in isolation from the other maritime countries."[69] But this unity, Jarman realized after the war, should not be based solely on economic grounds. "The common dangers which officers and seamen faced during this war have led to a realisation that their rightful prosperity and security are interdependent," Jarman told a rally in support of the seamen's charter, a platform for international sailors' rights.[70] World order, like internal union order and economic progress, depended on each other.

Jarman's promotion of world order included cooperation with unions from third-world countries. Chapter 2 illustrated his commitment during the war to pan-European unionism in the Belgian, Danish, Dutch, French, Polish Seafarers Federation and to paternalism in relation to the Chinese Seamen's Union. During and after the war he also supported the creation of a federation of Indian sailors' unions in Britain and India to bring some order to the chaotic situation among South Asian sailors—but wanted to ensure that it was firmly under the control of reliable non-nationalist leaders and amenable to participation in a corporatist national maritime board.[71]

World order, in turn, depended on the agreement of working people. In 1944 Jarman argued that the postwar global order depended on the cooperation of the wartime Allies. This cooperation would continue after the war, he maintained, because of the actions of the working classes of the world:

> The alliance that binds our nations together in this war is more than a diplomatic document. It is an alliance written in blood and cemented by a common sacrifice of the British, American and Russian people. And it is a pledge underwritten by the organized workers of Britain and America, by the organized workers of all the United Nations. I find the strongest guarantee that the alliance will not be broken to be embodied in the fact that it is not merely a pledge of governments—it is a vow taken by the peoples, and especially by the working people of these United Nations.[72]

(Of course, working-class participation did not mean direct democracy.)

Jarman thought that despite the differences between Communists and non-Communists, the World Federation and the international unity it represented were indispensable to world peace: "If we cannot as trade unionists overcome internal dissensions and conflicting viewpoints, how can we hope to influence the coming peace settlement? We must set an example of unity, solidarity, and mutual forbearance in pursuit of the common cause."[73] Labor unity seemed achievable in 1944 and 1945. But without unity, without "mutual forbearance," conflict would be inevitable and the world doomed to repeat the patterns of the interwar years.

TUC Internationalism

The wartime and immediate postwar experiences of the trade unions encouraged international undertakings. At the same time, political conflict within the union movement, as well as profound misgivings about the role of trade unions in government, gave form to the development of bureaucratic internationalism. The leaders of the TUC unions had distinct interests in internationalism that developed not only from their shared concerns as British people fighting the Axis and hoping to build a new world but also from their organizations' internal political conditions, their relations with government, their economic perceptions, and their belief in the power of solidarity. The leaders' own Socialist inclinations pushed them to seek corporatist solutions to class conflict and to the insecurities of the workers. This inclination should have led them—ironically—to avoid fighting for a worker-based world order, but they feared losing power to a potentially hostile government or being rejected by their members for seeking too much compromise. Because control of their autonomous realm promised labor the key to preventing future wars and to calming intramural strife, the unions seized the opportunity offered by the unsettled state of world diplomacy during World War II to create a new form of international relations.

As the outlines of global politics changed, the TUC found it difficult to change course. Despite the right-wing leadership's efforts, rank-and-file resistance and the strength of the leftists defeated an attempt at creating a red scare comparable to that in the CIO. Acceptance of the legitimacy of Soviet interests in world affairs was so strong that the TUC leadership had to be very careful not to appear to be the source of the break with the Communists in the World Federation. The popularity of its international commitments severely limited the expression of anticommunism by the leadership.

Further slowing the TUC's adherence to the battle lines of the cold war was the reluctance of the union movement to give up the glory that the international sphere had promised in exchange for the relative subservience required by American-oriented anticommunism and government dictates in the cold war. The comparative weakness of British anticommunism—there was certainly anti-Soviet and anti–Communist Party feeling but nothing on the scale of what occurred in the United States—flowed from the political and intellectual predicament of the British union movement and of British labor in general. The comparative weakness can also be attributed to the greater political strength of labor in Britain compared with the United States, a strength that allowed the unions to avoid being compelled by the right to demonstrate their loyalty to the nation by sacrificing the pro-Soviet side of their movement.

Despite these contrasts, U.S. and British unionists shared an intellectual crisis in the late forties. Understanding what the collapse of the mid-1940s order meant—the ideological upheaval it engendered—requires an examination of what happened on the other side of the Atlantic, inside the borders of the new leader of the world.

Part 3

The Americans

While working in a California shipyard during World War II, Katherine Archibald found that fear clouded her coworkers' dreams for the future. Although they had suffered little in the war compared with Asians or Europeans, "they yet believed that the happiest of tomorrows would be the day when the war should end and the time when war as a practice should forever cease." But this dream seemed unachievable: "Though the termination of the war was confidently expected almost any day, no one among those to whom I spoke seriously expected that war as an institution would be abolished, no one seriously expected that the machinations of the statesmen would really establish world-wide unity. Speculation was already rife about the next enemy, the next battlefield and the best ways of avoiding the perils of the inevitable next war."[1]

Labor internationalism in the United States was deeply related to its analog in Britain. Workers and union leadership responded to the same global forces, the war and the possibility of a new world order. They also grappled with similar domestic influences, the union relationship with the state, internal divisions over communism and rank-and-file militancy, underlying attitudes toward foreigners and foreign affairs.

Yet the Americans also contrasted greatly with their overseas counterparts. The structure of the labor movement with two competing national federations, the enormous diversity of the U.S. working class, the political weakness of labor, and, not least, the enormous difference in the U.S. role in the emerging global system of power led American internationalism down a significantly different path.

This section explores the twists and turns of internationalism in the United States in order to illuminate the sources of the Americans' role in the World Federation. This exploration requires a consideration of the nature of American working-class thought because American workers played a dramatically different role in world labor than their brothers and sisters overseas. Chapters 7 and 8 deal with the powerful yet conflicted ideas and actions of workers in the United States. Chapters 9 and 10 focus on the Congress of Industrial Organizations (CIO) and its efforts to secure a place for itself in the global order. The CIO had to grapple with problems that arose from a divided rank-and-file, a powerful competitor—the American Federation of Labor (AFL)—a changeable government, and demanding friends abroad. Ultimately, the intertwined questions of this section revolve around what American workers and unions could accomplish in the world and what the world would do to them in turn.

7

"A House Divided against Itself": American Workers and the World

In contrast to Great Britain, working-class thought in the United States during the 1940s was deeply divided about U.S. foreign policy and about the makeup of the postwar order.[1] Although workers, especially those in CIO unions, tended to be more sympathetic to the USSR and more internationalistic than the country at large, deep ideological cleavages prevented the emergence of a unified working-class voice on foreign policy issues. Consensus on the U.S. role in the world never completely developed, although by the end of the decade working-class and middle-class conceptions began to converge.[2]

Social divisions within the American working class and the split in the American labor movement between the CIO and AFL allowed a minority of politically active workers, who lacked overwhelming popular support, to exert great influence on the CIO's foreign policy. (The policy of the AFL remained in the control of the top leadership and was largely disconnected from rank-and-file sentiment.)[3] These articulate involved people with a variety of left-leaning political perspectives provided the impetus for the CIO's actions in the World Federation. Nevertheless, mass sentiment did not move America's workers to unite around a single way of thinking or to feel overwhelmingly positively—or, for that matter, negatively—toward the Soviet Union or people from other countries (with the exception of hatred of the Japanese). In contrast with the history of British workers, the story of American working-class thought before the cold war is a story of what did not happen.

Despite the lack of a coherent position on world issues and the diversity of working-class groups, a common pattern of thought had emerged by the end of the 1940s. This pattern, based not in class conceptions but in an ideology of Americanism, a synthetic U.S. nationalism, sustained the CIO's foreign policy. However, this ideology did not provide a powerful base for the CIO's internationalism, an underlying weakness that had grave consequences both for the CIO and for international trade unionism. Working-class thought and the social makeup of U.S. society that informed it are thus at the center of the problem of labor foreign policy. In turn, understanding the evolution of working-class thinking about foreign affairs in the 1940s and grasping the role this thinking played in international labor politics require a comprehension of the broader ideology and politics of the diverse elements of American labor.

Contemplating a New World Order

In addition to powerful ethnic and nationalist feelings, most American workers viewed international politics from a perspective informed by their experiences as workers in an unequal society. They believed that international issues affected working people differently than other groups in society. Foremost in their thinking was the prospect of a repetition of the economic crisis of the thirties, which would lead almost inevitably to another war.[4] For instance, only 20 percent of a group of workers surveyed in 1942 expected "favorable economic conditions" after the war.[5] One worker explained the connection of economics and world war: "It's money and raw goods and poor living that caused most of this war."[6] The solutions to these problems, moreover, were not clear. Workers remained divided by their ideologies, political leanings, and national background.

Surveys in the United States, unlike those taken in Great Britain, often showed no statistically significant difference in surveys of middle-class and working-class opinion about specific foreign policy issues. This cross-class unity reflects the integrating function of the dominant working-class way of thinking. (I examine the reasons for this common American approach at the end of this chapter.[7]) Working-class and middle-class people did answer survey questions similarly, but they often did so for different reasons. The distinct working-class sources of foreign policy thought had much to do with the economic and social insecurity of the diverse groups of U.S. workers. In the case of the small group of class-conscious union workers, these feelings gave rise to a unique working-class attitude.

A distinct working-class culture thrived in the United States during the 1940s. Its most self-conscious version centered on the labor movement, but even those who did not participate actively in the life of labor had class-tinted ways of understanding the world. Those who expressed ideas most similar to those of British workers, and thus in line with the thinking of the union leadership, tended to be union workers with a strong sense of class identity. O. G. Overcash, a union activist in Muncie, Indiana, for instance, believed deeply in international solidarity based on working-class comradeship. "When the workers of the world work and play together," he wrote James Carey, vice president of the CIO, in 1943, "no Dictator can rule them long."[8] Men and women like Overcash, whose lives revolved around the labor movement (he was the education chairman for Local 287 of the United Auto Workers), found international solidarity a compelling ideal. The unions also awoke internationalist feeling among workers. "We can't stay on our side of the pond anymore," a union carpenter explained. "It's one world now and we got to go in and do our share. The Union's taught me that. Workers everywhere want it fair for all."[9]

The best hope for the future, according to international-minded workers, was a just political and economic order. In portraying his postwar vision, one Hartford, Connecticut, aircraft worker underlined the identification of economic issues with the problem of war: "I hope that the United States will win the war and that there won't be any more wars afterwards and that everyone has a job and can live right and that there are no hard times like we have been having in the last years."[10]

The alternative to war and depression was some sort of international organization, a system that recognized the needs of working people. Many stressed that the U.S. role should not be to dominate the future international order. According to another aircraft plant worker in 1942:

> He [President Roosevelt] wants some kind of international police or some sort of organization to police the world. I don't want my boy [an infant] to have to go over and fight in another 20 years. Woodrow Wilson was right. I see the only way to have peace is through some kind of international understanding. The world is getting smaller. They can even fly across oceans now at 300 miles an hour. What protection is the Atlantic? We can't expect to have a wall around ourselves anymore. We've got to live with the rest of the world. . . . We should have better knowledge of what other people are like, how they think, and what kind of world they want for themselves.[11]

Another man in the same plant agreed about the U.S. role in the postwar era: "And as far as policing the world's concerned, that's like dictatorship—what we're fighting this war to overcome. (We should remember) Americanism might be just as objectionable to others as the Nazis are to us."[12] Similarly, an oiler in a New Orleans shipyard told an interviewer from the Office of War Information: "What are the fruits of the last war? This war. But if they have a set of right regulations for a league of nations, that would do it."[13]

To those most supportive of labor's role in keeping the peace, the World Federation held great promise. Murray Curran wrote his uncle, Philip Murray, the CIO president, that he hoped the WFTU would be "a powerful force for a real world peace since it stands to reason that if those who work for a living can unite on a world-wide basis, then certainly the governments of this world can resolve their differences by means short of total war."[14] International solidarity seemed a compelling basis for a new world order to class-conscious union workers in the United States, just as it did to their British counterparts.

Even among those who thought more pessimistically about the future, class concerns figured prominently. A shipyard worker in the Mississippi delta explained: "It wasn't Hitler himself that started this war. It wasn't the population of one country that started this war. It takes a group to make the agitation; and it takes two to make a fight."[15] Many workers believed that the upper class caused wars, so avoiding economic problems and the wars that grew out of them seemed to be the natural solution. Another shipyard worker explained that "this war is just a businessman's affair . . . and those guys who make the profits out of it are going to keep it going as long as they can. . . . It wasn't Hitler and Hirohito by themselves who began this war. . . . It was the big fellows all over the world who wanted the war, and so they got it."[16] The biggest danger for the future was that international affairs would be as they had been before the war. President Franklin Delano Roosevelt's responsiveness to the concerns of working people made this war different from previous ones, according to one West Coast worker: "But if the Republicans win out in the [1944] election, then it'll be a war like any other run for the benefit of the rich at the expense of the working guys."[17]

Yet relatively few workers thought actively about postwar plans and methods of avoiding future conflicts. Indeed, union activists worried that apathy might overwhelm their hopeful plans. "There are a few of us "who are really concerned with the post-war world," wrote Private Irving Salert, a former activist in the United Electrical, Radio, and Machine Workers of America. "No one speaks much about it. Most of us want something better [than] what we have had until now. Maybe the younger statesmen of labor can lead the fight. I hope they will for our sakes."[18] Similarly, Stanley Ruttenberg, also a GI and later research director for the CIO, worried about the apathy and ignorance of the other soldiers: "There's very little understanding of what we're fighting for and why. . . . Only the desire to get home means something. That attitude and lack of appreciation of the reasons for the fighting, etc has serious implications for the Post-War Period. . . . I fear for the future if some effort isn't made to instill into the men of the Armed Services some conceptions of a real and lasting peace."[19]

Many workers lacked a strong commitment to the ideals of the war, whether of national interest or of internationalism, such as those articulated in the Atlantic Charter. Strikes and other forms of industrial conflict continued, and apathy was widespread. A large propaganda apparatus developed to counteract these feelings but without tremendous success.[20] Katherine Archibald, the shipyard observer, was dismayed to find that shipyard workers worked hard to avoid the draft and scoffed at one man who decided to join the merchant marine. "You're just being a sucker for all the flag waving that's going on these days," one cynical man told the recruit.[21] Commitment to the patriotic effort did exist, nevertheless, but mostly in the form of support for the soldiers whose lives were on the line, not for the principles articulated by the government.[22] "The issues of the war," a disturbed Archibald found, "other than those expressed on the simple terms of hatred of Hitler or the Japanese, were almost completely lacking in meaning to the average shipyard worker."[23] Disappointed in her expectations, or at least hopes, that the workers she met would form part of a unified society, Archibald misunderstood the evidence of common working-class hatred of war and cynicism about politics. A union official in Milwaukee complained about such feelings among workers in his plant: "Their minds are a blank as far as the war is concerned. If you say something to most of them about the war, they look at you like, 'who the hell are you a company stooge?'"[24]

Cynicism about official politics and propaganda pervaded working-class thinking. One aircraft plant worker was generally quite cynical about the way the world was presented in the media and distrustful of many commonly believed facts: "I have a book published in 1918 full of propaganda stuff about atrocities. Yet these were later proved to be false. When I see these stories now I wonder if that's true."[25] More succinctly, a working-class woman observed: "All them politicians is as crooked as a cowpath, anyhow."[26] A leader of a United Electrical local in Chicago, probably a Communist, complained that the workers "have no clear understanding of what the war is about." Nevertheless, he claimed that, as a result of union educational campaigns, "as a group, I think the CIO membership has a better understanding of the war than any other group in the country."[27]

Opinions about U.S. involvement in the war also revealed economic differences. In April 1942, before U.S. troops were actively involved in the fighting, many more poor people than wealthier ones thought the United States was doing all it could to win the war.[28] One man expressed the economic side of his thinking on the justness of the war: "What I like about this war . . . is that rich men's sons are dying in it along side the sons of ordinary people."[29]

Those workers who felt most strongly about international issues had some sort of identification with people overseas. Powerful ethnic differences affected how people envisioned the goals of the war and the war itself. An Office of War Information survey of July 1942 found first-generation immigrants more committed to the war than any other group. Second-generation workers were somewhat less interested in the war, and "old American" groups (those with northern European backgrounds whose families immigrated before the Civil War) were the least concerned. The survey concluded that "the degree to which the worker is emotionally tied up with a European country shows some relationship to how earnest he is."[30] Lack of ideological and political interest in world affairs was thus a matter of identification: "Usual talk about freedom as put to him does not meet any strongly felt need since it depends upon his ability to identify himself with subject peoples abroad—a skill [at] which he does not show himself particularly adept (except, of course, for the foreign born worker)."[31] The ethnic and racial diversity of U.S. society militated against a unified working-class foreign policy. Archibald noticed similar lack of interest in the war:

> Although newspaper headlines constantly told of battles fought, ships torpedoed, and cities bombed, days passed in the shipyards when I heard no reference to these events. I knew one worker, to be sure, who kept maps pinned above his bench and traced on them the progress of the armies of the Allies; but he was a foreigner whose English was scarcely understandable and who was thought crazy by his fellows. A placid ignorance enveloped the strange place names of the war, and the conflict assumed an air of vast distance and unreality.[32]

Archibald's study convinced her that the disunity was the most serious problem plaguing the United States during the war. This lack of intellectual coherence—with only a minority enthusiastically endorsing midforties internationalism—had a profound effect on the evolution of working-class thought about foreign relations.

"Almost Everybody Just Don't Trust the Russians"

Popular attitudes toward the USSR before the war were even more mixed than those about the war. From 1917 on, American labor was seriously divided about the legitimacy of the USSR. Reflecting their acceptance of the U.S. economic system and their aversion to Socialist parties, the top leaders of the AFL distrusted and disliked the Bolsheviks. The AFL opposed Roosevelt's recognition of the USSR in 1933 and resolutely refused to have anything to with Soviet trade unions throughout the prewar decades. Still, a strong minority of trade unionists looked favorably on the USSR; many of these unionists were centered in Chicago and other midwestern cities where the Socialist Party had strong support.[33] The American Communist Party, for instance, drew many of its leaders, most prominently William Z. Foster, from the milieu of the unions. Many others had been active union organizers and members.[34] Beyond the Communist left, the USSR received widespread sympathy, if not unthinking support, from a large portion of the trade union movement. Unions such as the Amalgamated Clothing Workers of America and the International Ladies' Garment Workers' Union, with their large radical, Jewish, and Italian memberships, expressed their members' open thinking with delegations and aid to the young Soviet regime.[35] Into the 1930s the USSR remained quite popular among non-Communist trade unionists, more popular than with the public at large. Walter and Victor Reuther's journey to work in the USSR in 1933–34 showed a typical attraction to the Soviet Union at the time. Many other trade unionists made the same pilgrimage, returning with an appreciation (often later denied) of Soviet industrial and labor policy.[36] Although this group could not and did not mount an effective campaign against the leadership of the AFL on foreign policy issues, positive feelings for the Soviet Union helped define the left wing of the labor movement and found expression in the CIO.

During the 1930s, the "red decade" in Eugene Lyon's phrase, the Soviet Union gained popularity in the United States.[37] The Soviets' new foreign policy line, which began in 1933–34 and ended the confrontational "third period," promoted a united front against fascism. This shift in policy benefited the American Communist Party, which was now free to make alliances with other left-wing groups. It is difficult to separate Soviet popularity from other sources of Communist strength in the United States. Still, much of the Communist Party's limited success during this time came from its members' organizational abilities and participation in the unions and other popular movements.[38]

The Nazi-Soviet pact had a devastating effect on many of the middle-class united front groups that the Communist Party had so energetically promoted and were such an essential part of middle-class leftist political culture in the United States during the 1930s.[39] Between the summer of 1939, when the pact was signed, and the summer of 1941, when the Germans invaded the USSR, the loyalty of American intellectuals and middle-class political activists to Roosevelt's foreign policy clashed with the Communists' loyalty to Stalin's policy. The Communists' position on the pact destroyed their support among a key component of the New Deal–Popular Front coalition. As serious for the Communists was that anti-Communists were emboldened to move against their factional opponents in the CIO unions, passing resolutions and amending union constitutions that had banned Communists and fascists from membership and had equated communism with nazism.[40] Communist success depended on the coincidence of American and Soviet foreign policy.

Despite the increase in success for the anti-Communists in labor, the Communist Party's core of support among working people did not decline as much as might have been expected. True, anti-Communist activists were emboldened, and communism became an important factional issue for the first time in the CIO.[41] Nevertheless, in many cases the Communist Party was able to make up its lost ground by championing militant workers who refused to compromise their interests to military preparedness for a war they hoped to avoid entering. Former Communist Party chairman Earl Browder exaggerated when he later claimed that "the split of a few hundred intellectuals like [Granville] Hicks did not weaken the Party." But he was essentially, though not numerically, right to add that the intellectuals' "places were taken by ten times as many trade unionists, who were basically isolationist and admired Stalin for 'turning isolationist' and the American Communists for their practical qualities."[42] The party lost membership during the Nazi-Soviet pact period but never went below its 1938 total. In the 1940 elections the Communist Party improved its showing in ten large states and, had it not been ruled off the ballot in its stronghold of New York, it probably would have exceeded its previous showings.[43] Among the working class, communism's appeal had somewhat different sources than in the middle class. Yet because the international role of the USSR encouraged opposition to the war, the Communists took a militant approach to labor problems, thereby replacing their lost support. Foreign relations once again underlay Communist strength—and weakness.

The persistence of Communist power in labor probably also depended on the unwillingness of average workers to shift too rapidly from antiwar thinking or to readily give up their relatively positive image of the Soviet Union. As Ralph Levering notes: "During the eighteen months from the end of 1939 to the German attack on Russia in June 1941 there was little or no change in American attitudes toward Russia. The changes that occurred were largely favorable."[44] Surprisingly, the USSR weathered the Nazi-Soviet pact with its image in the United States somewhat intact.

Once the USSR entered the war, the Soviet Union became increasingly popular. Although pro-Soviet feeling was not overwhelming in the working class, it was more common there at the outset of U.S. involvement in the war than in other parts of the society. In a spring 1942 survey, for instance, poorer people in cities were more likely than wealthier ones to favor close cooperation with the USSR after the war and less likely to oppose such relations.[45] The economic status of respondents did not reveal the stark contrasts found in Britain, but a class trend of stronger dislike among people with high incomes and minority pro-Sovietism among poorer people suggests that the USSR's following in the United States had a distinct class factor.

In general, the middle class was intellectually more flexible than the working class. Initially, more working-class men and women than those in other socioeconomic groups thought the USSR would stay in the war. As official U.S. opinion came to emphasize the importance of the alliance with the USSR, culminating in the Moscow conference of August 1942, white-collar approval and trust of the Soviets increased substantially, whereas working-class opinion changed much less dramatically.[46]

By the summer of 1943, with the war going well for the Allies but before Roosevelt and Stalin's first meeting, more middle- and upper-class respondents than working-class ones believed the USSR and Great Britain likely to cooperate with the United States after the war. The lower levels of confidence among workers probably reflect a general cynicism about diplomacy and international cooperation, whereas those in upper levels had greater confidence in the ability of governments to achieve agreements. The lower levels of confidence also show that working-class opinion was somewhat less likely to fluctuate with the changing posture of the U.S. government.[47]

Cynicism and distrust regarding the Soviets were common among U.S. workers, in dramatic contrast with the British enthusiasm. At Moore Drydock in California female workers refused to let visiting Russian stewards use their bathroom: "Girls complain to me that they don't like to have those dirty Russian stewardesses in their rest rooms. . . . Almost everybody just don't trust the Russians," said a guard at the dock.[48] One worker at a New Jersey aircraft plant told an interviewer from the Office of War Information that the reports of great Soviet victories after Stalingrad were slanted and that "I would like to know what is really going on."[49] Most workers at the shipyard where Archibald worked believed that the United States and the USSR would fight each other in the next war.[50] Underlining the different British and American working-class attitudes toward the USSR was that Soviet trade union delegations received only moderately enthusiastic welcomes in the United States. In one case delegates were excluded from a General Motors plant with no protest from workers.[51]

Those who thought positively of the Soviets tended to blend Soviet military prowess and the idea of a workers' state. In this respect, workers shared the sentiment of the middle and upper classes in the United States.[52] In 1942 a southern union worker spelled out the connection between the strength of Soviet resistance to the German onslaught, the legitimacy of the Soviet government, and its relationship with the United States: "Russia is fighting for her way of life just like we are for ours. It must be what the people want or they wouldn't fight like they do. I'm for helping them and keeping hands off their government."[53]

It seems likely that the CIO unions had a higher proportion of pro-Soviet thinkers than other areas of society. Rank-and-file support for the opening of a second front in Europe is a good indicator. The CIO organized a "Win the War Rally" in New York City with such luminaries as Sidney Hillman, president of the Amalgamated Clothing Workers; Mike Quill of the Transport Workers' Union; Joseph Curran, president of the National Maritime Union; Charlie Chaplin; Mayor

Fiorello La Guardia; U.S. Representatives Emanuel Celler and Adam Clayton Powell Jr. of New York; and pro–New Deal senators Claude Pepper of Florida and James Mead of New York. It drew 100,000 people. Two weeks later Chicago's Grant Park overflowed with union members attending a similar rally.[54]

Naturally, the union movement's success in turning out huge crowds in favor of helping the USSR depended on a broader rise in Soviet popularity. One sociologist wrote of Americans as whole in 1944: "We distrust and dislike Communism, but we recognize the permanence of the Russian system and are beginning to take a realistic point of view that we must learn to get along with the Soviets."[55] A majority of the American people accepted the Soviet Union as a legitimate partner in world affairs at mid-decade. Reflecting this opinion, the vast majority of Americans agreed with Soviet demands for Polish territory.[56] By the fall of 1944, according to Paul Willen, "only seven per cent of the American people . . . foresaw an aggressive Russia in the postwar period." "The American people," Willen concludes, "were soft on Communism in the wartime period."[57]

Many people changed their ideas about the USSR during the war. The strength of the Red Army and the courage of the Soviet people warmed American hearts in bodies of all class backgrounds. Government and media portrayal of the USSR familiarized more people with the Soviets and undoubtedly increased confidence in the ability of the United States and the USSR to work closely with each other after the war. CIO vice president James Carey's first contacts with Soviet trade unionists convinced this anti-Communist activist of the distinction between domestic and foreign Communists. At the World Trade Union Conference in January 1945 Carey told a group of soldiers in England, "I got a different impression of the Soviets than I had. I don't like American Communists because they don't have the courage to put their cards on the table, but the Russians were different. There was no trickery, no intrigue."[58] The new improved Soviet image in American minds was based on the political compromises made by Roosevelt in creating the Grand Alliance and in planning for the postwar era; it encouraged optimism about the prospects for international unity. "They talked straight from the shoulder," James Carey said of the international unionists.[59]

Yet behind this optimism American workers remained deeply divided about how the world should be organized and, indeed, about who the legitimate participants would be. By the mid-1940s no powerful consensus had emerged among labor's rank-and-file. The ideas of the working class about foreign relations remained unclear and contradictory—hardly a strong basis for internationalism. Fractured and cynical, workers nonetheless sought ways to overcome disunity at home and abroad. Would their ways of achieving domestic consensus undercut or support internationalism after the war?

8

Americanism and Internationalism

As the Grand Alliance gave way to the cold war, a white steelworker from the South told an interviewer: "I hear the commentators on the radio and one says one thing and another one another thing, and I don't know what is right. You almost have to be your own commentator."[1] The ideas this man, and millions of people like him, drew on for commenting on the world reflected the enormous social and cultural divisions of the country. Ethnic and racial divisions permeated the American working class and helped to prevent the evolution of a cohesive working-class voice in foreign relations. The great divide between the CIO and the AFL represented not only a conflict of union styles and programs but also the fragmented nature of the American working class. Sources of commonality, such as shared class and labor experiences, countered this fragmentation but did not overcome it.

Yet workers did eventually espouse a relatively unified vision of themselves and their nation in the world based on an ideology growing from the Americanism promoted earlier by the right and the cultural pluralism promoted by the left. However, this uneasy and complicated synthesis of nationalist and pluralist ideas, as it existed in the midforties, did not immediately offer a powerful explanation for what was happening as the cold war ripped apart the assumptions of the Roosevelt era. Americanism, a complicated and contradictory set of ideas about what made an American, nonetheless spurred the evolution of cold war liberalism, a more coherent and formal ideology that posited foreign anticommunism and domestic liberalism as the solution to the social and political conflicts of the forties. The development of Americanism and of its estranged sibling, cold war liberalism, was, in turn, deeply tied to the efforts of workers to become their own commentators.

Great cultural gaps and social tensions characterized American society in the midtwentieth century. More than one in four Americans in 1940 were immigrants or the children of immigrants. One in ten were African American.[2] The industrial workers organized by the CIO had an even higher proportion of first- and second-generation Americans. Surprisingly, despite the work of a legion of historians, the connection between ethnicity, class, politics, and international affairs remains almost entirely unexplored. Yet the social and cultural makeup of the working class had a profound influence on how people thought and, in turn, on how American labor responded to the cold war and the new position of world preeminence for the United States.

Ethnicity, Race, and Religion

Surprisingly, religion was not as important a factor as ethnicity in affecting international thought. It is often argued, for instance, that Catholic workers, influenced by the teaching of the church and the activism of anti-Communist priests, disliked and distrusted the USSR.[3] Reality, however, was more complex. Attributing uniform beliefs to American Catholics is an oversimplification based on the assumption that groups like the anti-Communist Association of Catholic Trade Unionists (ACTU) spoke for all Catholic workers. The problems of radicalism and the issues of loyalty to church doctrine actually divided Catholic communities. As one historian of Catholic politics in the United States has found, "ethnic rivalries, organizational immaturity, and extremely rapid growth prevented the development of a truly unified, coherent American Catholicism."[4] The Catholic establishment in the United States had sought several times during the thirties and forties to force or at least convince American Catholics to support conservative causes in the world. For instance, although the overwhelming majority of church organs opposed the Republicans in the Spanish Civil War, average Catholics were divided evenly over the war.[5] Similarly, although Catholics in 1944 were more likely than Protestants to think the Soviets would take over Europe after World War II, the majority of both faiths thought the Russians would not be a danger.[6] Ethnicity and nationality are generally better predictors of opinion than religion.[7]

Nevertheless, the thinking of Catholics in American labor bears examination, not only because of the large number of Catholics, many of them quite devout, in leadership positions but also because Catholicism did play a role in forming labor opinion and policy on international affairs. Among the CIO leadership, Catholic influence was quite strong. Nearly 40 percent of 133 CIO leaders surveyed in 1946 were Catholic or of Catholic backgrounds. Three of the five original members of the CIO executive board were Catholic.[8] Although no exact figures are available, estimates count more than one third of all CIO members as Catholics in 1948, a fraction somewhat larger than their proportion in the population at large.[9] According to one study, Catholics were more likely to be union members than were members of any other religious group, except Jews who joined in comparable proportions. (Nonbelievers were the most likely to be unionists.)[10]

However, neither the high percentage of Catholic leaders nor the large number of Catholic rank-and-filers resulted in the CIO's adopting a particularly "Catholic" foreign policy. The opinions of church leaders were not simply mirrored by Catholic union members. Indeed, many of those counted as Catholics, such as the Mike Quill of the Transport Workers' Union, Joe Curran of the National Maritime Union, and the UE's Albert Fitzgerald, were Communist supporters. In the still all-too-few close studies of working-class ethnic communities, the range of rank-and-file Catholic opinion has become apparent. Ronald Schatz and Joshua Freeman have found that Catholic workers did not necessarily take anti-Communist stands in internal union politics. More often, factional or ethnic concerns predominated. For instance, Freeman found in his study of New York's transit workers that a coalition of radical Irish Republicans and Communists was able to win the support of an essentially conservative, Irish Catholic workforce.[11] Similarly, Steve Rosswurm found working-class opposition to church involvement in union affairs.[12] The issues of radicalism, communism, and support for the consensus foreign policy of the CIO divided Catholics. On occasion, such factionalism set brother against brother, as in the case of the UE's largest local, Pittsburgh's 601, where Mike and Tom FitzPatrick battled for the leadership of Popular Front and anti-Communist factions.[13] Devout Catholics often found ways to harmonize or, perhaps more accurately, compartmentalize their religious selves and their identities as unionists, ethnics, or Americans.

Except in the area of aid to Great Britain before Pearl Harbor, Catholic workers did not substantially depart from their Protestant, Jewish, and nonconfessional colleagues in their opinions on foreign affairs.[14] Almost immediately after the German invasion of the USSR, Catholics, like most Americans, overwhelmingly favored the Soviet side.[15] Pro-Soviet feeling could be expressed quite strongly. A Catholic milling machine operator of French-Canadian extraction claimed in 1942: "Stalin is the most maligned man in the world today. Before Russia was in the war they said that he was a dirty dictator hated by his people, that they wouldn't fight in Finland. But look what a fight they're putting up. Whoever is still writing that kind of stuff about our best ally should be put in a concentration camp."[16]

While the dominant opinion in clerical circles was decidedly antileft, and entirely anti-Communist, Catholic communities spawned diverse political groups. The church took the lead in organizing anti-Communist forces among Catholic workers and in the union movement as a whole. The most prominent Catholic union organization, the Association of Catholic Trade Unionists (ACTU), participated in numerous internal trade union battles and articulated a corporatist version of unionism.[17] (The influence of this corporatist doctrine on union leaders is treated in Chapter 9.) ACTU "provided the Doctrinal oil for the anti-Communist machines," Norman McKenna, a Catholic activist and later a labor specialist for the U.S. Information Agency, once remarked.[18] By the late forties ACTists, as they called themselves, were a presence in most CIO unions, even among the committed left-wing longshoremen. ACTists, both union members and their clerical advisers, spearheaded factional fights against Communists in several CIO unions, including United Electrical, the United Auto Workers (UAW), and the International Longshoremen's and Warehousemen's Union (ILWU). Ultimately attaining a membership of only ten thousand, ACTU, like the larger Communist Party, had much a wider influence than membership figures suggest. One estimate places the number of ACTU supporters in the labor movement at close to 100,000.[19]

Despite its numerical strength, it is not clear how powerful the support for ACTU actually was. A union's adherence to the ACTU line may not necessarily have represented its position on foreign affairs.[20] For instance, even in the flagship San Francisco local of the Communist-led ILWU, ACTU had an active group. Yet as one longshoreman friendly to the anti-Communists in the local recalled, the popular Catholic president of Local 10, Jim Kearney, "never used it in the union in meetings or privately."[21] All but one of the CIO's Communist-leaning leaders were from Catholic backgrounds, and their unions and supporters had large proportions of Catholics.[22] Even within ACTU, left-leaning Catholic activists at first opposed the organization's obsession with fighting Communists. During 1937–38 John Cort of the CIO's United Office and Professional Workers, along with Tim O'Brien of the Catholic Union of the Unemployed, George Donahue of the International Longshoremen's Association, and Edward Scully, a lawyer for the Catholic Labor Defense League, tried to push ACTU toward the Popular Front. Although this group failed to shift ACTU from its ideological course, its attempt reveals the diversity of opinion in the Catholic labor community about the danger of communism.[23]

The Grand Alliance period slowed ACTU's activities considerably. The anti-Communist organization failed to expand between 1942 and 1945, and many of its chapters suspended operations.[24] During the mid-1940s foreign policy, especially support for the USSR, and the internal consensus of the CIO militated against church power in the labor movement. Anti-Communists, for instance, learned that mobilizing Catholic transit workers against their Communist-allied leaders before 1947 was "a little like trying to melt an iceberg with a match."[25] Similarly, efforts to turn internal factional fights in the UAW into battles over U.S. foreign policy, UAW historian Martin Halpern has found, did not succeed, except during the Nazi-Soviet pact period. In general, foreign policy did not become a central issue in internal union conflicts until after 1947.[26]

Catholicism did not play a decisive role in forming working-class thought, although the church certainly affected union politics. More important than religious identification in influencing thoughts on international affairs was national background. Many immigrant and second-generation communities were deeply divided over the problem of communism and change in their or their parents' homelands. By the 1940s radical leadership had been eliminated in most communities, especially among Italian Americans, but community members remained deeply divided ideologically.[27]

A common explanation for the American public's support of the cold war is that Americans, usually of the first or second generation, strongly resented Soviet domination of their Eastern European homelands. It is true that the dominant groups in the Polish, Hungarian, Czech, and other communities vocally protested the imposition of Communist regimes in their homelands. Yet the image of completely unified anti-Soviet communities distorts a complex reality. Although pro-Soviet or -Communist government positions were certainly in the minority, they nonetheless had a powerful following, especially during and after the war. For instance, people with a background in eastern Poland tended to resent the Soviets far more than their compatriots from the west, who had suffered more at the hands of the Germans.[28]

Support for the Communists, for tolerance of the Soviet Union, and for a new world order could be found in varying degrees in most ethnic groups. A survey of 1946 and 1948 UAW convention delegates by Halpern found greater support in the union for the Communist-centrist alliance among those with eastern European, Italian, and Greek names. The eclectic anti-Communist group led by Walter Reuther received more support from those with British, French, German, and Dutch names.[29] Irish Americans dominated the anti-Communist ACTU, making up as much as 75 percent of the organization's membership.[30] Eastern European Jews, south Slavs, and Finns disproportionately supported Socialist and Communist causes.[31]

Communist influence in ethnically identified communities carried over into support for the Popular Front that led the CIO and for the coalition's foreign policy. According to Peter Friedlander, generalizing from the history of one UAW local: "Among such groups as the Armenians, the Rumanians, the Hungarians and the south Slavs, the Communist party had an influence far beyond its numbers, functioning in many ways as *the* legitimate political organization for many parts of the community. In the Ford Plant in Dearborn these groups formed an important part of the constituency for the [Communist] party, the CIO and New Deal—and ultimately for the left wing in the UAW."[32] In the Slovenian working-class community in Cleveland, UAW activist Leo Fenster told Halpern, the major cultural organizations were left wing, and most people felt "that socialism was a thing that would come."[33] Much of the Communist left's strength came from first-generation immigrants who, Milwaukee UAW leftist Harold Christoffel recalled, "had a background of . . . worker solidarity."[34] Friedlander found that Appalachians tended to support the right.[35] Despite these proclivities, no ethnic group was entirely Communist or Socialist, left or right.[36] Rather, ethnic political identity resulted from diverse forces, at times responding to class or racial concerns, at other moments resulting from American national issues. The result was, in James Gregory's phrase, "a shifting populism."[37]

African American workers were another source of support for the CIO leadership's consensus on foreign policy. The CIO factions all gave verbal support to racial equality. However, their reactions to the challenge of integrating the union movement, and creating and maintaining an interracial workforce, varied not according to the ideology of particular factions but according the political and social pressures brought to bear on them.[38] Nevertheless, in industries with large black workforces the CIO joined in black struggles for civil rights. In the area of foreign policy (except in relation to African and other colonial issues, which I discuss shortly), once black workers came to support the integrationist CIO leadership, they also came to support the consensus within the CIO on foreign policy.

Americanism provided a powerful unifying awareness to the diverse working class in the United States.[39] Ethnic American workers felt insecure in the nature of their Americanness. Members of minority groups—Jews, Slavs, Poles, French Canadians, blacks, Finns, and so on—all sought to fit into majority society. The major cultural achievement of the CIO and the New Deal was a politics of cultural pluralism that provided minority Americans with a legitimate avenue to American self-consciousness. Communist Party chief Earl Browder's declaration that "Communism is twentieth-century Americanism," was the most astounding example of the left-leaning nature of this form of Americanist thinking.[40] But a wide of variety of leftists and liberals also laid claim to a tradition of American democracy, appropriating Abraham Lincoln, Thomas Jefferson, Tom Paine, and the American Revolution as icons. Patriotism provided the intellectual glue that bound American workers together. Even the cynical shipyard workers studied by Katherine Archibald felt the patriotic urge quite strongly: "When the Shipyard band closed its noontime concerts with the 'Star Spangled Banner,' almost all men within hearing distance rose to their feet and took off their hats and here and there a tear was wiped away by a work hardened hand."[41] The Communists embraced this musical patriotism, starting their meetings with the *Star Spangled Banner* rather than the *Internationale.*[42] The contrast with Britons' enthusiastic singing of the *Internationale* or the *Red Flag* at rallies is striking.[43]

During the first quarter of the twentieth century, many on the right had attempted to use Americanism to homogenize what was, to them, a dangerously diverse society, but by the 1940s Americanism had taken on a new meaning. In contrast to the right-wing version, midcentury Americanism, as interpreted by the working class and the left, stressed the value of cultural diversity and the radical democratic elements of the American political tradition. Patriotism did not necessarily force people to the right. Under the Roosevelt administration, Americanism coexisted with internationalism. In fact, the ideas of cultural pluralism inherent in New Deal Americanism could easily be transferred to the multiple nations of the world and used to justify acceptance of a major Soviet role in world affairs. One New England union newspaper echoed Lincoln in explaining this application of pluralism to world politics: "We let a world of many peoples, of many faiths, races, and nationalities, become a house divided against itself and before we can put that house together again, many millions of the world's finest young men must die."[44] Just as people of all ethnic backgrounds and value systems could become Americans in a culturally plural system, so could all nations of any political system (except for aggressive fascism) participate in the United Nations.

Americanism was important as an ideology, not because American workers felt themselves safely part of a consensual social system but because of their insecure sense that they stood outside such a system. The main cultural victory of the working-class movement of the 1930s and 1940s was the definition of a pluralist society that legitimized ethnic identity. But this victory was not entirely secure. Loyalty to an American ideal of plural unity in the face of the problem of a fractured nation and world helped immigrant and second-generation Americans define their role in the emerging conflict about labor and communism in the United States and abroad.

The red scare of the late 1940s and 1950s was in a sense a battle about the legitimacy of the role of the working class and the left in the United States—a legitimacy that came increasingly to be defined in terms of loyalty to the U.S. side in the cold war. For the culturally diverse American working class, it was a battle fought on an uneven field.

Cold War and Public Opinion

Mobilization for the cold war did not evoke an immediate response among the American people as a whole. A survey by the University of Michigan's Survey Research Center in April 1947, shortly after President Harry Truman's call for aid to Greece and Turkey, found the public unsure and unenthusiastic about the direction of U.S. foreign policy: "Although a majority of the public are willing to 'go along' on most of the important issues of current foreign policy, it cannot be said that public opinion is strongly mobilized in support of that policy. Much of people's thinking on these issues is tentative and uncertain, lacking in any real conviction."[45] The surveyors found that more people disapproved of sending military supplies to Greece than approved.[46] In its initial stages the U.S. position in the cold war was not a popular stance. A combination of war weariness, apathy, and resurgent isolationism manifested itself in resistance to continued or renewed mobilization. This resistance was especially apparent among soldiers still stationed overseas.[47] This lack of popularity, while easily overstated, nonetheless underscored the ambiguous confused reactions of Americans to the cold war order.

By 1948 many in the State Department worried about the lack of public support for U.S. foreign policy. The political opponents of the cold war, albeit ultimately defeated, nonetheless seemed quite powerful at the time. In an effort to mobilize working-class opinion against the United States, Communists, especially the Soviets, accused the U.S. government of doing Wall Street's bidding. Domestically, Henry Wallace demanded that U.S. foreign policy "no longer heed the advice of the Big Brass or Wall Street."[48] Wallace's campaign to reverse the tide of U.S. foreign policy appeared to be gaining strength during late 1947 and early 1948.[49] His run for the presidency, which ultimately turned into a rout for the left, still mobilized strong political forces. Wallace threatened the possibility of an alliance of the American left with European third-force opponents of the division of the world into two spheres. However unlikely such an alliance might have been, the U.S. government took no chances and mounted a dramatic campaign to "scare the hell out of the country,"as Republican senator Arthur Vandenberg put it.[50]

One response by the State Department in 1948 was to commission a study to disprove the argument that U.S. foreign policy represents "the interest of big businessmen, militarists, imperialists, reactionaries, etc." The department's findings, however, did not reflect a clear grassroots endorsement of U.S. foreign policy. Still, the report's authors engaged in some wishful thinking. Contrary to the findings of a number of surveys they examined, State Department researchers found that "Americans in the lower income and educational brackets . . . show a marked tendency to be more suspicious and critical of Russia than those in higher brackets."[51] The report's figures, however, contradict this finding. Far more wealthier and better educated people were fearful of the USSR and endorsed specific measures to counteract it.[52] One Roper study, ignored in the State Department report, found only a third of factory workers in favor of the Marshall Plan.[53] The suspicions that working-class people voiced about the USSR were part of a generally cynical world view in which no government could trusted. American workers, unlike their British counterparts, were not inclined to take the Soviet side in conflicts. Nonetheless, most could not bring themselves to immediately abandon the hopes of the midforties.

Class distinctions did affect foreign policy thinking. The middle and upper classes and the highly educated formed their opinions in a manner more reflective of government opinion, that is, they followed the party line. "For the better informed portion of the public," wrote University of Michigan researchers in 1947, "attitudes toward the United States–Russian relations are more highly integrated with specific events of the past few months and more subject to change as the tenor of world affairs shifts."[54] Reflecting their support of the nuances of government policy, better educated and wealthier Americans were more inclined to favor getting tough with the Soviets.[55]

Distrusting official thinkers more than middle- and upper-class people, workers tended to maintain more consistent ideas about the USSR. As late as the fall of 1948, after the Berlin blockade and the Czech coup, the 19 percent of Americans who thought Soviet expansion "should not be a matter of U.S. concern" tended to have only a grammar school education and to earn less than $1,000 per year.[56] Although the majority of American workers agreed on the necessity of confronting the USSR, the small portion of the total population opposed to this aggressive policy was disproportionately working class.

Rather than reflecting "broad stereotyped beliefs," working-class thought attempted to harmonize wartime images of honorable Soviet patriots with the new reality of perplexing international conflict.[57] In some cases working people tried to explain away Soviet behavior as the work of a few bad men. The Soviet people themselves wanted to avoid conflict with the United States, many workers thought, but dangerous individuals in the USSR's government threatened the peace. "I feel there is a party in Russia like there was in Germany," a steelworker worried in 1946, "warmongers who want war. I don't think Stalin wants war. He wants peace just like we do."[58] Equally guilty of causing conflict, at least according to the wife of a steelworker in 1946, were American anti-Communists: "If certain radicals [government conservatives] in the United States would keep their mouths shut and not talk so much it wouldn't irritate people over there."[59]

Underlying some working people's distrust of the direction of U.S. foreign policy was an isolationist rejection of the anti-Communist internationalism that threatened to draw the United States deeper into international conflict. U.S. policy before 1947 sought to avoid conflict and therefore did not create as much anxiety among isolationist workers. Under the Truman Doctrine, however, American involvement in the global fight against communism became the essence of policy. Further reinforcing worker isolationism, sociologist Steven Withey of the University of Michigan noted in 1948, was that "some in the lower educational and lowest informational brackets do not separate domestic and foreign problems in their thinking."[60] Foreign policy had to apply to people's experience. Willard Townsend, vice president of the CIO and head of the largely African American Transport Service Employees, reassured a State Department official in 1947 that "the ordinary member [of his union] is largely concerned with working conditions, wages, etc., and is not deeply interested in international developments."[61] One working-class woman with an eighth-grade education explained to Withey that she opposed foreign aid "'cause we got a lot of people over here to help and work out their problems."[62]

Domestically, anticommunism received tepid support among union members in the midforties. Unionists, regardless of political belief, had been labeled as Communists for too long, and workers remained suspicious of people outside the union movement who were attacking labor Communists. In 1948 one person, probably a miner, explained this line of thought: "It seems as if someone wants to better himself or someone else he gets called a Communist. There are so many definitions. Just seems that anyone who doesn't agree with what is going on is classified as a Communist. But seems to me men should have the right to say what they want to. They called Roosevelt a Communist because of what he was doing. They call [John L.] Lewis a Communist, but he has done more for the miners than anyone ever did."[63] A key element of the CIO's organizing philosophy had been the cooperation of all political factions, which of course was not always perfectly practiced. Yet strong support existed for the idea that Communists had a legitimate place in the labor movement. One former UAW member told Archibald that "you got to have some Communists to make a union good."[64] In unions with a strong Communist presence workers often believed, as did one middle-of-the road San Francisco longshoreman, that although they opposed their union's Communist-inclined leader "on issues," it was "nothing personal," and "his political beliefs, what they were, didn't bother me."[65] This is not to argue that American workers were pro-Communist in any significant numbers. Rather, they were not innately anti-Communist; the fear of reds needed (and, of course, received) fanning from sources external to the working class itself, such as the churches, the press, and the state.

The CIO membership overwhelmingly supported its leaders' initial opposition to the antilabor tide of the late forties. As the left lost power in the late forties, the idea of Americanism had became increasingly associated with the right and with loyalty to the Western cause in the cold war. The idea that un-American activities were those that supported New Deal foreign policy threatened the achievements of the Americanized groups that made up the New Deal coalition. For a time in the late 1940s the union movement attempted to use the images and ideology of Americanism to defend its Popular Front politics and its power in society in general. Resistance to the antilabor pressures of the postwar period were couched in patriotic terms. Spokesmen constantly referred to the numbers of CIO members who had fought in the war. They tried to make patriotism work for them because, in the words of one slogan coined by a member of UAW Local 272, "we veterans didn't fight for union busting."[66]

The main political battle of the union movement in 1946–47 was against the Taft-Hartley Act, which was enacted over Truman's veto in 1947. Dubbed the "slave labor act" by the unions, Taft-Hartley eliminated the closed shop, increased presidential power to intervene in strike situations, and required union leaders to swear to affidavits certifying they were not Communists in order to use the machinery of the National Labor Relations Board (NLRB). CIO and, indeed, AFL leaders, vehemently opposed Taft-Hartley.[67] In the spring of 1947, shortly after the president's speech announcing the Truman Doctrine and the launching of the administration's loyalty campaign, a half-million workers staged a half-day strike and 200,000 joined in a downtown Detroit demonstration against the Taft-Hartley bill.[68] For two years after its passage all the CIO's top officers and the majority of CIO officials nationwide refused to sign the required affidavits. They received strong support from members who resented government interference in the internal affairs of the unions and supported the Popular Front thinking that underlay the CIO–New Deal coalition and formed the basis of the union movement's foreign policy. For instance, in creating visual attacks on Taft-Hartley, rank-and-file activists took to heart the idea promoted by the CIO that this was a "slave labor act." Floats in an enormous Labor Day parade in Detroit in 1947 had workers in chains pulling top-hatted capitalists or being whipped by bosses.[69]

But the use of Americanist imagery and patriotic thinking to resist the shift in U.S. politics did not succeed. The specter of government action and the potentially disastrous effects of withdrawal of NLRB services for violating the non-Communist provisions of Taft-Hartley eventually swung the tide against the left and destroyed any remaining support for the unions' policy of tolerance of Communists at home and abroad. Nevertheless, the complete turn by the non-Communists against the Communist Party took approximately two years after the Republican victories in the 1946 elections.

American workers as a whole had not immediately supported the resurgent right wing of labor and rarely supported the extreme right in U.S. politics as a whole. (Senator Joseph McCarthy's strongest support came from the traditional bases of the Republican right, the small-town middle class. Although the most consistently anti-McCarthy group was professionals, workers who belonged to unions were more likely to oppose him than those not in unions.[70]) Nor did liberal anticommunism, although attractive to many, immediately win overwhelming support in the working class. Walter Reuther's victory in the UAW in 1946 marked the beginning of the end for Communists in that union, but his triumph had more to do with personal ability than foreign policy. In most CIO unions the years from 1945 to 1947 were, in Joshua Freeman's phrase, "the Indian summer . . . of the Popular Front."[71]

Yet as the pressure for patriotic conformity mounted, ethnic Americans were faced with a challenge: abandon what remained of their left-internationalistic thinking, abandon the hope of increasing labor power in society, and demonstrate loyalty to the foreign policy of the United States. The alternative was to lose their claim to Americanness. Combined with the growing anger and horror among Americans of Eastern European extraction about Communist takeovers of their homelands, the changing conception of Americanism effectively eliminated the intellectual basis of mid-1940s internationalism in the United States and in the labor movement. The cumulative effect of this intellectual shift, and of the practical measures threatened by the right against continued labor and liberal cooperation with the Communists, such as Taft-Hartley, was the end of the Popular Front in the union movement and the beginning of the purges. By the end of the decade the pro-Soviet left was on its own.

Imperial Aspirations

Even more than in attitudes toward the cold war, American ideas about decolonization and the rise of the third world proved complex and uncohesive. With the telling exception of African Americans, most workers supported a two-sided U.S. policy in relations with less industrialized nations. On the one hand, they opposed the creation of an American empire after the war. On the other, most workers expected the United States to play a dominant role in world affairs, ensuring that the future would not bring renewed war, privation, or challenges to

U.S. hegemony. "We might be asked to protect small countries," a mechanic in a rubber factory explained, "but we have no interest in dominating them. We shall have plenty to do here to continue our own government and to get things right again."[72] A New Orleans shipyard worker put it concisely: "We don't want power for ourselves. We preach freedom; why not have it for others? We have the Monroe Doctrine. Why not let that take care of it."[73] The Monroe Doctrine, which claimed an active role for the United States in Western Hemisphere affairs but excluded European imperial powers, provided a common model for how people conceived of the American century. Some working-class thinkers advocated a noninterventionist world role and regretted past U.S. practices in Latin America. "We got to be careful with South America," a Texas carpenter warned. "They don't trust us too well. We're big and they're little. We got to really be good neighbors and keep hands off—not try to run them any more'n we try to [run] Russia."[74]

Race-based hatred of the Japanese during the war formed a large part of the underside of American attitudes toward foreigners. Although some African Americans were less antagonistic toward the Japanese, among white workers hatred of the Japanese grew out of anger at a supposedly inferior race's attack on its betters. Archibald noticed the contrasting perceptions of Japanese and Germans: "Anger against the Germans was mainly channeled . . . toward the single leader or the single group deemed to have misguided a worthy folk, but anger against the Japanese was directed against a nation and a people, and with the publicizing of every new Japanese atrocity the bloodthirsty shouted for the annihilation of the foe down to the veriest babe."[75] Hatred of the Japanese—manifested in actions that ranged from brutal atrocities committed by U.S. soldiers in the Pacific to the interning of innocent Japanese Americans on the West Coast to the atomic bombing of Hiroshima and Nagasaki—revealed a society-wide fear and aggressiveness toward non-Europeans.[76] Among the radical longshoremen, anti-Japanese feeling led to ugly incidents even after the war ended.[77] The long history of American racial attitudes and racial conflict in the United States prefigured attitudes toward the rise of the third world and the end of colonialism.

Yet racial awareness was not the only lens for viewing the empires. American workers, like Americans in general, disliked Britain's imperial role both because they recalled the historical conflicts with their country's former ruler and because they believed empires in general to be illegitimate. Many blamed the British for the war. "It's America that's fighting Britain's war," one woman complained at a California shipyard. One of her colleagues agreed: "We're doing just what we did in the last war . . . saving Britain and her empire with the blood of our boys."[78] One southern steelworker strongly distrusted Great Britain in part because of its colonial role: "I've worked with British people, and I know them. I always judge a country by its people. I always thought they were selfish. . . . England went to war with Germany for doing the same thing England did in the past, I think if India wants to be by itself, it should. England is reaping a harvest from India and always has."[79] A Chicago woman resented that her brother "had to give his life for the protection of English colonies," and "our men at home must work 11 hours a day with an allowance of 2 lbs of meat a week . . . while the British get our food and fine wools."[80]

Positive ideas about Britain, of course, were widespread. Yet the favorable conceptions had much to do with nostalgia for "Merrie England" or appreciation for plucky resistance to the Germans but little to do with the imperial side of Great Britain. Discussions of Britain often trivialized the country, as UAW president R. J. Thomas did after meeting King George VI and Queen Consort Elizabeth, remarking that instead of fearsome tyrants, "they're mighty nice people."[81] But it was as an imperial power that Great Britain posed the biggest problem for international affairs. For left-leaning trade unionists the victory of the Labour Party in the 1945 elections reinforced the likelihood that the postwar era would be a better and more peaceful one. One union member wrote to CIO president Murray shortly after the Labour landslide: "I am particularly heartened, not necessarily by the victory of Labor [*sic*] itself, but more by the determined awakening of the people there and by the profound effect the event will have on the stand-pat reactionaries over here and throughout Europe. . . . Pray God that our people will be gifted with the vision to perceive the real and patent potential which the British Labor landslide has furnished us."[82] The left's reaction to the Labour victory underscored the critical role Britain, as the world's greatest imperial power, played in the thinking of internationally minded Americans.

Identification with colonial liberation movements, however, conflicted with Americans' racial conceptions. In one telling instance, three trade unionists who supported the Indian National Congress met with UAW officials and asked for help in getting rid of British domination. George Addes, vice president of the UAW and a member of the union's left-wing faction, offered them help in sending letters to local unions and making radio broadcasts but could offer little more. "The Indians originally had sought to have the UAW sponsor a mass meeting in Detroit but George felt it might be a flop," explained one man who attended the meeting.[83]

Americans from all classes believed the United States would have to take a stronger role in the world. One California steelworker, for instance, believed the failings of foreigners required the United States to assume the mantle of world power: "I want a United States Army, Navy and Air Force that can whip the world anytime they turn around. We will have to police the world. . . . The Europeans are a bunch of sheep. They are not equal to our kind. We are educated and think for ourselves. . . . We will have to take a front seat in international affairs. If we are going to fight these wars, we had better take care of things afterwards. . . . There's only one way to do it—Force. That's all that talks."[84] More aggressive people thought the United States would have to be even more interventionist than it had been. A worker in Detroit thought the United States deserved some compensation for saving the world: "I imagine we'll be taking over some parts of different countries which will be payment for what we have done. We should get something out of it."[85] A southern railroad worker expressed the contradictory impulses of American internationalist thinking. He believed that the best way to prevent another war was "don't allow 'em to prepare again. Watch them close. Be fair to 'em. Don't let 'em build up. Can't trust 'em, particularly the Japs. Never forget Pearl Harbor. Send the Secret Service over there. This country is too lenient, too nice to them."[86]

African Americans, unlike the majority of U.S. workers, identified strongly with people in colonized countries. They criticized Britain's imperial role and even attributed the country's problems in the world to racist thinking. A housewife in Philadelphia told an Office of War Information (OWI) surveyor: "England's something like this country—so busy trying to keep the black man down they wasn't prepared for the enemy. I don't like England's attitude now. She seems to rather lose the war than give those people in India a free government."[87] The most "militant feeling," according to one OWI report, came from a Detroit laborer: "England always treated the colored people bad. India's been a slave for years, and now they just want to be free so they can fight the Japs. But England just shoots in the mobs and kills the people. If I were an Indian, I'd say to England 'kill us, kill everybody, let the Japs come in, let the whole world go to hell, but I want my freedom now. I don't want any promises.'"[88] Black Americans' critical attitude toward imperial powers reflected their sense of oppression in the United States and gained strength from blacks' increasing willingness to militantly combat their subjugation at home. Activism had increased during the war with, among other indicators, the first grassroots political movement, the march on Washington threatened by trade unionist A. Philip Randolph if Roosevelt did not end discrimination in federal agencies and businesses with federal contracts. The war heightened African Americans' critical awareness of the world.[89]

Black newspapers and middle-class community leaders pressured the labor movement to improve its stance on issues involving colonized and less industrialized nations in the World Federation. The CIO's "Lily-White delegation" to the world conference in 1945, complained Ollie Stewart of the *Afro-American*, "fumbled an opportunity" to place itself at the center of the fight against colonialism. Although African delegates to the world conference sought the creation of "an international FEPC [Fair Employment Practices Commission]," as Stewart put it, the CIO ended up helping a segregated South African trade union federation get a seat on the World Federation's executive board.[90] "Somebody on the high command of the CIO made a big mistake," *Pittsburgh Courier* editor P. L. Prattis wrote in 1945, "when no Negro delegate was included in the delegation to the World Trade Union Conference in Paris."[91] Those who felt most strongly about the European imperial systems had experienced a form of colonialism themselves. The great divisions of experience and circumstance that divided the American working class appeared, naturally enough, in attitudes toward world affairs.

Weak Internationalism

Concerns for economic and personal safety, grievances against the more privileged, and a belief in American world responsibility created the common elements of working-class thinking on international affairs. As a whole, U.S. workers lacked a unifying sense of themselves as members of a distinct class. Although a politically important and active minority of the American working class enthusiastically supported labor internationalism in the mid-1940s, the majority was either doubtful, unconcerned, or worried by the prospect of continued cooperation with the USSR in the context of a global organization.

Class-influenced ways of looking at foreign policy nevertheless affected the thinking of millions of workers. The role of the United States in the world was a central problem for all Americans in the 1940s. However, working-class thought on foreign issues failed to have a powerful influence in any single direction in trade union affairs. The root of this failure was that working people in the United States did not develop a unified critical stance toward the state and the U.S. role in the world. In Britain the working class's socialism and its critique of foreign policy grew from a widely held insight that the institutions and policies of government did not serve average people's interests. In the United States, although many thought working peoples' interests were only poorly served, the vast majority did not envision any thorough-going alternative to the current system. Without a unified sense of class and of the need for enormous social and political change, Americans proved unable to translate their diverse feelings about world order into a consistent oppositional program. Instead, a variety of Americanism proved to be the main unifying element in working-class thought in this period.

Although one segment of the working class expressed labor-internationalist ideas, working-class Americanism also included conceptions of national greatness that derived from the advance of U.S. power in the world. Even as the United States grew in stature and involvement in world affairs from the nineteenth to the twentieth century, eventually committing hundreds of thousands of lives to the wars of Europe and Asia, American workers struggled to improve their lives and to create the kind of society they would like to live in. Thus American working-class thinking about the world had two sides in the 1940s. One revolved around the desirability or necessity of exercising American power to dominate the world, presumably benevolently. The other side, drawing on the pluralist tradition, valued noninterventionism and favored a multilateral world system. Between 1941 and 1947 the unifying ideology of Americanism fit neatly into the political program of the Popular Front that guided the CIO in its internal and external politics. During these years there was no cold war in American labor, with some notable exceptions such as in the UAW. The pluralist tolerant side of Americanism extended to Communists at home and abroad. By 1948, however, political and cultural change had redefined Americanism to eliminate this toleration of communism.

The minority of workers who thought largely in class terms formed the group that supported labor internationalism; the internationally inclined were synonymous with the active politically minded core of the unions. Those who supported the World Federation, or internationalism in general, had some identification with people abroad. The CIO's leaders—Communist and non-Communist, Catholic, Protestant, Jew, and atheist— depended on this core of support for their foreign policy, far more than did the leadership of the TUC or AFL. Although the leadership of the trade unions, especially the top leadership of the CIO, favored global corporatism, the American unions entered the international arena with limited support, in contrast to the enormous force propelling TUC leaders into global cooperation. Acting with only a partial mandate, the U.S. union leaders were able to act decisively only when the prevailing political winds within and without labor were favorable. Beholden to only a minority of workers, the CIO leaders were free to pursue their international project by helping to create the World Federation and to initially oppose the cold war. Yet the shallowness of rank-and-file internationalism and the evanescence of members' ideology provided the CIO with few resources to defend its global policy as the world's climate chilled in the late forties. The freedom that the lack of a working-class consensus allowed the CIO leadership turned out to be an empty gift, for no group in the United States was powerful enough to stand up to the forces of the cold war.

9

"A Positively Mystical Vision": The CIO and the Politics of Internationalism

"We are confronted with an entirely new constellation of forces," James Carey, leader of the Congress of Industrial Organizations, informed a 1945 meeting of the newly formed World Federation of Trade Unions. Peace in the coming years would be ensured, he argued, because by "a happy geographical accident—[two] great powers occupying vast continents and controlling vast resources in areas that are non-competitive, [are the] dominating and directing force in the future course of history."[1] Carey's optimism proved unfounded, for even without clear conflicts of national interest—as he interpreted them—the two great powers steered history onto a course of intense, bitter, and often deadly conflict. In the face of this conflict, however, Carey and his colleagues in the CIO championed a foreign policy based on the belief that with the defeat of the Germans and Japanese and the dissolution of the great empires, nothing could effectively prevent worldwide harmony. The leaders of the CIO remained committed to this thinking, even when it proved dangerous to their domestic political success.

The disintegration of the wartime alliance between the United States and the Soviet Union had profound effects on the American labor movement. Despite the dynamism and excitement surrounding its creation and extraordinary growth in the 1930s, and its formidable political power in the mid-1940s, the CIO was in crisis in 1948–49. Although many causes of the shift in CIO fortunes in the 1940s were domestic, the evaporation of midforties hopes for a cooperative world order played a decisive role in that upheaval.

Much more than the leadership of the Trades Union Congress, during the 1940s the top officers of the CIO sincerely believed in an internationalism that embraced the USSR and the third world in a system of global labor-based bureaucracy. Unlike the TUC, the CIO lacked a powerful right wing. As a consequence little debate occurred regarding the need for the CIO to participate in the formation of a new trade union international along with the Soviets.[2] Moreover, until 1947 the dominant political groups in the CIO—liberal Democrats, Socialists, and Communists—agreed on the need for a cooperative world order. This ideology about world affairs derived from a conception of the proper relationship between labor and government, combined with a belief in the benevolent role the people of the United States should play in the world. These internationalist ideas grew from what can best be described as a "New Deal" foreign policy: a combination of realistic respect for the rights of nations to pursue their national interest and of idealistic faith in the power of worldwide organizations to create a better world. The cultural and political pluralism intrinsic to the New Deal was behind these ideas about how to reform the world system. The idea of cultural pluralism in national politics could easily be translated to the global level, where each country could retain its national interest while being a citizen of the world. In 1945 this foreign policy thinking reached its apotheosis in the formation of the World Federation of Trade Unions and the United Nations. The midforties were a time of tremendous success for the CIO, confirming the organization's role at the center of the transformation of world politics.

The shift in U.S. foreign policy between 1946 and 1948 pushed the CIO out into the cold. Unwilling to give up on the midforties vision and still believing in working with foreign Communists, the CIO remained loyal to these ideas of mid-decade. The industrial unionists faced political disaster.

The crisis the CIO faced forced its liberals to rethink their conceptions of world and domestic politics and to develop a labor version of cold war liberalism. Its time of rapid membership gains largely over, the industrial unions' federation faced a hostile Republican Congress and an equivocal Democratic president (albeit one elected with labor support).

By 1948 the CIO's tolerance of Communists within its membership and its commitment to a Rooseveltian foreign policy without Roosevelt threatened to bring down the wrath of official Communist hunters and to destroy the gains made by labor in the previous fifteen years. The cold war also benefited the organization's right-wing competitor, the American Federation of Labor, making the AFL a potent warrior against perceived threats to American interests around the world. As the idea of a world led by the common people receded into memory, displaced by the reality of a fervent battle of superstates, the CIO found itself tied to outmoded and potentially self-destructive policies. A few years after its triumphant participation in the creation of the World Federation, the CIO was fighting for its political life.

Why the CIO joined in attempts to create a new world order, and why it continued to pursue these hopes years after they proved hollow, are explored in this and the next chapter. Commitment to the ideology and practice of internationalism on the part of the unions' leaders, an evolving relationship with the U.S. government, competition with the AFL, and the interaction of Communists and non-Communists in the CIO all played crucial roles in determining how the organization acted in world affairs.

Makers of CIO Foreign Policy

Unlike their British counterparts, American workers were deeply divided about the legitimacy of the USSR and its role in world politics. Also unlike the British, the CIO's leaders were more consistently on the left—in a general sense—than the members of the unions they led. The absence of strong, working-class, pro-Soviet inclinations in the United States limited the influence of grassroots opinion on the conflict about communism at home and abroad. As a consequence, concern for the rank-and-file was relatively less important in the decision making by the leadership of the CIO than of the TUC. More critical for the Americans were the role of leadership thinking, factional issues, and the unions' relation to the government. This chapter concentrates on a small group of non-Communist leaders at the top of the CIO hierarchy, notably Sidney Hillman, Philip Murray, James Carey, and Walter Reuther, who exercised an inordinate influence on the ideology and practice of labor internationalism in the 1940s. Few Communist officials appear as actors, simply because they lacked the power to decide CIO policy. Their actions were important, but their thinking lies outside the scope of this work.

Hillman, Murray, Carey, and Reuther shared a common antipathy to the CIO's Communist faction, and all had been partisans in union battles with the Communist Party. Despite these experiences, they worked closely with Communists at home and abroad throughout the forties—with the critical exception of Reuther.

Hillman had organized effective anti-Communist campaigns during the 1920s as president of the Socialist-inclined Amalgamated Clothing Workers. Like many other Socialists, however, the Lithuania-born union leader had been a supporter of the Russian Revolution and had even organized a cooperative clothing factory during the Soviets' New Economic Policy.[3] Although he was distrustful of the Communists within his organization, Hillman was willing to work with them when they did not challenge his or the labor movement's position, and he cooperated with them during the creation of the CIO in the 1930s. But fearful for the safety of labor, especially during the Nazi-Soviet pact period, when the Communists were out of step with the mainstream, the Clothing Workers' president had no hesitation about supporting internal purges.[4] Once the United States and the USSR were in alliance, Hillman executed an about-face and worked with the left once again. Indeed, his commitment to an alliance with the Communist left led to startling symbolic and practical actions. In 1944 he refused to attend a protest rally after the imprisonment and presumed murder of Polish Socialists Victor Alter and Henry K. Ehrlich by the Soviet secret police. More practically, he supported the right of Communists to run for office under the banner of the American Labor Party in New York. This led to a split in the party and the founding of the anti-Communist Liberal Party.[5]

Hillman's flexibility did not indicate a lack of conviction. Rather, his characteristic role in his union, in labor relations, and in national and international politics was, as Steve Fraser notes, that of "the quintessential mediating figure whose notable later accomplishments depended on his ability to communicate across the borders of class and culture."[6] The ability to mediate conflicts brought Hillman great success. A close adviser to President Roosevelt, Hillman held a succession of government positions during the war and was instrumental in re-electing FDR in 1944 through the CIO's Political Action Committee. President Truman also respected Hillman, telling Henry Wallace that of all American unionists, "Hillman has the best brains of the lot."[7] Hillman was unable, however, to establish as good a relationship with Truman as he had with Roosevelt.

More than any other man, Hillman came to embody the hopes of American labor for a new world brought about through the World Federation and the UN. Although at times a cynical political operative, Hillman nonetheless held deeply idealistic views of what the world ought to be. "He had," remembered Jacob Potofsky, his successor at the Clothing Workers, "a profound belief in the United Nations."[8] According to another Amalgamated official, Frank Rosenblum, Hillman truly believed that "a single unified international organization of trade unions had an excellent chance of making a vital contribution toward the maintenance of an enduring peace."[9] Hillman occupied a place unmatched by any other trade unionist in the U.S. labor movement. Imbued with the Popular Front spirit of the CIO, Hillman actively worked for a powerful union movement and for liberal social change. He was a skilled politician who could handle well the difficult internal politics of international labor. Much of the early success of the World Federation can be attributed to Hillman's diplomatic abilities. Hillman, who died in July 1946, did not live to see the failure of one of the greatest accomplishments of his diplomacy, the World Federation.

Philip Murray, who succeeded the charismatic John L. Lewis as president of the CIO in 1940, lacked both his predecessor's dynamism and Hillman's political talents.[10] Nonetheless, he was an effective mediator whose understated unpolished style matched the CIO's needs after the stormy Lewis years. Like Hillman, he was a veteran of anti-Communist factional battles in his old union, the United Mine Workers (UMW). After leaving Lewis's shadow in the UMW, the devoutly Catholic Murray took over the leadership of the Steel Workers Organizing Committee (SWOC), which became the United Steel Workers of America (USWA) in 1942. The rapid top-down organization of the steel industry shut out the Communists; the SWOC/USWA had only a small far left presence. Although he surreptitiously supported anti-Communist activists in the labor movement and reportedly funneled money to anti-Communist insurgents in one union, Murray for the most part sought compromise until the purges of the Communist unions in 1949.[11]

The CIO president's willingness to work with Communists alarmed J. Edgar Hoover, who worried in 1942 "that Philip Murray will receive the wholehearted support of Moscow in the event he needs it, because the Russians believe in him."[12] Had the Scottish-born Murray known of the FBI director's fears, he might have easily calmed them, for although he grew up in a Labourist milieu, he was the most suspicious of the three leaders about Soviet intentions. Lee Pressman, the CIO's general counsel and a Communist, recalled that Murray refused to go to the World Trade Union Conference because he was "instinctively reluctant to sit there with Russians. . . . It simply went against his grain."[13] Although Murray hoped that the World Federation would "bring beneficial results to the peoples of all the Nations throughout the world," his distrust of the Soviets caused him to let Hillman and Carey run the machinery of CIO foreign policy.[14] Until it was completely clear that the CIO's connections to the Communists were going to bring disaster, Murray, despite his hands-off approach, supported the unions' Popular Front consensus.

Unlike the other three, James Carey had lost control of his union, the United Electrical, Radio, and Machine Workers (UE), to a Communist-led faction in 1941. Despite this experience with the Soviets' acolytes, Carey, who had become president of the UE at twenty-five and CIO secretary treasurer two years later, believed the USSR to be a legitimate force in world affairs. Indeed, the ambitious, somewhat intemperate Carey was the chief non-Communist champion of the World Federation after Hillman's death. Like his colleagues, Carey felt ambivalent about the Soviets and criticized them for particular acts such as the murder of Alter and Ehrlich in 1943.[15] He did not, however, become a strong anti-Soviet until 1949. A liberal Catholic like Murray, Carey had close ties to the Association of Catholic Trade Unionists. However, he turned to ACTU more for its help in fighting the Communists in the UE than because he believed in its conservative labor creed. Carey thought labor's role in national and international affairs was to be reformist.[16]

Walter Reuther's role was different from those of Carey, Hillman, and Murray. Reuther is a difficult man to easily categorize but in many ways was one of the brightest lights of the non-Communist left. Of the same generation as Carey, he had risen with the United Auto Workers as one of the most able union organizers of his time. Like Hillman, he had direct experience with the Soviet Union, which he gained from working in a Russian automobile plant in Gorki in 1934. Although a Socialist during the thirties, he had been quite sympathetic to the Soviet Union and had worked in coalition with Communists in the early years of the UAW. His factional position shifted in the 1940s and he opposed the Communists after the war. Despite toning down his socialism, he provided a strong leftist voice in national politics, making headlines with social-democratic plans to amalgamate the airplane industry during the war and with his demand to review the books of General Motors in the 1946 auto strike. His victory over the Communist-backed candidate for the presidency of the UAW in 1946 ensured his centrality to the anti-Communist drive in the CIO in the late forties. His political savvy led him to the presidency of the CIO after Murray died in 1952 and to the head of the AFL-CIO's industrial division after the two organizations merged in 1955. Reuther's creative formulations helped turn anticommunism from the province of the right to an essential element of the left later in the forties. He was in many ways the great synthesizer of cold war liberalism.

Together these four men designed and carried out CIO foreign policy; more than any other individuals, they were responsible for what the CIO did. Still, they did not and could not act independently; rather, they based their actions on the CIO's philosophy of internationalism and adjusted to political and diplomatic realities.

The Internationalism of the CIO

The CIO's foreign policy rested on two apparently contradictory prescriptions for the ills of the world. One was economic, the other political. In an attempt to convince the World Federation to endorse the Marshall Plan for aid to Europe, Carey characteristically portrayed his organization's economic goals in late 1947: "I am here to talk to you not about ideologies, because we have no American ideologies to export, but about food, and coal, and fertilizers, and agricultural machinery, and power plants, and transportation, and cotton, and steel."[17] Like so many other purveyors of American largess, from Woodrow Wilson forward,

Carey claimed to be free of ideologies and respectful of national self-determination. Confronted by a Foreign Service officer in 1944 with the charge that the CIO's ideas of foreign policy amounted to "social and labor imperialism," Carey retorted: "If what you say is true, I am going to stop talking about the Atlantic Charter and talk in very practical terms. We are going to have to influence every country we do business in and it might as well be a good influence."[18]

The CIO leadership shared the consensus of various economists and political leaders about the profound interconnection of the domestic and world economies. In 1945 FDR's Executive Committee on Economic Foreign Policy, for instance, argued, in Secretary of Labor Frances Perkins's words: "Unless there is a domestic program to maintain a high level of productive employment in the United States it would be almost impossible to achieve our goal of more liberal conditions for international trade."[19] Although the committee's recommendations were far less social-democratic than the CIO's consensus, they nonetheless argued for a program of domestic economic stimulation connected to foreign trade.[20]

Carey had anticipated this thinking in 1944: "What we want here in this country we also want for workers outside our borders." He claimed the world needed a fundamentally liberal order: "The world must be internationalized." This meant free trade, free access to raw material for all, free travel, and limitations on the power of individual states. "The alternative to cartels, reaction, and war," he explained carefully, "is democratic government within the state, democratically-controlled world organization and peace."[21]

However, economic expansion as a solution to the problems of the world was not enough, the CIO men realized. Economic causes might be at the root of war, but economic change alone could not prevent future crises.[22] They commonly believed, as Lou Harris, a member of the Oil and Chemical Workers Union, told Carey, that "it is folly to hope for this expansionist economic order without the existence of a united political force on an international scale to work for these measures." The United Nations could become this force, Harris argued, but it needed bolstering from international labor.[23] Carey agreed, telling a radio audience in 1946: "We must make a decision now to work together with all the other nations of the earth not to outlaw war, but to abolish the practices that breed war."[24] However, governments alone could not be trusted to do the job: "The time has passed when any one people can entrust the sole decision of political questions to any group of political office holders competent though they might be. The people of this country must make their personal contributions to functions of government."[25]

Hillman similarly emphasized the role of working people in international affairs. The World Trade Union Conference and the Yalta Conference "complement each other," Hillman told a prowar rally at Madison Square Garden in March 1945. The conference in the Crimea had affirmed the unity of the Allied governments in creating a just peace after the war against fascism, "but if the lofty objectives agreed upon by Prime Minister Churchill, Marshall Stalin, and President Roosevelt are to be realized, they must have the full support and understanding, not only of these leaders and the governments of the other United Nations, but of their people as well," Hillman said.[26] Hillman's commitment to the principles of institutionalized cooperation was legendary. His hopes for the abilities of the World Federation struck some observers as "positively 'mystical.'"[27]

Carey, like most other CIO leaders, believed that the unions, as representatives of the people, had a particular responsibility and unmatched ability to influence the course of international affairs. In February 1947 Carey maintained that by getting to know the unions of the world, the CIO would help prevent war between the USSR and the United States. "We don't believe that the United States Government, dealing with the Soviet government alone," he told a group of student officers at the Industrial College of the Armed Forces, "can bring about that kind of relationship that will maintain peace. Governments alone cannot do the job." Unions, however, could "cut across every economic, social, and political question, and we do it through the instruments that we create."[28] The union movement could bring about a different kind of international relations, a system in which differences between Communists and non-Communists were overcome in the mutual pursuit of a better life for all. Cooperation between competing groups and parties was not only possible but the best method of running the world.

As late as 1948, CIO leaders who were deeply involved in anti-Communist organizing within the union movement still believed the formal unity of diverse political groups to be the best solution to ideological conflicts. O. A. Knight, president of the Oil and Chemical Workers, suggested that factional strife in the Mexican labor movement could be cured if representatives from all the competing groups, including Communists, met in a large democratic forum.[29] Similarly, Willard S. Townsend, CIO vice president and president of the United Transport Service Employees, claimed in 1947 "that the problem of Communist influence within the WFTU was not a matter of great concern to the officers of his union" because the most basic principle of the World Federation was cooperation.[30]

The CIO's foreign policy never resolved the contradiction between spreading the politics of productivity based on U.S. economic power, which reproduced worldwide the economic and social divisions the unionists decried at home, and building a democratic world order. The CIO's consensus on foreign policy grew from a common philosophy that endorsed an American version of social democracy.[31] Hillman's efforts in the 1920s to bring peace to the intensely competitive garment industry served as a model for the CIO's vision of political economy.[32] Philip Murray proposed a plan in 1941, actually conceived by the liberal Roman Catholic intellectual John A. Ryan, to govern the wartime economy by a series of industrial councils.[33] Walter Reuther's more famous proposal to produce five hundred planes a day by eliminating corporate lines in the aerospace industry well expressed the unionists' bureaucratizing conceptions.[34] These plans received broad support among union activists and officials.[35] Even the AFL endorsed substantial corporative approaches to labor issues during the war.[36]

The CIO's plans for the national economy eliminated the dangers posed by conflicts of interest by balancing the demands of the opposing parties in a formal setting, much as the National Labor Relations Board defused the dangers of industrial conflicts by moving them from the workplace to the hearing room.[37] Further, the role of administrative boards in the CIO's plans underscored the union leaders' belief in the importance of centralized planning to ensure prosperity. As a natural extension of domestic programs, the CIO endorsed world-encompassing organizations without second thoughts.

The CIO leaders articulated a labor variation of the dominant ideas of world order best termed the Rooseveltian vision. President Roosevelt, in fact, was in favor of institutionalizing the Anglo-Soviet-American union cooperation of the alliance years. The Rooseveltian new world order not only responded to new realities of world power but reflected the domestic political and social vision of the New Deal, broadly conceived.

Roosevelt believed the UN should encompass the three main components of world politics. At the Teheran Conference he illustrated his idea of a world organization to Churchill and Stalin by drawing three circles on a napkin: in the first was the great powers; in the second, the "40 United Nations"; and in the third, the social institutions of the planned organization.[38] The UN, like the National Labor Relations Act, would regularize and defuse conflicts by bringing them into an institution underwritten by the power of the permanent members of what would become the Security Council. Through their control of the Security Council, the great powers of the world, especially Britain, the United States, and the USSR, would benevolently dominate the world in order to prevent atavistic challenges to peace such as that posed by fascism. Democracy in the new system would be ensured in different ways through what would become the General Assembly and by the social organizations. The opposition of democracy and Security Council power reflected the two implicit divisions of the new system, the coalition of the Grand Alliance versus the mass of the world nations on one side, and, on the other, the mass of people represented by the social organizations versus the state system. Both aspects were mirrored within the World Federation by the cooperation of Americans, British, and Soviets on the executive board and the more democratic conferences.

The CIO leadership accepted the Rooseveltian philosophy so strongly that the shifting political climate at the beginning of the cold war failed to elicit a change in line. CIO leaders continued to fight for their foreign policy in terms familiar to anyone on the left wing of the New Deal, even after American-Soviet relations began to deteriorate.

R. J. Thomas, president of the UAW from 1939 to 1946, provides an excellent example. In a 1946 letter to pro–New Deal senator Harley Kilgore of West Virginia, Thomas, who had just been unseated as president of the UAW by Reuther, vented his frustrations at the direction of U.S. policy in the year after Roosevelt's death: "But even more urgently the American people want to know the role of profit hungry American corporations at the present time in creating international conflict and seeking to light the fuse for a third world war. . . . Special hatred has been directed against those spokesmen of a democratic and peaceful foreign policy—Franklin Roosevelt and Henry Wallace. . . . Dangerous misunderstanding has been created in the post-war world."[39]

Because Thomas had only a small power base and believed deeply in the principles of the Popular Front, he had earlier been the choice of the Communists, Reutherites, and other militant factions to lead the Auto Workers after the defeat of incompetent conservative Homer Martin a few years earlier.[40] (Martin had been advised, not incidentally, by Jay Lovestone, former head of the Communist Party and later director of the AFL's rabidly anti-Communist Free Trade Union Committee.) Thomas's unwillingness to adapt to the changing political makeup of the UAW and the darkening atmosphere in the country at large consigned him to the vice presidency of his union and then ouster from office. "Thomas rattled around in the job," Carl Haessler, editor of the UAW's newspaper, recalled, "and did not have what it takes for a divided union. . . . That was his undoing."[41] Thomas preserved his now unpopular ideas about politics because of an inability to bend to political winds, which also excluded him from the mainstream of debate and power in the union movement.

On the other hand, his antagonist and successor, Walter Reuther, a gifted politician and an early practitioner of cold war liberalism, put together a coalition of anti-Communist left-wingers, Catholics, and opportunistic bread-and-butter unionists to gain control of the union—a grouping that presaged the urban side of the Truman coalition of 1948.[42] Reuther's takeover of the UAW marked the beginning of the end of official CIO tolerance for Communists, and the dynamic auto workers' leader became a strong opponent of the CIO's cooperation with the Soviets. Nevertheless, Reuther's first foreign-policy initiatives in 1946 attacked the three Allies for bypassing the UN, and he denounced Winston Churchill for "calling for an American-British Military alliance against Soviet Russia."[43] The issue of communism underlay the Auto Workers' factional fights but did not force a change in foreign policy—yet.

As the mobilization of national resources for the cold war that began in 1946 made the CIO's thinking—as it did R. J. Thomas's—increasingly anachronistic, the mainstream leaders searched for a new way of expressing their understanding of world politics. Some, like Thomas, failed to adapt and were brushed aside. Others in more secure positions found they could not simply adopt the AFL's vigorous anticommunism. Imitation of the AFL was impossible between 1946 and 1948, given the political makeup of the CIO and the inability of anticommunism as an ideology to satisfy the unionists' reformist urge.

The synthesis of anticommunism and reformism, which came to be called cold war liberalism, did not come easily to the CIO. It failed to immediately dominate CIO foreign policy because most cold war liberals more often than not gave priority to anticommunism over liberalism, a tendency that disturbed the union leadership.[44]

Shortly after President Truman called for aid to Greece and Turkey, for instance, Undersecretary of State Dean Acheson met with representatives of the AFL, CIO, and the Railway Brotherhoods to explain the necessity of intervening against the Communists there. Representatives of the AFL and Railway Brotherhoods enthusiastically pledged their support, even if it meant aiding brutally repressive royalists, but the CIO's delegation was much more equivocal, arguing that "the Greek people should be offered something other than Communism or Royalist-Fascism."[45] Despite this qualification, they agreed that "speedy help should be extended to Greece," with the caveat that democracy and trade unionism should be promoted "as Greek economic recovery takes place."[46] The substance of the CIO's concerns was, of course, ignored as the tendency of U.S. foreign policy to support the far right against the left asserted itself. The CIO did receive consideration from the State Department on this issue, however. Clinton Golden, a moderate intellectual staffer of the CIO who later headed the labor division of the Marshall Plan organization, joined the U.S. mission to Greece. He found himself frustrated by the precedence that the State Department gave to fighting communism over improving social conditions. His solution was to promote more labor participation in U.S. policy.[47] Golden, however, was ahead of the rest of the CIO in accepting the premises of cold war liberalism. The CIO, for instance, took no official position on the speech in which the president outlined the Truman Doctrine.[48]

Although their ideas eventually adapted to the changing times, the evolution of the CIO leaders' thinking about foreign affairs reflected the organization's shifting relationships to the main political currents of the time. The force of international relations, expressed in the cataclysm of World War II and the cold war, forced dramatic changes in the CIO's domestic circumstances as well.

Burying the Hatchet

International affairs had powerful effects on the relations of the AFL and CIO. U.S. entry into World War II stimulated renewed efforts at cooperation between the two centers. The underlying differences between the organizations on foreign and domestic issues, however, dissipated the good feelings of the early war years. The CIO's embrace of the Popular Front proved unacceptable to the AFL leadership. Cooperation on international affairs became impossible until 1950, both because of institutional competition—the AFL leadership believed itself the only legitimate representative of labor abroad—and because of ideological conflict, with the CIO's acceptance of Soviet legitimacy and the organization's positioning itself as the champion of the new world order. Even into the late forties, differing attitudes toward the Soviet Union precluded understanding between the two organizations and undercut their efforts to resist the inroads of antilabor forces at home.

The Japanese attack on Pearl Harbor spurred an epidemic of good feeling and passionate patriotism among local and national leaders of the CIO, AFL, and Railway Brotherhoods. Dan Tobin of the AFL's Teamsters asked for FDR's help in promoting such unity. Roosevelt agreed, saying, "The nation would be gratified if labor would agree to set aside all differences in this crucial hour when the safety of the nation and the freedom of the world [are] in danger."[49] Unionists readily responded to the appeal.

A joint meeting of union locals in San Francisco proposed to the rest of organized labor and the nation in general that "all factional, partisan and political differences be immediately forgotten."[50] The San Francisco unionists created a joint AFL-CIO Unity for Victory Committee and published newsletters and booklets.[51] Unionists in New Jersey visually likened the unity of the Allies to that of labor by joining the flags of the United States, the USSR, Great Britain, and China in a banner that read: "United Labor Smash Facism" (sic). In late December twenty thousand people celebrated labor unity at a rally in New York City.[52] Union officials cooperated in the national labor division of Citizens for Victory, a public pressure group devoted to the war effort.[53] By April AFL president William Green and the CIO's Philip Murray were willing to shake hands at a CIO-AFL hatchet-burying ceremony.[54]

More practically, the two organizations began to cooperate at the behest of President Roosevelt. They created the National Labor Victory Board and agreed to mediate jurisdictional disputes. Roosevelt played an active role in bringing the two sides together, holding mediation sessions and even suggesting to Murray the text of a letter to send to Green about cooperation.[55]

In part the AFL and CIO were undoubtedly prompted by the threat of pending legislation in Congress, such as that sponsored by Democratic representative Howard W. Smith of West Virginia, which used the war emergency to discipline the labor movement. Shortly before Pearl Harbor, Smith, along with Georgia Democrat Carl Vinson, introduced legislation presaging the Taft-Hartley Act of 1947, which outlawed the closed shop and instituted a thirty-day cooling-off period before strikes. Conservatives even proposed eliminating the forty-hour week.[56] To combat the resurgent antilabor feelings the CIO leaders pledged their loyalty to the patriotic struggle by promising not to strike for the duration of the war. But the no-strike pledge was not enough. They also agreed to fight antilabor legislation jointly and attempted to form a "United National Labor Council" to handle jurisdictional conflicts between members of the organizations, as well as to lay the basis for reunification.[57]

The American Labor Conference on International Affairs (ALCIA) grew out of this cooperative spirit and brought hundreds of American and exile labor leaders together to plan for the future and to aid the European Resistance. The conference, which was formed in the winter of 1943 and quickly gained a large membership, pledged to promote international democracy and to fight for "the establishment of an international order which guarantee[s] enduring peace" and "an economic system based on security of employment and development."[58] The Office of Strategic Services believed the conference had some potential: "The significance of the conference is suggested by the fact that it has laid the ground work for a permanent organization of American and European labor leaders which may prove to be a force in post-war international planning."[59]

Harmony in the ALCIA was brief. The AFL leaders who had facilitated its creation, notably David Dubinsky, a former Socialist and president of the International Ladies' Garment Workers Union (ILGWU), insisted on keeping CIO influence in the organization to a minimum. Dubinsky undoubtedly wanted to ensure that the ALCIA did not take positions favoring Communist and Soviet trade unions. The CIO representatives decided to resign en masse after the ALCIA—without consulting the CIO—coordinated an AFL postwar planning meeting in April 1944. "Our membership in your organization," they told Varian Fry, ALCIA's executive director, "has been nominal."[60] Carey refused to even participate in radio discussions hosted by the ALCIA.[61] The labor conference became a main think-tank for AFL foreign policy. Under Fry, Dubinsky, and exiled Social-Democrat Raphael Abramovich, the ALCIA developed the anti-Communist strategy that the AFL's overseas representatives, Irving Brown and Jay Lovestone, carried out.[62] The experiment in cooperation on international issues lasted barely a year and a half.

Labor diplomacy complicated CIO-AFL unity talks and quickly led to renewed rancor between leaders of the organizations.[63] Sir Walter Citrine had opened the Pandora's box as an emissary of the Anglo-Soviet Trade Union Committee in 1942. Citrine invited American unions to join the committee, but the AFL refused to meet with the Soviets.[64] The effort to join the allied labor movements in a formal alliance stalled almost immediately, and Citrine settled on simply creating an AFL-TUC committee in 1943. But this solution excluded the CIO and the Railway Brotherhoods at the AFL's behest. Once the AFL refused to meet with the Soviets, allow the CIO to join the AFL-TUC committee, or even permit pro-Soviet activity in the ALCIA, little could be salvaged of the conciliatory spirit of the first years of the war. Murray, infuriated by the TUC's snub, berated Citrine in early 1943: "Both you and they [the AFL] in the field of international labor collaboration can do just as you damn well please."[65]

Because the leaders of the CIO and the AFL could not agree on the proper international role for the United States, cooperation proved difficult in almost every area. In 1944 the chairman of the CIO's Latin American Affairs Committee, Jacob Potofsky, Hillman's second in command at the Clothing Workers, met with Matthew Woll, the AFL's Latin affairs specialist and executive board member, about forming a joint committee for Latin affairs. Potofsky claimed "he had made a sincere effort" but that Woll was unwilling to accept cooperation. Potofsky believed the AFL and CIO failed to work together because of their fundamentally different conceptions of international roles, with the CIO advocating a more neutral role for U.S. labor in Latin America and the AFL pressing for interventionism. (On the CIO in Latin America, see Chapter 10.) "Unity," Potofsky concluded, "while desirable must be based on similar objectives but apparently the objectives of the AFL are different from our own."[66] An attempt to sponsor jointly with the AFL an exchange program for Latin American union members in 1946 also failed.[67]

Foreign policy remained one of the chief stumbling blocks to AFL-CIO unity into the later part of the forties. In the antilabor atmosphere after the passage of the Taft-Hartley Act, the AFL and CIO once again sought to join forces, but international affairs kept them from reaching an agreement. At unity talks held in 1947 the CIO delegates reaffirmed their commitment to internationalism in the mold of the mid-1940s: "We argued that in the atomic age, there was a great and compelling need for international labor solidarity and understanding among the peoples of the world. Labor isolationism no less than political isolationism was narrow, dangerous and not conducive to the best interests of labor or our nation."[68]

Between 1941 and 1947 the AFL lost out in international affairs, while the CIO leaders rode the crest of a diplomatic wave that followed the contours of their basic social philosophy. Much has been made of the activities of the AFL's international representatives, Irving Brown and Jay Lovestone, in instigating the cold war in European labor, but their influence before 1948–49 has been overrated.[69] Although they make good villains (or heroes) they may not have been as relevant in the early years as is often thought. The two anti-Communists exerted little influence on German developments until the removal of the CIO's Mortimer Wolf from the commission responsible for labor in the U.S. zone in early 1946.[70] Even then the AFL had difficulty sending delegations around the American zone in Germany.[71] Similarly, the TUC resented AFL interference and heavy-handedness. The AFL's refusal to work with the All-Union Central Council of Soviet Trade Unions or the CIO forced it outside the mainstream of international affairs between 1941 and 1947.

Because the AFL was out of synch with the Allies' policies, it caused, in Anthony Eden's words, a "difficult situation" for Anglo-American-Soviet relations.[72] Citrine and many others in the TUC came to resent the AFL's obduracy. The refusal of the AFL to join an Anglo-American-Soviet committee, as well as its refusal to deal with the CIO in world affairs, left a "deep and bitter feeling between the AFL and TUC," the TUC's general secretary reported in 1945.[73] The AFL's envoys, Brown and Lovestone, developed a reputation for being manipulative and egocentric as much because they fought against the tide as because of their penchant for secretive behavior. AFL foreign policy, one TUC official told U.S. labor attaché Samuel Berger in London in the fall of 1947, was "too raw."[74] Even in mid-1948 Brown could not get the TUC to go along with his ambitious efforts to found a new pro–Marshall Plan organization to counter the World Federation.[75]

Only the ineffectiveness of the CIO's policies in late 1947 and 1948 gave its domestic competitor, the AFL, a chance to regain its lost position as champion of the American way of unionism around the world. The CIO began to move closer to the AFL after resistance to the Taft-Hartley Act and to the new direction of U.S. foreign policy proved ineffective. The threat to the liberal agenda from the antilabor right forced the CIO to jettison key elements of the New Deal alliance. Harry Truman's Fair Deal was a version of Roosevelt's politics stripped of its open acceptance of the Soviet Union abroad and its tacit uneasy acceptance of the Communists at home. Without the Communists inside the CIO and without the CIO inside the World Federation, the way was clear for the eventual reunification of the U.S. labor movement. But before this auspicious amalgamation, the CIO's leaders had to deal with their own Communist scourge.

The Communists at Home

Turmoil in the CIO delegation to the World Trade Union Conference greeted Sidney Hillman when he arrived a day late for the conference in February 1945. James Carey, who had acted as temporary leader, lacked the authority, patience, or skill to balance the Communist and non-Communist elements in the delegation. To make matters worse for the hot-tempered Carey, the man who had displaced him at the UE, Albert Fitzgerald, was also in the delegation. The two repeatedly clashed, their biggest conflict occurring over inviting the Lublin trade unionists to the conference. Carey did not oppose the Lublin invitation as such but wanted it tied to an invitation to the Italian trade union confederation. Fitzgerald, Carey complained to a U.S. embassy attaché in London, acted like a "babe in the woods" who was "only trying to be a good fellow," when in reality he was functioning as a stooge. The delegation faced an open split—until Hillman arrived. The veteran conciliator was able to smooth things over, and the delegation functioned more or less normally for the remainder of the World Conference.[76] This conflict and its resolution captured the dynamic of the factional conflict in the CIO. Although cooperation was the order of the day, vicious disputes were never far from the surface, especially in delicate areas like foreign policy.

Between 1939 and 1941 Communists had supported John L. Lewis's anti-Roosevelt position but quickly returned to the Popular Front when the USSR was invaded. After the Nazi-Soviet pact period Communist Party members and supporters within the CIO played an important role in the development of the CIO's international policy. Their importance came both from their ability to influence policy and from the efforts of their factional opponents to use foreign relations as a means of undercutting party members' popularity. As the government of the United States grew increasingly obsessed with the specter of communism in the aftermath of the war, however, the Communist left in the CIO became a dangerous burden, robbing the CIO of public legitimacy in the conduct of international affairs. Communist-led unions within the CIO, President Murray worried, were "targets, targets easily hit."[77]

Although Communists had been very active in building the CIO and led a number of the CIO unions, including one of the largest, the United Electrical Workers, they had an uneasy coexistence with other CIO groups.[78] Conflict based on political, personal, and factional grounds suffused the CIO and deeply affected its international policy. The Communists were only one faction among many, but at times they posed serious problems for the non-Communist leaders. These problems arose not only because of their contestation of power within the unions but also because of their support of the USSR, which acted as a lightning rod for antilabor sentiment. The problem of communism grew especially acute when the Communist Party adopted more militant political and industrial strategies, such as during the Nazi-Soviet pact period, or when the political atmosphere in the United States swung to the right, such as during the McCarthy era. Indeed, in 1940 the CIO convention passed—ironically, with the help of Communist delegates who thought they were making a tactical move—a resolution condemning communism and nazism. Yet the resolution carried no enforcement mechanism and was explained away as "a reassertion of the CIO's freedom from ideological domination of foreign origin."[79]

Before the right and middle of the CIO got rid of the Communist Party in the late forties, they had seen the Communists in a different light, often believing them to be legitimate opposition or allies. Unlike the TUC's middle and right wing, the CIO's dominant groups, with some notable exceptions, truly believed that the Communist Party could play a legitimate role. John L. Lewis's oft-quoted rhetorical question about the potential power of the Communist Party in the CIO—"Who gets the bird, the hunter or the dog?"—exaggerated his control over the organization but nonetheless expressed mainstream thinking: Communists were not dangerous and they could be effective partners.[80] One of the remarkable aspects of the CIO and of New Deal thinking in general was the idea that the left was a legitimate part of the political spectrum. That this now seems hard to believe is due to the revision of memory caused by the purges and anti-Communist demonology of the late forties and fifties.

The Nazi-Soviet pact broke down the New Deal alliance and spurred anti-Communist organizing in the CIO as communism became an important factional issue in the UAW and the UE.[81] But changes in United States and Communist politics after the USSR's entry into the war on Britain's side quickly ended this rehearsal for the cold war. The Nazi-Soviet pact period did not significantly reduce Communist Party power in the CIO, although it did dismay quite a number of sympathizers.

After the USSR joined the war, cooperation with the Soviets had great appeal for the anti-Communists in the CIO leadership, if only for the advantage it gave them in their conflicts with the Communist Party. Stanley Ruttenberg, a good friend of Carey's who became the CIO's education director after he left the military in 1946, enjoyed contemplating the pleasures of robbing the Soviet totem from the Communists. He wrote Carey in 1945: "I am even more anxious and curious to know how your trip to Moscow worked out. I know you had that secret [urge] to get their [goat]. The boys back in the UE must be pulling their hair out. To say nothing of some of your other 'friends' back in the states. You'll really be able to lay it to them on your return."[82]

Carey recommended that delegates of the faction-torn United Shoe Workers avoid international issues because this was the province of the CIO. If they did not heed his words, he warned, they would play into the Communists' hands: "There is no reason to destroy your organization by being too much concerned about Indonesia or China or some other matters that are so important to some people. You don't need the assistance of any other group in expressing policy on those questions. That is why we have a World Federation of Trade Unions."[83]

Factional conflicts overrode the knowledge that the Communists could be reasonable in international affairs. This obvious contradiction did not escape one Communist in 1945. He questioned R. J. Thomas, the internationalist president of the UAW, an organization that officially equated Communists and Nazis and banned them from top posts: "It is not presumption on my part to assume that you have found the Communists in the World's trade union congress 'pretty good guys.' Why should we in America be thought any different!"[84]

According to the Prague labor attaché, the internal balance of the CIO affected its foreign policy. He attributed the CIO's unwillingness to confront the Soviets and their allies in 1947–48 to "Left Wing Right Wing differences [from] home carried over" into the delegations to the World Federation.[85] Although the internal coalition of the CIO may have inhibited expression of anti-Communist sentiments at World Federation meetings, more important was the non-Communists' acceptance of Soviet legitimacy. Differences with the Communists rarely arose over strictly ideological issues.

Immediately before the purges, the split between supporters of Henry Wallace and those of Harry Truman for president was a major conflict in the CIO as a whole and definitely involved foreign policy issues, most notably controversy over support of the Marshall Plan.[86] But Marshall Plan opponents were quite weak, and the CIO's leaders had no trouble carrying their program. The Communists were not capable of imposing their will on the organization. Even the charismatic Harry Bridges, leader of the longshoremen, could not carry his own union in opposition to the European Recovery Program.[87] The Wallace presidential campaign, supported by Communists and others disenchanted with Truman's revisionist Rooseveltianism, threatened the CIO's carefully forged political connection to Truman. The 1948 election further emphasized to CIO moderates that the internal balance of the organization had to change.

The CIO leadership was careful all along to avoid participating in organizations that the Communists would control. Even during the middle of the war Philip Murray refused to have anything to do with the Communist-led Joint Anti-Fascist Refugee Committee. Instead, he convinced the CIO War Relief Committee to join with the AFL to form Refugee Relief Trustees, Inc., under the chairmanship of Edward Barsky.[88] Cooperation with the AFL was safer than being tied up with Communists.

In some of the big CIO unions, notably the Clothing Workers and the United Mine Workers, Communists had been eliminated from contention for power years earlier. In Murray's Steel Workers, effective centralized control (based on the imposition of the union on a largely unorganized rank-and-file after the signing of a contract with U.S. Steel and hundreds of other companies in 1937) precluded Communists from gaining support through their organizing activities.[89] But in many other CIO unions Communists provided effective leadership of local struggles and often gained national office. The rank-and-file upsurge that created the UAW owed much to the skill and perseverance of Communist and other radical organizers. Their presence in the faction-ridden UAW made it one of the main battlegrounds over communism in the CIO during the 1940s. Reuther successfully organized an anti-Communist bloc based both on ideological grounds—conservative Eastern European Catholics were a key group of supporters—and on personal loyalty to a militant leader.[90]

During the war "Reuther and his caucus allies," UAW newspaper editor Carl Haessler later recalled, "used the argument, not for the record but in caucus and in whispering efforts, . . . that the Communists were willing to undermine the union's position in order to help Russia."[91] Loyalty in factional struggles rested on ideological, factional, and practical grounds. Practical considerations arose if unionists thought the presence of Communists might impair the ability of their union to deliver the goods. Reuther gained power in the UAW in part because he championed labor militance at a time when many liberals, out of loyalty to the government, and Communists, out of support for the USSR, sought incentive pay, a postwar no-strike pledge, and other compromises of union power.[92] On the other hand, if members found the union effective, they kept their Communist leadership long into the cold war, as did the members of the West Coast locals of the International Longshoremen's and Warehousemen's Union and many UE locals.[93]

The connection of union factionalism and national loyalty arose repeatedly. During the Nazi-Soviet pact period in the Communist-controlled United Electrical Workers, right-wingers gained a big boost in their successful takeover of a formerly Communist-led local in Pennsylvania after the local's Communist leadership refused to sponsor a collection for an ambulance for Britain because it would aid the imperialists.[94] The Communists' overeagerness to support the foreign policy of the USSR occasionally discredited them in more amusing ways. A month before the Nazi invasion of the USSR, the Communist-led Plymouth (Michigan) UAW local introduced a resolution at the Wayne County CIO council condemning World War II as an imperialist venture, but the measure was tabled. In the month between council meetings the Germans invaded the USSR, so the Plymouth local introduced another resolution calling for U.S. participation in the war. Victor Reuther recounted: "So we had in the county meeting two resolutions from the same local advocating exactly opposite viewpoints. Someone moved to concur with both of them and it became quite a joke of course."[95]

The Communists, in the face of opposition from the CIO leadership, tried to use the international movement to their benefit. As relations with the Communists in the World Federation's secretariat deteriorated in the fall of 1947 and the winter of 1948, the anti-Communists moved to limit contacts by the CIO's left wing with the WFTU. The anti-Communists strenuously objected to any communication with the secretariat that the CIO's national office had not cleared first, and they complained hotly of previous incidents to Louis Saillant, general secretary of the World Federation. [96] Michael Ross, the CIO's international representative, feared that Saillant would receive "support from some quarters in both England and the United States even if the national centers of those countries take a position which he does not like."[97] When Carey flew on a mission to Moscow in the winter of 1948, he complained to the Russians first about "the feeling of the CIO . . . that they were being excluded from the WFTU" and that General Secretary Saillant was consulting with "less[er] CIO officials."[98]

The mainstream CIO factions kept the Communists from challenging their power. Before 1947–48 the union federation had tolerated limited Communist participation in policy formation, and the leadership was always careful to balance overseas delegations to ensure participation of the Communist factions. The CIO's pre-1948 policy toward internal Communists, like that toward those abroad, demonstrated a wary cooperativeness. The Communists for the most part had been reasonable partners in the organization and in the World Federation. But changing international and national politics made the Communists a danger. The CIO, however, had based a large part of both its organizational strategy and its diplomacy on the assumption that cooperation would continue. The purges of Communist-led unions conducted in 1948–49 were partly an effort to reconstitute the CIO on a new ideological basis. Instead, the CIO lost a big piece of its institutional identity and organizational dynamism, for liberal anticommunism proved a weak basis on which to build a union movement.

The CIO men searched for an apocryphal "middle way," which to them meant toleration of communism as long as it remained within legitimate bounds. Political circumstance eventually convinced them they had erred. The predicament of the CIO in the late forties—its promotion of a Rooseveltian foreign policy in a world without Roosevelt—became increasingly difficult.

10

"Neither Stalin nor Standard Oil": The Search for a CIO Identity

The CIO's formal diplomacy worked when the union leadership's thinking harmonized with the government consensus. With the shift in U.S. ideas about world politics in 1946–47, the CIO had to dramatically adjust its relationship to policy makers and to its counterparts in Europe and the third world. Moreover, the cold war required a reconceptualization of labor's world role.

The State Department and the CIO

The CIO's program for a new world order in the midforties depended on the organization's close relationship with the U.S. government in an international relations environment that was based on cooperation between the great powers and world labor. Sidney Hillman thought the trade unions in the World Federation could facilitate positive interactions among the USSR, Great Britain, France, and the United States. "The Federation," he told the Benjamin Cohen, a key adviser to Secretary of State James F. Byrnes in Paris, "could if properly utilized be helpful, particularly at working levels, in bringing about more friendly cooperation."[1] General Dwight Eisenhower, with whom Hillman consulted after the World Federation's founding convention in Paris in November 1945, agreed that the organization's role in Germany might "be helpful to them [U.S. occupation authorities] as they would be able to move freely in all zones."[2] The World Federation, as the embodiment of the popular base of the United Nations, could function successfully in the realm of policy—so long as the good relations of the alliance persisted. Just as the CIO depended in national affairs on continued political popularity, the success of the WFTU depended on favorable expectations from all sides.

The generally positive assessment of the World Federation in U.S. government circles during 1945 and 1946 grew from the organization's apparent fulfillment of the intentions of the Grand Alliance. More than simply a tactic, the alliance of the United States, Great Britain, and the USSR offered the basis for a new system of international relations after the war.[3] Between 1943 and 1946 the three major powers made plans for and actually began the development of institutions that would fulfill the promise of the alliance. All these efforts—creation of the United Nations, joint administration and reconstruction of liberated Europe, and global commitment to the decolonization process—depended on a continued willingness on the part of the great powers to work together in a spirit of compromise. Where practical cooperation was actually attempted, such as in the day-to-day running of the occupation of Germany in the first two years after the war, it proved remarkably successful.[4]

President Roosevelt had favored Anglo-American-Soviet labor cooperation in keeping with his general ideas of international amity. He endorsed the possibility of sending a CIO-AFL delegation to Britain in January 1942.[5] In July 1942 the TUC's Sir Walter Citrine met with Roosevelt to press him to intervene with the AFL to convince it to cooperate with the Soviet and British unions.[6] "Roosevelt had told me personally," Citrine reported, "that he was of the opinion that our proposal for an Anglo-Soviet-American Trade Union Committee was a good one and that the decision of the American Federation of Labor was a wrong decision and he would do his best to get such a committee formed."[7] The U.S. president's endorsement of trade union internationalism reflected his conclusion that the alliance should extend to more than simply military issues, which was an implicit acceptance of the legitimacy of the Soviet Union as a world power and of its inclusion in postwar global politics.

Roosevelt was concerned that the United States did not do enough to integrate labor into foreign relations. In response to a suggestion by Sumner Welles of the State Department, Roosevelt endorsed the creation of an extensive system of labor attachés at U.S. missions around the world. "It is indispensable," he wrote to Secretary of State Edward R. Stettinius in April 1944, "that we know what is going on in labor circles throughout the world."[8] This idea complemented one advanced earlier by White House adviser and labor economist Isador Lubin. Lubin, who had headed the Bureau of Labor Statistics and been an adviser to Hillman at the War Labor Board, suggested early in the war that "the morale of the working populations of the United Nations [the Allies] would be markedly improved," if U.S. missions abroad included "elder labor statesmen." Roosevelt agreed.[9]

Suspicions of the Soviets existed within the U.S. government, of course. The State Department's Soviet specialists had a long-standing anti-Bolshevik position; they had even opposed recognition of the USSR in 1933. The new wartime Soviet policy was, in effect, imposed on these hard-liners.[10] An assessment by the Office of Strategic Services (OSS) of the purpose of labor internationalism in Soviet foreign policy captured the ambiguities and misgivings of some foreign affairs professionals but, critically, reserved judgment on whether a new labor international would be used for dangerous goals. Although, the spies argued, "the Russians know the value of trade unions as mass organizations with the capacity to mobilize public opinion and exert political pressure . . . [they] are primarily interested in bringing to an end their isolation from the world trade union movement." Still, questions remained about Soviet intentions, the analysts believed, and the World Federation "might be of use in the future for the advancement of Communist aims."[11] Moscow-based hard-line analyst George Kennan expressed even fewer doubts: "To responsible Communist circles the international labor movement holds out great possibilities as an instrument of Soviet foreign policy."[12]

The government consensus found the fears of Kennan and the the OSS unjustified. A second OSS memorandum for newly sworn-in President Truman in May 1945 decided that the tricky negotiations to decide voting procedure in the World Federation had been resolved in favor of Western trade union interests. The intelligence analysts' worries were calmed because of Hillman's skillful diplomacy and because the Soviets "apparently really wanted a WFTU and were willing to compromise to get it." Because of the structure of the proposed World Federation, the OSS felt confident the Russians would not dominate the organization.[13] The State Department's Division of International Labor, Social, and Health Affairs also backed the CIO's diplomacy, much to the consternation of the AFL's foreign policy staff.[14]

In carrying out its resolutions to aid the reconstruction of world labor, the World Federation initially received tolerance if not wholehearted support from U.S. government agencies. In 1946 the United States facilitated a tour of the American zone in Germany by a high-level delegation from the WFTU. The decision was made at the highest levels to allow the World Federation to involve itself in union affairs in areas run by the U.S. military. In Germany during 1946 especially, the American administrators did what they could to help the World Federation analyze the needs of German labor.[15] In turn, the World Federation's report on Germany was an evenhanded treatment of developments in the different zones.[16]

A similar delegation to Japan also received top-level clearance in 1947. But this delegation, and later World Federation efforts to establish a liaison bureau for Germany, came too late to get fair treatment from the United States. U.S. occupation authorities resisted the WFTU's influence.[17]

The enormous difficulties of preserving the wartime alliance in 1946 had not immediately translated into cold war. Rather, American policy shifted almost aimlessly as contending elements of the State and War departments attempted to foist their analyses on an administration lacking consistent leadership. Intermittently in 1945 and increasingly in 1946 the World Federation and its U.S. proponents met with strong opposition from the State Department, American occupation authorities in Germany, and the White House. President Truman's refusal to reconsider the denial to the World Federation of a special position on the new United Nations Economic and Social Council foreshadowed the coming conflict. Despite an intensive lobbying effort by Hillman and Philip Murray, the State Department refused to budge on the issue in the days shortly before Roosevelt's death; Truman later reaffirmed the State Department's decision.[18] Stettinius worked so hard to ensure the San Francisco meeting establishing the UN would reject the World Federation's appeal that columnist Drew Pearson commented: "It looked as if he had taken some political lessons from boss Hague of Jersey City or boss Hanegan of St. Louis. He certainly used strong arm tactics to run roughshod over the opposition."[19] In this, the United States may have been following the British, for Foreign Secretary Anthony Eden and his successor, Ernest Bevin, lobbied the United States to rebuff the World Federation. Bevin told Stettinius the British "felt that it was quite improper for the WTUC as a private organization to have any formal relationship to the UN."[20]

After Roosevelt's death tension enveloped the Soviet-American relationship, but at first these problems were confined to the ministerial level. Ground-level cooperation in the administration of Germany did not end until December 1946 when Bizonia (a combination of the British and American zones) was created after the breakdown the previous July of the occupying powers' Council of Foreign Ministers in Paris.[21] For the world of labor the cold war started even later, in the fall of 1948, with the structural failure of the World Federation. Before then, the apparatus of the new world order functioned—usually problematically but occasionally with real success, as in Germany. From the fall of 1946 to the spring of 1947 U.S. foreign policy underwent a tremendous transformation, for the crystallization of anti-Soviet sentiment required the revision of almost all U.S. foreign policy. Reining in labor, however, proved more difficult than eliminating opposition within the government.

Until the end of 1946 the State Department's international labor experts believed that the WFTU was not an instrument of Soviet foreign policy, but the triumph of State Department hard-liners that fall forced a sharp reversal in assessment. In October 1946 Labor Section analyst John Fishburn discounted any Soviet threat in the World Federation in a report titled "Is the WFTU an Instrument of Russian Policy?" The Fishburn paper found that "the Russians have carefully avoided attempting to assert control" of the World Federation. Soviet desire to get along with the CIO and TUC, and their "opposition to an organization which would be regarded as Communist dominated," the report concluded, demonstrated that "there do not appear to be good grounds of any nature for regarding the WFTU as Soviet dominated."[22] Circulated to every office in the U.S. Foreign Service, Fishburn's paper articulated the midforties consensus that underlay the policy of the Grand Alliance: the Soviets were reasonable and responsible allies and could be trusted to work honestly in worldwide organizations.

Alarmed by Fishburn's positive analysis, John Hickerson, head of the State Department's division of European affairs, reacted aggressively. He commissioned a counterstudy by Ray Murphy, also of European affairs, in the late fall of 1946. Murphy's study, "The USSR and the World Federation of Trade Unions," predictably found that the World Federation was indeed a tool of the USSR, though the study provided no hard evidence for its conclusions. Murphy argued that the WFTU, meaning the organization's secretariat under the control of Louis Saillant, a leader of the French Resistance closely aligned with the Communists, had "never criticized the USSR," whereas it "extensively" criticized the United States and the United Kingdom.[23] Saillant's handling of day-to-day operations of the World Federation had undoubtedly been pro-Communist, but the report failed to show that the World Federation operated as a tool of the USSR.

Murphy argued that the CIO and the TUC had been unable to prevent the Soviets from committing the organization to such subversive positions as the idea that labor "concern itself with world political matters," and the resolution "to fight indefatigably in the national and international field, against any discrimination on the basis of race, color, or social position." Conceding that the World Federation's position reflected a consensus of world labor, the report nevertheless maintained that "the Russians frequently support causes or movements which may be most laudable, not, however, for constructive purposes, but in order to embarrass those who refuse to accept Soviet leadership."[24] Any organization in which the USSR could work as an equal to other nations was, by this reasoning, a tool of the Soviets. More than any particular act, the WFTU posed a danger because it encompassed the Soviets. Either the Soviets were under Western control, as in the UN, the report implied, or they would dominate the West.

State Department analysts gave resounding approval to Murphy's report.[25] Because they believed that it was impossible for the Russians to cooperate with non-Communists, cold warriors in the State Department had to conclude that Communists would dominate any organization if given the chance. Opponents of this analysis were afraid to raise their hands; no disagreements appear in the documents.

Murphy's report formed the intellectual basis of the reversal of State Department policy toward the World Federation. The World Federation could no longer be accepted—even with qualification—as perhaps a useful organization to promote liberal-style reconstruction and to help rid the world of imperialism and fascism. Rather, the WFTU was now a key battleground in the cold war. In retrospect the heady days of 1945 had been terribly mistaken. Revealingly, State Department analysts now remembered Sidney Hillman not as a labor statesman but as a dupe and probably a dangerous fellow traveler.[26]

Within the State Department those who had championed the CIO and international cooperation as part of the foreign policy of the alliance immediately became suspect. Otis Mulliken, the liberal chief of the Division of International Labor Affairs, was a prominent victim of the change in policy and of the government's new loyalty apparatus. The international labor division, one of the New Deal–influenced innovations in the State Department, did not survive the forties unscathed. The department removed Mulliken from his position in March 1947; he barely retained a job in the government after being charged with disloyalty at his dismissal hearing.[27] The unfounded charges of disloyalty underscored the ideological distance the government had traveled since 1945. In 1947 maintaining any sort of positive attitude toward USSR or the components of the new world order of the war years was tantamount to treason.[28]

Murphy's report, and Hickerson's agitation to promote it, alerted the State Department to the dangers of the World Federation as an instrument of Soviet foreign policy. Circulating the paper to all embassies, Dean Acheson asked for detailed investigations of the activities of the World Federation and Communist trade unions.[29] The results of the survey no doubt were disturbing.[30] Communists appeared to be everywhere, capitalizing on the popularity and legitimacy of the WFTU. Even the Chinese Association of Labor, which the CIO had championed in the World Federation as a great force for third-world progress, now appeared (erroneously, it turned out) to be a Communist front because it opposed the Kuomintang.[31] The State Department now viewed the World Federation's policies of encouraging multiparty trade unionism as fraught with danger. In a statement that summed up the new line on labor politics, Philip Sullivan, labor attaché in Japan, warned that labor unity "would be a threat to the success of our occupation."[32]

Despite the new evaluation of the World Federation, the State Department did not change course immediately and press the CIO to withdraw from the federation. Ultimately responsible for State's labor policy, Dean Acheson, the aristocratic undersecretary of state, did try to convince the CIO to "take a firmer and more active part in the WFTU as proponents of genuine trade union policies,"[33] that is, to aid non- or anti-Communist unions.[34] In calling for firmness, Acheson followed the prescription within the State Department that the Soviets could be controlled to the benefit of the United States—but only if the United States acted aggressively toward them.

Acheson told Carey and other CIO leaders in May 1947 that the nature of communism made it "impossible for the Soviet leaders to sit around a table, talk things over and reach rational agreements."[35] Acheson tried to drive home the need to abandon the assumptions of the mid-1940s, maintaining that the premise of the World Federation—that the Communists and non-Communists could work together—was not valid. The CIO diplomats disagreed with Acheson, arguing that it was indeed possible to make agreements and that the successes of the WFTU, especially in creating a German labor movement acceptable to both the British and Americans, proved it.[36] Similarly, two months later Elmer Cope, the American assistant general secretary of the WFTU, insisted in a conversation with Louis Wiesner, U.S. labor attaché in Berlin, that the WFTU was really a neutral instrument that could be used for good causes as well as those of the Soviets.[37]

CIO resistance to the suggestions of the cold warriors about how to deal with the Russians persisted into 1948. In December 1947 Samuel Berger, the active labor attaché in London who worked closely with Irving Brown of the AFL, worried that the CIO representatives at the World Federation, Michael Ross and Frank Rosenblum, would be "equally indecisive" in relations with the Communists. Berger volunteered to come back from London to pressure the CIO to join the TUC and "force M[arshall] Plan issue at February meeting WFTU Exbureau to the point of a breach," that is, to use the WFTU's refusal to endorse the Marshall Plan as a reason to break up the organization.[38] More cautious thinkers in the (now reformed) international labor division realized this plan might backfire because of Berger's close connections to the AFL. Instead, Paul Nitze of the European Recovery Plan, Hickerson, and the international labor division decided to get the secretary of state, or at least an undersecretary, to bring pressure to bear when the time was right.[39]

This more restrained policy paid off. The CIO eventually yielded to State Department pressure to support the Marshall Plan and, along with the TUC, helped to organize the European Recovery Program–Trade Union Advisory Conference that bypassed the World Federation.[40] By organizing the conference outside the World Federation, the CIO and the TUC avoided creating an immediate split in the World Federation, although it was never the same. Nevertheless, cold warriors in the field worried about the CIO leadership's unwillingness to adopt their way of thinking. "American observers here," reported one diplomat in Berlin during the trade unions' Marshall Plan conference, "consider Carey naive about [the] Soviets."[41]

Secretary of State George Marshall had given the keynote speech at the CIO convention in October 1947, but he only sought to ensure that labor would endorse the European Recovery Program. The CIO's support was no small thing, but Marshall, significantly, did not seek a labor confrontation with Communists at that time. The non-Communists probably would not have done so had he asked. The increase in government pressure to conform to the new diplomatic line irritated the touchy Carey. The Department of State, he complained to a reporter in January 1948, "keeps getting in our way."[42] Berger found Murray more sympathetic to a Truman doctrine for labor than Carey was: "Murray impressed me as far more practical and prepared to go very much further than Carey. He does not however know the facts and is influenced by Carey." Carey failed to see the necessity of pushing the Communists around when in his experience they had been quite reasonable. In this he carried Murray with him.[43] "We're too damned scared in dealing in this field," CIO Secretary Treasurer Carey complained.[44]

The CIO's commitment to the Rooseveltian world eventually weakened but only after it became clear its old policy could not function without government cooperation. The division between the CIO and the State Department hurt the practice of the CIO in foreign affairs. Operating a Grand Alliance foreign policy while the government mounted an almost feverish anti-Communist campaign became difficult, to say the least. Even the simpler elements of diplomacy, such as arranging binational conferences, proved increasingly troublesome. "It will be exceedingly embarrassing for the CIO and, of course, fatal to the objectives it hoped to accomplish," Michael Ross wrote to Carey, if the government interferes with the CIO's foreign relations.[45]

In the first ten months of 1948 the CIO leadership tried to pursue a two-track policy that was, in essence, contradictory. On one track, it sought to promote the Marshall Plan, both because it was part of the liberal internationalist program (which, not coincidentally, sought to preempt communism) and because the change in U.S. policy threatened to restore the primacy of the AFL in international labor affairs. On the other, the CIO leaders valued the World Federation both because of the leading role they had taken in creating it and because of the importance they attached to getting along with the Soviets. This contradictory policy pressed the CIO's diplomats into weak and often hopeless positions.

In early 1948, for instance, Carey and Michael Ross rushed off to Moscow to try to prevent the Soviets from reacting badly to the proposal for a conference of unions favoring the Marshall Plan, the European Recovery Plan–Trade Union Advisory Committee. But the task of the CIO's envoys was quixotic because the changed strategic alignments of the late 1940s made the assumptions of the WFTU and its approach to European reconstruction dangerously dated. Carey recognized the problem but refused to concede defeat. "It means that the WFTU has no reason to exist," he complained to Vasili Kuznetsov, leader of the All-Union Central Council of Trade Unions, "if it has no plans to implement its declarations for post-war relief and rehabilitation." Although he appreciated Carey's efforts to preserve the World Federation, Kuznetsov could not exactly endorse the Western position and expressed little sympathy with the CIO's predicament.[46]

Carey's diplomacy did succeed in convincing the Soviets not to condemn the Marshall Plan labor conference, but this success merely papered over the gap between the Communist and anti-Communist blocs. "The task of holding the WFTU together," Ross complained in February 1948, "is more difficult than we anticipated."[47] Indeed, the job shortly became impossible. In the fall of 1948 the CIO finally gave in to the power of anticommunism; as the leadership began a purge of Communist-led unions, it joined in the TUC plan to jettison the World Federation. Once out of the World Federation and with the Communist unions on the defensive, little now separated the CIO from the AFL. The cold war in labor had begun.

Neither Isolation nor Imperialism: The CIO versus the Empires

Changing international and national circumstances also rendered the CIO's policy in regard to third-world nations weak and irrelevant in the late forties. Before the cold war, however, the CIO had confidently pursued a noninterventionist role in the developing world. "Our Nation," James Carey told Allen Dulles at the 1945 United Nations Conference in San Francisco, "more than any other, but also along with Soviet Russia and China, can prosper and survive without exploitation of colonial peoples, and . . . it was therefore undesirable for the United States to line up with the colonial powers and in so doing take issue with Russia."[48]

Carey expressed a belief common among CIO leaders and trade unionists in general. The United States, unlike most other powerful nations, could and should oppose the colonial system as unethical and unnecessary. But the United States nevertheless had a special responsibility to help and guide the subject people of the world to freedom and participation in the world economy. Although the CIO leaders had distinct ideas about what sort of system they should lead people to, they felt quite uneasy about heavy-handed interventionism. The policy they settled on, in Philip Murray's words, "neither isolation nor imperialism," satisfied their desires for a moral foreign policy.[49] However, the problem they came to face, in addition to being blind to their own interventionism, was that their nation's leaders did not share their unwillingness to intervene around the world. Complicating its problems, the CIO faced competition from an AFL quite willing to aid imperialism as a manipulator of third-world labor.[50] In the end, conflicts within the third world, heightened by the worldwide cold war, made the CIO's benign program ineffectual. The CIO's idealistic policies disintegrated as the cooperative world order on which they were premised faded into memory.

Though the CIO rejected imperialism, the leaders' positions on the world role of the United States were ambiguous. Carey, for instance, ignored the brutal record of the Philippine-American War and claimed that U.S. colonial rule in the Philippines had been entirely benevolent: "Our American policy in the Philippine Islands for the last fifty years has been to [give] the Filipino people leadership and not to act as slave drivers."[51] Other nations may have been a bit alarmed by Carey's proposition that the U.S. relationship with the Philippines be extended to the rest of the world: "We believe the United States with its glorious tradition of democratic rule by the people must stand as a pattern to other nations, we can extend the benefits of democracy only by demonstration of its workability."[52] The United States should lead the world—but not in an imperious manner. In fact, colonial affairs and the development of a nonimperial world system were particular American concerns.[53]

Following this line of thought, the CIO took the lead in the development of the World Federation's colonial department, over the objections of Sir Walter Citrine, who opposed the World Federation's meddling in such affairs.[54] The CIO fought with the French, Dutch, Belgians, and British within the World Federation over colonial policy.[55] Michael Ross explained to the State Department that the CIO took the lead on colonial issues because "the Russians might want to use the WFTU as an instrument of its foreign policy through influence exerted upon dependent area labor organizations."[56] The CIO's policy was in fact popular among many third-world unionists, especially those from Latin America and India, where the CIO was perceived as an ally against British imperialism and Yankee arrogance.[57]

Here again the CIO was in line with the Rooseveltian system. The most difficult area of friction about postwar issues before President Roosevelt's death in April 1945, the problem of what to do with the British and French empires after the war, set the United States and the USSR against Britain. Within the U.S. government the dominant policy makers on the Joint Chiefs of Staff and in the White House, complained George Kennan, had "disgraceful anti-British and pro-Soviet prejudices."[58]

Once created, the Colonial Department of the World Federation promoted trade unionism in colonial territories, to the chagrin of the imperial countries' unions, which defended their empires. Even the French Communists were unwilling to sacrifice their domination of African labor. French left-winger Jean Laurain battled the CIO's Adolph Germer, head of the Colonial Department in 1946, over representation of African labor. Laurain insisted that the French Confédération Générale du Travail should represent the interests of the unions in the French possessions at the WFTU's Dakar conference. Laurain's demands jeopardized the World Federation's plans for creating an African division.[59] Germer resisted and the conference took place in the midst of great tension. African politics proved quite difficult for any side to stage-manage. In the end Germer concluded that the World Federation "was an open door for some of these Communists to reach into the whole colonial world and poison the minds of its population." He worried that the third world would remained trapped between imperialism and communism.[60]

The thinking behind the CIO's Latin policy expressed both the organization's expansiveness and its commitment to growth as the solution to the world's economic problems. In addition to opposing tariffs, "the CIO pledges itself on behalf of its own members and in the interests of those who toil for a living in the other Americas," the CIO's Committee on Latin American Affairs proclaimed, "to vigilantly safeguard the interest of the masses of the people in all inter-American accords and arrangements of an economic nature."[61] The organization also put itself on record as favoring free immigration and the protection of Mexican workers who labored in the United States. However, the official stance on immigration and protection of *braceros* did not translate into effective action.[62]

Although the CIO failed to accomplish much in its hemispheric policy, it became quite popular among Latin trade unionists, probably because of its refusal to meddle in their affairs. As a matter of policy the organization worked solely through established labor organizations such as the Confederación de Trabajadores de América Latina (CTAL). CTAL, led by the energetic pro-Communist Vincente Lombardo Toledano, united unions from sixteen countries and provided the CIO with an effective and legitimate avenue for relations with its southern counterparts. Latinos could easily contrast this low-key policy to the actions of the AFL, which sought to supplant leftist, nationalistic organizations. The members of the Latin American Affairs Committee, notably Jacob Potofsky of the Amalgamated Clothing Workers and Jack Knight of the Oil Workers, highly valued their relations with CTAL. They refused to cooperate with the AFL, for instance, on the Inter-American Labor Union Project, which arranged exchanges of unionists, because CTAL distrusted it.[63] "There is no doubt in our minds," Knight and Joseph Selly, the pro-Communist president of the American Communications Association, wrote after attending the 1945 convention of the Latin confederation, "that the CTAL is *the* labor movement in Latin America" (emphasis in the original).[64] The commitment of the CIO's Latin specialists to CTAL became difficult when the Latin organization was torn with internal conflicts in the late forties. Even so, the North Americans failed to develop a hemispheric policy beyond their relationship with CTAL and its constituents.

CTAL organizers, especially Lombardo Toledano, returned the CIO's trust by working actively to convince their constituents to support the war. This was not an easy task, as Knight and Selly noted: "The leadership of CTAL has had a most difficult political problem in attempting to bring to the peoples of Latin America a realization of their stake in the war against Fascism. The years of domination by British and American capital, the bitter memory of those economic and political policies which were characterized as 'Yankee Imperialism,' have left their mark."[65] Lombardo Toledano tried in 1943 to organize a pan-American labor conference to support the war effort but could not follow through, most likely because of a lack of resources.[66] Of course, pro-Soviet thinking in the Latin confederation probably played an equal if not more important role in mobilizing for the war. More important than the specific tasks Lombardo Toledano and his fellows could perform was that their legitimacy as an independent representative organization satisfied the CIO's wish to avoid what Potofsky called "a big stick impression."[67]

CIO wariness of the big stick methods and confidence in CTAL formed the two pillars of the noninterventionist program in Latin America. To some extent this policy may be attributed to lack of interest and resources for intervention. The CIO budgeted no money for its Latin American Affairs Committee in 1944.[68] But the CIO's isolationism, unlike the conservative variant popular in the United States during the 1930s, did not encompass a willingness to dominate this hemisphere. The Latin American Affairs Committee, for instance, decided to refer a request by Puerto Rican sugar workers for affiliation to the CIO to CTAL when it learned that the governor of Puerto Rico and the U.S. Department of the Interior were behind the move because "they regarded the CIO as a stabilizing force."[69] The members of the Latin American Affairs Committee did not want to take on the role of big brother in hemispheric labor.

Confident in their relationship with CTAL, the committee members lapsed into inaction. Their Spanish and English newsletter, the *Boletín,* had long breaks in publication. It took the committee nearly a year and a half to replace its executive secretary, leaving the CIO without anyone specifically responsible for relations with unions in the Americas between mid-1946 and the beginning of 1948. Until 1948, explained Ernst Schwarz, the new CIO secretary for Latin Affairs who tried valiantly to reactivate the committee, "the CIO's relationship with

Labor groups in Latin America had mostly been handled by the CTAL, and we were even anxious not to interfere directly."[70]

What led the CIO to try to reactivate its Latin labor policy was a split in CTAL that threatened the career of Lombardo Toledano and rendered the CIO's hemispheric strategy ineffectual. Although his battle with his comrades in the Confederación de Trabajadores de México centered on the proper relationship of the unions to the state in a period of economic crisis, it also involved disputes about the role of Communists in Mexican politics and can be considered similar to the battles about Communist power that split French and Italian labor at the same time.[71] In an effort to mediate the Mexican dispute, the Oil and Chemical Workers' Jack Knight traveled to Mexico in March 1948 to meet with Lombardo Toledano; his main opponent, Fernando Amilpa; and Saillant, general secretary of the World Federation. An active anti-Communist himself, Knight nonetheless believed the leftist position to be the legitimate one.[72] He found that his "conclusions about the split were almost identical" to those of Saillant.[73] Just six months before the purges of the Communist-led unions from the CIO, the CIO opposed the division of the Mexican labor movement along Communist–anti-Communist lines.

The conflict within Latin America's largest and most powerful trade union federation, the Confederación de Trabajadores de México, debilitated CTAL, put the World Federation in the difficult position of having a vice president unwillingly removed by his organization and rendered the CIO's Latin modus operandi unworkable. CIO policy toward the Southern Hemisphere had rested on relations with a nationalistic leader and an organization close to the Communist Party. With the crisis in Mexico and the overpowering pressure of the cold war, noninterventionism no longer benefited the CIO. CTAL struggled on for almost fifteen years but finally succumbed in the 1960s, with most of its constituents destroyed or underground. The AFL, on the other hand, profited greatly from the Mexican crisis and the legitimacy of anticommunism, founding an anti-Communist hemispheric federation that later became the regional arm of the International Confederation of Free Trade Unions.[74] For now, Ernst Schwarz, the CIO Latin affairs secretary, told Carey in 1949, the CIO "was on its own with Latin American Labor."[75] In Mexico, as almost everywhere in the world, the coalition unionism of the immediate postwar years on which the CIO had based its international policies turned out to be a failure.

Few tears were probably shed in the U.S. government over the failure of the CIO's Latin policy. As a part of the shift to a more aggressive foreign policy during the cold war, the State Department began to abandon the good neighbor policy in 1946.[76] Presaging the purge of the international labor section the next year, the department's Office of Inter-American Affairs, run by Assistant Secretary of State Spruille Braden, eliminated the office's labor relations division. The former head of the labor division, John Herling, had been a strong New Dealer and proponent of the idea "that participation by organized labor is indispensable to a genuine application of the Good Neighbor policy."[77] Braden communicated the shift in the department's methods to the AFL's Latin agent, Serafino Romualdi, reassuring Romualdi that he now had the government's endorsement for an interventionist anti-Communist program because "the Department had undergone a radical change and that in the future it will be guided by different policies."[78]

For the CIO the rebirth of interventionist thinking in the U.S. government eliminated one of the main props of its hemispheric program. Following a noninterventionist policy could not succeed, the CIO found, in a nation committed to something quite different. A world torn by intense ideological conflict was an inhospitable place for labor internationalism.

Erasing the Mystical Vision

The leaders of the Congress of Industrial Organizations eagerly joined in the creation of a new international of labor in 1943 as part of the construction of a bureaucratized world order devoted to economic improvements for all. They pursued close relations with the U.S. government and the proposed world institutions and expressed the belief that a New Deal–like corporatism would replace the class- and nation-based antagonisms of the prewar years. Active in helping European labor to rebuild itself after the incomprehensible horror of the war and serious in its commitment to being a good neighbor, the CIO expressed the generous side of American liberalism. Of course, the union leadership also desired the transformation of international politics because it would protect the economic well-being of American workers and give the CIO a major advantage over the AFL. The keystone of the CIO's foreign policy was a willingness to work and compromise with Communist unions, especially those of the USSR.

Unlike British workers, American union members were too divided on the issue of foreign communism to provide a strong popular base for any single international strategy, anti-Communist or pro-Soviet. As a result, American leaders had no one to rely on when the U.S. government began to demand loyalty to a new dogma, an intense commitment to fight communism everywhere in the world.

The increasing hatred and paranoia that typified international relations and domestic politics in the late forties eventually overwhelmed the Rooseveltian liberalism of labor's leaders. This destroyed the CIO's ambitions along with the broader dream of a new world order. The entire foreign policy edifice that the CIO had so enthusiastically constructed between 1944 and 1946—close relations with European, Soviet, and Latin trade unions; a major role in the reconstruction of world labor; and, of course, a central post in the new bureaucracy of peace—crumbled slowly but inevitably under the pressure of the growing antagonism of Communists and anti-Communists everywhere in the world.

With a feeling of undoubted urgency bordering on desperation, the CIO purged itself of vestiges of the Grand Alliance, both in its thinking and in its actual makeup, beginning in 1948. As the rift between the blocs deepened, the CIO was torn between its commitment to a fast-fading vision of a peaceful unified world and its hopes for integration into the domestic political economy. Deeply worried by the surge of antilabor sentiment after 1946 and loyal to a beleaguered Democratic Party coalition, liberals in the CIO furiously eliminated Communists from their ranks in the hope that this would achieve the integration in the economy or at least stave off a complete return to labor's pre–New Deal isolation. At the same time the CIO joined with other non-Communist unions in jettisoning the World Federation and creating a new anti-Communist international. The purges of the CIO and the breakup of the WFTU can best be understood as both the end of an era of cooperation—however uneasy—on the left and the beginning of a new period of aggressive cold war liberalism. To prepare for this brave new world, the leaders of the CIO had to demonstrate that they were no longer tainted by the thinking or the relationships of the past. The elimination of the Communist Party and the destruction of the World Federation demonstrated that the CIO leadership had overcome its past. The unionists had seen the errors of their ways and were now ready to fight, in the words of the International Confederation of Free Trade Unions, "to achieve a world free from the tyranny of Communist, Fascist, Falangist, and other forms of totalitarianism as well as from the domination and exploitation of concentrated economic power in the hands of cartels and monopolies."[79]

Now it was Walter Reuther's moment. In 1949, after the CIO and other anti-Communist unions left the World Federation of Trade Unions to found the International Confederation of Free Trade Unions, Reuther synthesized the new views of the CIO. The problem for Reuther and the CIO was that the AFL, which had waged a long-term campaign against the World Federation and developed its own foreign policy apparatus under Jay Lovestone, had effectively defined the role of anti-Communist trade unions in world affairs. The AFL maintained that the main political purpose of free trade unions, as the organization defined them, was to defeat communism. William Green, president of the AFL, thundered at the founding conference of the ICFTU in London: "The free trade unions of the world now face a world-wide totalitarian conspiracy. This conspiracy aims to foist on the workers of all free countries a system of economic exploitation and political oppression which would set labour back hundreds of years."[80] To meet such a challenge required a mass mobilization and effectively obsessive focus. For the AFL all other problems paled in comparison to the threat of communism.

Reuther, in turn, refused to "believe that our choice in the world today is between . . . Stalin and Standard Oil." (Supposedly, at this point one CIO leader whispered: "If it comes down to it I'll take Standard Oil.") The CIO leaders did not accept the AFL's single-minded formula. Rather, Reuther and his colleagues sought a different program: "The real challenge we face in the world is how to organise life so that we can achieve economic security and material well-being without sacrificing political and spiritual freedom." Unions should move "down the broad democratic middle where people may fight to have both bread and freedom." Echoing Reuther, Mike Quill, a former Communist and head of the Transport Workers' Union, complained that "fighting the Communists is not enough." He continued: "Had our State Department and the State departments of other countries been stronger in creating real democracy . . . we would not have to fear Communism."[81]

The CIO's leaders tried to preserve the reforming impulse of the New Deal in domestic and foreign affairs. At the same time they sought to combat domestic Communist factional opponents and preclude dangerous government intervention in their movement. The ultimate goal was to protect the union movement and some of the progressive drive that had exemplified American politics of the previous fifteen years. Yet the AFL's version of single-minded anti-Communist liberalism ultimately triumphed. The union centers reunited in 1955, three years after the deaths of Murray and the AFL's William Green, whose personal antagonism had kept the two organizations apart years after the ideological problem of Communists in the CIO had been solved. Still, the social-democratic inclinations of Reuther and the other CIO leaders continued to create friction with the AFL abroad in the 1950s and 1960s. Indeed, Reuther remained far more popular with the Socialist leadership of international labor than did Green's successor, George Meany.[82]

In foreign relations the AFL, untainted by any hint of the belief in a third force that the CIO leaders and their European Socialist friends endorsed, dominated international labor relations. Its power grew from its independent foreign policy apparatus, the Free Trade Union Committees, later the Institutes for Free Labor Development, and its close relationship to the State Department and even the Central Intelligence Agency. At the same time, constant conflict between the AFL,

CIO, and the Europeans in the International Confederation doomed that organization to ineffectuality throughout the 1950s.[83]

Despite the CIO's defensive maneuvering, the end of the era of international cooperation turned out to be disastrous for the union movement in the United States. Labor never again achieved the power or the legitimacy of the mid-1940s. Whatever the high ideals of the cold war liberals, neither their ideology nor political circumstances in general allowed a powerful role for unions in running national society or world politics. The "positively mystical vision" of the CIO dissolved in a polarized world.

Conclusion: Cynicism and Universalism—The World the Workers Lost

The cold war resulted in a great shrinking of human expectations. It marked a clear, though not final, end to hopes for universal world transformation based on political and social democracy, ideas that had been raised at the dawn of the modern era. The Grand Alliance period had rekindled a latent utopianism hidden by decades of depression and war. The renewed battles of world politics soon dampened this enthusiasm and made those who dreamed of a better world appear naive and deluded. In evaluating this period after the fact, observers have tended to dismiss the potential for establishing a new form of international relations. In this they reflect the disappointments of the era. Yet to the participants—unionists, politicians, diplomats, and average people—the mid-1940s had held great promise, a promise that, despite later arguments, was not entirely an illusion. The processes of popular thought and union politics outlined here confirm the enormous possibilities of that time.

In both the United States and Great Britain the cold war lacked immediate appeal among the working class and union leaders. Yet, as George Orwell had insightfully observed in 1941: "Patriotism is usually stronger than class hatred, and always stronger than any kind of internationalism."[1] Support for the international labor movement could not withstand the domestic political pressures of the cold war. In the United States worker apathy and a patriotic ideology undercut the left-leaning union leadership's initial efforts on behalf of world labor after the war. In Great Britain the anti-Communist leadership counteracted the leftist impulses of the rank-and-file. The weakness of labor internationalism in both cases resulted from the nature of working-class thinking, which was in turn based in essential aspects of people's experiences. The realities of the tremendous cultural diversity of the United States in a context of growing world power were essential influences on working-class thought there. Class unity in Britain stood in contrast with a fear that British greatness was slipping and a deep trust of the leadership. The net result for both the United States and the United Kingdom was a fundamental weakness in working-class support for internationalism.

Yet this weakness did not mean that the demise of the unified labor movement was inevitable. A common explanation advanced at the time was that the World Federation failed, as M. C. Bolle, a leader of the anti-Communist International Trade Secretariats, put it, because there was "a conflict within the WFTU about the very aims and methods of trade unionism."[2] More recently, Anthony Carew has agreed that this was "a headlong clash between . . . rival conceptions of trade unionism."[3] In general, these scholars find that the cold war had roots on every level of international relations because of the intrinsically opposed nature of East and West. In fact, the underlying weakness of the WFTU, and of political support for it in the United States and Britain, stemmed from sources other than those assumed by observers working within a cold war paradigm that posits inevitable and fundamental conflict between communism and liberalism or social democracy. The cold war–based analysis is not appropriate for the period from 1941 to 1947. The institutional split of 1949 had more to do with the union leaders' loyalties to the demands of their nations' foreign policies than it had with any disagreement about fundamental union practices. The unions in both East and West failed to act independently of state or party. The cold war in labor did not start on the bottom. It was imposed from the top.

Before its disintegration the World Federation began to chart a new course in world affairs, one that placed labor at the heart of the international system. The forties mark a clear end to a centuries-long era of European world dominance. The European subcontinent's preeminence had been shaken and fatally undercut by World War I and the Great Depression, but Europe remained at the center of the world system. The German effort to reorder the geography and structure of European power plunged the Continent into war, albeit without establishing a new world system of continental hegemony. Instead, the United States and the USSR came to dominate the Continent and indeed the world.[4] The bipolar system of the cold war years ended, perhaps permanently, the Eurocentric world system. The rise of Japan, the Chinese revolution, and Indian independence promised a new, more complex world system, with the third world at long last acting more as subject than object of history.[5] The reordering of the mid-1940s was more than an historical aberration. Rather, it marked a moment at which the great underlying economic and political changes of the previous forty years, combined with the disorder created by the war, rendered the remains of prewar international institutions and patterns of relationships obsolete. The effort to create a new world order was an attempt to come to grips with this new era. The struggle of the unions to build a labor-centered corporatist system occurred when the definition of the future world was, to a great degree, up for grabs. More than an interesting sidelight to the Grand Alliance and the cold war, the unions' activities were intrinsic to the vast changes underway in the forties, for the new world order meant more than a shift in centers of power.

At this moment of great global contingency the union movements of the world attempted to unite once again in order to alter the elite basis of international politics. Inheritor of a long history of democratic internationalism, world labor was also no newcomer to the project of institutionalization. Its most recent efforts at formal unity, the International Federation of Trade Unions, however, had proved its inability to overcome workers' nationalism during World War I. After the war the enormous successes of revolutionary communism split the left once again. The fight against fascism, which united labor in the Allied countries, also endowed it with an unprecedented legitimacy. But the unions did not simply translate their new power into a new world organization. As this book has shown, the Allied unions were limited by political circumstance, membership support, and ideology, but they forged a briefly effective organization. By embracing both the basic assumptions of trade unionism—the defense of workers' day-to-day interests—and the totalizing drive of social democracy, the creation of the World Federation of Trade Unions, despite its limitations, marked a high point of workers' century-old struggle for power and equity. The tradition of the workers' movement had been to seek to make the working class the greatest force in domestic and international affairs. The WFTU was, in effect, a corporatized version of a totalizing workers' movement, a social movement that sought to make workers the center of the historical process. The incorporation of unions into a bureaucratized world order, however, did not successfully contain the threat of social or international conflict.

The unions' creation of and disillusionment with the World Federation paralleled their nations' efforts to form the United Nations. Both labor and government experienced similar processes during the Alliance and the cold war. In the first half of this period, roughly 1942 to 1946, they attempted to carry through a modified version of what could be called their respective utopian traditions. The unions sought to create a worker-based international order, whereas the governing groups sought the rule of international law and global state-based institutions. Both envisioned an equitable world system. The intellectual roots of these two undertakings were a similar belief in the possibility that the world could indeed be transformed, that conflict could be contained. The collapse of these efforts in the second half of this period, 1946 to 1949, effectively ended widespread belief in the possibility of radically altering world politics. Instead, both unions and governments accepted severely limited goals and ideologies.

It was impossible to predict from the outset the unfortunate outcome of the unions' project or the new world order it sought to mold. Indeed, unionists and government ministers alike searched for models of how to transform the political and social circumstances of the mid-1940s into a better world. Corporatism provided one of the strongest patterns to follow. In this area Soviet influence was crucial. Both its military and economic significance and the supposedly corporatist model that the USSR offered the rest of the world in the forties made it a central focus of international affairs. A state that embraced the necessity of power and ruthlessness, while proclaiming the importance of workers' concerns and social democracy, appeared to many unionists to hold the key to the future. During the 1940s even anti-Communist union leaders such as Walter Citrine and Sidney Hillman found positive values in the Soviet system. Although the majority of American and British union officials were anti-Communist and opposed domestic Communist parties, they were not anti-Soviet. It is relatively easy to see the role of the capitalist powers in the system of the mid-1940s. Understanding the Soviet role, however, requires consideration of the relationship of a "workers's state" to a workers' order.

Soviet Foreign Policy and Trade Unionism

"The trade unions," Lenin declared shortly after the October Revolution, "are becoming the chief builders of the new society, for only the millions can build this society."[6] Although Communist thought places the working class at the center of the process of social change in the capitalist era, the role of trade unions has been problematic for Socialists and Communists since the early days of the movement. German Social Democrats, for instance, at first avoided any affiliation with trade unions because of their reformist nature. The solution worked out by most pre–World War I Social Democrats, including the Bolsheviks and Mensheviks, was that the parties would look after the future while the unions would look after improving things in the present. For the victorious Bolsheviks after 1917, however, the problem of unionism took on a new light. Although the state, claiming to represent the working class, now controlled the economy, labor conflict did not disappear.[7]

However, by 1928 Russian trade unions, in the words of U.S. trade unionist Robert Dunn, who visited Russia, "became themselves virtually a part of the machinery of government."[8] But labor opposition to simply serving the state was intense. Strikes, slowdowns, work actions, and an indirect resistance to state authority continued throughout the Soviet period. According to a compromise reached at the Tenth Party Congress in 1921, unions would still attempt to protect workers' rights; they were not to be simply transmission belts of communism. During the New Economic Policy of 1921–1928, unions followed this dual function more or less effectively. The militarization of the Soviet economy brought about by the first five-year plan, however, vastly extended state and union control over the labor force in order to increase the rate of production.[9] By the 1940s the Soviet trade unions had been for many years almost entirely subservient to the party and government. Yet rank-and-file disenchantment with the Soviet system led to serious labor conflict early in the war as workers resisted mobilization and the relocation of plants.[10] The desire of the Soviets for labor solidarity with the British and Americans was undoubtedly a response to this disgruntlement.

Vasili Kuznetsov, who took control of the All-Union Central Council of Soviet Trade Unions in 1944, launched a campaign to restore some power to the unions to protect workers but met with only marginal success.[11] Nevertheless, to outsiders inclined to look at the situation positively, the unions appeared to function effectively in a corporatized political economy. They presented one obvious model for the role of labor in the new world order.[12]

The Soviet government recognized the power over people's imaginations that its apparent acceptance of workers' incorporation bestowed. George Kennan, writing from Moscow in 1945, reported that "to responsible Communist circles the international labor movement holds out great possibilities as an instrument of Soviet foreign policy." Kennan observed that the Soviets still wanted front groups, but "it seems now to have been decided in Moscow that political parties especially those bearing the name 'Communist' are not always the most effective medium for such assertion of influence and emphasis has shifted . . . above all to organized labor."[13]

Despite Kennan's critical observation, the Soviet rulers could not easily manipulate the problems of class conflict, of workers and their organizations. Workers' thoughts were not so easily controlled. Even in the realm of Marxist theory the role of actual workers proved problematic. The central tenet of Marxism, that the working class would become the whole of society, militated against the idea of union subservience to the state. Workers' participation, as Communist philosopher Georg Lukács posited after the collapse in 1919 of the Béla Kun revolutionary government in Hungary, was essential to the overall project of Socialist transformation. In *History and Class Consciousness* Lukács revived Marx's early prizing of workers' action in a Hegelian dialectic of historical evolution and argued that the working class was the only historical phenomenon that could become the subject-object of history.[14] That is, in the process of becoming the whole of society by eliminating the capitalists, the workers would become at once the sole creators of history and the only creatures of it. Lukács, in a sad triumph for Communist conformity, later rejected his early philosophy as significantly flawed.[15] His revolutionary Marxist Hegelianism departed from Communist orthodoxy in a number of areas, but the idea of this self-totalizing working class raised more than philosophical issues. Among other problems, the work privileged an insurgent, revolutionary, and semi-anarchist working class. Lukács's rejection of his earlier work, in my reading, reflected the Communist Party's own fears of the working class.[16] Working-class power was something to be contained, controlled, and directed, not prized as promising the end of history.

Thus in philosophy and in trade union practice the Communists sought the use of trade union power without its dangers. The containment of working-class organization by its promoters had serious consequences both for the institutions of workers' power and for the ability of the left to conceive of world order. Soviet elites, like those in the West, had much to lose in a worker-centered order.

The United States, Britain, and the Politics of the New System

In the Western Hemisphere World War II was not simply a traditional European battle for perceived national interest pursued by the elites of the nation-states. From the vantage point of diplomatic archives and ministerial memoirs, such a perception may be inevitable, yet a broader view reveals the war's nontraditional character. The war demanded total commitment by the societies involved. Although this commitment was manipulated and, in effect, controlled by political, economic, and military elites, it nonetheless threatened to give rise to the kind of left-wing upsurge that occurred after World War I. From 1943 on, the politics of war, to use Gabriel Kolko's phrase, were a matter of whether the left or the right would triumph in Europe and whether the United States or the colonial powers would dominate postwar Asia. But the crucial difference from World War I was that this time the USSR was an ally in the equations of power. The World Federation thus expressed the realities of power and the potentials for worldwide change by promoting yet containing workers' power. The governments' limited support for the new union international was an incorporative response to the challenge of mass power in total war.

U.S. and British diplomats condemned the USSR for its unorthodox foreign policy but soon endorsed similar policies, promoting mass manipulation, propaganda, and subversion as critical instruments of the foreign policy of the cold war.[17] In the total war and in the cold war riven by ideology, national ambition, and fear, assumptions about how the world works, which were based on nineteenth-century concepts of national leadership, no longer held. Rather, international affairs in the 1940s were more than the wartime conferences of the great leaders, the sum total of disparate decisions or debates within foreign offices. Without explicit acknowledgment, U.S. and British foreign policy adapted to the realities of a mass-based international order.

Seen in this perspective, a new history of the Alliance and the growth of antagonism between East and West can be written. In Britain the TUC leadership was satisfied with the collapse of the original World Federation. In Peter Weiler's words the corporative relationship with the foreign and colonial policy apparatus of the British Labour government "was a source of pride to most TUC leaders."[18] The top ranks of the TUC saw their role in world affairs as a strong counterweight to the tendency toward radicalism of workers in Britain, the colonies, and, indeed, around the world. The TUC felt comfortable acting in concert with Labour, once the personal conflicts between Bevin and Citrine were overcome. Unity between the unions, the government, and the Labour Party provided the basis of the political compromise of the welfare state. But the British labor movement presided over a much-diminished great power.

Bevin's strategy of cooperating with the United States in containing communism and in bequeathing world dominance to the former colony secured Britain's place in the emerging American bloc, though at a price. As Bevin wrote to Prime Minister Clement Attlee: "For us as Britishers in between the two of them, our task is very difficult."[19] This world position paralleled the role the unions accepted in the domestic corporatist order. Unlike the nation, however, the unions bridled at their status, constantly seeking to revise to their benefit the terms, though not the basic assumptions, of the social bargain. National unity was precarious. Bevin blamed the left and, in a reflection of his English nationalism, "chiefly the Welsh," for opposition to Labour's demands for national sacrifice in order to assure its new relationship with the United States.[20] In contrast to the situation in the United States, however, the British unions were not involved in a fundamental conflict over status with the state and the political right. Despite occasional resistance, Labourism as a whole retained support, and the foreign policy strategy of the Labour government did not evoke mass opposition.

Americans in the forties, unlike the British, embarked on a new era of world power. The Roosevelt and Truman administrations were acutely conscious of the need for national consensus in the pursuit of international goals. Crucial to American success, policy makers believed, was the unity of the nation in a unified world. But if the world were not to be united, the United States would have to be even more so. As he was about to embark for the Paris Peace Conference of

1946, Secretary of State James F. Byrnes, flanked by Tom Connally, the Texas Democrat who was chairman of the Senate Foreign Relations Committee,and ranking Republican senator Arthur Vandenberg of Michigan, told an airport crowd that "there is no division between the great political parties as to the making of the peace." U.S. foreign policy makers were no longer political partisans; rather, "we are working together as Americans." Partisanship and politics had been overcome in the pursuit of world power, Byrnes emphasized: "We are deeply conscious that if we as a nation are to exert our influence on the affairs of the world, we must be united."[21] Unity at home was a necessary precondition to power abroad. Byrnes, a former senator and Supreme Court justice, had, as director of the Office of War Mobilization, presided over the resuscitation of the participation of big business in domestic affairs.[22] In a way, he was Sidney Hillman's nemesis, both in domestic and foreign arenas, and had been in large part responsible for Henry Wallace's dismissal from the Truman cabinet.[23] Unity in a divided world had to exclude the left. Nevertheless, Byrnes and other cold warriors articulated U.S. policy in universalist terms, though it would be a universe with the United States at the center.

The attempt to create an alternative form of universalism was the great ideological task of the contending sides in the cold war. Cold war liberalism was an attempt to salvage the remains of social democracy from its pernicious association with Soviet communism. But to maintain its power cold war liberalism compromised too much to become truly universal, either in domestic politics or in world affairs. Its most effective proponents, such as George Kennan, believed the continuation of social-democratic or, at least, reformist polices at home would be simply another weapon in the cold war. In his famous "Long Telegram" from Moscow arguing for a coherent anti-Soviet policy for the United States, Kennan emphasized the importance of domestic unity and prosperity: "Much depends on the health and vigor of our own society. World communism is like [a] malignant parasite which feeds only on diseased tissue. This is the point at which domestic and foreign policies meet. Every courageous and incisive measure to solve internal problems of our own society, to improve self-confidence, discipline, morale, and community spirit of our own people, is a diplomatic victory over Moscow worth a thousand diplomatic notes and joint communiques."[24]

The revival of anticommunism as the dominant ideology of U.S. politics and foreign policy required the elimination of what had been, in the 1930s and 1940s, two major streams of the political and foreign affairs of the United States. The first was the growth of labor power, as expressed in New Deal policies and in Roosevelt's reliance on labor activists in his election campaigns. The second was, of course, residual domestic sympathy for the main competitor of the United

States in world affairs.[25] Thus the Taft-Hartley Act, the opening gun in the war on union power, also heralded the Truman Doctrine as the center, and the liberals abandoned two key elements of the Roosevelt years.

The USSR predicated its foreign policy during the mid-1940s on both the cooperation of the major powers and on obtaining the sympathy of the working classes of the world. The leaders of the United States and Britain realized this, so they joined a battle of labor on two fronts. Overseas, the arena centered on Europe in the immediate postwar years, whereas at home the battleground was union politics and ideology. The British fought the first years of the cold war with a social-democratic political compromise, in which union power had to be preserved. In the United States the conflict similarly began with a liberal program but quickly evolved into a right-wing effort to discipline labor.[26] The new direction of worldwide social and international relations coincided with the final abandonment of domestic social transformation as a vision of U.S. and British union leaders. Although the TUC maintained its leftist urges, the cold war forced socialism into a purely national mold. In the United States the CIO participated actively in the creation of cold war liberalism. At the same time union leaders watched foreign affairs anxiously and ineffectively as the resurgent right went about "completely undermining the positive gains we've made," as the CIO's European representative, Jay Krane, put it.[27]

Many unionists later recalled that the WFTU had, from the start, been based on "misunderstanding and errors of judgment."[28] The revision of memory caused by the pressures of the cold war and red scare led many participants to deny they had ever truly believed in the principles of internationalism in the mid-1940s. Some, notably Citrine, may have never accepted the principles at heart, but many more found the World Federation and the ideas it stood for truly compelling. Yet they also later found the principles of the cold war convincing. Did the union leaders and members truly accept ideas that seemed, to their later selves, profoundly naive? Did they believe what they said? If they were lying, when were they lying? As problematic: What does it mean to say they lied when they acted like they believed something that they knew to be impossible (for instance the basic compatibility of the West and the USSR)?

These intellectual revisions among unionists had many parallels elsewhere, as the Americans and, to a lesser degree, the British came to deny their earlier belief in the possibilities of the East-West alliance or the Rooseveltian order. This process leaves historians with a difficult problem. Whom should they believe? The younger people who championed the new world order or their later selves, chastened by the cold war into a cynical realism? This problem has no easy solution, especially if it is likely (as it is) that unionists espoused, but did not believe, both positions. Indeed, we have much evidence that the same people both believed and disbelieved the contradictory stances. Such a contradiction does not simply reflect a state of confusion (on my or my subjects' parts). Rather, it reveals the complex process in which the great enthusiasms generated by the working-classes' interests conflicted with the power of their states and the structure of international relations, forcing working-class consciousness to yield to the wary cynicism of the contemporary era. Cultural theorist Slavoj Zizek has a useful formula for explaining the belief in ideology by people who should and do know better: "They know that in their activity they are following an illusion, but still they are doing it."[29] Zizek's formulation accounts for both the mixed feelings expressed about the original World Federation and the difficult development of a labor-based set of ideas during the cold war. The cynicism and wariness expressed or implicit in so much of the idealism of the mid-1940s was even more deeply characteristic of the ideology of the cold war. Few could truly believe in a utopian future in 1945, but many did nonetheless. With the cold war the sense of illusion (perhaps self-delusion) shifted, now attached to the virtue of the West in contrast to the Communists, but it did not disappear. The attempt was to adjust utopian dreams to the reality of power relations, although the transformation of those power relations proved too much of a challenge, both intellectually and practically.

The End of Internationalism?

From the revolutionary democracies of the late eighteenth century to the revolutionary Socialists of the early twentieth, the left around the world had sought to reconstitute the given order along more democratic lines. A main source of this radical democratic tradition was a universalistic impulse by which people generalized their own experiences.[30] By the 1940s such universalistically motivated internationalism had failed repeatedly, but a tremendous historical opportunity encouraged trade unionists to attempt a synthesis of bureaucracy and incorporation with workers' democratic impulses. Their failure was one of the final failures of the workers' movement to achieve even a very compromised version of the self-totalizing dialectic that Lukács proposed in the revolutionary 1920s.

Since the 1940s other movements with revolutionary aspirations have attempted to reconstitute themselves as the world order—but without success. The national liberation struggles of midcentury, which spawned pan-Arab, pan-African, and third-worldist movements, were the next battles in which people were briefly successful in their claims to universality. The movements of the 1960s and 1970s—from the youth movements that culminated in the uprisings of 1968 to feminism and gay/lesbian/bisexual/transgendered liberation—tried but have thus far failed to transform human relations. Feminism and nationalism remain great forces, of course, as do aspects of class struggle, but these contemporary movements remain unable (and perhaps do not want) to spread their appeal beyond their borders. In the intellectual realm the solipsism with which so many entertain themselves is the philosophical expression of the failure of these social and political movements. Without a movement with claims to totality, there is no universal thought. Realism in international relations theory, which revels in the Hobbesian basis of world politics, is as much a reflection of the collapse of the universalistic efforts as is postmodernism. Realism, the dominant paradigm for postwar international relations scholars and an embrace of the necessities of world power, was a retreat from the moralism and idealism of both cold war liberalism and the Popular Frontism that had preceded it.[31]

The failure of mid-1940s internationalism, and the global conflict that replaced it, significantly reduced the capacity of people around the world to conceive of alternatives to world conflict. This is borne out by the minimal understanding of the opportunities offered by the collapse of the USSR and the seeming end of the cold war (seeming because the cold war was both an East-West and a north-south—industrial–less industrial—conflict). The present seems to many a consolidation of the victory of the West against communism, whereas the future appears to be simply another version of the American century, this time in partnership with a united Europe. In other words, the 1990s have replaced a bipolar order with a unipolar one. Yet it is obvious that we are now continuing the transition to a polycentric world system and perhaps to a system in which national power centers no longer provide the main building blocks of the global structure.

This transition was apparent in the mid-1940s but was covered over by the struggles for loyalty in the cold war. Politicians, intellectuals, and labor leaders lack the vision to propose a new system of world order that would encompass the diverse powers of an increasingly complex and interdependent world or that would create and democratize global institutions capable of undergirding such a system. Instead, the fatuous celebration of globalization proceeds with only the marginalized left and the fanatically nationalist right pointing out the terrible price of the party. Because of the demands for political orthodoxy during the cold war, because of the suppression of the left's alternative, and because of the tremendous intellectual and—in a general sense—spiritual disappointment at the failure to create a better world system in the mid-1940s, we are confronted now with a profound failure of imagination. There is no equivalent in the 1990s of Sidney Hillman's and Cordell Hull's "mystical vision."

As in the 1940s the vast international upheaval today is a time when the possibilities of human progress could be enormous. Even more so than fifty years ago, however, these possibilities remain quite unlikely to be realized, considering that wholesale reforms are not even under consideration. Writing in 1946, German social theorist Max Horkheimer analyzed the uneasy combination of hope and fear in his time in a way that sheds light on our own: "The present potentialities of social achievement surpass the expectations of all the philosophers and statesmen who have ever outlined in utopian programs the idea of a truly human society. Yet there is a universal feeling of fear and disillusionment. The hopes of mankind seem to be farther from fulfillment today than they were even in the groping epochs when they were first formulated by humanists." Horkheimer attributed the sense of inevitable crisis to the failure of modern thinkers to replace reason in history with an effective theory of the connection between knowledge and human action. Without reason, or any useful substitute, people would be condemned to repeat the errors of the past and, if especially unlucky, to experience a "reemergence of the neo-barbarism recently defeated on the battlefields."[32]

The inability of individuals to understand their relation to the larger forces of history contributed to the international disasters of the 1940s and 1950s. Horkheimer's analysis suggests that two elements are necessary for people today to plan a better world system than has prevailed for fifty years. The first is the conception that an equitable democratic system is possible, that we can indeed conceive an alternative world order. The second is a series of broad social movements for such a system that would, like labor at its best moments, provide a democratic vision of how the world and domestic politics should operate. Although a sense of cynical reason and postmodern skepticism about universals undercuts such a project, they do not make it any less necessary.[33] In other words, the world needs to reinvent totality, to embrace a new universalism, if only a universalism that accepts its own impossibility.[34] Such a vision could help make the present moment of intense political and social ferment into something other than a new system of unequal power, overarching fear, and devastating war. Otherwise, like the unions of the 1940s, we will experience yet again the failure of reason and imagination.

Appendix

Survey 1. Feelings about Russians and Americans, London, March 1947

The survey was conducted in London in March 1947 and so is only somewhat generalizable to the rest of the country. Mass-Observation classified its respondents into four socioeconomic groups: upper class (A), middle class (B), "artisanal" or skilled workers (C), and unskilled workers (D). This survey had no A's. I determined averages for the working class by averaging the C and D results. The total number of respondents was not given.

			Socioeconomic Group					
	Men	Women	B	C	D	All	Labor	Conservative
What are your feelings now about Russians?								
Favorable	30%	17%	12%	22%	27%	23%	33%	15%
Unfavorable	41	43	60	36	40	42	31	45
Undetermined	25	27	24	28	24	25	27	30
Don't know	6	13	4	14	9	10	9	10
What are your feelings now about the Americans?								
Favorable	29%	15%	16%	26%	20%	22%	17%	15%
Unfavorable	50	42	60	48	40	46	54	45
Undetermined	15	23	20	16	23	19	16	30
Don't know	6	20	4	10	17	13	13	10

Source: Adapted from Tom Harrisson, draft of article for *Public Opinion Quarterly,* May 1947, FR2493, Mass-Observation Archive, University of Sussex, Brighton, U.K., p. 29.

Survey 2. Attitudes toward Foreigners, April 1943

This was a survey of Mass-Observation's informants (see chapter 3, note 8). The total number of respondents was not given but was probably in the range of 700, judging by similar surveys.

Feelings toward	1941	1943
Americans (U.S.)		
Favorable	27%	33%
Half and half	28	44
Unfavorable	26	21
Vague	19	2
Czechs		
Favorable	55	64
Half and half	9	12
Unfavorable	9	2
Vague	27	22
Dutch		
Favorable	47	73
Half and half	14	4
Unfavorable	11	5
Vague	28	18
French[a]		
Favorable	41	52
Half and half	12	32
Unfavorable	31	11
Vague	16	5
Poles		
Favorable	33	27
Half and half	20	39
Unfavorable	22	7
Vague	25	17

Source: Adapted from Mass-Observation, "Attitudes to Foreigners," April 1943, FR1669Q, Mass-Observation Archive, University of Sussex, Brighton, U.K.

a. Free in 1941, fighting in 1943.

Survey 3. World Role of the United States, Summer 1942

This survey is a typical example of American attitudes before the outlines of postwar world organization had become clear. The questions were whether the respondents thought that the United States should police the world, guarantee freedom of speech and religion, or improve working and living conditions around the globe.

	United States Should			
		Guarantee Free		
Occupation	Police the World	Speech	Religion	Improve Living/ Working Conditions Worldwide
Men (n = 2,345)				
White collar	90%	80%	84%	84%
Laborer	85	86	91	91
Farmer	86	81	84	84
Women (n = 2,203)				
Unemployed but husband was:				
White collar	89	84	88	89
Laborer	82	82	89	89
Farmer	81	79	88	83
Employed	86	84	89	88

Source: Adapted from Office of War Information, Division of Surveys, "Women and the War," 8/6/42, RG 44, Box 1798 E162, National Archives and Records Service, National Storage Center, Suitland, Md., tables 26a (females) and 26b (males).

Survey 4. Opinions about a Separate Peace between Russia and Germany, May 1942 and July 1942

On May 6–17, 1942, and again on July 1–11, 1942, survey respondents were asked, "Do you think Russia might make a separate peace with Germany without talking it over with her allies?"

	Yes		No		No Clear Response		
	May	July	May	July	May	July	Percentage of Change
Men[a]							
White collar	28%	25%	55%	66%	17%	9%	11
Laborer	24	26	60	57	16	17	3
Farmer	20	23	54	57	26	20	6
Women[b]							
Unemployed but husband was							
White collar	32	27	46	54	22	19	9
Laborer	27	21	44	52	29	27	8
Farmer	20	21	47	47	33	32	1
Employed	28	27	48	54	24	19	7

Survey 4. (*cont.*)

The agency obtained similar results on February 16–26, 1942, and again on July 1–11, 1942, when survey respondents were asked, "After the war is over do you think Russia can be depended on to cooperate with us?"

	Yes		No		No Clear Response		Percentage of Change
	May	July	May	July	May	July	
Men[c]							
White collar	42%	54%	42%	26%	16%	20%	16
Laborer	43	46	37	30	20	24	5
Farmer	43	44	33	23	24	33	10
Women[d]							
Unemployed but husband was							
White collar	32	43	45	29	23	28	16
Laborer	36	40	33	24	31	36	9
Farmer	31	36	28	25	41	39	5
Employed	36	45	37	27	27	28	10

Source: Adapted from Office of War Information, Division of Surveys, "Women and the War," 8/6/42, RG 44, Box 1798 E162, National Archives and Records Service, National Storage Center, Suitland, Md., tables 14a–17a (women) and 14b–17b (men).

a. For May, n = 1,779; for July, n = 1,767.

b. For May, n = 1,749; for July, n = 1,735.

c. For February, n = 2,345; for July, n = 1,767.

d. For February, n = 2,203; for July, n = 1,735.

Survey 5. Opinions of Allies, 1943

Survey repondents (n = 4,319) were asked, "Do you think England (Russia) can be depended on to cooperate with us after the war?" The results do not necessarily show the respondents' opinions of the countries involved.

	U.K. Will Cooperate	USSR Will Cooperate
Income level		
Prosperous	80%	49%
Average	79	47
Poor	73	43
Occupation		
Business and professionals	80	51
Farmers	79	43
Manual workers	76	45
Service workers	72	45

Source: Adapted from Office of War Information, Division of Surveys, "Special Memorandum No. 85, Attitudes toward International Problems," 8/31/43, RG 44, Box 1803 E164, National Archives and Records Service, National Storage Center, Suitland, Md., p. 9.

Survey 6. Religious Differences in Desire to Help England, 1940

Survey respondents (number unknown) were asked, "Which is more important: to help England at the risk of war or to stay out of war?" The margin of error was 4 percent.

Economic Status/Religion	Help England	Stay Out of War	No Opinion
Upper income			
Jews	76%	19%	5%
Protestants	60	37	3
Catholics	45	52	3
None	61	36	3
Middle income			
Jews	72	24	4
Protestants	51	45	4
Catholics	41	54	5
None	55	39	6
Lower income			
Jews	64	33	3
Protestants	43	49	8
Catholics	36	58	6
None	42	49	9

Source: Adapted from Hadley Cantril, "America Faces the War: The Reaction of Public Opinion," 12/16/40, RG 44, Box 1796, National Archives and Records Service, National Storage Center, Suitland, Md., table 3, p. 11.

Survey 7. Socioeconomic Characteristics and Attitude toward a "Tough" Approach to Russia, 1947

Income	Approval	Qualified Approval	Undecided	Qualified Disapproval	Disapproval
< $2,000 (34.1%)	6%	8%	14%	30%	41%
$2,000–3,999 (41.1%)	5	16	7	25	45
> $4,000 (23.1%)	15	6	3	29	46

Sources: Income distribution percentages from U.S. Bureau of the Census, *Statistical Abstract of the United States, 1948,* table 316, p. 285. Table adapted from Survey Research Center, "Public Attitudes toward Russia and United States–Russian Relations, Part 1: Attitudes toward United States–Russian Relations" (ms., Survey Research Center, 3/47), ISR Report #219, Institute for Social Research Library, University of Michigan, Ann Arbor, pp. 13, 21, table 9, appendix A.

Notes

Acc	Accession
ACWA	Amalgamated Clothing Workers of America Collection
CAB	Records of the Cabinet of His Majesty's Government
CIOST	CIO Secretary Treasurers Collection, Archives of Labor and Urban Affairs, Walter Reuther Library, Wayne State University, Detroit
Catholic	Department of Archives and Manuscripts, The Catholic University of America, Washington, D.C.
Churchill	Bevin Library, Churchill College, Cambridge, U.K.
Cornell	Labor Management Documentation Center, M. P. Catherwood Library, Cornell University, Ithaca, N.Y.
FO	Foreign Office, U.K.
FRUS	*Foreign Relations of the United States*
Hoover	Hoover Institution Archives, Stanford, Calif.
Imperial	Imperial War Museum, London
ISR	Institute for Social Research, University of Michigan, Ann Arbor
LAB	Ministry of Labour and National Service, U.K.
LSE	British Library of Economic and Political Science, London
M-O Archive	Mass-Observation Archive, University of Sussex, Brighton, U.K.
MOI	Ministry of Information
MRC	Modern Records Centre, University of Warwick, Coventry, U.K.
NARS	National Archives and Records Service, Washington, D.C.
NARS—Suitland	National Storage Center, Suitland, Md.
NUR	National Union of Railwaymen, U.K.
OF	President's Official Files
OWI	Office of War Information, United States
PPF	President's Personal Files (FDR)
PRO	Public Record Office, Kew, U.K.
PSF	President's Secretaries' Files (FDR)

R&A	Research and Analysis Report
RG	Record Group
Rhodes House	Rhodes House Library, Oxford
Roosevelt Library	Franklin D. Roosevelt Library, Hyde Park, N.Y.
Schevenels Papers	Walter Schevenels Papers
Taft Papers	Philip Taft Collection, Labor Management Documentation Center, M. P. Catherwood Library, Cornell University, Ithaca, N.Y.
TUC	Archives of the Trades Union Congress, Congress House, London (now at MRC)
UAW Presidents	Records of the Office of the President, United Autoworkers of America
Wayne State	Archives of Labor and Urban Affairs, Walter Reuther Library, Wayne State University, Detroit

Introduction

1. "Relationship of the World Federation of Trade Unions to the United Nations: Transcript of Meeting of Deputation to the Prime Minister from the Trades Union Congress," LAB 13/599-130373, p. 2, PRO.

2. Sidney Hillman to Truman, 10/31/45, ACWA, Acc 5619, Box 86, File 35, Cornell.

3. The Latin labor federation, Confederación de Trabajadores de América Latina (CTAL), first proposed a new world labor federation in 1942. However, CTAL, limited by finances and lacking close connections to the centers of world power, could not follow up on its proposal. Instead, the powerful unions of the developed countries took up the call for a world organization. Vincente Lombardo Toledano, CTAL president, was a major figure in this history. Rubens Iscaro, *Historia de la Federación Sindical Mundial* (Buenos Aires: Editorial Anteo, 1983), 26–27.

4. James B. Carey, "Report to President Murray, WFTU Vice President Hillman and the CIO Executive Board of WFTU Executive Committee Meetings Held in Moscow Beginning June 17th," n.d. [7/46], CIOST, Acc 185, Box 119, File: "World Federation of Trade Unions, Report on CIO Delegation, July 1946," p. 3, Wayne State.

5. M. Lazarev, "The World Federation of Trade Unions—Bulwark of the Working Class against Reaction," *TRUD,* 4/18/48, [translation by State Department Staff], RG 59, Decimal File: 800.5043/5-648, NARS.

6. Sidney Hillman, "One Voice for Sixty Million," *Collier's,* September 29, 1945.

7. For a fuller discussion of the nature of such transnational events, see Victor Silverman, "Is National History a Thing of the Past? On the Growing Reality of World History in the Twentieth Century," *European Legacy* 2 (April 1996): 696–702.

8. E. J. Hobsbawm, "Working-Class Internationalism," in *Internationalism in the Labour Movement, 1830–1940,* vol. 1, ed. Frits van Holthoon and Marcel van der Linden (Leiden, The Netherlands: Brill, 1988), 4. I often refer to the trades unions as active subjects (e.g.,

"the labor movements conceived"). Although this is a common shorthand for saying "the majority of the elected officials of the unions conceived," or in more representative cases, "the majority of the members of the unions and their elected and appointed officials conceived," this form of reference has some problems. The common belief in institutions as active subjects can obscure much about the reality of how groups of people act. Similar problems occur with national policies referred to as the actions of the "United States" or, somewhat more specifically, "Washington," "thinking, wanting, or doing" when in fact the writer means particular people or groups. These terms are abstractions that, while useful at times, often substitute for clear thinking about the nature of the historical actors to which they refer. I have tried to be careful in my use of such collective nouns, using them only when I feel they are justified, that is, when they refer to widespread phenomena or the result of a collective decision. Thus when I write that labor made "universalist claims," I believe that the ideas of universality were indeed shared by most union members and by the vast majority of their leaders.

9. Horst Lademacher has ably detailed the gap between ideology and practice in the evolution of labor internationalism in "Kosmopolitismus, Solidarität und Nation: Einige Bemerkungen zum Wandel von Begriff und Wirklichkeit im internationalen Sozialismus," in *Internationalism in the Labour Movement, 1830–1940,* vol. 2, ed. van Holthoon and van der Linden, 372–91.

10. Akira Iriye and Christopher Thorne ably examine the influence of cultural differences and imperial conflict in the diplomacy leading to the war in the Pacific and in the conduct of the war itself. Akira Iriye, *Power and Culture: The Japanese-American War* (Cambridge, Mass.: Harvard University Press, 1981); Christopher Thorne, *The Issue of War: States, Societies, and the Far Eastern Conflict of 1941–45* (London: Hamilton, 1985).

11. A good survey of the rise of this sort of thinking among the American elites is Robert A. Divine, *Second Chance: The Triumph of Internationalism in America During World War II* (New York: Atheneum, 1967).

12. Denis McShane, *International Labour and the Origins of the Cold War* (Oxford: Clarendon, 1992).

13. Ronald Radosh, *American Labor and U.S. Foreign Policy* (New York: Random House, 1969), 18–24.

14. Adolf Sturmthal, *Unity and Diversity in European Labor* (Glencoe, Ill.: Free Press, 1953), 116.

15. Horst Lademacher et al., "Der Weltgewerkschaftsbund im Spannungsfeld des Ost-West Konflikts," *Archiv für Sozialgeschichte* 18 (1978): 119–216, offer an early synthesis of the overall role of the World Federation. A good work on the breakup of the organization is Jean-François Michel, "La Scission de la Fédération Syndicale Mondiale," *Mouvement Social* (France) 117 (1981): 33–52. Sigrid Koch-Baumgarten and Peter Rütters give a solid introduction to the conflict between the World Federation and the International Secretariats, along with a helpful collection of documents, in their edited volume, *Zwischen Integration und Autonomie: Der Konflikt zwischen den IBS und dem WGB um den*

Neuaufbau einer Internationalen Gewerkschaftsbewegung, 1945–49 (Cologne, Germany: Bund-Verlag, 1991). Anthony Carew, *Labour Under the Marshall Plan* (Manchester, U.K.: Manchester University Press, 1987), examines the development of labor support for the Marshall Plan and the politics of productivity. Peter Weiler, *British Labor and the Cold War* (Stanford, Calif.: Stanford University Press, 1988), offers a detailed analysis of the close relationship of the TUC to the British government. Carolyn Eisenberg, "Working-Class Politics and the Cold War: American Intervention in the German Labor Movement," *Diplomatic History* 7 (Fall 1983): 283–306; Michael Fichter, *Besatzungsmacht und Gewerkschaften: Zur Entwicklung und Anwendung der U.S.-Gewerkschaftspolitik in Deutschland, 1944–88* (Berlin: Westdeutscher Verlag, 1982); and Rolf Steininger, "England und die deutsche Gewerkschaftsbewegung, 1945–46," *Archiv für Sozialgeschichte* 18 (1978): 41–118, consider international involvement in the fight over the structure of reconstructed German trade unions. Gene Sensenig, *Österreichisch-Amerikanische Gewerkschaftsbeziehungen, 1945 bis 1950* (Cologne, Germany: Pahl Rugenstein, 1987), places Austrian-American union relations in the context of U.S. world hegemony. Ronald Filippelli, *American Labor and Postwar Italy, 1943–53* (Stanford, Calif.: Stanford University Press, 1989), and Stephen Burwood, "American Labor, French Labor, and the Marshall Plan: Battleground and Crossroads" (paper delivered at the 9th Annual North American Labor History Conference, Detroit, October 22, 1987), are critical of the American labor role in France and Italy, finding close cooperation between U.S. labor and an anti-Communist U.S. government after 1945. In contrast, Irwin Wall, *L'Influence Americaine sur la Politique Française, 1945–54,* trans. Philippe-Etienne Raviart (Paris: Balland, 1989), esp. Chap. 4, argues that U.S. influences on French labor politics have been highly overrated. A significant portion of the literature focuses on the role of the American Federation of Labor—Roy Godson, *American Labor and European Politics* (New York: Crane Russak, 1976), finds that the AFL saved the Western world; and Radosh, *American Labor and U.S. Foreign Policy,* finds that the AFL may have been in league with the devil. On the left, Iscaro presents a classic pro-Communist version that attributes the problems in the World Federation to "imperialist intrigues" (*intriguas imperialistas*) in his *Historia de La Federación Sindical Mundial,* 53. Similar treatments can be found in Soviet and other Communist literature, including Boris Averyanov, "Soviet Unions and the World Trade Union Movement," *New World Review* (Moscow) 39, no. 2 (1971): 46–56; William Z. Foster, *Outline History of the World Trade Union Movement* (New York: International Publishers, 1956), 382–501; G. Bischoff, "Zur Internationalen Gewerkschaftsbewegung seit 1945," *Dokumentation der Zeit* (GDR) 5 (1972): 14–19.

16. The literature is quite extensive. Among the most thorough institutional works are John P. Windmuller, *American Labor and the International Labor Movement: 1940–53* (Ithaca, N.Y.: Cornell Institute of International Relations Reports, 1954); and Lewis Lorwin, *The International Labor Movement* (New York: Harper, 1953); Federico Romero, *The United States and the Reconstruction of the European Trade Union Movement, 1944–51,* trans. Harvey Fergusson II (Chapel Hill: University of North Carolina Press, 1992).

17. Research and Analysis Branch, OSS, "Russia's Role in the World Trade Union

Conference," R&A No. 2740, 1/15/45, RG 59, Decimal File: 550.4 London/1-1545. p. 6, NARS.

18. "Statement of Philip Murray, President of CIO Consultant to American Delegation," San Francisco, 5/7/45, CIOST, Acc 185, Box 68, File: "President Philip Murray, 1945," pp. 2–3, Wayne State.

19. Carey is quoted in Caffery [Paris] to Secretary of State, 2/19/48, RG 59, Decimal File: 800.5043/2-1948, NARS.

20. "Statement of Philip Murray, President of CIO,Consultant to American Delegation," San Francisco, 5/7/45, CIOST, Acc 185, Box 68, File: "President Philip Murray, 1945," p. 2, Wayne State.

21. Rostow is quoted in Jay Krane to Elmer Cope, 1/29/49 [misdated as 1948], Jay Krane Papers, Acc 614, Box 1, File #5: "CIO Paris Office, Jan. 12–March 16, 1949," Wayne State.

22. I use the terms *first, second,* and *third world* advisedly because they reflect the political alignments emerging in the forties. Third world refers to those countries not in the capitalist or Communist blocs and is an essentially political term. It includes colonized and independent nations.

23. World Trade Union Conference, *Report of the World Trade Union Conference* (London: TUC, 1945), 103.

24. The relationship of the World Federation to the third world has not yet been treated adequately. Gene Sensenig has made a good start, however. His interpretation was helpful here. Sensenig, *Österreichisch-Amerikanische Gewerkschaftsbeziehungen,* 142–67.

25. Louis Saillant, "Report on the Help of the World Federation Trade Unions to the Trade Unions in Colonial Countries or Mandated Territories," Moscow, June 1946, CIOST, Box 119, File: "WFTU Report on Help . . . ," Wayne State.

26. Ibid., 9.

27. Karl Marx and Frederick Engels, *Manifesto of the Communist Party,* in *Selected Works,* vol. 1 (Moscow: Progress Publishers, 1969), 124.

28. Marx and Engels seemed to recognize this problem, though they had no doubt that ultimately the workers would be a totalizing social force that would transform and become all of society. They argued in the *Manifesto* that the working class "must rise to be the leading class of the nation, must constitute itself *the* nation" (emphasis in the original). Nevertheless, the proletariat would not be national "in the bourgeois sense of the word." Yet the rise to national power, to becoming the sole legitimate political force in the nation, required adoption of certain bourgeois concerns for national interest—how else would the workers guide the nation if they did not believe in it? The problem of nationalism versus internationalism thus appears even in the thinking of the founders of modern communism. Marx and Engels, *Manifesto of the Communist Party,* 124.

A similar problem convinced nonsyndicalist Socialists that political parties rather than unions would be the best expression of working-class interest. Unions had to pursue the day-to-day interests of the workers, "limiting themselves to a guerrilla war against the effects of the existing system," in Marx's words, whereas the parties could take a longer perspective. The distrust of the short-range thinking of the unions was especially pronounced among German Social Democrats before the rise of Hitler and among the Bolsheviks. British Labourites had a better if still uneasy coexistence, whereas most North Americans dispensed with parties altogether. Karl Marx, *Wages, Price, and Profit,* in Marx and Engels, *Selected Works*, vol. 2, p. 75. See also Karl Kautsky, *The Social Revolution,* trans. A. M. Simons and May W. Simons (Chicago: Charles Kerr, 1910), 82–84; Carl Shorske, *German Social Democracy* (1955; reprint, New York: Russel and Russel, 1970), 11–16; V. I. Lenin, *What Is to Be Done?* in *Essential Works of Lenin,* ed. Henry M. Christman (New York: Bantam, 1966), 92–101.

29. Other critical factors in what could be called the deproletarianization of the left in the 1950s and 1960s were disillusionment with Soviet, or Communist, rule in Eastern Europe, the inability of Social-Democratic parties and their working-class bases to establish a transcendent form of socialism, the success of conservative forces in taming working-class organizations, and, not least, the rise of alternative totalizing movements—third-world nationalism, feminism, environmentalism, hippy culture, and the "New Class" of professional and union elites—which did not rely on the working class. See André Gorz, *Adieux au Proletariat* (Paris: Éditions Galilée, 1980); Alvin Gouldner, *The Intellectuals and the Rise of the New Class* (New York: Continuum, 1979); Giovanni Arrighi, "Marxist Century–American Century: The Making and Remaking of the World Labor Movement," in Samir Amin et al., *Transforming the Revolution: Social Movements and the World System* (New York: Monthly Review Press, 1990), 54–95.

30. See Enrique Krauze, *Caudillos Culturales de la Revolución Mexicana* (Mexico: Secretario de Educación Publica, 1985); Víctor Manuel Durand Ponte, *La Ruptura de la Nación* (Mexico: UNAM, 1986).

31. The governments established in the immediate aftermath of victory in Europe were almost universally coalitions dominated by Socialists, Communists, and, in some cases, antifascist conservatives. The pattern in Asia was quite different because of U.S. and Russian occupation policies there. See Gabriel Kolko, *The Politics of War: The World and U.S. Foreign Policy, 1943–45* (New York: Random House, 1969), 71–85, 96–98, 401–14; Hermann Weber and Dietrich Startz, eds., *Einheitsfront-Einheitspartei: Kommunisten und Sozial-Demokraten in Ost- und West-Europa, 1944–48* (Cologne, Germany: Verlag Wissenschaft und Politik, 1989).

32. Michael Ross to Leo Wertz [director of the Manpower Division, OMGUS], 1/8/47, Philip Taft Papers, Acc 5541, Box 5, File 22, Cornell.

PART 1: Ideas and Realities in the International Labor Community

1. Minutes, IFTU General Council Meeting, London, 3–4 September 1945, Schevenels Papers, Box 7, File 7, Hoover.

2. International Federation of Trade Unions, *Project for the Reconstruction of the International Trade Union Movement* (London: IFTU, 1944), Schevenels Papers, Box 8, File 7, Hoover.

Chapter 1: Communists, Socialists, and Liberals in International Labor

1. International Labour Office, "First Special International Trades Union Congress, London, November 22–27, 1920" (report, Geneva, 12 March 1921), Schevenels Papers, Box 8, File 6, Hoover, p. 2.

2. Ibid.

3. Ibid., 9. On the AFL's withdrawal from cooperation with the Socialists, see Lewis Lorwin, *The International Labor Movement* (New York: Harper, 1953), 81–85; and Philip Taft, *The AFL in the Time of Gompers* (New York: Harper, 1957), 330–40.

4. International Federation of Trade Unions, *Directives pour la Politique Economique,* (Amsterdam: IFTU, 1929), 9.

5. Resolution of the Moscow International Special Meeting, quoted in International Labour Office, "First Special International Trades Union Congress," 22–24.

6. See, for instance, Karl Kautsky, *The Dictatorship of the Proletariat,* trans. H. J. Stenning (Ann Arbor: University of Michigan Press, 1964).

7. International Labour Office, "First Special International Trades Union Congress," 24.

8. Ibid., 25.

9. Quoted in E. H. Carr, *Socialism in One Country: A History of Soviet Russia, 1924–26,* vol. 3 (Harmondsworth, U.K.: Penguin, 1972), 75.

10. General Council, British Trades Union Congress, *Russia and International Unity* (London: TUC, 1925), Schevenels Papers, Box 8, File 6: "IFTU Publications, Brochures, and Pamphlets," Hoover. See also Carr, *Socialism in One Country,* vol. 3, 543–601.

11. Lorwin, *International Labor Movement,* 148.

12. Ibid., 120.

13. International Federation of Trade Unions, *Triennial Report, 1933–35* (Paris: IFTU, 1937), 174.

14. Lorwin, *International Labor Movement,* 191.

15. Ibid., 175–83.

16. "Proposal of the Delegation of the Soviet Trade Unions," in Minutes, IFTU General Council, Oslo, 18 May 1938, Schevenels Papers, Box 7, File 7, Hoover.

17. Green to Citrine, 6/15/39, Philip Taft Papers, Acc 5541, Box 6, File 3, Cornell.

18. Isabelle Tombs argues that British Labour and unions muted their criticism of the Soviets in regard to the Soviets' execution of the Poles. She is right, yet the private discontent was substantial. Tombs, "Erlich and Alter, 'The Sacco and Vanzetti of the USSR': An Episode in the Wartime History of International Socialism," *Journal of Contemporary History* 23 (1988): 531–49.

19. Minutes, EITUC Committee I, Meetings of 2 November 1942 and 3 December 1942, Schevenels Papers, Box 8, File 1: "Minutes EITUC, General," Hoover.

20. IFTU, *Project for the Reconstruction of the International Trade Union Movement* (London: IFTU, 1944), 2.

21. Ibid., 7.

22. Minutes of EITUC General Council, London, 23 September 1943, Schevenels Papers, Box 8, File 1, Hoover.

23. Ibid.

24. Minutes, IFTU General Council Meeting, London, 3–4 September 1945, Schevenels Papers, Box 7, File 7, Hoover.

25. Walter Schevenels, "Toward Greater Unity in the World Trade Union Movement," *Trade Union World* 3 (January–February 1945): 3.

26. Denis McShane, *International Labour and the Origins of the Cold War* (Oxford: Clarendon, 1992); Anthony Carew, *Labour Under the Marshall Plan* (Manchester, U.K.: Manchester University Press, 1987).

27. Schevenels to Richard Nosworthy, 21 December 1944, Schevenels Papers, Box 6, File 8, Hoover.

28. *Daily Worker* (London), August 7, 1945.

29. Schevenels to A. Fabra Ribas, 29 March 1945, Schevenels Papers, Box 7, File 1, Hoover.

30. Schevenels to Citrine, 9 August 1945, Schevenels Papers, Box 7, File 2, Hoover.

31. McShane, *International Labour,* 5, 9, 63–78. See also Sigrid Koch-Baumgarten and Peter Rütters, *Zwischen Integration und Autonomie: Der Konflikt zwischen den IBS und dem WGB um den Neuaufbau einer Internationalen Gewerkschaftsbewegung, 1945–49* (Cologne, Germany: Bund-Verlag, 1991), 11–12.

32. Schevenels and the EITUC proposed that the new world federation unite the ITS and a confederation of national trade union centers. This was necessary, they believed, in order to balance national interests and the worldwide interests of workers in a particular industry. IFTU, *Reconstruction of the International Trade Union Movement,* 6.

33. "Address by Rt. Hon Sir Walter Citrine, KBE, to the House of Commons Trade Union Group on Wednesday, 8 July 1942, at 3 PM," 13 July 1942, Citrine Papers I, 4/10, p. 1, LSE.

34. Walter Schevenels, "Position of the IFTU and the steps to be taken in relation to the forthcoming World Trade Union Conference in Paris, September 1945," July 4, 1945, MSS 238/IF/1/60/1, MRC. For comparison, see Lorwin, *International Labor Movement,* 98–106.

35. "U.S.-Soviet Labor Committee Urged by CIO, AUCCTU Leaders; Carey Stresses Friendship," *Allied Labor News,* 10/16/45, CIOST, Acc 185, Box 117, File: "Paris Conf. September–October, Miscellaneous Material," Wayne State.

36. "Rough Draft of Transcript of Meeting of Members of the Foreign Service Division . . . to Hear Mr. James Carey," 9/22/44, CIOST, Acc 185, Box 46, File: "State Department Corres., 1941–43," p. 3, Wayne State.

37. Morton Goodman, "World Labor and Russian Power Politics," *New Leader,* January 27, 1945.

38. World Trade Union Conference, "Report of the Preparatory Committee," *Report*

of the World Trade Union Conference (London: TUC, 1945), Appendix A, 226–27. See also my fifth chapter.

39. Lutz Niethammer is one of the few historians who considers the thinking behind the Resistance coalition unions as representative of anything but an unimportant, and ultimately irrelevant, ideology. Niethammer, "Structural Reform and a Compact for Growth: Conditions for a United Labor Movement in Europe After the Collapse of Fascism," in *The Origins of the Cold War and Contemporary Europe,* ed. Charles Maier (New York: New Viewpoints, 1978), 203–43.

40. WTUC, *Report,* 113.

41. "Over Twenty Million Workers Represented at IFTU General Council Meeting," *Trade Union World* 3 (January–February 1945): 2.

42. IFTU General Council Meeting, [Minutes], London, 1–2 February 1945, Paul Tofahrn Papers, MSS 238/IF/1/55, p. 11, MRC.

43. William Green to Citrine, 14 February 1944, Schevenels Papers, Box 6, File 8, Hoover.

44. Schevenels to Green, 14 January 1944, Schevenels Papers, Box 6, File 8, Hoover.

45. For more on AFL voluntarism see Ruth Horowitz, *Political Ideologies of Organized Labor* (New Brunswick, N.J.: Transaction, 1978); Michael P. Rogin, "Voluntarism: The Political Functions of an Anti-Political Doctrine," in *The American Labor Movement,* ed. David Brody (New York: Harper and Row, 1971), 100–18.

46. *American Federationist,* October 1944.

47. On the TUC's liberalism see Henry Pelling, "The Working Class and the Origins of the Welfare State," in his *Popular Politics and Society in late Victorian Britain: Essays,* 2d ed. (London: Macmillan, 1979).

48. *American Federationist,* October 1944.

49. International Ladies Garment Workers, "Problems of International Trade Union Unity" [1944], Schevenels Papers, Box 9, File 4: "IFTU Publications, Reports."

50. Anthony Carew, "Conflict Within the ICFTU: Anti-Communism and Anti-Colonialism in the 1950s," *International Review of Social History* 41 (1996): 147.

51. EITUC, Minutes, 18 October 1943, reported in IFTU, *Reconstruction of the International Trade Union Movement,* 9.

52. The actual size of the committee's budget is a matter of dispute and was probably less than this enormous sum. The best estimate puts its actual budget in the first year at $200,000. Federico Romero, *The United States and the Reconstruction of the European Trade Union Movement, 1944–51,* trans. Harvey Fergusson II (Chapel Hill: University of North Carolina Press, 1992), 14; McShane, *International Labour,* 273; Carew, *Labour Under the Marshall Plan,* 63–69.

53. Green to Schevenels, 30 June 1945; Schevenels to Green, 19 December 1945; and Schevenels to Citrine, 3 August 1945, all in the Schevenels Papers, Box 7, File 2, Hoover.

54. Lorwin, *International Labor Movement,* 214–15.

55. International Confederation of Free Trade Unions, "Manifesto of the ICFTU," in

ICFTU, *Official Report of the Free World Labour Conference and of the International Confederation of Free Trade Unions* (London: TUC, 1949), 242.

56. Ibid., 95.

57. Ibid., 111.

58. Ironically, the AFL later came to see him as dangerously soft on communism and too much in the British pocket. See Carew, "Conflict Within the ICFTU."

Chapter 2: Chinese Sailors, Exile Unions, and the Limits of Practical Internationalism

1. An average wage at the time was less than £200 per year. IFTU Financial Statement, 1943, London, 31 December 1943, Schevenels Papers, Box 7, File 5, Hoover.

2. The IFTU's staff reflected both the international nature of the federation and the importance of the trade unionists to the exile governments. For example, Schevenels's assistant secretary, the Czech Jiri Stolz, was deeply involved in exile politics. *Lincolnshire Echo,* February 13, 1941; Jan Becko to Schevenels, 6 August 1943, Schevenels Papers, Box 6, File 7: "IFTU Correspondence, 1943," Hoover.

3. Undated untitled press release [1942?], CSFGB, Schevenels Papers, Box 10, File 4: "Subject File: France Correspondence, 1942," Hoover.

4. In 1940 the CGT's second-tier union leaders in France had organized the Comité de Coordination des Fédérations et unions départementales. [Unknown] to Schevenels, 30 September 1940, Schevenels Papers, Box 10, File 2: "France Correspondence, 1940," Hoover; Joseph Bondas to Schevenels, 2/11/1942, Schevenels Papers, Box 10, File 4: "France Correspondence, 1942," Hoover.

5. CSFGB to Roosevelt, Schevenels Papers, Box 10, File 4: "France Correspondence," Hoover.

6. CSF, untitled statement [n.d., 1942], Schevenels Papers, Box 10, File 1: "France Circulars," Hoover.

7. Schevenels to Hans Jahn, 16 July 1941, and Schevenels to Citrine, 11 August 1941, Schevenels Papers, Box 6, File 5: "IFTU Correspondence," Hoover.

8. Joseph Bondas to Schevenels, 2/11/1942, Schevenels Papers, Box 10, File 4: "France Correspondence, 1942."

9. Walter Schevenels to René Rous, 26 June 1941; P. Harries to Schevenels, 24 June 1941; Schevenels to Harries, 26 June 1941, "France Correspondence, 1943," Schevenels Papers, Box 10, File 3, Hoover.

10. Schevenels to Bolton, 22 May 1941, Schevenels Papers, Box 10, File 3: "France Correspondence, 1943," Hoover.

11. CSF, "Notes Syndicals," 25 February 1942, Schevenels Papers, Box 10, File 1: "France Circulars," Hoover; "Agreement Between the National Union of General and Municipal Workers and . . ." [n.d.], Schevenels Papers, Box 10, File 1: "France Circulars," Hoover.

12. Schevenels to Citrine, 8 July 1942, Schevenels Papers, Box 10, File 4: "France Correspondence, 1942," Hoover.

13. CSF, Rapport d'Activité: Année 1943, Schevenels Papers, Box 10, File 1: "France Circulars," Hoover.

14. Schevenels to René Rous, 13 June 1941, Schevenels Papers, Box 10, File 3, Hoover.

15. CSF, "Situation des membres 31 Mai 1941"; quotation in CSF, "Statement" [n.d., 1941], Schevenels Papers, Box 10, File 1: "Circulars," Hoover.

16. Schevenels to Oldenbroek, 28 March 1942, Schevenels Papers, Box 10, File 3: "France Correspondence, 1941," Hoover.

17. CSF, Rapport d'Activité: Année 1943," 1944, Schevenels Papers, Box 10, File 1: "France Circulars," Hoover.

18. CSF, "Situation des membres 31 Mai 1941."

19. IFTU, "Report on Activities 1942–43" [April 1943], Schevenels Papers, Box 8, File 1, p. 7, Hoover.

20. Ibid., 6.

21. IFTU Financial Statement, 1943, London, 31 December 1943, Schevenels Papers, Box 7, File 5, Hoover.

22. Schevenels to "Mr. J.," 10 January 1945, Schevenels Papers, Box 2, File 25: "Resistance," Hoover. The trade unions in the United States and Britain worked closely with the intelligence services during the war, though the exact extent of the cooperation remains unclear. See Federico Romero, *United States and the European Trade Union Movement, 1944–51*, trans. Harvey Fergusson II (Chapel Hill: University of North Carolina Press, 1992), 14; Denis McShane, *International Labour and the Origins of the Cold War* (Oxford: Clarendon, 1992), 79–80.

23. Feliks Szaraniec [delegate of the MS *Sobieski*] to Ministry of Industry, 5 February 1945, Box 476, File 910.1, TUC; H. Gawlik [delegate of the SS *Wilno*] to Ministry of Industry, 7 February 1945, Box 476, File 910.1, TUC; ITF Management Committee Minutes, 16 March 1945, MSS 159/1/4/39, MRC; ITF Executive Committee Minutes, 8/10 July 1945, MSS 159/1/3/53, MRC; W. Zeleszkiewicz and J. Fligiel [Polish Transport Workers, Naval Section, London] to Oldenbroek, 8 July 1945, MSS 159/3/D/55, MRC.

24. Schevenels to Joe Bain, 6 June 1945, Schevenels Papers, Box 7, File 1, Hoover.

25. Schevenels to Trade Union Center for German Workers in Great Britain, 11 August 1945, Schevenels Papers, Box 7, File: "IFTU Correspondence," Hoover.

26. Schevenels to Kupers, 30 January 1948, Schevenels Papers, Box 7, File 3, Hoover.

27. C. B. A. Behrens, the official historian of British merchant shipping in World War II, claims that "no foreign ships that were at sea when the Germans attacked in the West returned to enemy occupied territory." Many of these ships did not actually end up in British control. Some sailed only in neutral waters, others remained under their respective governments' control. A confusing melange of agreements, leases, and seizures effectively put the majority of the world's merchant fleet at Britain's direction. C. B. A. Behrens, *Merchant Shipping and the Demands of War* (London: HMSO, 1955), 91–103, quotation at 94.

28. Almost all Danish and French ships sailed under the Union Jack because there was no exile government to negotiate with the British. Behrens, *Merchant Shipping*, 101–2.

29. The figures do not include tankers. Behrens, *Merchant Shipping,* 113–18; "They Keep the Flag Flying," *Seaman,* October 1941; "Our Faith and Friendship Are Unshakable," *Seaman,* January–February 1942.

30. Union of Greek Seamen in Great Britain, "Annual Returns," 30 May 1946, Chief Registrar of Friendly Societies, FS12/411, PRO.

31. Through the war foreign ships averaged more than 25 percent of the British fleet. Figures compiled from Behrens, *Merchant Shipping,* 69.

32. "International Seamen's Conference," London, 4 September 1940, MSS 159/3/D/9, MRC.

33. ITF, "International Seamen's Conference," London, 18–19 September 1942, MSS 159/1/5/11, p. 2, MRC.

34. Ibid.

35. *Seaman,* December 1944.

36. Leathers to Jarman and Oldenbroek, 27 October 1942, MSS 159/3/D/69/A, MRC.

37. Noel-Baker to Jarman and Oldenbroek, 29 December 1942, MSS 159/3/D/69/A, MRC.

38. ITF, "Inter-Allied Wage Policy on Seamen's Wages" [1942], MSS 159/3/D/69/B, MRC; ITF, "Survey of Regulation of Hours and Overtime of Allied Seamen," 1 February 1943, MSS 159/3/D/69/A, MRC.

39. Patrick K. Fyrth, "Seaman's War," manuscript, Fyrth Papers, 87/42/1, Imperial, pp. 34–35.

40. "Revision of the Anglo-Chinese Agreement Regarding Chinese Seamen Serving on British Ships," 2 May 1944, FO371/41544, PRO.

41. Wong Kwok Hong to Chi Hork Fan, 14 July 1942, Postal and Telegraph Censorship Submission No. Liv 42,583/42, MT9/3692, PRO.

42. Liverpool Branch CSU to Foo Sang Kwe, 28 July 1942, Postal and Telegraph Censorship, Naval Section Censorship, Submission No. HOL/PO/22665/42, MT9/3692, PRO.

43. ITF Emergency General Council, "Report and Minutes," July 1941, MSS 159/1/2/29, pp. 16–17, MRC.

44. Ibid., 17.

45. Anglo-Saxon Petroleum Co., Ltd., to the Chairman, Liverpool Branch National Chinese Seamen's Union, 14 August 1942, MT9/3692, PRO.

46. H. W. Rowbottom [Anglo Saxon Petroleum] to N. A. Guttery, 27 April 1944, FO371/41544 PRO.

47. ITF, "Report on Activities . . . 1938 to 1946" (London: ITF, 1946), MSS 159/1/85, pp. 79–80, MRC.

48. During 1943 the Ministry of War Transport waited for Jarman's certification of the CSU, various minutes, MT9/3692, PRO.

49. ITF Emergency General Council, "Report and Minutes," July 1941, MSS 159/1/2/29, MRC.

50. ITF, "International Seamen's Conference," 18–19 September 1942, MSS 159/1/5/11, MRC.

51. Ibid.

Part 2: The British

1. Paul Tofahrn, "On the Eve of the World Trade Union Conference" [typescript], MSS 238/IF/1/45, MRC.

2. By "leaders" or "leadership" I refer to the members of the TUC General Council elected at the annual congress and the top officers and executives of the constituent unions. The leaders of the TUC, and thus the TUC itself, were dominated or led (depending upon one's opinion) by a group of moderate Labourites who had taken control of the TUC after the 1926 general strike. The National Union of General and Municipal Workers (NUGMW) and the Transport and General Workers' Union (TGWU) were the two largest constituents and exercised great power in determining overall policy.

3. In 1938 Harold Nicolson defined the basis of what can best be called Britain's "traditional" foreign policy: "For 250 years at least the great foundation of our foreign policy, what Sir Eyre Crowe called a 'law of nature,' has been to prevent by every means in our power the domination of Europe by any single Power or group of Powers." Quoted in Michael R. Gordon, *Conflict and Consensus in Labour's Foreign Policy, 1914–65* (Stanford, Calif.: Stanford University Press, 1969), x. The root purpose of this policy was to ensure that no power in the world was capable of threatening Britain's imperial and commercial preeminence. When combined with an ideological revulsion of communism, this traditional British policy made for an intense opposition to Soviet ambitions, especially because Communist ideology directly challenged the basis of Britain's economic and political empire.

Chapter 3: "Castles of Dreams"

1. ASW, *Monthly Journals* 81 (March 1940), MSS 78/ASW/4/1/20, MRC.

2. The British, in fact, were partially responsible for the developing East-West confrontation that had dire results for world labor's ambitions. See Ritchie Ovendale, ed., *The Foreign Policy of the British Labour Government, 1945–51* (Leicester, U.K.: Leicester University Press, 1984), esp. his "Introduction," 1–20, and D. Cameron Watt's "Britain, the United States, and the Opening of the Cold War," in *Foreign Policy of the British Labour Government,* 43–60.

3. Henry Pelling makes this argument in *The British Communist Party: A Historical Profile* (London: Black, 1958).

4. Peter Weiler, *British Labor and the Cold War* (Stanford, Calif.: Stanford University Press, 1988), 8; see also Gabriel Kolko, *Politics of War: The World and United States Foreign Policy, 1943–45* (New York: Random House, 1969).

5. George H. Gallup, *The Gallup International Public Opinion Polls: Great Britain, 1937–75*, vol. 1 (New York: Random House, 1976), 232, 377, 381, 446–47.

6. This is, of course, the classic problem and purpose of social history—discovering the world that the majority of people inhabited and that has been overlooked by those concerned with the higher reaches of status and power. In contrast to the historian of the lower classes of earlier centuries, the contemporary historian has a wealth, even an embarrassment, of sources. In part this is the result of better record keeping and the recourse to such modern techniques as oral history. A significant contrast in social dynamics is also responsible for the relative abundance of source material, for working people in Britain became more educated, articulate, and powerful than in earlier eras. Their contention for and occasional achievement of power necessarily generated an enormous historical record, although, as always, it takes great perseverance to learn the thinking and actions of the mass of people previously considered unimportant or unproblematic. Given the wealth of source material now available, including newspapers, letters, diaries, memoirs, and oral histories, it is quite possible to ascertain the history of working-class thought in the twentieth century.

7. For a discussion of contrasting survey techniques see A. Strauss and J. Corbin, *Basics of Qualitative Research* (Newbury Park, Calif: Sage, 1990).

8. Mass-Observation, founded in the thirties by Tom Harrisson, Charles Madge, and Humphrey Jennings, attempted to create an "anthropology of ourselves" by conducting fieldwork among the British people. By the mid-1940s Mass-Observation employed hundreds of observers around the country, recording what they saw and heard of daily life in public, in peoples' homes, workplaces, and pubs. The group also engaged in specific studies and during the war worked for the Ministry of Information. The records of Mass-Observation, housed at the University of Sussex, provide an incomparable resource for understanding popular culture and politics. The surveyors were most often anonymous. In references to M-O file reports (FR) and topic collections (TC), the authors and interviewers are often cited only by initials.

9. For examples of middle-class ideological flexibility at two key moments when both Communists and non-Communists went through ideological flip-flops, see OWI, Division of Surveys, "Women and the War," 8/6/42, RG 44, Box 1798, E162, no file; OWI, Division of Surveys, "Special Memorandum No. 85, Attitudes Toward International Problems," 8/31/43, RG 44, Box 1803, E164, no file, NARS—Suitland, Md.; Survey Research Center, "Public Attitudes Toward Russia and United States–Russian Relations, Part II: Attitudes and Beliefs About Russia" (paper, Survey Research Center 4/47), Institute for Social Research (ISR) Report #220, p. 32, ISR Library; Office of Public Affairs, Division of Public Studies, U.S. Department of State, "Special Report on American Opinion: Opinion of American Labor Organizations on International Questions, January 1, 1948–March 21, 1948," 3/24/49, RG 59, Box 19, File: "Curr. Attitudes of Am. Labor," p. 14, NARS; Mass-Observation, "Feelings About Russia," *Mass-Observation Bulletin,* March 23, 1943, p. 10, FR 1634, Mass-Observation Archive (hereafter M-O Archive), University of Sussex, Brighton; Angus Calder, *The People's War: Britain, 1939–45* (New York: Pan-

theon, 1969), 75; Bill Jones, *The Russia Complex: The British Labour Party and the Soviet Union* (Manchester, U.K.: Manchester University Press, 1977), 33–54.

10. Survey Research Center, "Public Attitudes Toward Russia and United States–Russian Relations, Part I: Attitudes Toward United States–Russian Relations" (paper, Survey Research Center, 3/47), ISR Report #219, p. ii, ISR Library.

11. Ibid., 13, 21.

12. On this issue see Noam Chomsky, *American Power and the New Mandarins* (New York: Pantheon, 1969), 309–20, 323–59; C. Wright Mills, *White Collar: The American Middle Classes* (New York: Oxford University Press, 1951), 324–54.

13. James E. Cronin, *Labour and Society in Britain* (London: Batsford Academic and Educational, 1984), 135.

14. David Butler and Jennie Freeman, *British Political Facts, 1900–60* (London: Macmillan, 1963), 233.

15. Gallup, *Polls: Great Britain,* 203.

16. L. E. Ransom, "Postscript" to "Where There's a Wheel: Experiences of an RAF M[otor] T[ransport] . . . During World War II," manuscript, 87/42/1, p. 1, Imperial.

17. Patricia Yu Lin, "Perils Awaiting Those Deemed to Rise Above Their Allotted Status: The Social Impact of Overseas Evacuation of British Children in the Second World War" (bachelor's thesis, Princeton University, Princeton, N.J., 1991).

18. Questionnaire of Ivy Streatham (pseudonym), cited in Yu Lin, "Perils Awaiting."

19. Walter Citrine, *In Russia Now* (London: Hale, 1942), 3.

20. J. H. Witte, "The One That Didn't Get Away," manuscript, J. H. Witte Papers, 87/12/1, pp. 155–59, Imperial.

21. John Lilley, letter to the editor, *Railway Review,* July 10, 1942, MSS 127/NU/4/1/30, MRC.

22. "Pro Bono Publico," letter to the editor, *Railway Review,* June 15, 1945.

23. NUR, "Proceedings and Reports . . . 1944: Reports to and Decisions of the Special Executive Meetings . . . ," September 1944, MSS 127/NU/1/1/35, p. 125, MRC.

24. Raphael Samuel argues that British Communists owed their successes in the thirties and forties to the development, or attempted development, of a form of national communism. Samuel's argument does make some sense, but he underestimates how much the Communists' success was the result of their identification as the party of Soviet-oriented internationalism. The Communists, like their counterparts in Labour, rode on the back of an upsurge in nationalism *and* internationalism. Raphael Samuel, "Communism in Britain" (paper presented at "Back to the Future" conference at South Bank Polytechnic, London, July 9, 1988); see also his "The Lost World of British Communism," *New Left Review* 154 (November–December 1985): 3–53; 156 (March–April 1986): 63–113; 165 (September–October 1987): 52–91; and *Patriotism: The Making and Unmaking of British National Identity* (New York: Routledge, 1989).

25. ASW, *Monthly Journals* 80 (June 1939), MSS 78/ASW/4/1/19, MRC.

26. On the problems of the achievement of corporate forms of industrial organization, see Michael Dintenfass, review of Keith Middlemas, *Politics in Industrial Society, Bulletin*

of the Society for the Study of Labour History 41 (Autumn 1980): 63–65; and Robert Lowe, "The Ministry of Labour: Fact and Fiction," *Bulletin of the Society for the Study of Labour History* 41 (Autumn 1980): 23–28.

27. G. A. W. Tomlinson, *Coal-Miner* (London: Hutchinson, n.d. [1937]), 92ff.

28. For more on working-class conservatism see Robert McKenzie and Allan Silver, *Angels in Marble: Working-Class Conservatives in Urban England* (London: Heineman, 1968); Alan J. Lee, "Conservatism, Traditionalism, and the British Working Class," in *Ideology and the Labour Movement,* ed. David E. Martin and David Rubinstein (London: Croom Helm, 1979). Hugh Cunningham takes the contrary view that the true symbols of patriotism, the monarchy, the church, and the empire were above party concerns. I disagree, as should be evident. Cunningham, "The Conservative Party and Patriotism," in *Englishness: Politics and Culture, 1880–1920,* ed. Robert Colls and Philip Dodd (London: Croom Helm, 1986), 283–307.

29. James Hinton takes a very different view of working-class nationalism in midcentury in his "Voluntarism versus Jacobinism: Labor, Nation, and Citizenship in Britain, 1850–1950," *International Labor and Working Class History* 48 (Fall 1995): 68–90.

30. Patrick K. Fyrth, "Seaman's War," manuscript, Fyrth Papers, 87/42/1, pp. 77–78, Imperial.

31. Bill Jones, *The Russia Complex: The British Labour Party and the Soviet Union* (Manchester, U.K.: Manchester University Press, 1977), treats the background of the Labour leadership's infatuation with the USSR and then argues that Soviet policy in the cold war brought an end to the Russia complex. In a more general study F. S. Northedge and Audrey Wells, *Britain and Soviet Communism: The Impact of a Revolution* (London: Macmillan, 1982), emphasize domestic factors.

32. The National Council of Labour roundly condemned the invasion in its policy document, *Labour's Aims in War and Peace,* (London: Lincoln Praeger, 1940). On the genesis of Labour's policy toward Finland see Trevor Burridge, *Clement Attlee: A Political Biography* (London: Cape, 1985), 162–63. Sir Walter Citrine got into the act after a tour of besieged Finland with *My Finnish Diary* (Harmondsworth, U.K.: Penguin, 1940).

33. TGWU, "General Secretary's Sixty-Ninth Quarterly Report," Appendix 1, "Minutes and Records of the General Executive Council," XVII (1940), MSS 126/T&G/1/1/18, p. 96, MRC.

34. ASW, *Monthly Journals* 81 (March 1940).

35. Bryn Roberts, "Book Review," *Public Employees Journal* (March 1940), MSS 281, MRC.

36. Mass-Observation, "Feelings About Russia," *Mass Observation Bulletin,* March 23, 1943, FR 1634, p. 10, M-O Archive.

37. G.H./L.E./D.H., "Survey 1940", 2 December 1940 and 12 December 1940, TC25/7/H, M-O Archive.

38. Mass-Observation, "Feelings About Russia," p. 10. Angus Calder concurs, finding

the public "strangely unimpressed by anti-Russian propaganda." Calder, *The People's War,* 75. Bill Jones finds this continuing support as well. Jones, *Russia Complex,* 33–54.

39. Both Jones, *Russia Complex,* and Northedge and Wells, *Britain and Soviet Communism,* collapse popular beliefs.

40. Winston Churchill, *The Grand Alliance* (Boston: Houghton Mifflin, 1951), 371.

41. Citrine, *In Russia Now,* 5.

42. This treaty, incidentally, assured the Soviets of British acceptance of their territorial interests in Eastern Europe by recognizing the USSR's 1940 borders, including the Baltic states and eastern Poland. This acceptance was duplicated among most working people, as this chapter demonstrates. On the treaty itself see Llewellyn Woodward, *British Foreign Policy in the Second World War,* vol. 2 (London: HMSO, 1971), 244–52.

43. *Railway Review,* September 5, 1941.

44. Citrine, *In Russia Now,* 5.

45. Security Executive, "The Communist Party: Policy of the Ministry of Information," 6 November 1941, FO371/29523, PRO.

46. Figures from James Hinton, "Coventry Communism: A Study of Factory Politics in the Second World War," *History Workshop* 10 (Autumn 1980): 90. For instance, the *Daily Worker* became the source for expert information about the Soviet Union. See Douglas Hyde, *I Believed* (1950; reprint, London: Reprint Society, 1952), 114–15.

47. E.G., "Mass Demonstration for the Opening of the Second Front, Trafalgar Square, London, 26 July 1942, TC25/8/J, M-O Archive.

48. Ibid.; E.G., "First Anniversary of the British-Soviet Alliance: Demonstration and Pageant at the Empress Hall, Earls Court, 20 June 1942," TC25/8/K, M-O Archive. Churchill understood the symbolic meaning of songs, describing Labourites and Conservatives, respectively, as "those who wholeheartedly sing 'The Red Flag' and those who rejoice to sing 'Land of Hope and Glory.'" Quoted in Leon D. Epstein, *Britain: Uneasy Ally* (Chicago: University of Chicago Press, 1954), 178.

49. Paul Addison, *The Road to 1945: British Politics and the Second World War* (London: Cape, 1975), 134–35.

50. [Walter Citrine] to R. Barber [Secretary, Bradford Trades Council], 9 October 1941, Box 51, File 947/520, TUC.

51. National Help for Russia Fund, "Accounts for the Period 23d September 1941 to 31st December 1945," Box 624, File 947/525, TUC.

52. H. W. Franklin, letter to the editor, *Railway Review,* September 26, 1941, MSS 127/NU/4/1/29, MRC.

53. Citrine, *In Russia Now,* 10.

54. Ibid., 13.

55. "Observitur," "Amongst the Nons: Canvassing Among the Hills," *Railway Review,* August 15, 1941, MSS 127/NU/4/1/29, MRC.

56. J.H., "Feelings About Russia," 20 November 1942, FR 1492, M-O Archive.

57. D.H., "Indirects," 6 December 1941, TC25/13/B, M-O Archive.

58. *Railway Review,* September 5, 1941. Conversely, according to one woodworker, Hitler's most damning crime was his effort to become a "rich man" by forcing people to buy copies of *Mein Kampf,* "a costly book." John Davison, letter to the editor, ASW *Monthly Journal,* January 1940.

59. MOI, "Home Intelligence Weekly Report, No. 114," 21 January 1943, INF1/292, PRO.

60. J.H., "Feelings About Russia," 20 November 1942, FR 1492, M-O Archive.

61. For a detailed study of industrial conflict in the war, see Richard Croucher, *Engineers at War* (London: Merlin, 1982). Also, Mass-Observation, *War Factory* (London: Gollanz, 1943); Mass-Observation, *People in Production* (London: Murray, 1942). For the general problem of social conflict in wartime, see Harold L. Smith, ed., *War and Social Change: British Society in the Second World War* (Manchester, U.K.: Manchester University Press, 1986), which offers a collections of essays detailing the continuation of gender, class, and cultural conflict during the war. This new literature revises an older thesis first introduced by the official histories of the war and developed by such historians as Arthur Marwick, that the war led to a vast social transformation because it at once brought social problems to the fore and helped Britons overcome their divisions. See Richard Titmuss, *Problems of Social Policy* (London: HMSO, 1950); Arthur Marwick, *War and Social Change in the Twentieth Century: A Comparative Study of Britain, France, Germany, Russia, and the United States* (New York: St. Martin's, 1974).

62. On the apprentice strikes see Stuart Bloomfield, "The Apprentice Boys' Strikes of the Second World War," *Llafur* 3 (Spring 1981): 53–67.

63. Croucher, *Engineers at War,* 87–90.

64. MOI, "Home Intelligence Weekly Reports, #50," 17 September 1941; MOI, "Home Intelligence Weekly Reports, #52," 1 October 1941, INF1/292, PRO.

65. MOI, "Home Intelligence Weekly Reports, #61," 3 December 1941, INF1/292, PRO. Not all factories were so easily affected—in some the cynicism was too deep. The Air Ministry reported that in one group of aircraft factories "the feeling is that the present output could be trebled. . . . The Russian campaign does not seem to have any effect on production" in these plants. Similar problems occurred in southern shipyards. However, in yards in the north, an observer noted, "Everyone sets to with a will and efficiency is very high." The observer attributed the contrast to the government's ownership of the southern shipyards, whereas private ownership was the rule in the north, although northern pro-Sovietism may have had an effect. Mass-Observation, "Report on Effects of Russian Campaign on Feelings about Industrial Output," 12 December 1941, FR 995, M-O Archive.

Enthusiasm for the USSR was manipulated or feigned by Communist activists in a number of plants. This manipulation makes some evidence of changing workplace conditions questionable, because the reporters may not have known the difference between coordinated Communist activity and spontaneous feeling. Often the evidence given for attitudes toward the USSR is the appearance of wall posters, chalking of slogans, and a new attitude on the part of shop stewards. Because many shop stewards were Communists and the party members controlled many of the stewards' organizations, it is plausible that stewards' attitudes may have differed from the mass of the workers'. The effect on labor attitudes may have been more apparent than real. Yet the response was too widespread to be simply a product of Communist public relations. Furthermore, enough right-wing and left-wing Labourites actively involved themselves in the agitation to ensure that pro-Soviet agitation did not solely originate with the Communist Party. Even so, some caution needs to be used to distinguish popular sentiment from organized activities of any party or faction. I have tried to distinguish manifestations of sentiments held by small groups of workers of any party from those held by the great mass of workers.

66. MOI, "Scottish Miners, Appendix II, Home Intelligence Weekly Report: No. 105," 8 October 1942, INF1/292, PRO.

67. MOI, "Home Intelligence Weekly Report: No. 82," 29 April 1942, INF1/292, PRO.

68. MOI, "Home Intelligence Weekly Reports," various 1941–43, INF1/292, PRO.

69. A.P.H., "Less Nonsense" [n.d., 1943], Bevin Papers, BEVN I, Box 6, File 14, Churchill.

70. Citrine, *In Russia Now.* The *Daily Herald* of London articles appeared November 10–20, 1941.

71. MOI, "Appendix 1: Impressions of the Visit of the Soviet Trades Union Delegation, Home Intelligence Weekly Report, No. 70," 4 February 1942, INF1/292, PRO.

72. [A. R. Rollin], "With the Soviet Trade Union Delegation: Description of Visit" [n.d., 1942], A. R. Rollin Papers, MSS 240/T/3/22, MRC.

73. C.M., "TUC Meeting for Russian Delegates, Empress Hall, Earl's Court," 25 January 1942, TC75/6/D, M-O Archive.

74. C. F. A. Warner, "Comments on Request for Testimony of USSR Delegation to House of Commons," 17 January 1942, FO371/32919a, PRO.

75. See Penny Summerfield, *Women Workers in the Second World War* (London: Croom Helm, 1984), 185–91.

76. *Yorkshire Evening Post,* January 5, 1942.

77. MOI, "Visit of the Soviet Trades Union Delegation, Home Intelligence Weekly Report No. 70," 4 February 1942, INF1/292, PRO.

78. MOI, "Home Intelligence Special Report, No. 36: Complacency in Factories" 9 December 1942, INF1/292, PRO.

79. M. W. Irwin, t/s manuscript, Irwin Papers, 89/5/1, p. 91, Imperial.

80. *Manchester Evening News,* January 1942 (day reference misplaced).

81. E.G., "Special Report: The Anglo-Soviet Trade Union Conference at the Albert Hall, London, 18 January 1942," TC25/8/K, M-O Archive.

82. MOI, "Special Report No. 36: Complacency in Factories," 9 December 1942, INF1/293, PRO.

83. *Manchester Evening News,* September 14, 1943; *St. Helens' Newspaper,* September 17, 1943. On the experience of the delegations in general see Denis McShane, "Unfriendly Delegations" (paper delivered at the 26th Linz Conference of the Internationale Tagung der Historiker der Arbeiterbewegung, September 1990, Linz, Austria).

Chapter 4: "What We Want We Shan't Get"

1. Mass-Observation, "Good and Bad Omens for the Post War World," *Mass-Observation Bulletin,* April–May 1945, FR 2234, M-O Archive.

2. Allan Bullock, *Ernest Bevin: Foreign Secretary* (London: Heinemann, 1983), 639; Anthony Adamthwaite, "Britain and the World, 1945–49: The View From the Foreign Office," *International Affairs* 61 (Spring 1985): 229.

3. Mass-Observation, "Various Indirects Collected During the Week of 15th March 1943," 22 March 1943, FR 1630, M-O Archive.

4. MOI, "Home Intelligence Weekly Report No. 158, 14 October 1943"; "Home Intelligence Weekly Report No. 184, 14 April 1944," INF1/292, PRO.

5. E.G., International Indirects, 25 October 1945, TC50/1/H, M-O Archive.

6. Mass-Observation, "World Organization and the Future: Changing Attitudes, February to June," 6 June 1946, FR 2397, M-O Archive.

7. Mass-Observation, "Attitudes to Russia, 7 November 1945, 11 April 1946," FR 2301, p. 8, M-O Archive.

8. Ibid., 9.

9. Blackburn to John and Lil Blackburn, 12 October 1945, V. F. G. Blackburn Papers, 88/19/1, Imperial.

10. Tom Harrisson and H. D. Willcock, "British Opinion Moves Toward a New Synthesis," *Public Opinion Quarterly* 11 (Fall 1947): 328–30.

11. Ibid., 330.

12. Leon D. Epstein, *Britain: Uneasy Ally* (Chicago: University of Chicago Press, 1954), 100.

13. Tom Harrisson, draft of article for *Public Opinion Quarterly,* May 1947, FR 2493, p. 29, M-O Archive. Middle-class people, Mass-Observation found, disapproved of the USSR and the United States in equally large numbers. In contrast, 44 percent of the working people surveyed disapproved of the Americans, and 38 percent disliked the Russians. Predictably, many more wage earners than middle-income people—24 percent to 12 percent, respectively—approved of the workers' state. For the results, see Survey 1 in the Appendix.

14. D.W., "Indirects," 6 December 1941, TC/25/13/B, M-O Archive.

15. MOI, "Home Intelligence Special Report No. 8: British Public Opinion and the United States," 23 February 1942, INF1/293, p. 7, PRO. Perhaps the greatest factual dispute in the debate about the USSR in the 1930s in Great Britain involved relative standard of living. See, for example, Sidney Webb and Beatrice Webb's favorable findings in *Soviet Communism: A New Civilization,* 3d ed. (London: Longmans, Green, 1944), 653–54, 698–714; and Walter Citrine's unfavorable ones in *I Search for Truth in Russia,* rev. ed. (London: Routledge, 1938), 63, 90–99, and passim.

16. Mass-Observation, "Attitudes to Foreigners," April 1943, FR 1669Q, M-O Archive. For the full results see Survey 2 in the Appendix.

17. See, for instance, the *Railway Review,* various issues for 1942.

18. Mass-Observation, "Anti-Americanism," 26 January 1947, FR 2454, M-O Archive.

19. A popular quip was that the Americans were "overpaid, over sexed and over here." Angus Calder, *The People's War: Britain, 1939–45* (New York: Pantheon, 1969), 307–11.

20. Harrisson, draft of article for *Public Opinion Quarterly*, p. 29.

21. G.S.T., "Russia," 7 November 1945, TC25/15/F, M-O Archive.

22. Walter Citrine, "America, 1943," vol. 2, diary, Citrine Papers, IV 1.4, p. 92ff, LSE.

23. Amalgamated Engineering Union, "Report of the AEU Delegation to the USA, March and April 1949" (London: [n.p.] 1949), William H. Stokes Papers, MSS 289/21/35, MRC.

24. Walter Citrine, *In Russia Now* (London: Hale, 1942), 113.

25. W. H. Stokes, "Trade Unions and Peace" [notes for speech], n.d. [1947], William H. Stokes Papers, MSS 289/30/69, MRC.

26. John Benstead, "Labour Party Conference," *Railway Review*, June 7, 1946, NUR Collection, MSS/NU/4/1/34, MRC.

27. Henry M. Pelling, *America and the British Left: From Bright to Bevan* (New York: New York University Press, 1957), 148–59.

28. For the classic expression of this doctrine see Winston Churchill, *Europe Unite: Speeches, 1947–48* (Boston: Houghton Mifflin, 1950). Geoffrey Warner points out that the Conservatives' adoption of European unification was more a handy political device to use against Labour than it was Tory dogma. The British, by rejecting the Schuman plan for integrating European coal and steel production and the Pleven plan for a European army, cast their lot with the Commonwealth and the United States. They did accept integration with Europe when the United States would be involved, as with NATO and the Marshall Plan. Geoffrey Warner, "The Labour Governments and the Unity of Europe, 1945–51," in *The Foreign Policy of the British Labour Governments*, ed. Ritchie Ovendale (Leicester, U.K.: Leicester University Press, 1984), 61–82; John Grahl, "A Fateful Decision? Labour and the Schuman Plan," in *Labour's High Noon: The Government and the Economy, 1945–51*, ed. Jim Fyrth (London: Lawrence and Wishart, 1993), 145–61.

29. The material that follows is based on Jerzy Zubrzycki, *Polish Immigrants in Britain* (The Hague: Martinus Nijhoff, 1956), which remains the standard work on the Polish presence in the United Kingdom. See also J. A. Tannahil, *European Volunteer Workers in Britain* (Manchester, U.K.: Manchester University Press, 1958); Kenneth Lunn, "The Employment of Polish and European Volunteer Workers in the Scottish Coalfields, 1945–50," in *Towards a Social History of Mining in the Nineteenth and Twentieth Centuries*, ed. K. Tenflede (Munich: Beck, 1992).

30. MOI, "Home Intelligence Weekly Reports, #134," 24 April 1943, INF1/292, PRO.

31. Mass-Observation, *Mass-Observation Bulletin*, May 10, 1943, FR 1676, p. 16, M-O Archive.

32. Mass-Observation found an increase in mixed feelings toward the Poles and a decline in both negative and positive ideas. Mass-Observation, "Attitudes to Foreigners," April 1943, FR1669Q, M-O Archive. See Survey 2 in the Appendix.

33. Mass-Observation, *Mass-Observation Bulletin*, May 10, 1943, 16.

34. Llewellyn Woodward, *British Foreign Policy in the Second World War,* vol. 2 (London: HMSO, 1971), 614–16.

35. Zubrzycki, *Polish Immigrants,* 57–58.

36. MOI, "Home Intelligence Weekly Reports: No. 164," 25 November 1943, INF1/292, PRO.

37. Zubrzycki, *Polish Immigrants,* 40ff.

38. Ibid., 82, 86.

39. Zygmunt Nagorski Jr., "Liberation Movements in Exile," *Journal of Central European Affairs* 10 (July 1950): 134.

40. Trades Union Congress, *Report of Proceedings at the 78th Annual Trades Union Congress* (London: TUC, 1946), 357.

41. Zubrzycki, *Polish Immigrants,* 170; Tannahil, *Volunteer Workers,* 57–65.

42. Among the unions refusing Poles membership were the Amalgamated Society of Woodworkers (ASW), the Amalgamated Engineering Union, the National Union of Railwaymen (NUR), and the National Union of Public Employees (NUPE). In most cases the locals and districts promoting anti-Polish positions were in the northwest and the Clyde regions. Both the railway union and the Transport and General Workers' Union (TGWU) originally supported the government position, but by 1947 all urged repatriation. NUPE, "Minutes of the Executive Council," 1 September 1946, MSS 281, MRC; NUR, "Proceedings and Reports, " for September 1946, September 1947, June 1947, March 1949, MSS 127/NU/1/1/39–45, MRC; ASW, *Monthly Journal* 87 (August 1947); ASW, "Minutes of the Executive Committee," August 1946, MSS 78/ASW/1/1/24, MRC; TGWU, *Minutes of the Executive Council,* XXV (16 September 1947), MSS 126/T&G/1/128, MRC.

43. Zubrzycki maintains that the TGWU's Polish sections promoted pluralism and tolerance because it kept in people's minds "the existence of the problem of Polish *Political* refugees" [his emphasis]. See *Polish Immigrants,* 101–102.

44. Nagorski, "Liberation Movements," 12.

45. Bullock, *Ernest Bevin: Foreign Secretary,* 274.

46. Zubrzycki, *Polish Immigrants,* 110.

47. MOI, "Home Intelligence Weekly Reports, No. 199," 27 July 1944, INF1/292, PRO.

48. Tannahil, *Volunteer Workers,* 57–65.

49. Kenneth Lunn, "Race Relations or Industrial Relations? Race and Labour in Britain, 1880–1950," *Immigrants and Minorities* 4 (July 1985): 21–22.

50. Zubrzycki, *Polish Immigrants,* 99–100.

51. Ibid., 208.

52. Although substantial work has been done in this area, until recently most has been institutionally oriented. Recently, scholars have turned their attention to a more social analysis. See Lunn, "Race Relations or Industrial Relations?"; Kenneth Lunn, "'Race' and Immigration: Labour's Hidden History," in *Labour's High Noon,* ed. Fyrth, 227–42; Laura Tabili, *We Ask for British Justice: Workers and Racial Difference in Late Imperial Britain*

(Ithaca, N.Y.: Cornell University Press, 1994); J. L. Watson, ed., *Between Two Cultures: Migrants and Minorities in Britain* (Oxford: Oxford University Press, 1977).

53. Leonard Bloom, "Introduction," in Kenneth Little, *Negroes in Britain: A Study of Racial Relations in English Society* (1948; 2d rev. ed., London: Routledge and Kegan Paul, 1972), 4.

54. The ports had a checkered history. See, for instance, Roy May and Robin Cohen, "The Interaction of Race and Colonialism: A Case Study of the Liverpool Race Riots of 1919," *Race and Class* 16 (October 1974): 111–26; Neil Evans, "The South Wales Race Riots of 1919," *Llafur* 3 (1983): 76–87; Tabili, *We Ask for British Justice,* passim.

55. Michael Banton, *The Coloured Quarter: Negro Immigrants in an English City* (London: Cape, 1955), 189.

56. There were exceptions, of course, such as the Scottish woman who lived with her British-Honduran husband in her parents' home. Marika Sherwood, *Many Struggles: West Indian Workers and Service Personnel in Britain, 1939–45* (London: Karia Press, 1984), 122.

57. Ibid., 74.

58. Ibid.

59. Ibid., 118; MOI, "Home Intelligence Special Report: No. 34, Hondurasian [*sic*] Lumbermen in Scotland," 3 December 1942, INF1/293, PRO.

60. MOI, "Home Intelligence Weekly Report: No. 41. Special Report on the Merseyside and Clydeside," 16 July 1941, INF1/292, PRO.

61. Mass-Observation, "Report on Foreign Seamen's Organisations in Liverpool," 11 August 1941, FR 819, quotation at p. 5, M-O Archive.

62. Ibid.

63. NUS Executive Council Minutes, 24 October 1947, MSS 175/1/1/10, MRC.

64. Lunn, "Race Relations," 24.

65. Little, *Negroes in Britain,* 249–51.

66. Patrick K. Fyrth, "Seaman's War," manuscript, Fyrth Papers, 87/42/1, p. 34, Imperial.

67. Richard Croucher, *Engineers at War* (London: Merlin, 1982), 201.

68. W.A.L., Extracts from Diary, 10/9/41–26/1/41, 10 September 1941, TC75/7/A, M-O Archive.

69. Banton, *Coloured Quarter,* 145.

70. Dryden made the comparison quite explicitly in 1690, when he suggested the English conquerors of Ireland should "Each bring his love a Bogland captive home; / Such proper pages will long trains become; / With copper collars and brawny backs / Quite to put down the fashion of our blacks." The reference to copper collars recalls those used on black slaves and many prisoners in general. Quoted in Little, *Negroes in Britain,* p. 190. Of course, treatment of the Christian (if papist) Irish was not exactly the same as that of blacks. The Irish did not, for instance, serve as slaves in the colonies, though conditions of indenture were indeed brutal. See Winthrop Jordan, *White over Black* (1968; reprint, New York: Norton, 1977), 87–88.

71. Little, *Negroes in Britain,* 255.

72. William Close, "William Close in the Second World War," manuscript, William Close Papers, 89/5/1, p. 5, Imperial.

73. Little, *Negroes in Britain,* 241.

74. Ibid., 244.

75. Kenneth O. Morgan, *Labour in Power, 1945–51* (Oxford: Oxford University Press, 1985), 184.

76. Little, *Negroes in Britain,* 254.

77. Louis Challoner, manuscript diary, Louis Challoner Papers, LCI/P479, p. 12.

78. MOI, "Home Intelligence Weekly Report: No. 58," 12 November 1941, INF1/292, PRO.

79. Hugh F. Wilson, "Changi to Burma," manuscript, 90/2/1, p. 21, Imperial.

80. MOI, "Home Intelligence Weekly Report: No. 58," 12 November 1941, INF1/292, PRO.

81. See, for instance, Partha Sarathi Gupta, *Imperialism and the British Labour Movement* (London: Macmillan, 1972); Nicholas Owen, "'Responsibility Without Power': The Attlee Governments and the End of British Rule in India," in *The Attlee Years,* ed. Nick Tiratsoo (London: Pinter, 1991), 167–89.

82. See Peter Weiler, *British Labour and the Cold War* (Stanford, Calif.: Stanford University Press, 1988), 27–52, for a critical analysis of the TUC's colonial policy in the 1930s. Weiler stresses the development of a corporative relationship between the government and the TUC as result of the 1930s collaboration in Trinidad and West Africa. For other critical views see Gupta, *Imperialism and the British Labour Movement,* 253; Sahadeo Basdeo, "The Role of the British Labour Movement in the Development of Labour Organisation in Trinidad, 1929–38," *Social and Economic Studies* 31 (March 1982): 40–73; Basdeo, "Walter Citrine and the British Caribbean Workers Movement During the Moyne Commission Hearing, 1938–39," *Journal of Caribbean History* (Barbados) 18 (1983): 43–59; Jeffrey Harrod, *Trade Union Foreign Policy: A Study of British and American Trade Union Activities in Jamaica* (Garden City, N.Y.: Doubleday, 1972). Marjorie Nicholson, *The TUC Overseas: The Roots of Policy* (London: Allen and Unwin, 1986), 215–53, presents a more sympathetic, even naive assessment of TUC policy. Unlike the U.S. conceptions of "free trade unionism" being developed at the time, the TUC promoted political involvement for unions along the model of the TUC and the Labour Party.

83. TUC Colonial Advisory Committee, Memorandum, 22 December 1937, Arthur Creech Jones Papers, Box 14, File 1, Rhodes House.

84. TGWU, "Minutes and Record of the Proceedings of the Ninth Biennial Delegate Conference" (London, n.d. [1941]), MSS 126/T&G/1/4/9, p. 32, MRC.

85. Quoted in Morgan, *Labour in Power,* 193.

86. Ibid., 190–92; quotation at 192.

87. Bevin to L. S. Amery, 24 September 1941, Bevin Papers, BEVN I, Box 3, File 1, Churchill.

88. The left-wing NUR called for immediate dominion status in 1944, while the ASW echoed the Labour Party line. NUR, "Proceedings and Reports for the Year 1944," February Special Executive Meeting, MSS 127/NU/1/1/35, MRC; ASW, *Monthly Journals* 83 (September 1942), MSS 78/ASW/4/22, p. 375, MRC.

89. TGWU, "Minutes and Record of the Proceedings of the Eleventh Biennial Delegate Conference" (London, n.d. [1947]), MSS 126/T&G/1/4/11, MRC.

90. In the ASW, for instance, many locals controlled by the right wing voiced their support for any effort to "settle the grievances of the Indian people," as the Newcastle branch put it. ASW, *Monthly Journals* 86 (March 1945): 104.

91. See ASW, *Monthly Reports,* December 1944, MSS 78/ASW/4/23, MRC.

92. H. L. Bullock, "The Indian Scene," (ASW) *Monthly Journals* 89 (March 1948).

93. Mass-Observation, *Peace and the Public* (London: Longmans, Green, 1947), 50. Mass-Observation's analyst believed that these figures understated nationalist sentiment because an internationalist answer was the expected reply, given Labour Party dogma. The author of the report stressed that such opinions were actually quite volatile and "reflect the atmosphere of the time." This critique seems designed to reassure patriots, because ideas always reflect their times—though this does not disprove the assertion that the ideas were volatile. Mass-Observation, "World Organisation and the Future: Changing Attitudes February to June," 6 June 1946, FR 2397, pp. 20, 53, 55, M-O Archive.

94. Ibid., 7.

95. Local economic power may have been a different issue, as Herbert Morrison, lord president of the council and Bevin's chief rival in the cabinet, exclaimed in rejecting the Schuman plan: "It's no good, we cannot do it, the Durham miners won't wear it." Quoted in Warner, "Labour Governments and the Unity of Western Europe," 73.

96. See, for instance, the extensive debates about workers' control in nationalized industries and whether nationalization of the railroads would change the work experience of the average railwayman in the *Railway Review* for 1947 and 1948. Leo Panitch maintains that Labour's policy and its role as an "integrative political party" contradicted the class militance that gave it strength. Panitch, *Social Democracy and Industrial Militancy: The Labour Party, the Trade Unions, and Incomes Policy, 1945–47* (Cambridge: Cambridge University Press, 1976), 1; see also Richard Hyman, "Praetorians and Proletarians: Unions and Industrial Relations," in *Labour's High Noon,* ed. Fyrth, 165–94.

97. J. W. Stafford, "On the Permanentway," *Railway Review,* March 2, 1945, MSS 127/NU/4/1/33, MRC.

98. Manchester Branch, CPGB, "Once More There Is Great News from Russia," *Factory News,* January 24, 1944, MSS 180/FN/6.ii, MRC.

99. Mass-Observation, *Peace and the Public,* 42.

100. David Butler and Jennie Freeman, *British Political Facts, 1900–60* (London: Macmillan, 1963), 124.

101. The Communist vote dropped precipitously in 1951 from 91,000 to 21,000 because, as part of its perennial effort to achieve unity with Labour, the Communist Party decided

to field only ten candidates, as opposed to one hundred the year before. Butler and Freeman, *British Political Facts,* 124; D. E. Butler, *The British General Election of 1951* (London: Macmillan, 1952), 49.

102. Butler, *Election of 1951,* 251–64.

103. James E. Cronin, *Labour and Society in Britain* (London: Batsford Academic and Educational, 1984), 132.

104. Mass-Observation, "Good and Bad Omens for the Postwar World," *Mass-Observation Bulletin,* April–May 1945, FR 2234, M-O Archive.

105. Harrisson, "British Opinion Moves Toward a New Synthesis," 339. For a classic study of the rise of mass culture and the deleterious effects of affluence on the Labour Party in the 1950s, see J. Goldthorpe and D. Lockwood, *The Affluent Worker in the Class Structure* (London: Cambridge University Press, 1969).

106. ASW, *Monthly Journals* 89 (April 1948).

107. Martin Harrison also found that expressions of political opinion in unions were mostly on the left. This does not prove, as he is careful to point out, that the rank-and-file always supported left-wing positions, only that the right did not use this forum. Harrison, *Trade Unions and the Labour Party Since 1945* (London: Allen and Unwin, 1960), 119–25.

108. Jacqueline Sax, Untitled survey on the Marshall Plan, 20 March 1948, FR 2575, p. 2, M-O Archive.

109. E.G., "International Indirects," 25 October 1945, TC50/1/H, M-O Archive.

110. Harrison, *Trade Unions and the Labour Party,* 123n. For more see Steve Fielding, "'Don't Know and Don't Care': Popular Political Attitudes in Labour's Britain, 1945–51," in *Attlee Years,* ed. Tiratsoo.

Chapter 5: "Hoodwinking Ourselves"

1. The most famous of these efforts were the talks of 1928 conducted by Bevin, Citrine, and Ben Turner, who then was chairman of the TUC and of the textile workers, with Sir Alfred Mond, head of the chemical giant ICI, and other liberal capitalists. The talks sought to establish cooperation between labor and industry, but the effort fell apart under the economic retrenchment brought on by the depression. See Alan Bullock, *Trade Union Leader, 1881–1940,* vol. 1 of *The Life and Times of Ernest Bevin* (London: Heinemann, 1960), 392–416; G. W. McDonald and H. Gospel, "The Mond-Turner Talks, 1927–33: A Study in Industrial Cooperation," *Historical Journal* 14 (Winter 1973): 807–29; Patrick Renshaw, "The Depression Years, 1918–31," in *Trade Unions in British Politics,* ed. Ben Pimlott and Chris Cook (London: Longman, 1982), 111–13.

2. The classic statement of 1920s opposition to the Communist Party is Walter Citrine, *Democracy or Disruption? An Examination of Communist Influences in the Trade Unions* (London: Trades Union Congress, 1928).

3. As with the CIO's Philip Murray, no one has written a good biography of Citrine. His two volumes of memoirs are *Men at Work* (London: Hutchinson, 1964) and *Two Careers* (London: Hutchinson, 1967).

4. Samuel Berger, "Labor Letter No. 7 (1944), 76th annual Conference of the TUC," 29 November 1944, Isador Lubin Papers, Personal Correspondence, Box 101, File: "British Labor News and Letters, 1944," Roosevelt Library.

5. Bevin to Woll, 20 February 1942, Bevin Papers, BEVN I, Box 6, File 55, Churchill.

6. On the National Minority Movement, the Communist-led insurgency, see Stuart Macintyre, *Little Moscows: Communism and Working-Class Militancy in Interwar Britain* (London: Croom Helm, 1980), 112–35; Roderick Martin, *Communism and the British Trade Unions, 1924–33: A Study of the National Minority Movement* (Oxford: Oxford University Press, 1969).

7. On the fight between left and right in the Labour Party, see Ben Pimlott, *Labour and the Left in the 1930s* (Cambridge, U.K.: Cambridge University Press, 1977).

8. Bullock, *Trade Union Leader,* 133–42; Stephen R. Graubard, *British Labour and the Russian Revolution, 1917–24* (Boston: Harvard University Press, 1956), 64–114.

9. See, for instance, Partha Sarathi Gupta, *Imperialism and the British Labour Movement* (London: Macmillan, 1972); Nicholas Owen, "'Responsibility Without Power': The Attlee Governments and the End of British Rule in India," in *The Attlee Years,* ed. Nick Tiratsoo (London: Pinter, 1991), 167–89.

10. The TUC's role in Spain is well detailed in Tom Buchanan, *The Spanish Civil War and the British Labour Movement* (Cambridge, U.K.: Cambridge University Press, 1991).

11. Bullock, *Trade Union Leader,* 624.

12. Quoted in Bullock, *Trade Union Leader,* 559.

13. Eden to Winston Churchill, 22 August 1941, PREM 4/21/3, PRO, quoted in Peter Weiler, *British Labor and the Cold War* (Stanford, Calif.: Stanford University Press, 1988), 56.

14. Quoted in Bill Jones, *The Russia Complex: The British Labour Party and the Soviet Union* (Manchester, U.K.: Manchester University Press, 1977), 35.

15. Citrine to Duff Cooper [copy of letter], 7 July 1941, Citrine Papers, I.4/7, LSE.

16. Paul Tofahrn, handwritten notes on Emergency General Council Meeting, IFTU, 7 December 1944, MSS 238/IF/1/48, MRC.

17. Citrine, *Two Careers,* 28.

18. Hugh Dalton, *The Second World War Diary of Hugh Dalton, 1940–45,* ed. Ben Pimlott (London: Cape, 1986), 783.

19. Ibid., 511.

20. Samuel Berger, "Labor Letter No. 7 (1944), 76th annual Conference of the TUC," 29 November 1944, Lubin Papers, Personal Correspondence, Box 101, File: "British Labor News and Letters, 1944," Roosevelt Library.

21. Quoted in A. Mcd. Gordon, "Report on the United States Labor Movement," 18 March 1944, BEVN I, Box 6, File 58, Bevin Papers, Churchill.

22. Although Citrine and Bevin generally claimed publicly that their differences were matters of style, not of substance, the conflict of the two most prominent trade unionists in the country inevitably affected matters of policy. See Bullock, *Trade Union Leader,* 591; Weiler, *British Labor and the Cold War,* 291n; Citrine, *Two Careers,* 357–58.

23. H. W. Franklin, "At the Blackpool TUC," *Railway Review* MSS 127/NU/4/1/30, MRC.

24. Keith Middlemas, *Politics in Industrial Society: The Experience of the British System Since 1911* (London: Andre Deutsch, 1979), 266–302.

25. Alan Bullock, *Minister of Labour, 1940–45*, vol. 2 of *The Life and Times of Ernest Bevin* (London: Heinemann, 1967), 142.

26. Middlemas, *Politics in Industrial Society,* 266–302, argues that Bevin expressed the dominant strain of TUC thinking in pushing for increased government control. It is true that Bevin sought corporatist solutions to labor problems during his tenure as minister of labor and national service. However, he offers little evidence that the trade unions as a whole willingly went along with this corporatist bias. Bullock, in *Minister of Labour,* says he believes Bevin worked miracles in getting the unions to agree to the level of control that they did. Both works understate the level of opposition within the TUC to such policies even in light of the national emergency. The unions successfully fought the elimination of collective bargaining and protested strongly against most control-of-labor rules, such as order 1305 of 1941, which made strikes illegal. Nevertheless, the unions were glad to obtain government protection. They were successful in achieving the best of both worlds; they had independence and government protection. On the union government relationship in the war see Denis Barnes and Eileen Reid, "A New Relationship: Trade Unions in the Second World War," in *Trade Unions in British Politics,* ed. Pimlott and Cook, 159–62, 165–67; Ian Taylor, "Labour and the Impact of War, 1939–45," in *The Attlee Years,* ed. Tiratsoo, 7–28.

27. Attlee to Bevin, 30 September 1941; and Bevin to Citrine, 24 September 1941, Bevin Papers, BEVN I, 3/1, Churchill.

28. Samuel Berger, "Bi-Monthly Labor Letter: No. 5," 1943, Lubin Papers, Personal Correspondence, Box 101, File: "British Labor, News and Letters, 1943," Roosevelt Library.

29. "Text of Official Communiqué of the Result of the Anglo-Soviet Trade Union Joint Committee," 26 October 1941, FO371/29640, PRO.

30. This is the argument made by James Hinton in "Coventry Communism: A Study of Factory Politics in the Second World War," *History Workshop* 10 (Autumn 1980): 90–118, and by Richard Croucher in *Engineers at War* (London: Merlin, 1982).

31. Trades Union Congress, *Report of Proceedings at the 73d Annual Trades Union Congress* (London: Cooperative Printing Society, 1941), 141.

32. Earnest Bell, "Transcription of Shorthand Notes Taken by Earnest A. Bell at First Meetings of Anglo-Soviet Trade Union Committee, Held in USSR, October, 1941," TUC, Box 625, File 947/230, pp. 13–14.

33. ASW, *Monthly Journal* 82 (July 1941).

34. ASW, *Monthly Journal* 82 (November 1941). The members of the executive council did pledge to fight for a return to straight time after the war.

35. ASW, *Monthly Journal* 85 (November 1943) and (December 1943).

36. ASW, *Monthly Journal* 85 (January 1944). At its meeting of November 26, 1943, the National Executive Council decided to censor the journal.

37. Minutes, National Executive Committee, ASW, 3 and 4 October 1944, MSS 78/ASW/1/1/22, MRC.

38. Frank Wolstencroft, "My Visit to Russia," ASW *Monthly Journal* 82 (December 1941).

39. Circular 16 dated from 1934 and had been passed to counteract the rise of the minority movement and the national unemployed workers' movement. It also forbade Trades Council contacts with proscribed organizations.

40. TGWU, "Minutes and Record of the Proceedings of the Tenth Biennial Delegate Conference, Held on August 2, 3, 4, and 5 1943," MSS 126/T&G/1/4/10, p. 34, MRC.

41. The General Council only grudgingly acceded to the lifting of the ban on Communists. It reserved the right to act against "disruption" because, as Citrine explained, the council members "are not convinced the disruptive tactics of the Communist Party have been abandoned." Of course, if this were the case, why retract the ban? Trades Union Congress, *Report of Proceedings at the 75th Annual Trades Union Congress* (London: Co-operative Printing Society, 1943), 337–39.

42. He did so in *Railway Review,* July 4, 1941.

43. In November 1941 G. W. Harrison of the Ministry of Labour spoke to Citrine's secretary, who told him that Citrine believed that whether to permit Potts's proposed trip was properly the Foreign Office's decision, but the refusal "must clearly be taken in the light of the arrangements made by the recent TU members to Russia, and that if Mr. Potts is allowed to go, other trade unions will [ask] for similar facilities." In other words, without taking a firm stance, Citrine was advising against the trip. This seems typical of his relationship with various government people, giving or taking advice without making it appear that it was given or taken. Potts finally got his trip to the USSR in 1942. Memo to Mr. [C. F. A.] Warner from Harrison [Ministry of Labour] 24 November 1941, FO371/29601, PRO. On the Fire Brigades' request see John Horner [secretary FBU] to Vincent Tewson [asst. general secretary, TUC], 28 October 1941, TUC, Box 51, File 947/520; F. R. Fermor [Hon. Sec. East Ham Trades Council] to Citrine, 12 September 1941, TUC, Box 51, File 947/520.

44. Vincent Tewson to F. R. Fermor, 31 October 1941, TUC, Box 51, File 947/520.

45. Citrine to Richard Law, 24 November 1941, FO371/29601, PRO.

46. Excerpt from AFL Executive Council minutes, 20 May 1942, Taft Papers, Box 6, File 3, Cornell.

47. "Transcription of Shorthand Notes Taken by Earnest A. Bell at First Meetings of Anglo-Soviet Trade Union Committee, Held in USSR, October, 1941," TUC, Box 625, File 947/230, pp. 14–15.

48. Ibid., 4.

49. Ibid.

50. World Trade Union Conference, *Report of the World Trade Union Conference* (London: TUC, 1945), 128.

51. Martin Harrison writes of arguments that unions should remain aloof from politics: "Such judgments spring either from wooly thinking or from a complete misappre-

hension of trade unionism. The unions have never been wholly isolated from politics, even in the days of the purest *laissez faire.*" Harrison, *Trade Unions and the Labour Party Since 1945* (London: Allen and Unwin, 1960), 13.

52. TUC, "Report of Meetings of Anglo-Soviet Trade Union Committee, Held at the Palace of Labour, Moscow, from June 25, 1943 to July 22, 1943, Inclusive," 2 September 1943, TUC, Box 625, File 947/233, minute #123.

53. Ibid.

54. Ibid., minute #124.

55. W. W. Craik, *Bryn Roberts and the National Union of Public Employees* (London: Allen and Unwin, 1955), 118–22.

56. F. R. Leggett, "Russian and British Trade Union Relations," 15 September 1943, LAB13/593, PRO.

57. Smollet to C. F. A. Warner, 8 October 1943, FO371/37055, PRO.

58. C. F. A. Warner, minute attached to Smollet to Warner.

59. Bryn Roberts, *The American Labour Split and Allied Unity* (London: Lawrence and Wishart, 1943), discussed the history of the AFL and CIO and gave a report of his travels in the United States during 1943. Not surprisingly for an industrial unionist, his work was heavily biased in favor of the CIO. Roosevelt to Roberts, 1/10/44, and Roberts to FDR, 12/17/44, PPF 8614, File: "Roberts, Bryn," Roosevelt Library.

60. Bryn Roberts, "The Rift in the American Trade Union Movement," *Public Employees Journal,* April 1943, MSS 281, pp. 10–11, MRC.

61. During the late 1930s and 1940s the National Union of Public Employees (NUPE) grew at an astounding rate, increasing its membership from 13,000 when Roberts took over the practically moribund organization in 1934, to 105,000 in 1945. This organizational achievement did not win NUPE friends in the two general unions that competed for the same membership. NUPE promoted corporatist joint industrial councils as the solution to the problems of the low-wage county workers it organized. But the existing joint councils often excluded NUPE at the behest of the NUGMW. So NUPE fought for the creation of a national joint industrial council and for national wage agreements—which the NUGMW and the TGWU resisted. In this case the big unions opposed corporatism because it threatened their position at the negotiating table and because it would have allowed NUPE to make inroads in their territory. In fact, by the midforties the upstart organization had a larger membership than the public employee sections of the big general unions.

NUPE also found that Labour-controlled county and municipal councils were just as hard to negotiate with as those controlled by Conservatives. This proved to be a salutary, though only partially learned, lesson for those who saw nationalization as a panacea. It also prepared NUPE for the difficult task of organizing workers in the National Health Service, which it attempted after 1945. Craik, *Bryn Roberts,* 61, 108, and passim.

Chapter 6: "A Grave and Conscious Moral Force"

1. "Speech by the Rt. Hon. Ernest Bevin," 9 February 1945, Bevin Papers, BEVN II, Box 5, File 1, Churchill.

2. Harriman to F. D. Roosevelt, 7 March 1942, PSF Diplomatic File, Box 37, File: "Great Britain: Harriman, W. Averell, 1941–42," Roosevelt Library.

3. David Dilks, ed., *The Diaries of Sir Alexander Cadogan* (London: Cassell, 1971), 780, quoted in Anthony Adamthwaite, "Britain and the World, 1945–49: The View from the Foreign Office," *International Affairs* 61 (Spring 1985): 225.

4. Ernest Bevin, "Memo on the Diplomatic Services" [n.d.], Bevin Papers, BEVN I, Box 2, File 1, Churchill.

5. Adamthwaite, "Britain and the World," 225.

6. A new and complex portrait of the workings of the cabinet and the Foreign office in creating Britain's cold war policy has emerged recently. According to this synthesis, Bevin, convinced by the hard-line anti-Soviets on the Foreign Office's permanent staff, such as Christopher F. A. Warner and Orme Sargent, sought to press the moderate members of the cabinet, notably Clement Attlee, to take a more confrontational line with the Soviets, especially over the Balkans. Attlee had a more sympathetic attitude toward the USSR than Bevin but was swayed by the force of his foreign secretary's arguments and bureaucratic maneuvers. The debate about the new line toward the USSR took place without the participation of cabinet left-wingers like Aneurin Bevan and Stafford Cripps. Raymond Smith, "A Climate of Opinion: British Officials and the Development of British Soviet Policy, 1945–47," *International Affairs* 64 (Autumn 1988): 631–47.

7. The evolution of Labour thinking about foreign policy and the USSR occupies a major place in the historiography. The main issue is how the British Socialists dealt with their self-proclaimed comrades in a country with national interests that apparently clashed with their own. An important strain of current thinking is that Labour willy-nilly gave up its idealism for a consensual policy that adhered to an alliance with the United States in order to protect British power, respond to a lack of balance on the Continent, and counter a revolutionary upsurge around the world. Both Victor Rothwell, *Britain and the Cold War, 1941–47* (London: Cape, 1982), and Bill Jones, *The Russia Complex: The British Labour Party and the Soviet Union* (Manchester, U.K.: Manchester University Press, 1977), advance this position. However, Elaine Windrich sees a consistent socialism in Labour's foreign policy, *British Labour's Foreign Policy* (Stanford, Calif.: Stanford University Press, 1952). The problem is solved by considering, as is done here and by Michael R. Gordon, the tensions between the power of Socialist thinking among the rank-and-file and the urge among the leaders to serve the nation. Gordon, *Conflict and Consensus in Labour's Foreign Policy, 1914–65* (Stanford, Calif.: Stanford University Press, 1969), esp. 285–89.

8. Minute by Sir Frederick Leggett, 17 February 1944, LAB13/596, PRO.

9. J. E. Coulson to J. A. R. Pimlott, 26 February 1944, LAB13/596, PRO.

10. Minute by A. D. K. Owen on file: "Italian General Confederation of Labour," 13 January 1945, FO371/49843, PRO.

11. George Hall to Bevin, 8 November 1943, LAB13/596, PRO; Bevin to Sir Frederick Leggett, 10 November 1943, LAB13/596, PRO.

12. Minute by A. D. K. Owen on file: "Italian General Confederation of Labour." See also Leggett to N. B. Ronald, 17 January 1943, FO371/49843, PRO.

13. Bevin to Halifax, 28 March 1944, Bevin Papers, BEVN I, 3/2, Churchill Library.

14. Ibid.

15. J. E. Coulson to J. A. R. Pimlott, 26 February 1944, LAB13/596, PRO.

16. Memorandum of meeting of Eden and Citrine, 20 December 1944, FO371/50776, PRO.

17. A. E. Carthy to Citrine, 7 July 1944, TUC, Box 475, File 910.1 II.

18. "Memorandum of Interview, Sir Walter Citrine and Mr. Eden," 20 December 1944, TUC, Box 477, File 910.11.

19. Ernest Bell to Owen, 28 December 1944, FO371/50776, PRO.

20. "Soviet Trade Union Delegation's Visit to Britain," *Soviet Monitor* (December 1, 1942) #5432, FO371/43441, PRO.

21. World Trade Union Conference, *Report of the World Trade Union Conference* (London: TUC, 1945), 226–27.

22. Antoni Kolodziej to TUC, 8 February 1945, TUC, Box 476, File 910.1.

23. WTUC, *Report,* 45.

24. Grew to Habana, 2/20/45, RG 59, 800.5043/2-2045, NARS.

25. WTUC, *Report,* 85ff.

26. TUC, International Committee Minutes, 16 January 1945, TUC, Box 1854, File 901.1.

27. *Afro American* (Washington, D.C.), October 13, 1945.

28. WTUC, *Report,* 194.

29. The conference took a leaf from Lord Balfour and amended the resolution with the caveat that the Jewish nation be established "respecting the rights and legitimate interests of other national groups." How this was to be accomplished was not specified. WTUC, *Report,* 186, 191. The problem of Palestine was one of the most difficult at the conference, but the TUC managed to avoid contradicting British policy at this time. Of course, this was quite easy because the policy, formulated in the McDonald White Paper of 1939, was terribly ambiguous. The TUC and Labour had been officially pro-Zionist for years. But once in power the problems of ruling the strife-torn country forced Labour to back down; it too was unable to come up with an effective policy. The vagueness of the call for a national home with respect for the rights of other peoples in the region gave the TUC great latitude in the coming years.

Much of the conflict took place outside the London County Hall, where the World Conference was held. It was quite difficult for the TUC to decide which were legitimate Palestinian trade unions and which were not. The Palestine Labour League, a Palestinian section of the Zionist-Socialist Histadrut, demanded, with the support of its parent organization and a number of Zionist lobbyists in London, a seat at the conference. The Palestinian organizations protested vehemently. For its part, the Histadrut tried to deny representation to the two Palestinian union centers, claiming the idea of a voluntaristic trade union movement was "almost alien in oriental climes." Anything the Arabs claimed could not be believed: "Arab workers have no opinion of their own. Any statement which may be made by them is only what has been put in their mouths [by] others." Over the loud protests of Palestinian unions, the TUC invited the Labour League to send an observer. The delegate, George Nassar, turned out to be quite corrupt, as the Arabs had charged; he even left his hotel without paying the bill. The quotation about Arab workers appears in General Federation of Jewish Labour in Palestine [Histadrut], Department of Relations with Arab Workers, "A Survey of Arab Labour Organizations in Palestine," January 1945, MSS 159/3/D/39, MRC. See also Citrine to Arab Labour League, 24 March 1944, TUC, Box 475, File 910.1 I; A. E. McGhee to TUC, 14 April 1945, TUC, Box 476, File 910.1 I.

30. S. V. Zakharov, "The World Trade Union Conference in London," *Mirove Khozyaisko I Moravaya Politika [World Economy and World Politics]* 4 (Moscow, April 1945), translation by Foreign Office staff, FO371/47935, PRO.

31. Among these were the railwaymen, the TGWU, the woodworkers, the postal workers, and others. For instance, in 1942 the woodworkers had more than four thousand members in the Republic of Ireland, almost half of its total Irish membership. The railwaymen had more than nine thousand Irish members in 1948. ASW *Monthly Journal* (March 1942); NUR, "Agenda and Decisions of the Annual General Meeting, 1949," MSS 127/NU/1/1/46, p. 47, MRC.

32. National Executive Committee Minutes, 13 April 1945, MSS 78/ASW/1/1/23, p. 118, MRC.

33. Trades Union Congress, *Report of the Proceedings at the 77th Annual Trades Union Congress* (London: Cooperative Printing Society, 1945), 143; TUC, *Proceedings* (1946), 68–69.

34. On the evolution of Labour policy toward Germany see Trevor Burridge, *British Labour and Hitler's War* (London: Deutsch, 1976), 57–67.

35. *Seaman,* unsigned editorial written by Jarman, July–August 1944, MSS 41 tc 152c, MRC.

36. ITF Executive Committee minutes, Zurich, 3 May 1946, MSS 159/1/3/55, MRC.

37. J. H. Benstead, "World Trade Union Congress," *Railway Review,* February 16, 1945.

38. WTUC, *Report,* 237; "Minutes of the Fourth Meeting of the Anglo-Soviet Trade Union Committee," 6 October 1944, TUC, Box 625, File 947/230.

39. Lewis Lorwin, *The International Labor Movement* (New York: Harper, 1953), 209–10.

40. A. M. Phillips to G. Dennys, 13 November 1945, LAB13/986, PRO.

41. Sir Arthur Street to Citrine, 18 December 1945, LAB13/986, PRO.

42. Godfrey Ince to Street, 19 November 1945, LAB13/986, PRO.

43. Citrine to Bevin, 29 October 1946, LAB13/986, PRO. Both U.S. and British mili-

tary authorities opposed Germany-wide trade unions. The British thought the German union leaders were much less reliable than the Americans did. On the general problem of the reconstruction of German unions see Carolyn Eisenberg, "Working-Class Politics and the Cold War: American Intervention in the German Labor Movement," *Diplomatic History* 7 (Fall 1983): 283–306; Peter Weiler, *British Labor and the Cold War* (Stanford, Calif.: Stanford University Press, 1988), 165–85; Niethammer, "Structural Reform and a Compact for Growth: Conditions for a United Labor Movement in Europe After the Collapse of Fascism," in *The Origins of the Cold War and Contemporary Europe,* ed. Charles Maier (New York: New Viewpoints, 1978), 201–43; Rolf Steininger, "England und die deutsche Gewerkschaftsbewegung, 1945–46," *Archiv für Sozialgeschichte* 18 (1978): 41–90.

44. Minute by G. Dennys, 3 April 1946, LAB13/986, PRO; Philip Nichols [ambassador to Czechoslovakia] to Bevin, 20 June 1947, FO/371/67613, PRO.

45. Horst Lademacher et al., "Der Weltgewerkschaftsbund im Spannungsfeld des Ost-West Konflikts," *Archiv für Sozialgeschichte* 18 (1978): 176–78.

46. Weiler, *British Labor and the Cold War,* 79.

47. G.H.H. [George Hall], "Annex to Memorandum for the War Cabinet," 23 March 1945, CAB66/63/wp (45)199, PRO.

48. Ibid.

49. H. L. Bullock and Will Lawther, "Interim Report of General Council Representatives Attached to the British Government Delegation to the United Nations Assembly, New York, October–December 1946," 18 December 1946, TUC, Box 1854, File 901, p. 3.

50. Cabinet Conclusions 5(46), 15 January 1946, CAB128/5/5(46)3, PRO.

51. ASW, *Monthly Journal* 87 (April 1946).

52. "Relationship of the World Federation of Trade Unions to United Nations: Deputation to the Prime Minister from the Trades Union Congress," 1 April 1946, LAB13/599, PRO.

53. Draft telegram, Bevin to Deakin, [no day] November 1946, PRO LAB 13/596; "Notes on discussion w/ Mr. Arthur Deakin with regard to the World Federation of Trade Unions on 24 April 1947," LAB13/596, PRO.

54. Weiler, *British Labor and the Cold War,* 80–82, 129–65.

55. George Woodcock, "Functions of Trade Unions in Nationalised Industries," ASW *Monthly Journal* 88 (October 1947) MRC MSS 78/ASW/4/27.

56. Weiler, *British Labor and the Cold War,* 72–77.

57. On the Merseyside rank-and-file movement see Arthur Marsh and Victoria Ryan, *The Seamen* (Hassocks, West Sussex, U.K.: Malthouse, 1988), 162–64. On the dock strike see Weiler, *British Labor and the Cold War,* 230–70.

58. The official historian of British merchant marine, C. B. A. Behrens, gives figures only for ships lost where sailors died. Behrens, *Merchant Shipping and the Demands of War* (London: HMSO, 1955), 178.

59. Ibid, 183; Marsh and Ryan, *Seamen,* 149.

60. Marsh and Ryan, *Seamen,* 161–62.

61. Ibid., 162.

62. C. Jarman, "Ginger for Communists," *Seaman,* May–June 1944, MSS 41/TC/152C, MRC.

63. NUS, "Report of the 53d Annual General Meeting . . . July 1945," MSS 175/4/24, MRC.

64. Ibid.

65. Jarman, review of *Men and Ships, Seaman,* May–June 1944, MSS 41/TC/152C, MRC.

66. London Rank and File Committee, *Anchors Aweigh,* January 1948, MSS 175/6/R&F/4/4, MRC.

67. "Seamen to Tackle Mischief on Liners," *Daily Herald* (London), May 20, 1949.

68. *Seaman,* unsigned editorial written by Jarman, January 1944, MSS 41/TC/152C, MRC.

69. *Seaman,* unsigned editorial written by Jarman, November 1944, MSS 41/TC/152C, MRC.

70. "Mr. Jarman's Speech, International Seafarer's Charter Meeting," 14 January 1946, MSS 175/6/JAR/10, MRC.

71. Bevin to Lord Pethick-Lawrence, 11 January 1946; Pethick-Lawrence to Bevin, 16 January 1946, L/E/9/976, India Office Library.

72. "Notes for Mr. Jarman" [copy of Jarman's speech given on the third anniversary of the Nazi invasion of the USSR], 23 June 1944, MSS 175/6/JAR/10, MRC.

73. *Seaman,* unsigned editorial written by Jarman, January 1944, MSS 41/TC/152C, MRC.

Part 3: The Americans

1. Katherine Archibald, *Wartime Shipyard: A Study in Social Disunity* (Berkeley: University of California Press, 1947), 213–14.

Chapter 7: "A House Divided against Itself"

1. Determining the characteristics of American working-class thought about foreign policy is more challenging than finding British working-class perceptions and ideas. Beyond the differences in population and diversity of working-class groups in the United States, the unavailability of good qualitative surveys makes it much harder to grasp how people here thought. U.S. social scientists concerned with public opinion did not often preserve long interviews with average people, as Mass-Observation did. Steven Withey's work for the University of Michigan's Institute for Social Research does use quotations to illustrate particular opinions, but it does not provide any description of the socioeconomic characteristics of the speaker. Although class repeatedly appears as a critical dividing line in opinion, with wealthier and better educated people more readily supporting government thinking, researchers draw few conclusions from this evidence. Perhaps such

little consideration is given to class for ideological reasons: the social scientists believed that class was not an important political factor in the United States and so they did not follow up on their findings.

2. Few studies exist on the relation of popular opinion to foreign affairs and the USSR. Those that do examine "public opinion" almost inevitably confine themselves to published opinion, newspaper editorials, policy statements, speeches by famous figures, and so on. How these ideas were received, a more difficult issue to investigate, has been largely neglected. The opinion of the wider public, especially of working people, is reflected in these works almost solely by the results of opinion polls. Interestingly, older works are the exceptions: Gabriel Almond, *The American People and Foreign Policy* (New York: Praeger, 1950); Thomas A. Baley, *The Man in the Street* (New York: Macmillan, 1948); M. Brewster Smith, "The Personal Setting of Public Opinion: A Study of Attitudes Toward Russia," *Public Opinion Quarterly* 11 (Winter 1947–48): 507–23. More typical are Peter G. Filene, *Americans and the Soviet Experiment, 1917–33* (Cambridge, Mass.: Harvard University Press, 1967); Michael Leigh, *Mobilizing Consent: Public Opinion and American Foreign Policy* (Westport, Conn.: Greenwood, 1976); Ralph Levering, *American Opinion and the Russian Alliance, 1939–45* (Chapel Hill: University of North Carolina Press, 1976); George Sirgiovanni, *An Undercurrent of Suspicion: Anti-Communist and Anti Soviet Opinion in World War II America* (New Brunswick, N.J.: Transaction, 1990), 73–115; Melvin Small, "How We Learned to Love the Russians: American Media and the Soviet Union During World War II," *Historian* 36 (May 1974): 455–78; Warren B. Walsh, "What the American People Think of Russia," *Public Opinion Quarterly* 8 (Winter 1944–45): 512–22.

3. Elizabeth McKillen treats resistance to the foreign policy of the AFL Executive Council in an earlier period. There is no good recent study of opposition to the AFL's foreign policy within the organization in the 1940s, even though opposition certainly existed. For instance, in 1944 a number of local leaders and some executives from the Culinary Workers, Teamsters, Painters, and Machinists advocated joining the Anglo-Soviet committee against the wishes of their leadership. McKillen, *Chicago Labor and the Quest for a Democratic Diplomacy* (Ithaca, N.Y.: Cornell University Press, 1995); Ward Coley [Local 6 Building Service Employees, AFL] to Ferdinand Smith, 19 April 1944, CIOST, Box 68, File: "President Philip Murray, 1944," Wayne State.

4. David Louis Sallach describes the importance of economic thinking, "enlightened self-interest," in the CIO's policy development process. However, he maintains that the unionists' concerns were almost wholly economic, misunderstanding the profound connection between economic and political thought in the CIO. For more on this issue see Chapter 9. David Louis Sallach, "Enlightened Self-Interest: The Congress of Industrial Organizations and Foreign Policy, 1935–55" (Ph.D. diss., Rutgers University, New Brunswick, N.J., 1983).

5. OWI, Division of Surveys, "Report Number 21: The War Worker's Point of View," 7/28/42, RG 44, Box 1786, File: "War Worker's Point of View," table 53, NARS—Suitland. Other surveys had similar results. See, for example, "After the War: Portrait of Gloom," 12 November 1941, PSF Subject Box 157, File: "Public Opinion Polls, 1935–41," Roosevelt Library.

6. OWI, Division of Surveys, "Report Number 25: Conceptions of the Role of America in World Affairs: Part I," 9/29/42, p. i, RG 44, Box 1786, no file, NARS—Suitland.

7. Differences between working-class opinion and middle-class opinion are quite small, often falling within the error of the surveys. The difficulty with these statistically oriented studies is that they don't explain why people thought the way they did, or if there were qualitative differences in the answers. See, for instance, Survey 3 in the Appendix.

8. O. G. Overcash to Carey, 6/13/43, CIOST, Acc 185, Box 132, File: "Report on Labor Conditions in Bolivia, 1943," Wayne State.

9. OWI, Division of Surveys, "Report Number 25: Conceptions of the Role of America in World Affairs: Part I," 9/29/42, p. i, RG 44, Box 1786, no file, NARS—Suitland.

10. OWI, Division of Surveys, "Report Number 21: The War Worker's Point of View," 7/28/42, RG 44, Box 1786, File: "War Worker's Point of View," p. 44, NARS—Suitland.

11. Paul Cressey, Intensive Interview #4-T19 [n.d., 12/?/42], RG 44, Box 1823 E168, File: "Paul Cressey Field Reports," p. 5, NARS—Suitland.

12. Ibid., 4.

13. Edgar A. Schuler, Weekly Report, 4/3/43, RG 44, Box 1824 E166, File: "Schuler Field Reports," p. 4, NARS—Suitland.

14. Murray [Curran] to Phil [Murray], 5/22/45, Murray Papers, file reference lost, Catholic.

15. Schuler, Weekly Report, p. 4.

16. Katherine Archibald, *Wartime Shipyard: A Study in Social Disunity* (Berkeley: University of California Press, 1947), 197.

17. Ibid., 198–99.

18. Irving Salert to Carey, n.d. [5/44], CIOST, Acc 185, Box 3, File: "Correspondence, Salert, Irving," Wayne State.

19. Ruttenberg to Carey, 1/1/44, CIOST, Acc 185, Box 3, File: Correspondence, "Ruttenberg, Stanley, Private Correspondence," Wayne State.

20. See, for instance, John Morton Blum, *V Was for Victory* (New York: Harvest/HBJ, 1976), 15–53; Richard Boyden, "The San Francisco Machinists from Depression to Cold War, 1930–50" (Ph.D. diss., University of California, Berkeley, 1988); Daniel Cornford and Sally Miller, eds., *American Labor in the Era of World War II* (Westport, Conn.: Praeger, 1995).

21. Archibald, *Wartime Shipyard,* 192.

22. Ibid., 196.

23. Ibid.

24. OWI, "Report Number 21: The War Worker's Point of View," p. 9.

25. Cressey, Intensive Interview #4-T19, p. 4.

26. Archibald, *Wartime Shipyard,* 200.

27. Herbert Passin, WPB [War Production Board] Study, Chicago, Illinois [n.d., ?/5/42], RG 44, Box 1824 E164, File: "Field Reports, Passin," pp. 6–7, NARS—Suitland.

28. The study found 71 percent of poor people (not defined in the survey report) thought this, as opposed to 49 percent of the upper-income group. Nationally, 62 per-

cent believed the United States was doing all it could. The statistics do not provide the number of informants in each survey, but these studies were usually on the order of n = 1,100. Hadley Cantril, Office of Public Opinion Research, "U.S. Opinion Toward British and U.S. War Effort" (paper, Princeton University, 4/10/42), RG 44, Box 1796, File: E162, pp. 2, 6, table 1, NARS—Suitland.

29. Archibald, *Wartime Shipyard,* 198.

30. OWI, "Report Number 21: The War Worker's Point of View," p. 4.

31. Ibid., 45.

32. Archibald, *Wartime Shipyard,* 187.

33. Philip Taft, *The AFL in the Time of Gompers* (New York: Harper, 1957), 448–51; McKillen, *Chicago Labor.*

34. Communists played an active role in building the American labor movement in the 1930s. They eventually led (or dominated, depending on the observers' ideological predilection) fifteen CIO unions, including the third-largest union in the CIO, the United Electrical Workers (UE). Communist Party members also played an important role in the growth of several other CIO unions, notably the United Auto Workers (UAW). The social makeup of Communist Party support has been the subject of much debate. Although the party in the 1920s was overwhelmingly made up of working-class immigrants, by the mid-1930s the party had diversified, gaining many middle-class and native-born members. The consensus of anti-Communist scholars is, in Nathan Glazier's words, that although the party styled itself as the "vanguard of the proletariat," it had "enormous difficulties in realizing this extravagant slogan." Glazier finds that "the party was rather more successful in becoming the 'vanguard of the intellectual and professional workers.'" Following this argument, party membership figures would mean little for this discussion. To the contrary, scholars more sympathetic to the Communist Party, such as Roger Keeran, find that Communists in the union movement, whatever the makeup of the party as a whole, were definitely part of an organic working-class leadership: "The Communists were legitimate and often outstanding trade unionists." For the purposes of this discussion, the debate about Communist legitimacy is beside the point, although working-class support for the party and for the party's central icon, the USSR, are connected. Of course, nonmembership in the party did not necessarily reflect a position on the USSR, but those in the party had—by definition—to be admirers of the Bolsheviks. Nathan Glazier, *Social Bases of American Communism* (New York: Harcourt, Brace, and World, 1961), 89–147, quotations at 130; Roger Keeran, *The Communist Party and the Auto Workers' Unions* (New York: International, 1980), 24. See also Steve Rosswurm, "Introduction," in *The CIO's Left-Led Unions,* ed. Steve Rosswurm (New Brunswick, N.J.: Rutgers University Press, 1992), 1–17.

35. Filene, *Americans and the Soviet Experiment,* 157–85.

36. Victor Reuther later claimed it was the brothers' experience in the USSR that turned them against communism. However, there is no contemporary evidence for this claim to an early anticommunism. Others had more difficult experiences. Andrew Smith, a Hungarian-born American Communist, became so disturbed by the inequities promoted by Soviet communism that he resigned from the party. Victor Reuther, interview by Jack

W. Skeels, 3/7/63, Oral History #96, Wayne State; Nelson Lichtenstein, "Walter Reuther and the Rise of Labor Liberalism," in *Labor Leaders in America,* ed. Melvyn Dubofsky and Warren Van Tine (Urbana: University of Illinois Press, 1987), 282, now superseded by Nelson Lichtenstein, *The Most Dangerous Man in Detroit: Walter Reuther and the Fate of American Labor* (New York: Basic, 1995); Andrew Smith, *I Was a Soviet Worker* (New York: Dutton, 1936).

37. Eugene Lyons, *The Red Decade: The Stalinist Penetration of America* (Indianapolis: Bobbs-Merrill, 1941).

38. See Harvey Klehr, *Heyday of America Communism: The Depression Decade* (New York: Basic, 1984), 365–85.

39. Ibid., 386–400; Irving Howe and Lewis Coser, *The American Communist Party: A Critical History* (New York: Praeger, 1962), 273–387.

40. John L. Lewis blocked an anti-Communist resolution from being passed by the CIO executive board in 1939. The Mine, Mill, and Smelter Workers; the International Woodworkers of America; the UE; and the UAW all had factional battles about anti-Communist resolutions at conventions during the Nazi-Soviet pact period. The UAW was the most important union to pass an anti-Communist clause. Bert Cochran, *Labor and Communism: The Conflict That Shaped American Unions* (Princeton, N.J.: Princeton University Press, 1977), 145, 148, 151, 192–95.

41. For the factional fight in the UE see James J. Matles and James Higgins, *Them and Us: Struggles of a Rank and File Union* (Boston: Beacon, 1974), 130–34. On the UAW see Martin Halpern, *UAW Politics in the Cold War Era* (Albany: State University of New York Press, 1988), 26.

42. Earl Browder, "The American Communist Party in the Thirties," in *As We Saw the Thirties: Essays on Social and Political Movements of a Decade,* ed. Rita James Simon (Urbana: University of Illinois Press, 1967), 244.

43. Klehr, *Heyday of American Communism,* 407.

44. Levering, *American Opinion and the Russian Alliance,* 35.

45. Wealthier people had more confidence in cooperation "more broadly conceived," such as a revived League of Nations, in this survey. OWI, Division of Surveys, "America Views the Post War World; Division of Surveys Report Number 14," 5/28/42, RG 44, Box 1784A, File: "America Views the Post-War World," table 14, NARS—Suitland.

46. See Survey 4 in the Appendix.

47. See Survey 5 in the Appendix.

48. Archibald, *Wartime Shipyard,* 207.

49. Cressey, Intensive Interview #4-T19, 4.

50. Archibald, *Wartime Shipyard,* 208.

51. *In Fact,* 8/13/45, R. J. Thomas Papers, UAW Presidents, Acc 115, Box 18, File: #6, "'B' Miscellaneous Correspondence, 9/26/45–8/3/45," Wayne State.

52. Levering, *American Opinion and the Russian Alliance,* 63–145.

53. OWI, Division of Surveys, "Report Number 25: Conceptions of the Role of America in World Affairs: Part I," 9/29/42, p. i, RG 44, Box 1786, No File, NARS—Suitland.

54. Levering, *American Opinion and the Russian Alliance,* 86; *CIO NEWS*, July 22 and August 15, 1942.

55. Walsh, "What the American People Think," 522.

56. Division of Public Liaison, Office of Public Affairs, U.S. State Department, "Public Attitudes on Foreign Policy, Special Report No. 55: Public Response to the Report of the Crimea Conference," 6/3/45, RG 59, Records of the Office of Public Opinion Studies: Box 1, File: "Public Attitudes on Foreign Policy Nos. 45–79, 11/23/44–2/27/46," NARS.

57. Paul Willen, "Who 'Collaborated' with Russia?" *Antioch Review* 14 (Fall 1954): 260.

58. Fred Perkins, Scripps-Howard staff writer, no title, contained in Perkins to Carey, 3/22/45, CIOST, Acc 185, Box 115, File: "WFTU, London Conference, February 1945, Correspondence," Wayne State.

59. Ibid.

Chapter 8: Americanism and Internationalism

1. Survey Research Center, "How Three People Feel About the International Situation" (paper), Survey Research Center, 4/46, ISR Report #231, p. 9, ISR Library.

2. U.S. Bureau of the Census, *Statistical Abstract of the United States, 1948* (Washington, D.C.: USGPO, 1948), 19, 37.

3. See, for example, George Q. Flynn, *American Catholics and the Roosevelt Presidency, 1932–36* (Lexington: University of Kentucky Press, 1968), xii–xiii, 121–94; Leo V. Kanawada Jr. is particularly bad at distinguishing between the "opinion makers" and American Catholics as a whole in *Franklin D. Roosevelt's Diplomacy and American Catholics, Italians, and Jews* (Ann Arbor, Mich.: UMI Research Press, 1982), 69–71.

4. David J. O'Brien, *America Catholics and Social Reform: The New Deal Years* (New York: Oxford University Press, 1968), 30.

5. One poll taken in 1936 showed 42 percent as pro-Republican, whereas a poll one year later found 30 percent supporting the Loyalists and 32 percent neutral. Cited in O'Brien, *American Catholics and Social Reform,* 89, 248n. Anticipating President Ronald Reagan's equation of the Nicaraguan contras with the Founders of the United States, the Catholic journal *Tablet* in 1937 compared Franco and the royalists to "our patriots of 1776." See O'Brien, *American Catholics and Social Reform,* 87.

6. Hadley Cantril, "Catholic Shift from Democrats," 7 September 1944, PSF Subject Box 157, File: "Public Opinion Polls, 1942–44," Roosevelt Library.

7. One need only briefly examine the differing levels of support for communism among nominal Catholics in Italy, France, Ireland, and Poland in this period to see that Catholicism or a Catholic background did not impose a uniform ideology on the working class. In these four countries, chosen arbitrarily, Catholicism did not form the dividing lines of groups or parties—except in the case of Northern Ireland, where religion has helped to define nationality.

8. Neil Betten, *Catholic Activism and the Industrial Worker* (Gainesville: Florida State University Press, 1976), 111–12.

9. The CIO refused to collect racial or ethnic information on its membership. Figures compiled from Betten, *Catholic Activism,* 110–11.

10. Ibid.

11. Joshua Freeman, *In Transit: The Transit Workers Union in New York City, 1933–66* (New York: Oxford University Press, 1989), vii. See also Ronald Schatz, *The Electrical Workers: A History of Labor at General Electric and Westinghouse, 1923–60* (Urbana: University of Illinois Press, 1983), 190–98.

12. Steve Rosswurm, "The Catholic Church and the Left-Led Unions: Labor Priests, the Labor Schools, and the ACTU," in *The CIO's Left-Led Unions,* ed. Steve Rosswurm (New Brunswick, N.J.: Rutgers University Press, 1992), 119–37.

13. Douglas Seaton, *Catholics and Radicals* (Lewisburg, Pa.: Bucknell University Press, 1981), 226; Schatz, *Electrical Workers,* 198–99.

14. In 1940 Hadley Cantril found that "religion has a very significant effect on opinion." It is impossible to tell from his study, however, whether the differences in attitude came from Catholic Irish Americans' resentment of Britain and Italian Americans' desire to avoid a war with their homeland or more generally Catholic ideas. One would assume Catholics of Polish and French backgrounds would be more likely to favor intervention than other groups. See Survey 6 in the Appendix.

15. In a survey taken in the summer of 1941, 65 percent of Catholics and 75 percent of Protestants and "non-members" wanted the USSR to win the war, whereas 7 percent of Catholics, 4 percent of Protestants, and 3 percent of the nonmembers favored the Germans. Twenty-one percent of Catholics, 17 percent of Protestants, and 16 percent of nonmembers did not choose a side. The size of the sample was not given. Hadley Cantril and Donald Rugg, Office of Public Opinion Research, "U.S. Opinion Toward Russia," 2/27/42, RG 44, Box 1796, File: E162, NARS—Suitland.

16. OWI, Division of Surveys, "America Views the Postwar World; Division of Surveys Report Number 14," 5/28/42, p. 12.

17. Seaton, *Catholics and Radicals,* provides a good introduction to the history of the Association of Catholic Trade Unionists (ACTU), stressing the critical role ACTists played in moving the CIO to the right. In contrast, I believe Seaton overemphasizes the effectiveness of the ACTists. Passim and esp. 234–45.

18. Quoted in Mel Piehl, *Breaking Bread: The Catholic Worker and the Origin of Catholic Radicalism in America* (Philadelphia: Temple University Press, 1982), 162; Seaton, *Catholics and Radicals,* 180n.

19. Seaton, *Catholics and Radicals,* 56.

20. In the 1930s liberal Catholic activists created a number of groups, ranging from the utopian Catholic Worker movement to the more materially minded ACTU. One important group, those around the magazine the *Christian Front,* renamed *Christian Social Action,* notably Richard Deverall, developed close relations with Catholic CIO leaders. Deverall later worked for the AFL's Jay Lovestone as a European representative, promoting what Deverall claimed was "the basic philosophy of the Popes and Sam Gompers." Quoted in Piehl, *Breaking Bread,* 151.

21. Reino Erkilla, interview by author, San Francisco, April 20, 1983.

22. The exception was Ben Gold of the International Fur and Leather Workers' Union. Seaton, *Catholics and Radicals*, 62.

23. Ibid., 77–99.

24. Ibid., 168.

25. Quoted in Freeman, *In Transit*, 281.

26. Martin Halpern, *UAW Politics in the Cold War Era* (Albany: State University of New York Press, 1988), 101, 114–15.

27. On the Polish American community see John J. Bukowczyk, "The Transformation of Working-Class Ethnicity: Corporate Control, Americanization, and the Polish Immigrant Middle Class in Bayonne, New Jersey, 1915–25," *Labor History* 25 (Winter 1984): 53–82. For Italian Americans see Charles Zappia, "Unionism and the Italian American Worker: A History of the New York City 'Italian Locals' in the International Ladies' Garment Workers' Union" (Ph.D. diss., University of California, Berkeley, 1994).

28. Gary Gerstle, in *Working-Class Americanism* (Cambridge, U.K.: Cambridge University Press, 1989), offers an intriguing explanation of the development of American labor conservatism. This conservatism, he argues, grew out of immigrant workers' desire to Americanize themselves, a drive that combined readily with an indigenous Catholic conservatism and led them to readily embrace cold war dogma. Although this is an accurate analysis of some of the supports underlying labor conservatism, especially for the small group of first- and second-generation French Canadian immigrant workers he studies, he nevertheless does not come to grips with the importance of New Deal internationalism. Unable to integrate the twists and turns of union ideology that had been influenced by foreign policy, Gerstle dismisses the conservative unionists' embrace of the USSR during World War II without reflecting. He asserts that their turn to New Deal internationalism "could never be more than a tactical maneuver, an evil that would be tolerated only as long as the war against the fascists had to be fought" (286). Unfortunately, he does not provide evidence for this assertion, leaving the reader unsure of why this particular twist of foreign policy thinking was tactical, whereas the others reflected the true nature of working-class thought.

Nelson Lichtenstein and Mike Davis have offered similar explanations but more convincingly tied to world events. Both argue that the rise of the right in labor corresponded to a groundswell of anticommunism in ethnic Eastern European communities. The source of this anti-Communist upsurge, Lichtenstein explains, was "the entry of the Red Army into Eastern Europe late in the war[, which] had an electrifying impact upon Slavs and Hungarians who comprised as much as half of the industrial union membership." Unfortunately, neither scholar offers evidence for this change in feeling. Although the effect of the Soviet Union's reorganization of Eastern Europe was undoubtedly key in moving Eastern European communities to the right, Davis and Lichtenstein date the switch too early—by as much as three years in some cases. The governments of national resistance set up in the wake of the Red Army in 1945 were not universally rejected by American ethnics. The Communist repression that began in February 1947 in Hungary and culminated in the Czech coup a year later fatally undercut the Communist and leftist presence in American ethnic communities. See Gerstle, *Working-Class Americanism*; Nelson Lichtenstein, "The Making of the Postwar Working Class: Cultural Pluralism and Social Structure in World War II," *Historian* 51 (November 1988): 42–63; Mike Davis, *Prisoners of the American Dream: Politics and Economy in the History of the U.S. Working Class* (London: Verso, 1986), 88–90. Compare these versions to the more nuanced Stephen Meyer, *Stalin over Wisconsin: The Making and Unmaking of Militant Unionism, 1900–50* (New Brunswick, N.J.: Rutgers University Press, 1992).

29. Halpern, *UAW Politics*, 129–30.

30. Seaton, *Catholics and Radicals*, 57–58.

31. Nathan Glazier, *Social Bases of American Communism* (New York: Harcourt, Brace, and World, 1961), 42, 130–33.

32. Peter Friedlander, *Emergence of a UAW Local, 1936–39: A Study in Class and Culture* (Pittsburgh, Pa.: University of Pittsburgh Press, 1975), 123.

33. Halpern, *UAW Politics*, 129.

34. Quoted in Halpern, *UAW Politics*,, 129. Nathan Glazier found this pattern repeated for the Communist Party as a whole. Glazier, *Social Basis of American Communism*, 38–89.

35. Friedlander, *Emergence of a UAW Local*, 125.

36. See James N. Gregory, *American Exodus: The Dustbowl Migration and Okie Culture in California* (New York: Oxford University Press, 1989), 150–71; Glazier, *Social Basis of American Communism*, 130–31.

37. Gregory, *American Exodus*, 150.

38. The CIO officially committed itself to ending racial discrimination. Yet the practices of its constituents varied greatly, and racial issues played an important part in factional battles, if only sub rosa. African Americans used their position in divided unions to increase their political position and to ensure fair treatment on such issues as seniority and hiring. The breakthrough organization of the Ford Motor Co. in 1940–41, which had a large black workforce, boosted the strength of the left in the UAW. The Communist-aligned leadership of Ford Local 600 at the huge River Rouge plant derived much of its support from black workers. Roger Keeran claims that Communists were generally on the right side of racial issues and thereby gained strong support from black workers. This is only partly true. The UAW leadership as a whole supported black rights in the workforce and in society at large. In some instances, especially UAW Packard Local 190, left-wing supporters of UAW leader George Addes catered to the racist sentiments of the union's largely Polish American and southern membership. The problems posed by the hate strikes of 1942–43 also perplexed the UAW leadership of all factions. It was only under great pressure from black community leaders and union activists that the UAW took punitive action against hate strikers. Despite the problems, as Meier and Rudwick note, under the left-center coalition "the UAW-CIO International emerged as black Detroit's most helpful and outspoken ally." Once in control of the union, the Reuther faction continued this alliance. The CIO's most integrated unions, the National Maritime Union and the Ma-

rine Cooks and Stewards Union, were Communist led, and in the left-led ILWU, blacks provided the Communists with crucial support in severely divided locals such as San Francisco's Local 10. But, as often as not, the unions integrated because the workforce was integrated; to not integrate would have been to not organize. The United Electrical Workers, for instance, organizing a largely white industry, had poorly developed racial policies. August Meier and Elliot Rudwick, *Black Detroit and the Rise of the UAW* (Oxford: Oxford University Press, 1979), 106–107, 126–30, 208, quotation at 174; Keeran, *The Communist Party and the Auto Workers' Unions* (New York: International, 1980), 231–35; Victor Silverman, "Left-Led Unions and Racism: A History of the Integration of ILWU Local 10, 1940–60" (paper, University of California, Berkeley, 1983); Silverman, "Race and Radical Unionism: A History of the Marine Cooks and Stewards" (honors thesis, Department of History, University of California, Berkeley, 1984); Donald Chrichtlow, "Communist Unions and Racism," *Labor History* 17 (Spring 1982): 165–97.

39. There is substantial dispute about whether the cultural and political unity created by the labor version of Americanism and the working-class version of mass culture empowered the working class. See Lizabeth Cohen, *Making a New Deal: Industrial Workers in Chicago, 1919–39* (New York: Cambridge University Press, 1990); Thomas Gobel, "Becoming American: Ethnic Workers and the Rise of the CIO," *Labor History* 29 (Spring 1988): 173–98; Gerstle, *Working-Class Americanism*; Christopher Lasch, *The Agony of the American Left* (New York: Knopf, 1969); Warren Susman, *Culture as History: The Transformation of American Society in the Twentieth Century* (New York: Pantheon, 1984); Davis, *Prisoners of the American Dream.*

40. Quoted in Joseph Starobin, *American Communism in Crisis, 1943–57* (Berkeley: University of California Press, 1972), 45.

41. Katherine Archibald, *Wartime Shipyard: A Study in Social Disunity* (Berkeley: University of California Press, 1947) 186.

42. Starobin, *American Communism in Crisis,* 45.

43. See my Chapter 3.

44. Quoted in Gerstle, *Working-Class Americanism,* 290.

45. Survey Research Center, "Public Attitudes Toward American Foreign Policy, Part I: Patterns of Attitudes Toward American Foreign Policy" (paper, Survey Research Center, 5/47), ISR Report #222, p. iii, ISR Library.

46. The exact figures in answer to the question "How do you feel about our sending military supplies to Greece?" were Approve, 11 percent; Approve with qualifications, 23 percent; Undecided/don't know, 23 percent; Disapprove (with qualifications), 16 percent; Disapprove, 23 percent; not ascertained, 4 percent; $n = 625$. Survey Research Center, "Public Attitudes Toward American Foreign Policy; Part I" (paper, Survey Research Center, 5/47), ISR Report #222, table 1, p. 17, ISR Library.

47. Steven Ashby, "Shattered Dreams: The American Working Class and the Origins of the Cold War, 1945–49" (Ph.D. diss., University of Chicago, 1993).

48. Quoted in Richard J. Walton, *Henry Wallace, Harry Truman, and the Cold War* (New York: Viking, 1976), 174.

49. Ibid., 181–203.

50. Quoted in Richard Freeland, *The Truman Doctrine and the Origins of McCarthyism: Foreign Policy, Domestic Politics, and Internal Security, 1946–48* (New York: New York University Press, 1985), 89. He develops this argument more fully.

51. "Special Report on American Opinion: Social, Educational, and Economic Differences in U.S. Opinion Toward Russia" [n.d.], RG 59, Office of Public Opinion Surveys, U.S. State Department, Public Opinion on Foreign Countries and Regions; Soviet Union and Eastern Europe; Box 45, File: "Russian Reports Misc., 1948," p. 1, NARS.

52. Yet a 1946 Survey Research Center poll found that slightly more union members than nonmembers thought the USSR to be unfriendly, but this difference was well within the error margin of the poll. "Special Report on American Opinion: Social, Educational, and Economic Differences in U.S. Opinion Toward Russia" [n.d.], RG 59, Office of Public Opinion Surveys, U.S. State Department, Public Opinion on Foreign Countries and Regions; Soviet Union and Eastern Europe; Box 45, File: "Russian Reports Misc., 1948," p. 3, NARS. The poll cited by the State Department was Survey Research Center, "Public Attitudes Toward Russia and United States–Russian Relations, Part II: Attitudes and Beliefs about Russia" (paper, Survey Research Center 4/47), ISR Report #220, p. 32, ISR Library.

53. The sample included 417 factory workers, 312 professionals and executives, and 345 salaried workers. Roper Organization, "Special Report on American Opinion: Opinion of American Labor Organizations on International Questions, January 1, 1948–March 21, 1948," 3/24/49, RG 59, Office of Public Affairs, Division of Public Studies, Box 19, File: "Curr. Attitudes of Am. Labor," p. 14, NARS.

54. Survey Research Center, University of Michigan, "Public Attitudes Toward Russia and United States–Russian Relations, Part I: Attitudes Toward United States–Russian Relations" (paper, Survey Research Center, 3/47), ISR Report #219, pp. ii, 13, 21, ISR Library.

55. See Survey 7 in the Appendix.

56. [Steven Withey], Survey Research Center, "Attitudes Toward United States–Russian Relations" (paper, Survey Research Center, 10/48), ISR Report #229, p. 31, ISR Library.

57. Survey Research Center, "Public Attitudes Toward Russia and United States–Russian Relations, Part I," ISR Report #219, p. ii.

58. Survey Research Center, "How Three People Feel About the International Situation" (paper, Survey Research Center, 4/46), ISR Report #231, p. 9, ISR Library.

59. Ibid., 15.

60. [Withey], Survey Research Center, "Attitudes Toward Russian and United States–Russian Relations," ISR Report #229, p. 2.

61. Memorandum of conversation with Townsend, 2/11/47, RG 59; 841.504-WFTU/2-1147, NARS.

62. Steven Withey and Survey Research Center, "Three Americans Discuss Foreign Affairs" (paper, Survey Research Center, 1/50), ISR Report #234, p. 2, ISR Library.

63. I am guessing that this speaker is a miner because of the reference to Lewis. [Withey],

Survey Research Center, "Attitudes Toward Russian and United States–Russian Relations," ISR Report #229, p. 59.

64. Archibald, *Wartime Shipyard,* 212.

65. Erkilla interview. Howard Kimmeldorf found a similar reaction to radicalism, though he also found a strong strain of working-class militance supporting the leadership in the ILWU. Kimmeldorf, *Reds or Rackets: The Making of Radical and Conservative Unions on the Waterfront* (Berkeley: University of California Press, 1988), 127–51, 159–69.

66. The slogan is reproduced in a photograph in Halpern, *UAW Politics,* 167.

67. Nonetheless, many made use of Taft-Hartley in factional and jurisdictional conflicts. The literature on the Taft-Hartley Act is substantial. On the leadership's initial opposition to Taft-Hartley see Harvey A. Levenstein, *Communism, Anti-Communism, and the CIO* (Westport, Conn.: Greenwood, 1981), 216–19. The political process leading up to passage and the act's effects on the union movement, labor relations, and labor law are examined in Arthur F. McClure, *The Truman Administration and the Problems of Postwar Labor* (Rutherford, N.J.: Fairleigh Dickinson University Press, 1969), 162–83; Christopher L. Tomlins, *The State and the Unions: Labor Relations, Law, and the Organized Labor Movement in America, 1880–1960* (Cambridge, U.K.: Cambridge University Press, 1985), 247–316; Irving Richter, *Labor's Struggles, 1945–50: A Participant's View* (Cambridge, U.K.: Cambridge University Press, 1994).

68. Halpern, *UAW Politics,* 202.

69. Ibid., 168, 201–203.

70. Michael Paul Rogin, *Intellectuals and McCarthy: The Radical Specter* (Cambridge, Mass.: MIT Press, 1967), 236.

71. Freeman, *In Transit,* 267.

72. OWI, Division of Surveys, "America Views the Postwar World; Division of Surveys Report Number 14," p. 3.

73. Edgar A. Schuler, Weekly Report, 4/3/43, RG 44, Box 1824 E166, File: "Schuler Field Reports," p. 4, NARS—Suitland.

74. OWI, Division of Surveys, "Report Number 25: Conceptions of the Role of America in World Affairs: Part I," 9/29/42, RG 44, Box 1786, p. i, NARS—Suitland.

75. Archibald, *Wartime Shipyard,* 191.

76. John Dower describes well the range of this type of hatred in *War Without Mercy: Race and Power in the Pacific War* (New York: Pantheon, 1986), 3–15, 33–73.

77. Harvey Schwartz, "A Union Combats Racism: The ILWU's Japanese-American 'Stockton Incident' of 1945," *Southern California Quarterly* 62 (Summer 1980): 161–76.

78. Archibald, *Wartime Shipyard,* 203–204.

79. Survey Research Center, "How Three People Feel About the International Situation," ISR Report #231, p. 11.

80. Alice Kernmer to F. D. Roosevelt, 1 May 1943, OF 48A, England, File: Miscellaneous, 1943, Roosevelt Library.

81. "Thomas Finds British Rulers 'Nice People,'" *Washington Daily News* (Pullman), February 17, 1945.

82. Peter J. Flynn to Murray, 7/31/45, Murray Papers, file reference misplaced, Catholic.

83. D. P. Connery to R. J. Thomas, 10/6/42, R. J. Thomas Papers, UAW Presidents, Acc 115, Box 9, File: #6, "Miscellaneous Correspondence, 1942," Wayne State.

84. OWI, Division of Surveys, "Report Number 25: Conceptions of the Role of America in World Affairs: Part I," p. iii.

85. The Office of War Information maintained that this was a minority viewpoint. Division of Surveys, "America Views the Post War World; Division of Surveys Report Number 14," p. 4A.

86. Edgar A. Schuler, Weekly Report, 4/3/43, RG 44, Box 1824 E166, File: "Schuler Field Reports," p. 4, NARS—Suitland.

87. OWI, Division of Surveys, "Anti-British Attitudes of Negroes," 10/3/42, RG 44, Box 1784, File: "Survey's Special Reports # 24," p. 4, NARS—Suitland.

88. Ibid., 4.

89. See Neil Wynn, *The Afro-American and the Second World War* (New York: Holmes and Meier, 1976); Patrick S. Washburn, *A Question of Sedition: The Federal Government's Investigation of the Black Press During World War II* (New York: Oxford University Press, 1986); Joe William Trotter Jr., *Black Milwaukee: The Making of an Industrial Proletariat, 1915–45* (Urbana: University of Illinois Press, 1985), 147–95; Richard Polenberg, *War and Society: The United States, 1941–45* (Philadelphia: Lippincott, 1972), 99–130.

90. *Afro-American* (Baltimore), December 13, 1945.

91. P. L. Prattis, *Pittsburgh Courier*, October 13, 1945.

Chapter 9: "A Positively Mystical Vision"

1. [James B. Carey], Hand-written notes for speech to Paris meeting, n.d. [9/45], CIOST, Acc 185, Box 117, File: "World Federation of Trade Unions, Paris Conference, Sept.–Oct. '45, Miscellaneous Material," Wayne State.

2. Early proposals for American-Anglo-Soviet cooperation did come from the Communist left. Lewis Merril of the United Office and Professional Workers suggested a delegation to the USSR in October 1941. F. D. Roosevelt to Frances Perkins, 8 October 1941, OF 142 AFL, Box 2, File 1941, Roosevelt Library.

3. Matthew Josephson, *Sidney Hillman: Statesman of American Labor* (New York: Doubleday, 1952), 261–67. Steven Fraser, *Labor Will Rule: Sidney Hillman and the Rise of American Labor* (New York: Free Press, 1991), 178–89.

4. As part of the abortive red scare of 1939–40, Hillman pushed the Clothing Workers to ban Communists from staff or elected positions and promoted a purge of other Communists in defense industries. Minutes of the General Executive Board, 11/14/40, ACWA, Acc 5619, Box 166, File 1, Cornell; Harvey A. Levenstein, *Communism, Anticommunism, and the CIO* (Westport, Conn.: Greenwood, 1981), 150–51.

5. Hillman to Alex Rose [American Labor Party secretary], 1/22/44, Rose and George Counts to Hillman, 1/25/44 OF 4910, File: "Hillman, Sidney 1942–45," Roosevelt Library; Fraser, *Labor Will Rule*, 517–22.

6. Steve Fraser, "Sidney Hillman: Labor's Machiavelli," in *Labor Leaders in America,* ed. Melvin Dubofsky and Warren Van Tine (Urbana: University of Illinois Press, 1987), 210.

7. Quoted in Henry A. Wallace, *The Price of Vision: The Diaries of Henry A. Wallace,* ed. John Blum (Boston: Houghton Mifflin, 1973), 529. Thanks to Alan Lawrence for this reference.

8. Jacob Potofsky, interview by Neil Gold, 7/6/64, ACWA, Acc 5619, Box 188, File 1, p. 322, Cornell.

9. Quoted in John P. Windmuller, *American Labor and the International Labor Movement: 1940–53* (Ithaca, N.Y.: Cornell Institute of International Relations Reports, 1954), 111.

10. Murray, a modest, unpretentious man, has been overshadowed by more charismatic labor leaders. There is no published biography of the man who led the CIO through some of its most challenging years.

11. Ronald Schatz, "Philip Murray and the Subordination of the Industrial Unions to the United States Government," in *Labor Leaders in America,* ed. Dubofsky and Van Tyne, 252.

12. Hoover also claimed the Russians "considered Philip Murray to be the most promising man in unionism today, and that some day he will be one of the most powerful men in America." J. E. Hoover to Adolf A. Berle, 7/28/42, RG 59, Decimal File: 841.5043/118, NARS.

13. Lee Pressman interview, Columbia Oral History Project, quoted in Levenstein, *Communism, Anticommunism, and the CIO,* 194n.

14. Murray to Philip M. Curran, 5/18/45, Murray Papers, Collection 5, Box A4, Catholic.

15. Carey to Wilmer Tate, 7/6/43, CIOST, Acc 185, Box 2, File Corres.: "Misc. Persons T," Wayne State.

16. As with Murray, there is no good biography of James B. Carey. Ronald Schatz discusses Carey's thinking in *The Electrical Workers: A History of Labor at General Electric and Westinghouse, 1923–60* (Urbana: University of Illinois Press, 1983), 96–99. Carey did not like his allies in the anti-Communist effort, informing one ACTist that "the New York ACTU outfit is a boil on the face of Labor's progress." Carey to John Cort, 5/22/43, CIOST, Acc 185, Box 1, File Corres.: "Misc. Persons co," Wayne State.

17. James B. Carey, "CIO Views Regarding American European Aid, Presented to WFTU Executive Board, Paris, November 18–24, 1947," 11/24/47, RG 59 Decimal File: 800.5043/12-247, p. 14, NARS.

18. Rough draft of transcript, "Meeting of Members of the Foreign Service Division . . . to Hear Mr. James Carey," 9/22/44, CIOST, Acc 185, Box 46, File: "State Department Corres., 1941–43," p. 6, Wayne State. On the popularity of this sort of economism among U.S. internationalists as a whole, see Charles Maier, "Politics of Productivity," *International Organizations* 31 (Fall 1977): 607–33; Alan Wolfe, *America's Impasse: The Rise and Fall of the Politics of Growth* (Boston: South End, 1981), 13–48.

19. Perkins to Roosevelt, 31 March 1945, PSF Departmental Files, Box 57, File: "Labor: Perkins, Frances," Roosevelt Library.

20. Executive Committee on Economic Foreign Policy, "Formulation of a Full Employment Program with Reference to Economic Foreign Policy," 23 February 1945, PSF Departmental Files, Box 57, File: "Labor: Perkins, Frances," Roosevelt Library.

21. James Carey, "What Labor Wants," Speech at the USWA [United Steel Workers of America] 4th District Convention, 10 December 1944, CIOST, Box 136, File: "Speeches, James Carey, 1944," Reuther Library.

22. David Louis Sallach and David Milton argue that the basis of the CIO's foreign policy was its concern for avoiding economic problems for the unions' members. This is only partially true, for they believed economic issues were intimately tied to political ones, and they truly feared war. Sallach, "Enlightened Self-Interest: The Congress of Industrial Organizations and Foreign Policy, 1935–55" (Ph.D. diss., Rutgers University, New Brunswick, N.J., 1983); David Milton, *The Politics of U.S. Labor* (New York: Monthly Review Press, 1982), 11–12.

23. Harris to Carey, 5/21/45, CIOST, Acc 185, Box 3, File: "Harris, Lou," Wayne State.

24. Harry Read [Carey's executive assistant] to Franklin Schaffner, 8/5/46, CIOST, Acc 185, Box 9, File: "Americans United For World Government," Wayne State.

25. Ibid.

26. "Address by Sidney Hillman, Madison Square Garden, March 12, 1945," ACWA, Acc 5619, Box 171, File 5, Cornell.

27. Josephson, *Sidney Hillman,* 646. Cordell Hull's enthusiasm for an international organization seemed similar to Hillman's. According to envoy Robert Murphy, Hull was "almost mystical in his approach" to promoting the United Nations. Murphy, *Diplomat Among Warriors* (Garden City, N.Y.: Doubleday, 1964), 208. See also Cordell Hull, *Memoirs,* vol. 2 (New York: Macmillan, 1948), 1314–15.

28. James B. Carey, "Organized Labor and the National Economy—The Congress of Industrial Organizations. Lecture given by J. B. Carey for the Economic Mobilization Course at the Industrial College of the Armed Forces Washington, D.C.," 2/17/47, CIOST, Acc 185, Box 48, File: "War Department, 1947," pp. 7–8, Wayne State.

29. Saillant to Knight, 4/6/48; Knight to Potofsky, 4/12/48, CIOST, Acc 185, Box 84, File: "Latin American Affairs Committee, O. A. Knight's Trip to Mexico, 1948," Wayne State.

30. Memorandum of conversation with Willard Townsend, 2/11/47, RG 59, Decimal File: 841.504-WFTU/2-1147, NARS.

31. On the social-democratic impulse in U.S. politics see Nelson Lichtenstein, "From Corporatism to Collective Bargaining: Organized Labor and the Eclipse of Social Democracy in the Postwar Era," in *Rise and Fall of the New Deal Order,* ed. Gary Gerstle and Steve Fraser (Princeton, N.J.: Princeton University Press, 1989), 122–52.

32. The Clothing Workers and New York clothing manufacturers established joint boards for settling wage and other disputes in 1924. They had earlier set up one of the first arbitration systems in the world. Hillman and his union were also involved in a variety of Socialist/cooperative ventures, including unemployment insurance, banking, and housing. Josephson, *Hillman,* 245–67, 272–74, 319–26.

33. See Philip Murray, "Labor and Responsibility," *Virginia Quarterly* 16 (April 1940): 267–78; Schatz, "Philip Murray," 248–49; Murray to F. D. Roosevelt, 22 November 1941, PPF 5640, File: "CIO, 1938–41," and Murray to Roosevelt, 11 March 1941, OF 2546, Box 2, File: "CIO, 1941," Roosevelt Library.

34. Nelson Lichtenstein discusses both proposals in *Labor's War at Home: The CIO in World War II* (Cambridge, U.K.: Cambridge University Press, 1982), 85–89.

35. See, for instance, the variety of resolutions in Roosevelt's files: OF 407, Box 3, Labor File: "January March 1942," Roosevelt Library. Typical is the resolution by the United Rubber Workers' Local 125, Pontiac, Michigan, of March 19, 1942, which asks for legislation to "remove monop[o]ly, greed and excess profit from the war and defense effort."

36. The CIO in coalition with the AFL and the U.S. Chamber of Commerce even proposed an extensive plan for "industrial peace" that included a national committee of business and labor that would adopt a code of behavior for key economic actors. As David Brody has noted, the two sides had deeply divergent ideas of the meaning of this noble-sounding plan. The committee fell apart when the CIO and AFL demanded greater inroads into "managerial prerogative" than the businessmen were willing to concede. The 1945–46 General Motors strike, with its union demand that the auto giant reveal its financial ability to pay a wage increase, was indeed as much a result of demands for increased wages as it was for a basic change in the power relationship between the UAW and management. "Proposal for Industrial Peace for the Consideration of the American People," 3/5/45; Roosevelt to Green, Johnston [U.S. Chamber of Commerce], and Murray, 3/28/45, OF 407, Box 4, File: "1945," Roosevelt Library; David Brody, "The Uses of Power I: Industrial Battleground," *Workers in Industrial America: Essays on the Twentieth-Century Struggle* (New York: Oxford University Press, 1980), 173–214.

37. On the National Labor Relations Act as a formalizer, and thus defuser, of conflict see Christopher L. Tomlins, *The State and the Unions: Labor Relations, Law, and the Organized Labor Movement in America, 1880–1960* (Cambridge, U.K.: Cambridge University Press, 1985), 197–243.

38. Robert Sherwood, *White House Papers of Harry Hopkins*, vol. 2 (London: Eyre and Spottiswoode, 1949), 784.

39. R. J. Thomas to Sen. Harley M. Kilgore, 9/27/46, R. J. Thomas Collection, Acc 115, Box 34, File 12: "Mead, Sen. James M. Senate War Investigating Committee, 1946," UAW President's Office, Wayne State.

40. Martin Halpern, "The 1939 UAW Convention: Turning Point for Communist Power in the Auto Union?" *Labor History* 33 (Spring 1992): 190–216.

41. Carl Haessler, interview by Jack W. Skeels, 11/27/59–10/24/60, Oral History #42, Wayne State, p. 167.

42. The factional battles in the UAW are, second to the split between the AFL and CIO, the most studied conflicts in the history of institutional labor. See Irving Howe and B. J. Widdick, *The UAW and Walter Reuther* (New York: Praeger, 1973); Bert Cochran, *Labor and Communism: The Conflict That Shaped American Unions* (Princeton, N.J.: Princeton University Press, 1977), esp. 272–96; Roger Keeran, *Communist Party and the Auto Work-*

ers' Unions (New York: International, 1980); Victor Reuther, *The Brothers Reuther and the Story of the UAW: A Memoir* (Boston: Houghton Mifflin, 1976); Jack W. Skeels, "The Development of Political Stability Within the United Automobile Workers' Union" (Ph.D. diss., University of Wisconsin, Madison, 1957; Martin Halpern, *UAW Politics in the Cold War Era* (Albany: State University of New York Press, 1988); Nelson Lichtenstein, *The Most Dangerous Man in Detroit: Walter Reuther and the Fate of American Labor* (New York: Basic, 1995), 248–70.

43. Quoted in Halpern, *UAW Politics,* 101.

44. William Appleman Williams saw anticommunism and liberalism as two contradictory parts of a repeating pattern of U.S. foreign relations. He found a "surface pattern" of commitment to noninterventionism and concern for democratic development. Yet a deeper "fundamental antagonism" to revolution pressed the United States to abandon its professed democratic aims in order to repress revolutionary change. In the case of the CIO, interest in democracy outweighed opposition to communism for the time being. Williams, *The Tragedy of American Diplomacy* (1959; rev. ed., New York: Dell, 1962), 4. Mary Sperling McAuliffe provides an insightful institutionally oriented introduction to the evolution of cold war liberalism in *Crisis on the Left: Cold War Politics and American Liberals* (Amherst: University of Massachusetts Press, 1978).

45. Memorandum: Ross to Murray, 3/20/47, CIOST, Acc 185, Box 132, File: "International Affairs Dept. Correspondence, 1946–47," Wayne State.

46. Ibid.

47. Federico Romero, *The United States and the Reconstruction of the European Trade Union Movement, 1944–51,* trans. by Harvey Fergusson II (Chapel Hill: University of North Carolina Press, 1992), 84–87; Lawrence Wittner, *American Intervention in Greece, 1943–49* (New York: Columbia University Press, 1982), 135–85, 208–10.

48. McAuliffe, *Crisis on the Left,* 23.

49. E.M.W. to FDR, 9 December 1941, PPF 3189, File: "American Federation of Labor, 1940–44," Roosevelt Library.

50. *CIO News,* December 15, 1941.

51. The booklet was *The Battle of America: The Fighting Plans of AFL-CIO-RR Brotherhoods and Independent Unions* (San Francisco: Labor's Unity for Victory Committee, 1942); Mervyn Rathborne [secretary treasurer, California State Industrial Union Council–CIO] to F. D. Roosevelt, 26 June 1942, President's Official Files, OF 407, Box 3, Labor File: "May–June 1942," Roosevelt Library.

52. *CIO News,* December 22, 1941.

53. See Samuel Shore [ILGWU], to F. D. Roosevelt, 12 March 1942, President's Official Files, OF 407, Box 3, Labor File: "April 1942," Roosevelt Library.

54. *CIO News,* April 13, 1942.

55. See W. Green to Murray, 23 May 1942, and FDR memo 2, June 1942, President's Official Files, OF 407, Box 3, Labor File: "May–June 1942," Roosevelt Library.

56. See Lichtenstein, *Labor's War at Home,* 70, 96–97.

57. *CIO News,* June 6, 1942.

58. Varian Fry to Carey, 3/19/43, CIOST, Acc 185, Box 8, File: "Am. Labor Conference on Intl. Affairs," Wayne State; Quotation from OSS Foreign Nationalities Branch, Report of Public Meeting: American Labor Conference on International Affairs June 12, 1943, 7/5/43, RG 59, Decimal File: 811.5043/130, p. 4, NARS.

59. Ibid., 1.

60. Clinton Golden to Varian Fry, 6/17/44; Emile Rieve to Fry, 5/8/44; Samuel Wolchok to Fry, 6/12/44; Louis Hollander, Abraham Siller, Irving Abramson, John Green, and J. Raymond Walsh to Fry, 6/20/44, CIOST, Acc 185, Box 8, File: "Am. Labor Conference on International Affairs," Wayne State.

61. Varian Fry to Carey, 12/9/44, CIOST, Acc 185, Box 8, File: "Am. Labor Conference on Intl. Affairs," Wayne State.

62. Anthony Carew, *Labour Under the Marshall Plan* (Manchester, U.K.: Manchester University Press, 1987), 62–63.

63. The difficulties the CIO and AFL had in joining forces cannot, of course, be attributed solely to international affairs. The most significant problem in the meetings themselves was an inability on both sides to compromise on a structure for solving jurisdictional issues. See Circular Letter to CIO Executive Board and Staff from P. Murray, 4/3/43, CIOST, Acc 185, Box 68, File: "President P. Murray, 1943," Wayne State.

64. Windmuller, *American Labor,* 22–24.

65. [n.a.], "Conference Between British Trade Union Delegation and Congress of Industrial Organizations," 13 February 1943, TUC Archives, Box 625, File 947/232.

66. Minutes of meeting of CIO Committee on Latin American Affairs, 6/16/44, CIOST, Acc 185, Box 83, File: "Latin American Affairs Committee," Wayne State.

67. Samuel Guy Inman, "Inter-American Labor Union Project: Report of Activities of the Director," 5/18/46, CIOST, Acc 185, Box 1, File: "Correspondence, Misc persons, K," Wayne State.

68. [n.a.], "Report on AFL-CIO Unity Talks," 5/1/47, UAW Presidents, Acc 261, Box 61, File #2: "Cio, Murray, Philip, 1947," p. 10, Wayne State.

69. Irwin Wall has recently questioned the important role usually attributed to U.S. labor in the split of Fource Ouvrier from the French CGT. Irwin Wall, *The United States and the Making of Postwar France, 1945–54* (Cambridge, U.K.: Cambridge University Press, 1991).

70. Robert Murphy to Secretary of State; Transmits report "The World Federation of Trade Unions and the German Labor Movement" by Louis Wiesner, 7/32/47, RG 59, Decimal File: 800.5043/7-3147, p. 9, NARS.

71. Memorandum of Conversation: "Relationship of WFTU to invitation to AFL to Visit Germany," 5/2/46, RG 59, Decimal File: 862.5043/5-246, NARS.

72. "We have watched with some anxiety," Anthony Eden informed U.S. Ambassador John Winant, "the difficult situation which has been created by the differing views among American and British trade union organizations on the subject of relations with the Russian trade unions." Winant to Secretary of State, 4/7/44, *Foreign Relations of the United States, 1944* (hereafter, *FRUS*), vol. 2, p. 1022.

73. Paul Tofahrn, "Notes on IFTU General Council Meeting," London, 3 September 1945, MSS 238/IF/1/68, MRC.

74. Samuel Berger to Secretary of State, Subject: "Analysis of the 79th annual Conference of the British Trades Union Congress," 9/25/47, RG 59, Decimal File: 841.5043/9-2547, p. 5, NARS.

75. The TUC originally opposed Brown's attempt to "develop [an] active and vigorous ERP-TU" because it's "not a trade union issue." London to Secretary of State 6/14/48, RG 59, Decimal File: 841.5043/6-1448, NARS.

76. Grew to Habana, 2/20/45, RG 59, Decimal File: 800.5043/2-2045, NARS.

77. Quoted in Schatz, "Philip Murray," 252.

78. The literature on Communist activity in the CIO is extensive but, like the study of communism in general, is more often than not partisan, mired in old debates about Communist legitimacy and perfidy. Some of the better recent works: Levenstein, *Communism, Anti-Communism, and the CIO;* Cochran, *Labor and Communism;* Keeran, *Communist Party and the Auto Workers' Unions;* Howard Kimmeldorf, *Reds or Rackets: The Making of Radical and Conservative Unions on the Waterfront* (Berkeley: University of California Press, 1988).

79. Nunn, "CIO Convention, Atlantic City," 5 December 1940, OF 2546, Box 1 CIO, 1940, Roosevelt Library.

80. Quoted in Cochran, *Labor and Communism,* 97.

81. In the UE, a Communist-led group ousted Carey from leadership. In the UAW the unity slate of Communists, Socialists, and liberal Catholics, which had ousted opportunistic president Homer Martin, began to fracture, which led to intense ideological and factional conflicts. Keeran, *Communist Party and the Auto Workers' Union,* 186–225; Schatz, *Electrical Workers,* 96–99.

82. Stanley Ruttenberg to James Carey, 10/21/45, CIOST, Acc 185, Box 3, File: "Stanley Ruttenberg," Wayne State.

83. "Transcript: Remarks of James B. Carey, Secretary Treasurer, Congress of Industrial Organizations, Convention of United Shoe Workers, Atlantic City, N.J., October 9, 1946," 10/9/46, CIOST, Acc 185, Box 136, File: "Speeches, James Carey, 1946," Wayne State.

84. W. I. Davies to Thomas, 8/28/45, R. J. Thomas Collection, UAW Presidents, Acc 115, Box 21, File 16, "D" Miscellaneous Corres. 9/24/45–7/30/45, Wayne State.

85. Steinhardt [Praha] to Secretary of State, 6/11/47, RG 59, Decimal File: 800.5043/6-1147, NARS.

86. Richard J. Walton, *Henry Wallace, Harry Truman, and the Cold War* (New York: Viking, 1976), 274–87.

87. Charles P. Larrowe, *Harry Bridges: The Rise and Fall of Radical Labor in the United States,* 2d ed. rev. (Westport, Conn.: Hill, 1977), 292–93.

88. Murray to Curran, 2/22/44, CIOST, Acc 185, Box 68, File: "President Philip Murray, 1944," Wayne State.

89. Lichtenstein, *Labor's War at Home,* 24–25; Levenstein, *Communism, Anticommunism, and the CIO,* 49–52.

90. For the role of Catholic workers see Chap. 3, and Lichtenstein, "Walter Reuther," 187–93.

91. Haessler interview, 144–45.

92. Lichtenstein, *Labor's War at Home,* 214–15.

93. Kimmeldorf, *Reds or Rackets,* 163–69; Schatz, *Electrical Workers,* 204–205, 225–26.

94. Schatz, *Electrical Workers,* 192.

95. "Oral History Interview of Victor Reuther," interview by Jack W. Skeels, 3/7/63, Oral History #96, p. 36, Wayne State.

96. Memorandum: Ross to Murray, 3/20/47, CIOST, Acc 185, Box 132, File: "International Affairs Dept. Correspondence, 1946–47," Wayne State; "Report of Conference with Soviet Trade Unionists, [February] 25–26, 1948," 3/?/48, CIOST, Acc 185, Box 120, File: "WFTU-ERP, European Trip of J.B.C., Feb.–March 1948, Moscow Conf. Report," p. 12, Wayne State.

97. Ross to Murray, 2/16/48, CIOST, Acc 185, Box 68, File: "President Philip Murray, 1948–51," p. 4, Wayne State.

98. "Report of Conference with Soviet Trade Unionists, [February] 25–26, 1948," 3/?/48, CIOST, Acc 185, Box 120, File: "WFTU-ERP, European Trip of J.B.C., Feb.–March 1948," p. 1, Wayne State.

Chapter 10: "Neither Stalin nor Standard Oil"

1. Benjamin Cohen, Memorandum of Conversation, Subject: "World Federation of Trade Unions," 11/2/45, RG 59, Decimal File: 550.4 Paris/11-245, NARS.

2. Ibid. Hillman returned Eisenhower's goodwill, remarking that the general was the "only man" who could guide Germany into a democratic future. Stephen Ambrose, *Eisenhower*, vol. 1 (1890–1952) (New York: Simon and Schuster, 1983), 409.

3. See Diane S. Clemens, *Yalta* (London: Oxford University Press, 1970), 28–95; Robert Dallek, *Franklin D. Roosevelt and American Foreign Policy* (Oxford: Oxford University Press, 1979), 406–528; Walter LaFeber, *America, Russia, and the Cold War,* 5th ed. (New York: Knopf, 1985), 8–28. For a sample of assessments of the alliance as tactical or naive, see Gaddis Smith, *American Diplomacy During the Second World War* (New York: Wiley, 1969), 1–21; Herbert Feis, *Churchill, Roosevelt, Stalin: The War They Waged and the Peace They Sought* (Princeton, N.J.: Princeton University Press, 1957); John Lewis Gaddis, *The United States and the Origins of the Cold War* (New York: Columbia University Press, 1972), 7–62.

4. The American in charge of the occupation, General Lucius Clay, found the Soviets remarkably cooperative. Jean Edward Smith, "General Clay and the Russians: A Continuation of the Wartime Alliance in Germany, 1945–48," *Virginia Quarterly Review* 64 (1988): 20–36.

5. Roosevelt to Isador Lubin, 13 January 1942, OF 142, Box 2, File: "1942," Roosevelt Library.

6. "Memorandum of Interview with Mr. J. Winant and Sir Walter," 7/27/42, Citrine

Papers, I. 4/10b, LSE; "Conference Between British Trade Union Delegation and Congress of Industrial Organizations," 2/13/43, Box 625, File 947/232, TUC Archives.

7. Transcription of "Special Meeting of [TUC] General Council on 12 August 1942," 9/18/42, Citrine Papers, I. 4/10, p. 2, LSE.

8. V.A.H., re: presidential memorandum for Dr. Lubin, 4/7/44, OF 407, Box 4, File: "January–July 1944," Roosevelt Library.

9. Lubin to F. D. Roosevelt, 11 March 1942, OF 499, Box 1, File: "International Labor Conference, 1942–43," Roosevelt Library.

10. Horst Lademacher et al. also found this to be the case, "Der Weltgewerkschaftsbund im Spannungsfeld des Ost-West Konflikts." *Archiv für Sozialgeschichte* 18 (1978): 120–21.

11. OSS, Research and Analysis Branch, "Russia's Role in the World Trade Union Conference," Research & Analysis No. 2740, 1/15/45, RG 59, Decimal File: 550.4 London/1-1545, pp. iv, 12, 50, NARS.

12. Kennan to Secretary of State, 1/26/45, RG 59, Decimal File: 800.5043/1-2645, NARS.

13. OSS, "Memorandum for the President," 5/13/45, *Declassified Documents Retrospective,* 316E Fiche 803, pp. 5, 9.

14. Serafino Romualdi, *Presidents and Peons: Recollections of a Labor Ambassador* (New York: Funk and Wagnalls, 1967), 73.

15. Manpower Directorate, Allied Control Authority, "Statements of the Zonal Manpower Directorates on the Status of Trade Unions in Each Zone and Their Structure," 7/46, CIOST, Acc 185, Box 40, File: "Military Govt for Germany, 1946–49," Wayne State.

16. The World Federation's report did find that denazification was more advanced in the Soviet zone and that the Russians devoted more resources to aiding the reconstruction of the unions, all of which was true. It did criticize overcentralization of the unions in the eastern zone. It is important to recall, however, that at this point the unions there were, as in the other zones, Resistance coalitions. Communist domination was several years away. "Report of the Commission of the World Federation of Trade Unions to Investigate Conditions in Germany," CIOST, Acc 185, Box 117, File: "Paris Conf. September–October, Reports," pp. 5–7, Wayne State. For an attack on the World Federation for painting an unjustifiably positive portrait of conditions in the Soviet zone see Robert Murphy to Secretary of State, Transmitting Report, "The World Federation of Trade Unions and the German Labor Movement," by Louis Wiesner, 7/23/47, RG 59, Decimal File: 800.5043/7-3147, NARS.

17. Lademacher et al., "Weltgewerkschaftsbund," 148–72; General Clay to Saillant, 2/20/48, CIOST, Acc 185, Box 40, File: "Military Govt for Germany, 1946–49," Wayne State.

18. Stettinius to Roosevelt, 4/10/45, *Foreign Relations of the United States, 1945* (hereafter *FRUS*), vol. 1, p. 240. For Truman's rejection see pp. 372, 405, 482, 1442.

19. Drew Pearson, "Washington Merry-Go-Round," *Washington Post,* May 22, 1945.

20. Bevin to Stettinius, 9/5/45, *FRUS, 1945,* vol. 1, p. 1442.

21. William Roger Louis, *Imperialism at Bay: The United States and the Decolonization of the British Empire, 1941–45* (New York: Oxford University Press, 1978), 19–26, 350–65.

22. John Fishburn, "Is the WFTU an Instrument of Russian Policy?" 10/15/46, RG 59, Decimal File: 800.5043/6-2347, NARS.

23. Ray Murphy, "The USSR and the World Federation of Trade Unions," RG 59, Decimal File: 800.5043/6-2347, p. 4, NARS. Peter Weiler also analyzes this and the Fishburn paper cited in note 22. However, he does not note the political process that the change in the State Department involved. Weiler, *British Labor and the Cold War* (Stanford, Calif.: Stanford University Press, 1988), 69–71.

24. "The USSR and the World Federation of Trade Unions," RG 59, Decimal File: 800.5043/6-2347, pp. 5–6, NARS.

25. Dean Acheson liked Murphy's original draft but decided that it needed to be "less contentious." The report was widely read, and I could find no memos that articulate disapproval. Acheson to Hickerson, 1/15/47, RG 59, Decimal File: 800.5043/6-2347, NARS.

26. For the portrait of Hillman the fellow traveler see Robert Murphy to Secretary of State, 7/23/47, which transmits the report, "The World Federation of Trade Unions and the German Labor Movement," by Louis Wiesner, RG 59 Decimal File: 800.5043/7-3147, pp. 2, 7ff, NARS.

27. Carey to Acheson, 3/26/47, CIOST, Acc 185, Box 46, File: "State Department Corres., 1947," Wayne State; Mulliken to Carey, 5/11/47, CIOST, Acc 185, Box 46, File: "State Department Corres., 1947," Wayne State.

28. This was why the loyalty hearings instituted by the Truman administration were so devastating. The literature on the purges of the State Department is enormous. A good synthesis is David Caute, *The Great Fear: The Anti-Communist Purge Under Truman and Eisenhower* (New York: Simon and Schuster, 1978), 267–345. Richard Freeland effectively demonstrates the close interrelationship of foreign policy and domestic paranoia in *The Truman Doctrine and the Origins of McCarthyism: Foreign Policy, Domestic Politics, and Internal Security, 1946–48* (New York: New York University Press, 1985).

29. Acheson, "Circular: The World Federation of trade unions," 6/23/47, RG 59, Decimal File: 800.5043/6-2347, NARS.

30. John F. Simmons [Quito] to Secretary of State, "Subject: Relationship Between Ecuadorian Labor and the World Federation of Trade Unions," 8/22/47, RG 59, Decimal File: 800.5043/9-1047; Harold Tewell [Habana] to Secretary of State, Subject: "Relations Between the World Federation of Trade Unions and Cuban Labor Organizations," 8/22/47, RG 59, Decimal File: 800.5043/8-2247; Stanton Griffis [Warsaw] to Secretary of State, "Subject: The World Federation of Trade Unions," 8/8/47, RG 59, Decimal File: 800.5043/8-1147; Charles E. Dickerson Jr. [Pretoria] to Secretary of State, "Subject: Activities of the World Federation of Trade Unions in the Union of South Africa," 8/8/47, RG 59, Decimal File: 800.5043/8-847; Paul W. Meyer [Shanghai] to Secretary of State, "Transmitting Memorandum of Conversation Between Members of Shanghai's Labor Organization and Willis R. Etter," 8/4/47, RG 59, Decimal File: 800.5043/8-447; Lowell Pinkerton [Beirut] to Secretary of State, 8/1/47, RG 59, Decimal File: 800.5043/8-147; all in NARS.

31. Paul W. Meyer, American consul in Shanghai, to Secretary of State, "Transmitting

Memorandum of Conversation Between Members of Shanghai's Labor Organization and Willis R. Etter," 8/4/47, RG 59, Decimal File: 800.5043/8-447, NARS.

32. Memorandum: Philip B. Sullivan to T. W. Holland, 2/27/47, RG 59, Decimal File: 800.5043/2-2747, p. 3, NARS.

33. Acheson had little sympathy for trade unions or the USSR despite his friendship with Alger Hiss and his tarring by McCarthy. A graduate of Harvard and Yale, one-time assistant secretary of commerce, and successful lawyer before joining the government, Acheson had close ties to many U.S. corporations opposed to trade union activity in their overseas operations. Caute, *Great Fear,* 44–45; Dean Acheson, *Present at the Creation: My Years at the State Department* (New York: Norton, 1969), 238–40.

34. Memorandum of Conversation: "The CIO Position in the World Federation of Trade Unions," 5/19/47, RG 59, Decimal File: 800.5043/5-1947, NARS, p. 1.

35. Ibid., 3.

36. Ibid., 2.

37. Robert Murphy to Secretary of State; Transmits report, "The World Federation of Trade Unions and the German Labor Movement," by Louis Wiesner 7/23/47, RG 59, Decimal File: 800.5043/7-3147, p. 18, NARS.

38. Callman [U.S. embassy in London] to Douglass, Hickerson, and Bohlen, 12/30/47, RG 59, Decimal File: 800.5043/12-3047, NARS.

39. Swayzee to Nitze and Hickerson, 1/7/48; Hickerson to Gallman, 1/12/48, both in RG 59, Decimal File: 800.5043/12-3047, NARS.

40. See Anthony Carew, *Labour Under the Marshall Plan* (Manchester, U.K.: Manchester University Press, 1987), 76–77.

41. Chase to Secretary of State, 3/2/48, RG 59, Decimal File: 800.5043/3-248, NARS.

42. "Copy of Article on Press Ticker," 1/2/48, CIOST, Acc 185, Box 120, File: "WFTU-ERP, European trip of J.B.C., 1948, Records Taken Abroad," Wayne State.

43. Memorandum of Conversation, "Participants Mr. Philip Murray, Mr. James Carey, Mr. Clinton Golden, Mr. Samuel D. Berger, March 20, 1948," 3/23/48, RG 59, Decimal File: 800.5043/3-2348, NARS.

44. "Copy of Article on Press Ticker," 1/2/48, CIOST, Acc 185, Box 120, File: "WFTU-ERP, European trip of J.B.C., 1948, Records Taken Abroad," Wayne State.

45. Ross to Carey, 9/28/47; Helen D. Kissane to Carey, 10/27/47, CIOST, Acc 185, Box 132, File: "International Affairs Dept. Correspondence, 1946–47," Wayne State.

46. "Report of Conference with Soviet Trade Unionists, [February] 25–26, 1948," March 1948, CIOST, Acc 185, Box 120, File: "WFTU-ERP, European Trip of J.B.C., Feb.–March 1948, Moscow Conf. Report," quotation at p. 11, Wayne State.

47. Ross to Murray, 2/16/48, CIOST, Acc 185, Box 68, File: "President Philip Murray, 1948–51," p. 1, Wayne State.

48. Carey to Murray, 5/19/45, CIOST, Acc 185, Box 68, File: "President Philip Murray, 1945," p. 6, Wayne State.

49. Philip Murray, "CIO International Policy" [message sent to Jewish Labor Day

Convention], n.d. [9/44], CIOST, Acc 185, Box 68, File: "President Philip Murray, 1944," Wayne State.

50. The AFL's role in manipulating labor in Latin America to the benefit of the United States has been extensively documented. Ronald Radosh, *American Labor and U.S. Foreign Policy* (New York: Random House, 1969), 348–435; Henry Berger, "Union Diplomacy: American Labor's Foreign Policy in Latin America, 1932–55" (Ph.D. diss., University of Wisconsin, Madison, 1966); Harvey Levenstein, *Labor Organizations in the United States and Mexico: A History of their Relations* (Westport, Conn.: Greenwood, 1971); Gabriel Ross, *El Neocolonialismo Sindical* (Buenos Aires: Ediciones de La Linea, 1974).

51. James B. Carey, "Recording for OWI Broadcast to Philippine Islands," 7/6/45, CIOST, Acc 185, Box 136, File: "Speeches, James Carey, 1945," p. 4, Wayne State.

52. Ibid., 5.

53. Carey to Murray, 5/19/45, CIOST, Acc 185, Box 68, File: "President Philip Murray, 1945," p. 6, Wayne State.

54. Weiler, *British Labor and the Cold War,* 79; Lademacher et al., "Weltgewerkschaftsbund," 175–76.

55. Lademacher et al., "Weltgewerkschaftsbund," 177–79.

56. Memorandum of Conversation: "Carey and Ross Visit to Moscow," 6/11/46, RG 59, Decimal File: 800.5043/7-1146, NARS.

57. On relations with Indian unions see D. P. Connery to R. J. Thomas, 10/6/42, Thomas Collection, UAW Presidents, Acc 115, Box 9, File #6: "Miscellaneous Correspondence, 1942," Wayne State.

58. George Kennan, *Memoirs, 1925–50* (Boston: Little, Brown, 1967), 257. Kennan recalled that on a visit to Germany in the fall of 1945 he had to "sit alone with a very high ranking military officer at Ambassador Robert Murphy's house in Berlin and . . . endure reproaches leveled at me, and at us 'State Department people' generally, for our anti-Soviet attitudes and our inability 'to get along with the Russians'—an inability which, I was permitted to understand, we could easily overcome if we would only take example from the military establishment" (257). See also Louis, *Imperialism at Bay;* Christopher Thorne, *Allies of a Kind: The United States, Britain, and the War against Japan, 1941–45* (New York: Oxford University Press, 1978).

59. J. T. Fishburn, "Pan-African Information Conference of WFTU," 12/6/46, RG 59, Decimal File: 800.5043/12-646, NARS.

60. Adolph F. Germer, interview by Jack W. Skeels, 11/22/60, Oral History #38, Wayne State.

61. CIO, "Present and Post War Program of the Committee on Latin American Affairs," 1944, CIOST, Acc 185, Box 83, File: "Latin American Affairs Committee, 1944," p. 1, Wayne State.

62. See Ernesto Galarza, *Merchants of Labor: The Mexican Bracero Story* (Charlotte, N.C.: McNally and Loftin, 1964), 17–58.

63. Samuel Guy Inman, "Inter-American Labor Union Project: Report of Activities of

the Director, May 18, 1946," CIOST, Acc 185, Box 1, File: "Correspondence, Misc persons, K," pp. 8–9, Wayne State.

64. O. A. Knight and J. P. Selly, "Report on CTAL Convention, Cali, Colombia, December 10 to 15," 1/11/45, CIOST, Acc 185, Box 84, File: "Latin American Affairs Committee, 1945," p. 1, Wayne State.

65. Ibid.

66. Lombardo Toledano to Murray, 9/6/43, CIOST, Acc 185, Box 83, File: "Latin American Affairs Committee, 1941–43," Wayne State.

67. Minutes of Meeting of CIO Committee on Latin American Affairs, 4/12/45, CIOST, Acc 185, Box 84, File: "Latin American Affairs Committee, 1945," p. 3, Wayne State.

68. Minutes of Meeting of CIO Committee on Latin American Affairs, 6/16/44, CIOST, Acc 185, Box 83, File: "Latin American Affairs Committee," p. 4, Wayne State.

69. Minutes of Meeting of CIO Committee on Latin American Affairs, 4/12/45, CIOST, Acc 185, Box 84, File: "Latin American Affairs Committee, 1945," pp. 3–4, Wayne State.

70. Schwarz to Carey, 2/21/49, CIOST, Acc 185, Box 84, File: "Latin American Affairs Committee, 1949," Wayne State.

71. Lombardo Toledano was leader of the Mexican teachers' union, a close ally of nationalist Mexican president Lázaro Cardénas's, and a founder of the main Mexican union federation and the CTAL; he had emerged as a spokesman for Latin and third-world issues. His energy, skills, and political importance also won him a place on the World Federation's executive board. But in 1947 Lombardo Toledano, who claimed to be Marxist (but not a Communist), crossed swords with two of the *Cinco Lobitos* (five wolves of the unions)—Fernando Amilpa, who was general secretary of Confederación de Trabajadores de México (CTM) and an important member of the ruling Partido Revolucionario Institucional, and Fidel Velazquez, who later came to rule the CTM with an iron hand. Amilpa, Velazquez, and Lombardo Toledano had presided over the integration of the CTM into the governing system of Mexico, a relationship that worked well enough during the wartime boom. Postwar inflation, however, led to tremendous unrest among Mexican workers, but the CTM, because of its loyalty to the government, could not respond. Lombardo Toledano, however, could and, along with several other prominent union leaders, supported militant workers in railways, mining, and petroleum, among other industries. Amilpa and the progovernment elements in the CTM retaliated by kicking out Lombardo Toledano and his allies. The repression of militant labor that ensued, known as *El Charrazo,* ensured the subservience of labor to government during the fifties and sixties. It also reassured the United States, as Ian Roxborough argues, that the Mexican government would be a reliable ally in the cold war. Roxborough, "The Mexican Charrazo of 1948: Latin American Labor from World War to Cold War," Helen Kellogg Institute for International Studies, Working Paper #77 (Notre Dame, Ind.: Helen Kellogg Institute, University of Notre Dame, 1986). See also Dan La Botz, *The Crisis of Mexican Labor* (New York: Praeger, 1988), 65–99, which presents a fairly effective Trotskyist critique of Mexican labor history; Enrique Krauze, *Caudillos Culturales de la Revolución*

Mexicana (Mexico: Secretaria de Educación Publica, 1985); Antonio Rivera Flores, *La Derrota de Lombardo Toledano* (Queretaro, Mexico: Universidad Autónoma de Queretaro, Centro de Investigaciones Sociología, 1984).

72. Knight was falsely accused in a federal loyalty hearing (he was a dollar-a-year employee of the Commerce Department) of being a Communist. He had actually been actively opposed to the Communists during his tenure as an officer of the Oil Workers and as a vice president of the CIO. In fact, he presided over one of the trials of Communist-led unions during the purges of the CIO. Ray Davidson, *Challenging the Giants: A History of the Oil, Chemical, and Atomic Workers International Union* (Denver, Colo.: Oil, Chemical, and Atomic Workers International Union, 1988), 235–39; Harvey A. Levenstein, *Communism, Anticommunism, and the CIO* (Westport, Conn.: Greenwood, 1981), 302. Thanks to Nancy and Jeff Quam-Wickham for these references.

73. Knight to Potofsky, 4/12/48, CIOST, Acc 185, Box 84, File: "Latin American Affairs Committee, O. A. Knight's trip to Mexico, 1948," Wayne State.

74. The AFL's organization was the Confederación Inter-Americana de Trabajadores, which became the Organización Regional Inter-Americana de Trabajadores, the regional arm of the International Confederation of Trade Unions. Radosh, *American Labor and U.S. foreign Policy,* 365–75; Hobart A. Spalding Jr., *Organized Labor in Latin America* (New York: New York University Press, 1977), 251–76.

75. Ernst Schwarz to Carey, 2/21/49, CIOST, Acc 185, Box 84, File: "Latin American Affairs Committee, 1949," Wayne State.

76. As the State Department was changing its inter-American office, Truman sought military aid for Latin nations. Latin policy, like the overall policy of containment, moved rapidly from an economic to a military strategy. Roger Trask, "The Impact of the Cold War on United States–Latin American Relations," *Diplomatic History* 1 (Summer 1977): 271–84.

77. John Herling to Carey, 5/10/46, CIOST, Acc 185, Box 1, File Corres.: "Misc. Persons H," Wayne State.

78. Romualdi to Woll, Meany, and Dubinsky, 4/15/47, quoted in Radosh, *American Labor and U.S. Foreign Policy,* 368; Romualdi, *Presidents and Peons,* 73.

79. International Confederation of Free Trade Unions, "Manifesto of the ICFTU," *ICFTU Report, 1949* (London: ICFTU, 1949), 242.

80. Ibid., 90.

81. Ibid, 92.

82. Nelson Lichtenstein, *The Most Dangerous Man in Detroit: Walter Reuther and the Fate of American Labor* (New York: Basic, 1995), 331–45.

83. Anthony Carew, "Conflict Within the ICFTU: Anti-Communism and Anti-Colonialism in the 1950s," *International Review of Social History* 41 (1996): 147.

Conclusion

1. George Orwell, *The Lion and the Unicorn: Socialism and the English Genius* (London: Secker and Warburg, 1941), 26.

2. Quoted in Anthony Carew, *Labour Under the Marshall Plan* (Manchester, U.K.: Manchester University Press, 1987), 71.

3. Anthony Carew, "The Schism Within the World Federation of Trade Unions," *International Review of Social History* 29 (1984): 335; Denis McShane and Robert Zieger concur. See McShane, *International Labour and the Origins of the Cold War* (Oxford: Clarendon, 1992); and Robert Zieger, *The CIO, 1935–55* (Chapel Hill: University of North Carolina Press, 1995), 261–67.

4. A. W. DePorte, *Europe Between the Superpowers* (New Haven, Conn.: Yale University Press, 1979), provides a helpful framework for understanding the place of Europe in the bipolar system.

5. A good, if abstract, explication of the entrance of the third world into the global system is contained in S. P. Varma, *International Systems and the Third World: A Study in Changing Perspectives* (New Delhi: Vikas, 1988).

6. Quoted in Vasili Prokhorov, *Lenin and the Trade Unions* (Moscow: Novosti Press Agency, 1970), 11.

7. The opening of the archives in the countries of the former Soviet Union has stimulated a renaissance in Soviet labor history. See Lewis Siegelbaum and Ronald Suny, eds., *Making Workers Soviet* (Ithaca, N.Y.: Cornell University Press, 1994).

8. Robert W. Dunn, *Soviet Trade Unions* (New York: Vanguard, 1928), 20. Dunn was a research director of the Amalgamated Textile Workers in 1919–21, publicity director of the Russian-American Industrial Corporation, and technical adviser to the U.S. trade union delegation to Russia in 1927.

9. See Sheila Fitzpatrick, "War and Society in the Soviet Context: Soviet Labor Before, During, and After World War II," *International Labor and Working-Class History* 35 (Spring 1989): 37–52; Donald Filtzer, *Soviet Workers and Stalinist Industrialization: The Formation of Modern Soviet Production Relations, 1928–41* (Armonk, N.Y.: Sharpe, 1986).

10. Jeffrey Rossman, "Rebellion on the Home Front: Cultures of Resistance in a Russian Working-Class Community, June–December 1941" (paper delivered at the eleventh North American Labor History Conference, Wayne State University, October 20–22, 1995).

11. Emily Clark Brown, *Soviet Trade Unions and Labor Relations* (Cambridge, Mass.: Harvard University Press, 1966), 57–58.

12. Corporatism is not the best concept for analyzing the Stalinized Soviet system, however, because corporatism implies plural centers of power. For a survey of the debate about corporatism as an explanation of Soviet trade unionism and politics in general, see Blair Ruble, *The Applicability of Corporatist Models to the Study of Soviet Politics: The Case of Trade Unions,* Carl Beck Papers in Russian and East European Studies, paper 303 (Pittsburgh, Pa.: Russian and East European Studies Program, University of Pittsburgh, 1983).

13. Kennan to Secretary of State, 1/26/45, RG 59, Decimal File: 800.5043/1-2645, p. 2, NARS.

14. Georg Lukács, *History and Class Consciousness: Studies in Marxist Dialectics,* trans. Rodney Livingstone (1968; Cambridge, Mass.: MIT Press, 1971).

15. See Lukács's "Preface to the New Edition" in *History and Class Consciousness*, xvii–xxxviii.

16. For more on this in the Hungarian case see Gyorgy Konrad and Ivan Szelezny, *The Intellectuals on the Road to Class Power,* trans. A. Arato and R. E. Allen (New York: Harcourt, Brace, Jovanovich, 1979).

17. In order to win the war, the mass of society was called into action, not just as soldiers but as workers, citizens, and society as a whole. Yet this mass involvement in a total war was not like a flow of water from a faucet, able to be turned on and off almost at will. In democratic systems certainly, and even in dictatorial ones, support of the mass of society for particular policies, or at least for the basic tenets of diplomacy, is absolutely necessary. Moreover, social conflict engendered by the dislocations and stresses of the war could not be contained; society was in part out of the control of its elites.

Concentrations of power, empowerment of leadership, structures of society, and politics do indeed allow leaders to influence or manipulate mass opinion. However, the relationship of elite and mass that is behind international relations is not as simple as most historians have believed. Many diplomatic historians have ignored the role of the public, let alone the working class. Those who do investigate international relations on a broader level generally treat public opinion as a secondary factor affecting the process of diplomacy. Most scholars agree with Melvin Small, following Walter Lippmann, that the relationship between public and policy makers is more or less one sided. Although public opinion can constrain the activities of leaders, "if anything it is more accurate to say that the president determines public opinion through his appeals to patriotism and his ability to control the information which contributes to the development of that opinion." Small, "How we Learned to Love the Russians: American Media and the Soviet Union During World War II," *Historian* 36 (May 1974): 457; Walter Lippmann, *Public Opinion* (New York: Harcourt, Brace, 1922).

The problem with this sort of thinking is not that is it wrong, though it is not entirely accurate in specifics, but that it remains mired in very limited assumptions about just what international relations are or were, and, as important, how people make up their minds about foreign policy. If the role of public opinion is considered solely as a factor in the decision-making process of the forties, these assumptions limit the ability of historians to comprehend the totality of the war and the new structures that, abortively it is true, brought new elements into the international scene.

18. Peter Weiler, *British Labor and the Cold War* (Stanford, Calif.: Stanford University Press, 1988), 275.

19. Quoted in Francis Williams, *A Prime Minister Remembers: The War and Post-War Memoirs of the Rt. Hon. Earl Attlee* (London: Heinemann, 1961), 158.

20. Quoted in Alan Bullock, *Ernest Bevin: Foreign Secretary* (London: Heinemann, 1983), 395.

21. James F. Byrnes, *Speaking Frankly* (New York: Harper, 1947), 236.

22. John Morton Blum, *V Was for Victory* (New York: Harvest/HBJ, 1976), 116–46; Richard Polenberg, *War and Society: The United States, 1941–45* (Philadelphia: Lippincott, 1972), 164–82; Bruce Catton, *Warlords of Washington* (New York: Harcourt Brace, 1948).

23. Ronald Messer argues that Byrnes was a transitional figure between the era of Stettinius, Roosevelt, and Harry Hopkins, who had promoted the Grand Alliance, and the era of Truman, Marshall, and Acheson, who were unflinching cold warriors. I follow Patricia Dawson Ward in placing Byrnes in the more committed anti-Soviet camp from the start. His championship of business interests in the early forties and his memoirs alone reflect the strength of his antipathy to communism or anything resembling it. Ronald L. Messer, *End of An Alliance: James F. Byrnes, Roosevelt, Truman, and the Origins of the Cold War* (Chapel Hill: University of North Carolina Press, 1982); Patricia Dawson Ward, *The Threat of Peace: James F. Byrnes and the Council of Foreign Ministers* (Kent, Ohio: Kent State University Press, 1979). On Byrnes and Wallace see Byrnes, *Speaking Frankly,* 239–43.

24. George F. Kennan, "Long Telegram," in *Major Problems in America Foreign Policy Since 1945,* vol. 2, ed. Thomas Paterson (Lexington Mass.; Heath, 1989), 280.

25. Interestingly, some works on the history of anticommunism in the CIO fail to effectively consider the role of foreign policy within the union movement. Bert Cochran's often convincing analysis attributes the CIO's self-destructive purges of Communist-led unions and Communists to its dependence on the government, because the CIO's success left it no option but to fall in line and "respond unhesitatingly to the bugle call." He thus finds that the influence of foreign affairs moved in only one direction—from the world diplomatic sphere to the U.S. government and only then to the CIO. As a consequence of this thinking, he devotes a bare three pages to actual events in the world of international labor and makes only one mention of the World Federation in his book. Cochran, *Labor and Communism: The Conflict That Shaped American Unions* (Princeton, N.J.: Princeton University Press, 1977), 317–19, quotation at 315.

Harvey Levenstein places foreign policy more at the center of the conflict with labor, but he too sees the process as almost solely one of the threat of government retaliation: "Communist opposition to the government's foreign policy threatened to turn the CIO into the core of an opposition political movement that would be strong enough to spread disquiet in Washington but weak enough to invite massive retaliation by a government armed with extensive formal and informal power over the labor movement." Although this is true enough, Levenstein does not recognize the revision of the CIO's non-Communist thinking that was underway at the same time. Fear of retaliation was one factor but certainly not the only reason that foreign policy was a crucial issue for the CIO.

26. Many have underestimated the importance of the left's tradition that was embodied in the CIO leadership's conception of domestic politics. For example, Warren Susman writes, "By 1948, when C. Wright Mills published his *The New Men of Power,* few Ameri-

cans on the Left retained any illusion about the significant role organized labor had in fact played in sustaining the existing American system." Susman fails to provide any evidence for this assertion, because there isn't any. In reality, the role of labor in achieving a better world and society was still a matter of great contention. Mills's perceptive book was a part of the process of reassessment caused by the ongoing political and social conflict that both revealed and created the political compromises of the union movement. Susman, *Culture as History: The Transformation of American Society in the Twentieth Century* (New York: Pantheon, 1984), 76; C. Wright Mills, *The New Men of Power: America's Labor Leaders* (New York: Harcourt, Brace, 1948). On the collapse of the CIO's social-democratic program see Nelson Lichtenstein, "From Corporatism to Collective Bargaining: American Labor and the Eclipse of Social Democracy in the Postwar Era," in *The Rise and Fall of the New Deal Order, 1930–80,* ed. Gary Gerstle and Steve Fraser. (Princeton, N.J.: Princeton University Press, 1989), 122–52.

27. Jay Krane to Elmer Cope, 11/17/48, Jay Krane Papers, Acc 614, Box 1, File: "#2, CIO Paris Office, Nov. 15–25, 1948," pp. 1, 4, Wayne State.

28. Adolf Sturmthal, *Unity and Diversity in European Labor* (Glencoe, Ill.: Free Press, 1953), 116.

29. Slavoj Zizek, *The Sublime Object of Ideology* (London: Verso, 1989), 33.

30. Alvin Gouldner explains this process as the result of the efforts of a pseudo-universal class, the new class, which supersedes the old moneyed elite as a new cultured elite. The new class, although only one section of society, is able to claim universality through what he calls a form of "the false consciousness of the cultural bourgeoisie." Gouldner, *The Future of Intellectuals and the Rise of the New Class* (New York: Continuum, 1979), 10–15, 75, 85–87.

31. On realism See Walter Lippmann, *U.S. Foreign Policy: Shield of the Republic* (Boston: Little, Brown, 1943); George Kennan, *American Diplomacy, 1900–50* (Chicago: University of Chicago Press, 1951); Edward Hallet Carr, *The Twenty Years' Crisis, 1919–39: An Introduction to the Study of International Relations,* 2d ed. (London: Macmillan, 1946). A good survey of contemporary realism is Robert O. Keohane, ed., *Neorealism and Its Critics* (New York: Columbia University Press, 1986). A critique is Richard Falk, *The End of World Order: Essays in Normative International Relations* (New York: Holmes and Meier, 1983).

32. Max Horkheimer, *Eclipse of Reason* (1947; reprint, New York: Seabury Press, 1974), v–vi.

33. For an explication of cynical reason see Peter Sloterdijk, *Critique of Cynical Reason,* trans. Michael Eldred (Minneapolis: University of Minnesota Press, 1987).

34. Ernesto Laclau and Chantal Mouffe's ideas of radical democracy attempt this. See Laclau and Mouffe, *Hegemony and Socialist Strategy: Toward a Radical Democratic Politics* (London: Verso, 1985).

Bibliography

Manuscript Collections

Archives of Labor and Urban Affairs, Walter Reuther Library, Wayne State University, Detroit

Acc 185, CIO Secretary-Treasurers Collection

Acc 261, R. J. Thomas Collection and Walter Reuther Collection, Records of the UAW President's Office

Acc 614, Jay Krane Papers

Bevin Library, Churchill College, Cambridge, U.K.

Ernest Bevin Papers

Clement Attlee, Correspondence

British Library of Political and Economic Science, London

Lord Citrine Papers

Department of Archives and Manuscripts, Catholic University of America, Washington, D.C.

Philip Murray Papers

John Brophy Papers

Franklin D. Roosevelt Library, Hyde Park, New York

Adolf A. Berle Papers

Isidor Lubin Papers

Frances Perkins Papers

President's Official File

President's Personal Files

President's Secretary's Files

Henry A. Wallace Papers

Hoover Institution Archives, Stanford University, Palo Alto, Calif.

Walter Schevenels Papers

Lawrence Todd MS

Imperial War Museum, Department of Documents, London
Twenty-Eight Collections of Personal Papers
Labor Management Documentation Center, M. P. Catherwood Library, Cornell University, Ithaca, N.Y.
Records of the Amalgamated Clothing Workers of America
Philip Taft Papers
Mass-Observation Archive, University of Sussex, Brighton, U.K.
File Reports
Topic Collections
Modern Records Centre, University of Warwick, Coventry, U.K.
MSS 78, Records of the Amalgamated Society of Woodworkers
MSS 126, Records of the Transport and General Workers Union
MSS 127, Records of the National Union of Railwaymen
MSS 159, Records of the International Transport Workers' Federation
MSS 180, Richard Croucher Deposit
MSS 175, Records of the National Union of Seamen
MSS 233, David Michaelson Papers
MSS 238, Paul Tofahrn Papers
MSS 240, A. R. Rollin Papers
MSS 281, Records of the National Union of Public Employees
MSS 289, William H. Stokes Papers
National Archives and Records Service, National Storage Center, Suitland, Maryland
Acc 66A, Records of the Department of Labor, Office of International Labor Affairs
RG 44, Office of War Information, Division of Surveys
RG 208, Office of War Information, Miscellaneous Records
National Archives and Record Service, Washington National Records Center, Washington, D.C.
RG 59, Records of the Department of State
RG 174, Records of the Secretary of Labor
Oriental and India Office Library, British Library, London
Sir Maurice Garnier Hallet Collection
L/E, India Office Records, Economic Departments
Public Record Office, London
CAB66, War Cabinet, Memoranda
CAB128, War Cabinet, Conclusions
FO371, Foreign Office Correspondence
FO800, Ernest Bevin Papers
FS12, Chief Registrar of Friendly Societies
INF1, Ministry of Information
LAB13, Ministry of Labour and National Service, Overseas Department
MT9, Ministry of War Transport
PREM4, Prime Minister's Correspondence

Registry, Trades Union Congress, London
Archives of the Trades Union Congress (now housed at the Modern Records Centre, University of Warwick, Coventry, U.K.)
Rhodes House Library, Oxford
Arthur Creech Jones Papers
Fabian Colonial Bureau Collection
Tamiment Library, New York University, New York
Archives of the National Maritime Union

Periodicals (1939–49)

Afro American (Washington, D.C.)
Anchors Aweigh (Liverpool)
CIO NEWS (Washington, D.C.)
Daily Herald (London)
Factory News (Coventry)
Collier's (New York)
Humber Clarion (Coventry)
Lincolnshire (U.K.) *Echo*
Manchester (U.K.) *Evening News*
Mass-Observation Bulletin (London)
Mirove Khozyaisko I Moravaya Politika [World Economy and World Politics] (Moscow)
Monthly Journals (Amalgamated Society of Woodworkers, London)
New Leader (London)
Pittsburgh (Pa.) *Courier*
Public Employees Journal (National Union of Public Employees, U.K.)
Railway Review (National Union of Railwaymen, U.K.)
Seaman (National Union of Seamen, U.K.)
Soviet Monitor (Moscow)
St Helens' (U.K.) *Newspaper*
Trade Union World (IFTU, U.K.)
Washington Post (Washington, D.C.)
Washington Daily News (Pullman, Wash.)
Yorkshire (U.K.) *Evening Post*

Interviews

Erkilla, Reino. Interview by author. April 20, 1983. San Francisco.
Germer, Adolph F. Interview by Jack W. Skeels. November 22, 1960. Oral History 38, Wayne State University.
Haessler, Carl. Interview by Jack W. Skeels. November 27, 1959–October 24, 1960. Oral History 42, Wayne State University.

Potofsky, Jacob. Interview by Neil Gold. July 6, 1964. Acc 5619, Box 188, File 1, ACWA, Cornell University.

Reuther, Victor. Interview by Jack W. Skeels. March 7, 1963. Oral History 96, Wayne State University.

Published Works

Acheson, Dean. *Present at the Creation: My Years at the State Department.* New York: Norton, 1969.

Adamthwaite, Anthony. "Britain and the World, 1945–49: The View from the Foreign Office." *International Affairs* 61 (Spring 1985): 223–35.

Addison, Paul. *The Road to 1945: British Politics and the Second World War.* London: Cape, 1975.

Almond, Gabriel. *The American People and Foreign Policy.* New York: Praeger, 1950.

Ambrose, Stephen. *Eisenhower.* Vol. 1 (1890–1952). New York: Simon and Schuster, 1983.

Archibald, Katherine. *Wartime Shipyard: A Study in Social Disunity.* Berkeley: University of California Press, 1947.

Arrighi, Giovanni. "Marxist Century–American Century: The Making and Remaking of the World Labor Movement." In *Transforming the Revolution: Social Movements and the World System.* Edited by Samir Amin, Giovanni Arrighi, André Gunder Frank, and Immanuel Wallerstein. New York: Monthly Review Press, 1990.

Averyanov, Boris. "Soviet Unions and the World Trade Union Movement." *New World Review* (Moscow) 39, no. 2 (1971): 46–56.

Baley, Thomas A. *The Man in the Street.* New York: Macmillan, 1948.

Banton, Michael. *The Coloured Quarter: Negro Immigrants in an English City.* London: Cape, 1955.

Barnes, Denis, and Eileen Reid. "A New Relationship: Trade Unions in the Second World War." In *Trade Unions in British Politics.* Edited by Ben Pimlott and Chris Cook. London: Longman, 1982.

Basdeo, Sahadeo. "The Role of the British Labour Movement in the Development of Labour Organisation in Trinidad, 1929–38." *Social and Economic Studies* 31 (March 1982): 40–73.

———. "Walter Citrine and the British Caribbean Workers Movement During the Moyne Commission Hearing, 1938–39." *Journal of Caribbean History* (Barbados) 18 (1983): 43–59.

Behrens, C. B. A. *Merchant Shipping and the Demands of War.* London: HMSO, 1955.

Benstead, J. H. "World Trade Union Congress." *Railway Review,* February 16, 1945.

Betten, Neil. *Catholic Activism and the Industrial Worker.* Gainesville: Florida State University Press, 1976.

Bischoff, G. "Zur Internationalen Gewerkschaftsbewegung Seit 1945." *Dokumentation der Zeit* (GDR) 5 (1972): 14–19.

Bloom, Leonard. "Introduction." In *Negroes in Britain: A Study of Racial Relations in English Society.* Edited by Kenneth Little. 1948. 2d rev. ed., London: Routledge and Kegan Paul, 1972.

Bloomfield, Stuart. "The Apprentice Boys' Strikes of the Second World War." *Llafur* 3 (Spring 1981): 53–67.

Blum, John Morton. *V Was for Victory.* New York: Harvest/HBJ, 1976.

Brody, David. "The Uses of Power I: Industrial Battleground." *Workers in Industrial America: Essays on the Twentieth-Century Struggle.* New York: Oxford University Press, 1980.

Browder, Earl. "The American Communist Party in the Thirties." In *As We Saw the Thirties: Essays on Social and Political Movements of a Decade.* Edited by Rita James Simon. Urbana: University of Illinois Press, 1967.

Brown, Emily Clark. *Soviet Trade Unions and Labor Relations.* Cambridge, Mass.: Harvard University Press, 1966.

Buchanan, Tom. *The Spanish Civil War and the British Labour Movement.* Cambridge, U.K.: Cambridge University Press, 1991.

Bukowczyk, John J. "The Transformation of Working-Class Ethnicity: Corporate Control, Americanization, and the Polish Immigrant Middle Class in Bayonne, New Jersey, 1915–25." *Labor History* 25 (Winter 1984): 53–82.

Bullock, Alan. *The Life and Times of Ernest Bevin.* Vol. 1: *Trade Union Leader, 1881–1940.* London: Heinemann, 1960.

———. *The Life and Times of Ernest Bevin.* Vol. 2: *Minister of Labour, 1940–45.* London: Heinemann, 1967.

———. *Ernest Bevin: Foreign Secretary.* London: Heinemann, 1983.

Burridge, Trevor. *British Labour and Hitler's War.* London: Deutsch, 1976.

———. *Clement Attlee: A Political Biography.* London: Cape, 1985.

Butler, David E. *The British General Election of 1951.* London: Macmillan, 1952.

Butler, David E., and Jennie Freeman. *British Political Facts, 1900–60.* London: Macmillan, 1963.

Byrnes, James F. *Speaking Frankly.* New York: Harper, 1947.

Calder, Angus. *The People's War: Britain, 1939–45.* New York: Pantheon, 1969.

Carew, Anthony. "The Schism Within the World Federation of Trade Unions." *International Review of Social History* 29 (1984): 297–335.

———. *Labour Under the Marshall Plan.* Manchester, U.K.: Manchester University Press, 1987.

———. "Conflict Within the ICFTU: Anti-Communism and Anti-Colonialism in the 1950s." *International Review of Social History* 41 (1996): 147–81.

Carr, Edward Hallet. *The Twenty Years' Crisis, 1919–39: An Introduction to the Study of International Relations.* 2d ed. London: Macmillan, 1946.

———. *Socialism in One Country, 1924–26: A History of Soviet Russia.* 9 vols. 1964. Reprint, Middlesex: Penguin, 1972.

Catton, Bruce. *Warlords of Washington.* New York: Harcourt Brace, 1948.
Caute, David. *The Great Fear: The Anti-Communist Purge Under Truman and Eisenhower.* New York: Simon and Schuster, 1978.
Chomsky, Noam. *American Power and the New Mandarins.* New York: Pantheon, 1969.
Chrichtlow, Donald. "Communist Unions and Racism." *Labor History* 17 (Spring 1982): 165–97.
Churchill, Winston. *Europe Unite: Speeches, 1947–48.* Boston: Houghton Mifflin, 1950.
———. *The Grand Alliance.* Boston: Houghton Mifflin, 1951.
Citrine, Walter. *Democracy or Disruption? An Examination of Communist Influences in the Trade Unions.* London: Trades Union Congress, 1928.
———. *I Search for Truth in Russia.* Popular ed. rev. London: Routledge, 1938.
———. *My Finnish Diary.* Harmondsworth, U.K.: Penguin, 1940.
———. *In Russia Now.* London: Hale, 1942.
———. *The Grand Alliance.* Boston: Houghton Mifflin, 1950.
———. *Men at Work.* London: Hutchinson, 1964.
———. *Two Careers.* London: Hutchinson, 1967.
Clemens, Diane S. *Yalta.* London: Oxford University Press, 1970.
Cochran, Bert. *Labor and Communism: The Conflict That Shaped American Unions.* Princeton, N.J.: Princeton University Press, 1977.
Cohen, Lizabeth. *Making a New Deal: Industrial Workers in Chicago, 1919–39.* New York: Cambridge University Press, 1990.
Cornford, Daniel, and Sally Miller, eds. *American Labor in the Era of World War II.* Westport, Conn.: Praeger, 1995.
Craik, W. W. *Bryn Roberts and the National Union of Public Employees.* London: Allen and Unwin, 1955.
Cronin, James E. *Labour and Society in Britain.* London: Batsford Academic and Educational, 1984.
Croucher, Richard. *Engineers at War.* London: Merlin, 1982.
Cunningham, Hugh. "The Conservative Party and Patriotism." In *Englishness: Politics and Culture, 1880–1920.* Edited by Robert Colls and Philip Dodd. London: Croom Helm, 1986.
Dallek, Robert. *Franklin D. Roosevelt and American Foreign Policy.* Oxford: Oxford University Press, 1979.
Dalton, Hugh. *The Second World War Diary of Hugh Dalton, 1940–45.* Edited by Ben Pimlott. London: Cape, 1986.
Davidson, Ray. *Challenging the Giants: A History of the Oil, Chemical, and Atomic Workers International Union.* Denver, Colo.: Oil, Chemical, and Atomic Workers International Union, 1988.
Davis, Mike. *Prisoners of the American Dream: Politics and Economy in the History of the U.S. Working Class.* London: Verso, 1986.
DePorte, A. W. *Europe Between the Superpowers.* New Haven, Conn.: Yale University Press, 1979.

Dilks, David, ed. *The Diaries of Sir Alexander Cadogan.* London: Cassell, 1971.

Dintenfass, Michael. Review of Keith Middlemas, *Politics in Industrial Society. Bulletin of the Society for the Study of Labour History* 41 (Autumn 1980): 63–65

Divine, Robert A. *Second Chance: The Triumph of Internationalism in America During World War II.* New York: Atheneum, 1967.

Dower, John. *War Without Mercy: Race and Power in the Pacific War.* New York: Pantheon, 1986.

Dunn, Robert W. *Soviet Trade Unions.* New York: Vanguard, 1928.

Durand Ponte, Victor Manuel. *La Ruptura de la Nación.* México: Universidad Nacional Autónoma de México, 1986.

Eisenberg, Carolyn. "Working-Class Politics and the Cold War: American Intervention in the German Labor Movement." *Diplomatic History* 7 (Fall 1983): 283–306.

Epstein, Leon D. *Britain: Uneasy Ally.* Chicago: University of Chicago Press, 1954.

Evans, Neil. "The South Wales Race Riots of 1919." *Llafur* 3 (1983): 76–87.

Falk, Richard. *The End of World Order: Essays on Normative International Relations.* New York: Holmes and Meier, 1983.

Feis, Herbert. *Churchill, Roosevelt, Stalin: The War They Waged and the Peace They Sought.* Princeton, N.J.: Princeton University Press, 1957.

Fichter, Michael. *Besatzungsmacht und Gewerkschaften: Zur Entwicklung und Anwendung der U.S.-Gewerkschaftspolitik in Deutschland, 1944–88.* Berlin: Westdeutscher Verlag, 1982.

Fielding, Steve. "'Don't Know and Don't Care': Popular Political Attitudes in Labour's Britain, 1945–51." In *The Attlee Years.* Edited by Nick Tiratsoo. London: Pinter, 1991.

Filene, Peter G. *Americans and the Soviet Experiment, 1917–33.* Cambridge, Mass.: Harvard University Press, 1967.

Filippelli, Ronald. *American Labor and Postwar Italy, 1943–53.* Stanford, Calif.: Stanford University Press, 1989.

Filtzer, Donald. *Soviet Workers and Stalinist Industrialization: The Formation of Modern Soviet Production Relations, 1928–41.* Armonk, N.Y.: Sharpe, 1986.

Fitzpatrick, Sheila. "War and Society in the Soviet Context: Soviet Labor Before, During, and After World War II." *International Labor and Working-Class History* 35 (Spring 1989): 37–52.

Flores, Antonio Rivera. *La Derrota de Lombardo Toledano.* Queretaro, Mexico: Universidad Autónoma de Queretaro, Centro de Investigaciones Sociologica, 1984.

Flynn, George Q. *American Catholics and the Roosevelt Presidency, 1932–36.* Lexington: University of Kentucky Press, 1968.

Foster, William Z. *Outline History of the World Trade Union Movement.* New York: International, 1956.

Fraser, Steve. "Sidney Hillman: Labor's Machiavelli." In *Labor Leaders in America.* Edited by Melvyn Dubofsky and Warren Van Tine. Urbana: University of Illinois Press, 1987.

———. *Labor Will Rule: Sidney Hillman and the Rise of American Labor.* New York: Free Press, 1991.

Freeland, Richard. *The Truman Doctrine and the Origins of McCarthyism: Foreign Policy, Domestic Politics, and Internal Security, 1946–48.* New York: New York University Press, 1985.

Freeman, Joshua. *In Transit: The Transit Workers Union in New York City, 1933–66.* New York: Oxford University Press, 1989.

Friedlander, Peter. *Emergence of a UAW Local, 1936–39: A Study in Class and Culture.* Pittsburgh, Pa.: University of Pittsburgh Press, 1975.

Fyrth, Jim, ed. *Labour's High Noon: The Government and the Economy, 1945–51.* London: Lawrence and Wishart, 1993.

Gaddis, John Lewis. *The United States and the Origins of the Cold War.* New York: Columbia University Press, 1972.

Galarza, Ernesto. *Merchants of Labor: The Mexican Bracero Story.* Charlotte, N.C.: McNally and Loftin, 1964.

Gallup, George H. *The Gallup International Public Opinion Polls: Great Britain, 1937–75.* Vol. 1. New York: Random House, 1976.

Gerstle, Gary. *Working-Class Americanism.* Cambridge, U.K.: Cambridge University Press, 1989.

Glazier, Nathan. *Social Bases of American Communism.* New York: Harcourt, Brace, and World, 1961.

Gobel, Thomas. "Becoming American: Ethnic Workers and the Rise of the CIO." *Labor History* 29 (Spring 1988): 173–98.

Godson, Roy. *American Labor and European Politics.* New York: Crane Russak, 1976.

Goldthorpe, J., and D. Lockwood. *The Affluent Worker in the Class Structure.* London: Cambridge University Press, 1969.

Gordon, Michael R. *Conflict and Consensus in Labour's Foreign Policy, 1914–65.* Stanford, Calif.: Stanford University Press, 1969.

Gorz, André. *Adieux au Proletariat.* Paris: Éditions Galilée, 1980.

Gouldner, Alvin. *The Future of Intellectuals and the Rise of the New Class.* New York: Continuum, 1979.

Grahl, John. "A Fateful Decision? Labour and the Schuman Plan." In *Labour's High Noon: The Government and the Economy, 1945–51.* Edited by Jim Furth. London: Lawrence and Wishart, 1993.

Graubard, Stephen R. *British Labour and the Russian Revolution, 1917–24.* Boston: Harvard University Press, 1956.

Gregory, James N. *American Exodus: The Dustbowl Migration and Okie Culture in California.* New York: Oxford University Press, 1989.

Gupta, Partha Sarathi. *Imperialism and the British Labour Movement.* London: Macmillan, 1975.

Halpern, Martin. *UAW Politics in the Cold War Era.* Albany: State University of New York Press, 1988.

———. "The 1939 UAW Convention: Turning Point for Communist Power in the Auto Union?" *Labor History* 33 (Spring 1992): 190–216.

Harrison, Martin. *Trade Unions and the Labour Party Since 1945.* London: Allen and Unwin, 1960.

Harrisson, Tom (and H. D. Willcock). "British Opinion Moves Toward a New Synthesis." *Public Opinion Quarterly* 11 (Fall 1947): 328–30.

Harrod, Jeffrey. *Trade Union Foreign Policy: A Study of British and American Trade Union Activities in Jamaica.* Garden City, N.Y.: Doubleday, 1972.

Hillman, Sidney. "One Voice for Sixty Million." *Collier's,* September 29, 1945.

Hinton, James. "Coventry Communism: A Study of Factory Politics in the Second World War." *History Workshop* 10 (Autumn 1980): 90–118.

———. "Voluntarism versus Jacobinism: Labor, Nation, and Citizenship in Britain, 1850–1950." *International Labor and Working Class History* 48 (Fall 1995): 68–90.

Hobsbawm, E. J. "Working-Class Internationalism." In *Internationalism in the Labour Movement, 1830–1940.* Vol. 1. Edited by Frits van Holthoon and Marcel van der Linden. Leiden, The Netherlands: Brill; 1988.

Horkheimer, Max. *Eclipse of Reason.* 1947. Reprint, New York: Seabury Press, 1974.

Horowitz, Ruth. *Political Ideologies of Organized Labor.* New Brunswick, N.J.: Transaction, 1978.

Howe, Irving, and Lewis Coser. *The American Communist Party: A Critical History.* New York: Praeger, 1962.

Howe, Irving, and B. J. Widdick. *The UAW and Walter Reuther.* New York: Praeger, 1973.

Hull, Cordell. *Memoirs.* Vol. 2. New York: Macmillan, 1948.

Hyde, Douglas. *I Believed.* 1950. Reprint, London: Reprint Society, 1952.

Hyman, Richard. "Praetorians and Proletarians: Unions and Industrial Relations." In *Labour's High Noon: The Government and the Economy, 1945–51.* Edited by Jim Furth. London: Lawrence and Wishart, 1993.

International Confederation of Free Trade Unions. "Manifesto of the ICFTU." In *ICFTU Report, 1949.* London: ICFTU, 1949.

———. *Official Report of the Free World Labour Conference and of the International Confederation of Free Trade Unions.* London: TUC, 1949.

International Federation of Trade Unions. *Directives pour la Politique Economique.* Amsterdam: IFTU, 1929.

———. *Triennial Report, 1933–35.* Paris: IFTU, 1937.

———. *Project for the Reconstruction of the International Trade Union Movement.* London: IFTU, 1944.

Iriye, Akira. *Power and Culture: The Japanese-American War.* Cambridge, Mass.: Harvard University Press, 1981.

Iscaro, Ruben. *Historia de la Federación Sindical Mundial.* Buenos Aires: Editorial Anteo, 1983.

Jones, Bill. *The Russia Complex: The British Labour Party and the Soviet Union.* Manchester, U.K.: Manchester University Press, 1977.

Jordan, Winthrop. *White over Black.* 1968. Reprint. New York: Norton, 1977.

Josephson, Matthew. *Sidney Hillman: Statesman of American Labor.* New York: Doubleday, 1952.

Kanawada, Leo V. Jr. *Franklin D. Roosevelt's Diplomacy and American Catholics, Italians, and Jews.* Ann Arbor, Mich.: UMI Research Press, 1982.

Kautsky, Karl. *The Social Revolution.* Translated by A. M. Simons and May W. Simons. Chicago: Kerr, 1910.

———. *The Dictatorship of the Proletariat.* Translated by H. J. Stenning. Ann Arbor: University of Michigan Press, 1964.

Keeran, Roger. *The Communist Party and the Auto Workers' Unions.* New York: International, 1980.

Kennan, George. *American Diplomacy, 1900–50.* Chicago: University of Chicago Press, 1951.

———. *Memoirs, 1925–50.* Boston: Little, Brown, 1967.

———. "Long Telegram." In *Major Problems in America Foreign Policy Since 1945.* Vol. 2. Edited by Thomas Paterson. Lexington Mass.; Heath, 1989.

Keohane, Robert O., ed. *Neorealism and Its Critics.* New York: Columbia University Press, 1986.

Kimmeldorf, Howard. *Reds or Rackets: The Making of Radical and Conservative Unions on the Waterfront.* Berkeley: University of California Press, 1988.

Klehr, Harvey. *Heyday of America Communism: The Depression Decade.* New York: Basic, 1984.

Koch-Baumgarten, Sigrid, and Peter Rütters, eds. *Zwischen Integration und Autonomie: Der Konflikt zwischen den IBS und dem WGB um den Neuaufbau einer Internationalen Gewerkschaftsbewegung, 1945–49.* Cologne, Germany: Bund-Verlag, 1991.

Kolko, Gabriel. *The Politics of War: The World and United States Foreign Policy, 1943–45.* New York: Random House, 1969.

Konrad, Gyorgy, and Ivan Szelezny. *The Intellectuals on the Road to Class Power.* Translated by A. Arato and R. E. Allen. New York: Harcourt, Brace, Jovanovich, 1979.

Krauzé, Enrique. *Caudillos Culturales de la Revolución Mexicana.* Mexico: Secretario de Educación Publica, 1985.

La Botz, Dan. *The Crisis of Mexican Labor.* New York: Praeger, 1988.

Laclau, Ernesto, and Chantal Mouffe. *Hegemony and Socialist Strategy: Toward a Radical Democratic Politics* London: Verso, 1985.

Lademacher, Horst. "Kosmopolitismus, Solidarität und Nation: Einige Bemerkungen zum Wandel von Begriff und Wirklichkeit im Internationalen Sozialismus." In *Internationalism in the Labour Movement, 1830–1940.* Vol. 2. Edited by Frits van Holthoon and Marcel van der Linden. Leiden, The Netherlands: Brill, 1988.

Lademacher, Horst, Jürgen C. Heß, Herman J. Langveld, and Henk Reitsma. "Der Weltgewerkschaftsbund im Spannungsfeld des Ost-West Konflikts." *Archiv für Sozialgeschichte* 18 (1978): 119–216.

LaFeber, Walter. *America, Russia, and the Cold War.* 5th ed. New York: Knopf, 1985.

Larrowe, Charles P. *Harry Bridges: The Rise and Fall of Radical Labor in the United States.* 2d. ed. rev. Westport, Conn.: Hill, 1977.

Lasch, Christopher. *The Agony of the American Left.* New York: Knopf, 1969.

Lee, Alan J. "Conservatism, Traditionalism, and the British Working Class." In *Ideology and the Labour Movement.* Edited by David E. Martin and David Rubinstein. London: Croom Helm, 1979.

Leigh, Michael. *Mobilizing Consent: Public Opinion and American Foreign Policy.* Westport, Conn.: Greenwood, 1976.

Lenin, V. I. *What Is to Be Done?* In *Essential Works of Lenin.* Edited by Henry M. Christman. New York: Bantam, 1966.

Levenstein, Harvey A. *Labor Organizations in the United States and Mexico: A History of their Relations.* Westport, Conn.: Greenwood, 1971.

———. *Communism, Anti-Communism, and the CIO.* Westport, Conn.: Greenwood, 1981.

Levering, Ralph. *American Opinion and the Russian Alliance, 1939–45.* Chapel Hill: University of North Carolina Press, 1976.

Lichtenstein, Nelson. *Labor's War at Home: The CIO in World War II.* Cambridge, U.K.: Cambridge University Press, 1982.

———. "Walter Reuther and the Rise of Labor Liberalism." In *Labor Leaders in America.* Edited by Melvyn Dubofsky and Warren Van Tine. Urbana: University of Illinois Press, 1987.

———. "The Making of the Postwar Working Class: Cultural Pluralism and Social Structure in World War II." *Historian* 51 (November 1988): 42–63.

———. "From Corporatism to Collective Bargaining: American Labor and the Eclipse of Social Democracy in the Postwar Era." In *The Rise and Fall of the New Deal Order, 1930–80.* Edited by Gary Gerstle and Steve Fraser. Princeton, N.J.: Princeton University Press, 1989.

———. *The Most Dangerous Man in Detroit: Walter Reuther and the Fate of American Labor.* New York: Basic, 1995.

Lippmann, Walter. *Public Opinion.* New York: Harcourt, Brace, 1922.

———. *U.S. Foreign Policy: Shield of the Republic.* Boston: Little, Brown, 1943.

Little, Kenneth. *Negroes in Britain: A Study of Racial Relations in English Society.* 1948. 2d rev. ed., London: Routledge and Kegan Paul, 1972.

Lorwin, Lewis. *The International Labor Movement.* New York: Harper, 1953.

Louis, William Roger. *Imperialism at Bay: The United States and the Decolonization of the British Empire, 1941–45.* New York: Oxford University Press, 1978.

Lowe, Robert. "The Ministry of Labour: Fact and Fiction." *Bulletin of the Society for the Study of Labour History* 41 (Autumn 1980): 23–28.

Lukács, Georg. *History and Class Consciousness: Studies in Marxist Dialectics.* Translated by Rodney Livingstone. 1968. Cambridge, Mass.: MIT Press, 1971.

Lunn, Kenneth. "Race Relations or Industrial Relations? Race and Labour in Britain, 1880–1950." *Immigrants and Minorities* 4 (July 1985): 1–39.

———. "The Employment of Polish and European Volunteer Workers in the Scottish Coalfields, 1945–50." In *Towards a Social History of Mining in the Nineteenth and Twentieth Centuries.* Edited by K. Tenflede. Munich: Beck, 1992.

———. "'Race' and Immigration: Labour's Hidden History." In *Labour's High Noon: The Government and the Economy, 1945–51*. Edited by Jim Furth. London: Lawrence and Wishart, 1993.

Lyons, Eugene. *The Red Decade: The Stalinist Penetration of America.* Indianapolis, Ind.: Bobbs-Merrill, 1941.

Macintyre, Stuart. *Little Moscows: Communism and Working-Class Militancy in Interwar Britain.* London: Croom Helm, 1980.

Maier, Charles. "Politics of Productivity." *International Organizations* 31 (Fall 1977): 607–33.

Marsh, Arthur, and Victoria Ryan. *The Seamen.* Hassocks, West Sussex, U.K.: Malthouse, 1988.

Martin, Roderick. *Communism and the British Trade Unions, 1924–33: A Study of the National Minority Movement.* Oxford: Oxford University Press, 1969.

Marwick, Arthur. *War and Social Change in the Twentieth Century: A Comparative Study of Britain, France, Germany, Russia, and the United States.* New York: St. Martin's, 1974.

Marx, Karl. *Wages, Price, and Profit.* In Karl Marx and Frederick Engels, *Selected Works.* Vol. 2. Moscow: Progress, 1969.

Marx, Karl, and Frederick Engels. *Manifesto of the Communist Party.* In *Selected Works.* Vol. 1. Moscow: Progress, 1969.

Mass-Observation. *People in Production.* London: Murray, 1942.

———. *War Factory.* London: Gollanz, 1943.

———. *Peace and the Public.* London: Longmans, Green, 1947.

Matles, James J., and James Higgins. *Them and Us: Struggles of a Rank-and-File Union.* Boston: Beacon, 1974.

May, Roy, and Robin Cohen. "The Interaction of Race and Colonialism: A Case Study of the Liverpool Race Riots of 1919." *Race and Class* 16 (October 1974): 111–26.

McAuliffe, Mary Sperling. *Crisis on the Left: Cold War Politics and American Liberals.* Amherst: University of Massachusetts Press, 1978.

McClure, Arthur F. *The Truman Administration and the Problems of Postwar Labor.* Rutherford, N.J.: Fairleigh Dickinson University Press, 1969.

McDonald, G. W., and H. Gospel. "The Mond-Turner Talks, 1927–33: A Study in Industrial Cooperation." *Historical Journal* 14 (Winter 1973): 807–29.

McKenzie, Robert, and Allan Silver. *Angels in Marble: Working-Class Conservatives in Urban England.* London: Heineman, 1968.

McKillen, Elizabeth. *Chicago Labor and the Quest for a Democratic Diplomacy.* Ithaca, N.Y.: Cornell University Press, 1995.

McShane, Denis. *International Labour and the Origins of the Cold War.* Oxford: Clarendon, 1992.

Meier, August, and Elliot Rudwick. *Black Detroit and the Rise of the UAW.* Oxford: Oxford University Press, 1979.

Messer, Ronald L. *End of an Alliance: James F. Byrnes, Roosevelt, Truman, and the Origins of the Cold War.* Chapel Hill: University of North Carolina Press, 1982.

Meyer, Stephen. *Stalin over Wisconsin: The Making and Unmaking of Militant Unionism, 1900–50*. New Brunswick, N.J.: Rutgers University Press, 1992.

Michel, Jean-François. "La Scission de la Fédération Syndicale Mondiale." *Mouvement Social* (France) 117 (1981): 33–52.

Middlemas, Keith. *Politics in Industrial Society: The Experience of the British System Since 1911*. London: Deutsch, 1979.

Mills, C. Wright. *The New Men of Power: America's Labor Leaders*. New York: Harcourt, Brace, 1948.

———. *White Collar: The American Middle Classes*. New York: Oxford University Press, 1951.

Milton, David. *The Politics of U.S. Labor*. New York: Monthly Review Press, 1982.

Morgan, Kenneth O. *Labour in Power, 1945–51*. Oxford: Oxford University Press, 1985.

Murphy, Robert. *Diplomat Among Warriors*. Garden City, N.Y.: Doubleday, 1964.

Murray, Philip. "Labor and Responsibility." *Virginia Quarterly* 16 (April 1940): 267–78.

Nagorski, Zygmunt Jr. "Liberation Movements in Exile." *Journal of Central European Affairs* 10 (July 1950): 129–44.

National Council of Labour. *Labour's Aims in War and Peace*. London: Lincoln Praeger, 1940.

Nicholson, Marjorie. *The TUC Overseas: The Roots of Policy*. London: Allen and Unwin, 1986.

Niethammer, Lutz. "Structural Reform and a Compact for Growth: Conditions for a United Labor Movement in Europe After the Collapse of Fascism." In *The Origins of the Cold War and Contemporary Europe*. Edited by Charles Maier. New York: New Viewpoints, 1978.

Northedge, F. S., and Audrey Wells. *Britain and Soviet Communism: The Impact of a Revolution*. London: Macmillan, 1982.

O'Brien, David J. *American Catholics and Social Reform: The New Deal Years*. New York: Oxford University Press, 1968.

Orwell, George. *The Lion and the Unicorn: Socialism and the English Genius*. London: Secker and Warburg, 1941.

Ovendale, Ritchie, ed. *The Foreign Policy of the British Labour Governments, 1945–51*. Leicester, U.K.: Leicester University Press, 1984.

Owen, Nicholas. "'Responsibility Without Power': The Attlee Governments and the End of British Rule in India." In *The Attlee Years*. Edited by Nick Tiratsoo. London: Pinter, 1991.

Panitch, Leo. *Social Democracy and Industrial Militancy: The Labour Party, the Trade Unions, and Incomes Policy, 1945–47*. Cambridge, U.K.: Cambridge University Press, 1976.

Pelling, Henry M. *America and the British Left: From Bright to Bevan*. New York: New York University Press, 1957.

———. *The British Communist Party: A Historical Profile*. London: Black, 1958.

———. "The Working Class and the Origins of the Welfare State." In *Popular Politics and Society in late Victorian Britain: Essays*. 2d ed. London: Macmillan, 1979.

Piehl, Mel. *Breaking Bread: The Catholic Worker and the Origin of Catholic Radicalism in America.* Philadelphia: Temple University Press, 1982.

Pimlott, Ben. *Labour and the Left in the 1930s.* Cambridge, U.K.: Cambridge University Press, 1977.

Polenberg, Richard. *War and Society: The United States, 1941–45.* Philadelphia, Pa.: Lippincott, 1972.

Prokhorov, Vasili. *Lenin and the Trade Unions.* Moscow: Novosti Press Agency, 1970.

Radosh, Ronald. *American Labor and U.S. Foreign Policy.* New York: Random House, 1969.

Renshaw, Patrick. "The Depression Years, 1918–31." In *Trade Unions in British Politics.* Edited by Ben Pimlott and Chris Cook. London: Longman, 1982.

Reuther, Victor. *The Brothers Reuther and the Story of the UAW: A Memoir.* Boston: Houghton Mifflin, 1976.

Richter, Irving. *Labor's Struggles, 1945–50: A Participant's View* Cambridge, U.K.: Cambridge University Press, 1994.

Roberts, Bryn. *The American Labour Split and Allied Unity.* London: Lawrence and Wishart, 1943.

Rogin, Michael Paul. *The Intellectuals and McCarthy: The Radical Specter.* Cambridge, Mass.: MIT Press, 1967.

———. "Voluntarism: The Political Functions of an Antipolitical Doctrine." In *The American Labor Movement.* Edited by David Brody. New York: Harper and Row, 1971.

Romero, Federico. *The United States and the Reconstruction of the European Trade Union Movement, 1944–51.* Translated by Harvey Fergusson II. Chapel Hill: University of North Carolina Press, 1992.

Romualdi, Serafino. *Presidents and Peons: Recollections of a Labor Ambassador.* New York: Funk and Wagnalls, 1967.

Ross, Gabriel. *El Neocolonialismo Sindical.* Buenos Aires: Ediciones de la Línea, 1974.

Rosswurm, Stephen, ed. *The CIO's Left-Led Unions.* New Brunswick, N.J.: Rutgers University Press, 1992.

Rothwell, Victor. *Britain and the Cold War, 1941–47.* London: Cape, 1982.

Roxborough, Ian. "The Mexican Charrazo of 1948: Latin American Labor from World War to Cold War." Helen Kellogg Institute for International Studies, Working Paper 77. Notre Dame, Ind.: University of Notre Dame, 1986.

Ruble, Blair. *The Applicability of Corporatist Models to the Study of Soviet Politics: The Case of Trade Unions.* Carl Beck Papers in Russian and East European Studies, paper 303. Pittsburgh, Pa.: Russian and East European Studies Program, University of Pittsburgh, 1983.

Samuel, Raphael. "The Lost World of British Communism." *New Left Review* 154 (November–December 1985): 3–53; 156 (March–April 1986): 63–113; 165 (September–October 1987): 52–91.

———. *Patriotism: The Making and Unmaking of British National Identity.* New York: Routledge, 1989.

Schatz, Ronald. *The Electrical Workers: A History of Labor at General Electric and Westinghouse, 1923–60.* Urbana: University of Illinois Press, 1983.

———. "Philip Murray and the Subordination of the Industrial Unions to the United States Government." In *Labor Leaders in America.* Edited by Melvyn Dubofsky and Warren Van Tine. Urbana: University of Illinois Press, 1987.

Schevenels, Walter. "Toward Greater Unity in the World Trade Union Movement." *Trade Union World* 3 (January–February 1945): 3.

Schwartz, Harvey. "A Union Combats Racism: The ILWU's Japanese-American 'Stockton Incident' of 1945." *Southern California Quarterly* 62 (Summer 1980): 161–76.

Seaton, Douglas. *Catholics and Radicals.* Lewisburg, Pa.: Bucknell University Press, 1981.

Sensenig, Gene. *Österreichisch-Amerikanische Gewerkschaftsbeziehungen, 1945 bis 1950.* Cologne, Germany: Pahl Rugenstein, 1987.

Sherwood, Marika. *Many Struggles: West Indian Workers and Service Personnel in Britain, 1939–45.* London: Karia Press, 1984.

Sherwood, Robert. *White House Papers of Harry Hopkins.* Vol. 2. London: Eyre and Spottiswoode, 1949.

Shorske, Carl. *German Social Democracy.* 1955. Reprint, New York: Russel and Russel, 1970.

Siegelbaum, Lewis, and Ronald Suny, eds. *Making Workers Soviet.* Ithaca, N.Y.: Cornell University Press, 1994.

Silverman, Victor. "Is National History a Thing of the Past? On the Growing Reality of World History in the Twentieth Century." *European Legacy* 1 (April 1996): 696–702.

Sirgiovanni, George. *An Undercurrent of Suspicion: Anti-Communist and Anti-Soviet Opinion in World War II America.* New Brunswick, N.J.: Transaction, 1990.

Sloterdijk, Peter. *Critique of Cynical Reason.* Translated by Michael Eldred. Minneapolis: University of Minnesota Press, 1987.

Small, Melvin. "How We Learned to Love the Russians: American Media and the Soviet Union During World War II." *Historian* 36 (May 1974): 455–78.

Smith, Andrew. *I Was a Soviet Worker.* New York: Dutton, 1936.

Smith, Gaddis. *American Diplomacy During the Second World War.* New York: Wiley, 1969.

Smith, Harold L., ed. *War and Social Change: British Society in the Second World War.* Manchester, U.K.: Manchester University Press, 1986.

Smith, Jean Edward. "General Clay and the Russians: A Continuation of the Wartime Alliance in Germany, 1945–48." *Virginia Quarterly Review* 64 (1988): 20–36.

Smith, M. Brewster. "The Personal Setting of Public Opinion: A Study of Attitudes Toward Russia." *Public Opinion Quarterly* 11 (Winter 1947–48): 507–23.

Smith, Raymond. "A Climate of Opinion: British Officials and the Development of British Soviet Policy, 1945–47." *International Affairs* 64 (Autumn 1988): 631–47.

Spalding, Hobart A. Jr. *Organized Labor in Latin America.* New York: New York University Press, 1977.

Starobin, Joseph. *American Communism in Crisis, 1943–57.* Berkeley: University of California Press, 1972.

Steininger, Rolf. "England und die deutsche Gewerkschaftsbewegung, 1945–46." *Archiv für Sozialgeschichte* 18 (1978): 41–118.

Strauss, A., and J. Corbin. *Basics of Qualitative Research.* Newbury Park, Calif.: Sage, 1990.

Sturmthal, Adolf. *Unity and Diversity in European Labor.* Glencoe, Ill.: Free Press, 1953.

Summerfield, Penny. *Women Workers in the Second World War.* London: Croom Helm, 1984.

Susman, Warren. *Culture as History: The Transformation of American Society in the Twentieth Century.* New York: Pantheon, 1984.

Tabili, Laura. *We Ask for British Justice: Workers and Racial Difference in Late Imperial Britain.* Ithaca, N.Y.: Cornell University Press, 1994.

Taft, Philip. *The AFL in the Time of Gompers.* New York: Harper, 1957.

Tannahil, J. A. *European Volunteer Workers in Britain.* Manchester, U.K.: Manchester University Press, 1958.

Taylor, Ian. "Labour and the Impact of War, 1939–45." In *The Attlee Years.* Edited by Nick Tiratsoo. London: Pinter, 1991.

Thorne, Christopher. *Allies of a Kind: The United States, Britain, and the War against Japan, 1941–45.* New York: Oxford University Press, 1978.

———. *The Issue of War: States, Societies, and the Far Eastern Conflict of 1941–45.* London: H. Hamilton, 1985.

Tiratsoo, Nick, ed. *The Attlee Years.* London: Pinter, 1991.

Titmuss, Richard. *Problems of Social Policy.* London: HMSO, 1950.

Tombs, Isabelle. "Erlich and Alter, 'The Sacco and Vanzetti of the USSR': An Episode in the Wartime History of International Socialism." *Journal of Contemporary History* 23 (1988): 531–49.

Tomlins, Christopher L. *The State and the Unions: Labor Relations, Law, and the Organized Labor Movement in America, 1880–1960.* Cambridge, U.K.: Cambridge University Press, 1985.

Tomlinson, G. A. W. *Coal-Miner.* London: Hutchinson, n.d. (1937).

Trades Union Congress. *Report of Proceedings at the 73d Annual Trades Union Congress.* London: Cooperative Printing Society, 1941.

———. *Report of Proceedings at the 75th Annual Trades Union Congress.* London: Cooperative Printing Society, 1943.

———. *Report of the Proceedings at the 77th Annual Trades Union Congress.* London: Cooperative Printing Society, 1945.

———. *Report of Proceedings at the 78th Annual Trades Union Congress.* London: Cooperative Printing Society, 1946.

Trask, Roger. "The Impact of the Cold War on United States–Latin American Relations." *Diplomatic History* 1 (Summer 1977): 271–84.

Trotter, Joe William Jr. *Black Milwaukee: The Making of an Industrial Proletariat, 1915–45.* Urbana: University of Illinois Press, 1985.

U.S. Bureau of the Census. *Statistical Abstract of the United States, 1948.* Washington, D.C.: USGPO, 1948.

U.S. Department of State. *Foreign Relations of the United States, 1944.* Vol. 2. Washington: USGPO, 1966.

———. *Foreign Relations of the United States, 1945.* Vol. 1. Washington: USGPO, 1967.

Varma, S. P. *International Systems and the Third World: A Study in Changing Perspectives.* New Delhi: Vikas, 1988.

Wall, Irwin M. *The United States and the Making of Postwar France, 1945–54.* Cambridge, U.K.: Cambridge University Press, 1991.

Wallace, Henry A. *The Price of Vision: The Diaries of Henry A. Wallace.* Edited by John Blum. Boston: Houghton Mifflin, 1973.

Walsh, Warren B. "What the American People Think of Russia." *Public Opinion Quarterly* 8 (Winter 1944–45): 512–22.

Walton, Richard J. *Henry Wallace, Harry Truman, and the Cold War.* New York: Viking, 1976.

Ward, Patricia Dawson. *The Threat of Peace: James F. Byrnes and the Council of Foreign Ministers.* Kent, Ohio: Kent State University Press, 1979.

Warner, Geoffrey. "The Labour Governments and the Unity of Europe, 1945–51." In *The Foreign Policy of the British Labour Governments.* Edited by Ritchie Ovendale. Leicester, U.K.: Leicester University Press, 1984.

Washburn, Patrick S. *A Question of Sedition: The Federal Government's Investigation of the Black Press During World War II.* New York: Oxford University Press, 1986.

Watson, J. L., ed. *Between Two Cultures: Migrants and Minorities in Britain.* Oxford: Oxford University Press, 1977.

Watt, D. Cameron. "Britain, the United States, and the Opening of the Cold War." In *The Foreign Policy of the British Labour Government, 1945–51.* Edited by Ritchie Ovendale. Leicester, U.K.: Leicester University Press, 1984.

Webb, Sidney, and Beatrice Webb. *Soviet Communism: A New Civilization.* 3d ed. London: Longmans, Green, 1944.

Weber, Hermann, and Dietrich Startz, eds. *Einheitsfront—Einheitspartei: Kommunisten und Sozial-Demokraten in Ost- und West-Europa, 1944–48.* Cologne, Germany: Verlag Wissenschaft und Politik, 1989.

Weiler, Peter. *British Labor and the Cold War.* Stanford, Calif.: Stanford University Press, 1988.

Willen, Paul. "Who 'Collaborated' with Russia?" *Antioch Review* 14 (Fall 1954): 259–83.

Williams, Francis. *A Prime Minister Remembers: The War and Post-War Memoirs of the Rt. Hon. Earl Attlee.* London: Heinemann, 1961.

Williams, William Appleman. *The Tragedy of American Diplomacy.* 1959. Rev. ed., New York: Dell, 1962.

Windmuller, John P. *American Labor and the International Labor Movement: 1940–53.* Ithaca, N.Y.: Cornell Institute of International Relations Reports, 1954.

Windrich, Elaine. *British Labour's Foreign Policy.* Stanford, Calif.: Stanford University Press, 1952.

Wittner, Lawrence. *American Intervention in Greece, 1943–49.* New York: Columbia University Press, 1982.

Wolfe, Alan. *America's Impasse: The Rise and Fall of the Politics of Growth.* Boston: South End, 1981.

Woodward, Llewellyn. *British Foreign Policy in the Second World War.* Vol. 2. London: HMSO, 1971.

World Trade Union Conference. *Report of the World Trade Union Conference.* London: TUC, 1945.

Wynn, Neil. *The Afro-American and the Second World War.* New York: Holmes and Meier, 1976.

Zieger, Robert. *The CIO, 1935–55.* Chapel Hill: University of North Carolina Press, 1995.

Zizek, Slavoj. *The Sublime Object of Ideology.* London: Verso, 1989.

Zubrzycki, Jerzy. *Polish Immigrants in Britain.* The Hague: Martinus Nijhoff, 1956.

Unpublished Secondary Works

Ashby, Steven. Shattered Dreams: The American Working Class and the Origins of the Cold War, 1945–49. Ph.D. diss., University of Chicago, 1993.

Berger, Henry. Union Diplomacy: American Labor's Foreign Policy in Latin America, 1932–55. Ph.D. diss., University of Wisconsin, Madison, 1966.

Boyden, Richard. The San Francisco Machinists from Depression to Cold War, 1930–50. Ph.D. diss., University of California, Berkeley, 1988.

Burwood, Stephen. American Labor, French Labor, and the Marshall Plan: Battleground and Crossroads. Paper delivered at the 9th Annual North American Labor History Conference, October 22, 1987, Detroit.

McShane, Denis. Unfriendly Delegations. Paper delivered at the 26th Linz Conference of the Internationale Tagung der Historiker der Arbeiterbewegung, September 1990, Linz, Austria.

Rossman, Jeffrey. Rebellion on the Home Front: Cultures of Resistance in a Russian Working-Class Community, June–December 1941. Paper delivered at the eleventh North American Labor History Conference, October 20–22, 1995, Wayne State University, Detroit.

Sallach, David Louis. Enlightened Self-Interest: The Congress of Industrial Organizations and Foreign Policy, 1935–55. Ph.D. diss., Rutgers University, New Brunswick, N.J., 1983.

Samuel, Raphael. Communism in Britain. Paper presented at "Back to the Future" conference, July 9, 1988, South Bank Polytechnic, London.

Silverman, Victor. Left-Led Unions and Racism: A History of the Integration of ILWU Local 10, 1940–60. Seminar paper, University of California, Berkeley, 1983.

———. Race and Radical Unionism: A History of the Marine Cooks and Stewards. Honors thesis, Department of History, University of California, Berkeley, 1984.

Skeels, Jack W. The Development of Political Stability Within the United Automobile Workers' Union. Ph.D. diss., University of Wisconsin, Madison, 1957.

Survey Research Center. How Three People Feel About the International Situation. Paper, Survey Research Center, 4/46. ISR Report #231, ISR Library.

———. Public Attitudes Toward Russia and United States–Russian Relations, Part I:

Attitudes Toward United States–Russian Relations. Paper, Survey Research Center, 3/47. ISR Report #219, ISR Library.

———. Public Attitudes Toward Russia and United States–Russian Relations, Part II: Attitudes and Beliefs About Russia. Paper, Survey Research Center 4/47. ISR Report #220, ISR Library.

———. Public Attitudes Toward American Foreign Policy, Part I: Patterns of Attitudes Toward American Foreign Policy. Paper, Survey Research Center, 5/47. ISR Report #222, ISR Library.

———. [Steven Withey]. Attitudes Toward United States–Russian Relations. Paper, Survey Research Center, 10/48. ISR Report #229, ISR Library.

———. Three Americans Discuss Foreign Affairs. Paper, Survey Research Center, 1/50. ISR Report #234, ISR Library.

Yu Lin. Patricia. Perils Awaiting Those Deemed to Rise Above Their Allotted Status: The Social Impact of Overseas Evacuation of British Children in the Second World War. Bachelor's thesis, Princeton University, Princeton, N.J., 1991.

Zappia, Charles. Unionism and the Italian American Worker: A History of the New York City "Italian Locals" in the International Ladies' Garment Workers' Union. Ph.D. diss., University of California, Berkeley, 1994.

Index

Acheson, Dean, 170–71, 257n.33
ACTU. *See* Association of Catholic Trade Unionists
Adamthwaite, Anthony, 101
Addes, George, 140
AFL. *See* American Federation of Labor
AFL-CIO unity: AFL-CIO Unity for Victory Committee, 155; foreign policies as barrier to, 157–59, 252n.63; hatchet-burying ceremony, 155; impossibility of, before WWII, 155; Pearl Harbor attack and, 155; Roosevelt's promotion of, 155, 156; Taft-Hartley Act and, 157, 158. *See also* American Labor Conference on International Affairs (ALCIA)
African American workers: CIO foreign policy and, 132, 141–42; CIO support of civil rights for, 132, 243–44n.38; hate strikes of 1942–43, 243n.38; identification with colonized countries, 141–42
African politics in the WFTU, 175
ALCIA. *See* American Labor Conference on International Affairs
Allgemeiner Deutscher Gewerkschaftsbund, 29
All-Union Central Council of Soviet Trade Unions (AUCCTU): agreement to avoid British Communists, 97; delegation sent to TUC (1943), 65; Green's opposition to, 25–26; IFTU refuses demands of, 23–24; viewed by British as free trade union, 30–31. *See also* Anglo-Soviet Trade Union Committee (ASC)
Alter, Victor, 26, 147, 148
Amalgamated Clothing Workers of America, 24, 122–23
Amalgamated Society of Woodworkers (ASW): Poles banned by, 222n.42; policies toward the Irish, 104–5; power struggles during the war, 94–95
American Communist Party. *See* Communist Party of the United States of America
American Federation of Labor (AFL): AFL-TUC committee, 157; ALCIA conference and foreign policy of, 156–57; anticommunism of, 2, 22, 30, 32–34, 154, 179–81; British union cooperation eschewed by, 166; cold war in European labor and, 158; domination of international labor relations, 180; foreign policy of, 117, 156–57, 236n.3; Free Trade Union Committee created by, 34, 180, 209n.52; free trade unionism defined by, 30, 32–33; ICFTU founded by, 34–35; IFTU affiliation (1937), 25–26; IFTU too revolutionary for (1920), 22; independent Communist trade unions countering, 24; "industrial peace" proposal, 250n.36; Institutes for Free Labor development, 180; intervention in Latin America, 157, 175, 177, 258n.50, 260n.74; leaders' disconnection from rank-and-file, 117; pro-imperialism of, 174, 258n.50; Taft-Hartley Act opposed by, 137–38, 246n.67; TUC antagonized by, 158, 252n.72; USSR distrusted by, 122; WFTU participation refused by, 33–34; WTUC and, 4, 32. *See also* AFL-CIO unity
Americanism: of American workers, 127; of ethnic American workers, 132–33, 244n.39; importance of, as ideology, 133; internationalism and, 133; in mid-century vs. early twentieth

century, 133; red scare and, 133; Taft-Hartley Act and, 137–38. *See also* Nationalism
American Labor Conference on International Affairs (ALCIA), 156–57
American Labor Party, 147
American workers: African American, 132, 141–42, 243–44n.38; apathy about postwar world, 120; British blamed for war by, 139–40; cold war's lack of appeal for, 183; cynicism about politics among, 121; lack of consensus among, 117, 118; lack of war ideals among, 120–21; Marshall Plan disfavored by, 135; middle-class opinions compared to, 118, 124–25, 237n.7, 239n.45; nationalism of, 117, 127; racism of, toward Japanese, 139; social and cultural makeup of, 128–33; weak internationalism of, 142–43; working-class culture, 118–20
—attitudes of: toward less industrialized nations, 138–39; toward the British, 139–40; toward the USSR, 117, 122–26, 135–36, 178, 236n.2, 245 nn.52–53; toward the war, 115, 119–22, 237–38n.28; toward U.S. foreign policy, 117, 119, 140–41, 235–36n.1
Amilpa, Fernando, 177
Anders, Wladyslaw, 72
Anglo-Chinese Agreement of 1940, 43
Anglo-Russian treaty of 1942, 58, 217n.42
Anglo-Saxon Petroleum, CSU strike of 1942, 44
Anglo-Soviet Trade Union Committee (ASC): AFL-CIO disagreements over, 157; leftists excluded from, 96–97; re-creation of, 30, 96; Soviet-British vicissitudes and, 97; Soviet demand for second front endorsement by the TUC, 97–98; WFTU's origins in, 4
Anticolonialism: American, and racism, 140; of British workers, 78; of the CIO, 173–75
Anticommunism: of the AFL, 2, 22, 30, 32–34, 154, 179–81; AFL-CIO conflicts over, 179–80; of American Catholics, 128, 129–31; American workers' unconcern for, 135–37; anti-Soviet feeling vs., 84; British, and the Grand Alliance, 57–65, 84, 89, 101; of British workers, 83–84; of CIO leaders, 146; as dominant U.S. ideology, 190–91, 263n.25; of the ICFTU, 34–35; of the IFTU, 40; Marshall Plan and, 7, 34–35, 135, 161, 172–73; Nazi invasion of the USSR and, 57–58, 88–89; Nazi-Soviet pact and, 123; New Deal foreign policy and, 137; in the NUS, 111; Taft-Hartley Act and, 137–38, 157, 158, 191, 246n.67; U.S. unions' principle of cooperation and, 151
Archibald, Katherine: on Americanism of ethnic American workers, 132–33; on American workers' attitudes toward the war, 115, 120–21, 122; findings on anticommunism, 136
ASC. *See* Anglo-Soviet Trade Union Committee
Asfour, J., 104
Association of Catholic Trade Unionists (ACTU): anticommunism of, 128, 130–31; Carey's ties to, 148–49; Grand Alliance and, 130–31; union support for, 130, 241n.20
ASW. *See* Amalgamated Society of Woodworkers
Attlee, Clement, 189
AUCCTU. *See* All-Union Central Council of Soviet Trade Unions

Bakunin, Mikhail, 2
Bankole, T. A., 104
Banton, Michael, 75–76
Barsky, Edward, 162
Behrens, C. B. A., 211n.27
Belgian, Danish, Dutch, French, Polish Seafarers Federation (BDDFP), 40, 42
Benstead, John, 70–71, 105
Berger, Samuel, 158, 171
Bevan, Aneurin, 99
Bevin, Ernest: character of, 86; Citrine contrasted with, 86; conflicts with Citrine, 90–92, 102, 108, 227n.22; corporatist bias of, 228n.26; foreign policy, Benstead's critique of, 70–71; hands-off policy toward the WTUC, 102–3; imperialism defended by, 80; influence on British cold war policy, 231n.6; lobbying for U.S. to rebuff the WFTU, 168; Polish refugees and, 74; Popular Front opposed by, 87; relations with USSR, 67; rise to power, 52; on Soviet relations with British trade unions, 87; strikes forbidden by, 61; traditional British foreign policy supported by, 101; TUC delegates to ECOSOC dismissed by, 107–8; U.S. cold war politics accepted by, 50, 189; "voluntaryism" espoused by, 91; WTUC opposed by, 89, 100; WTUC speech of, 100
Big business, and U.S. foreign policy, 134–35
Blackburn, Victor, 68
Black-white relations: African American workers, 132, 141–42, 243–44; in Britain, 75–76, 78. *See also* People of color; Racism

Bolle, M. C., 184
Bonafide trade unions: CSU's difficulties being recognized as, 44–45; definitions of, 29; WFTU tour of Britain and, 106
Braden, Spruille, 178
British Honduran lumberjacks in Scotland, 76–77, 223n.59
British imperialism: American censure of, 139–40; Labour's defense of, 79; union leaders' defense of, 79–80. *See also* Colonized peoples; People of color; Racism
British seamen: hierarchy of races among, 77–78; internationalism of, 56, 110–13; postwar denazification programs, 105; race relations in seaports, 77. *See also* Refugee sailors
British workers: anticommunism of, 83–84; anxiety about postwar foreign relations, 67; attitudes toward colonized peoples, 75, 76, 78–79, 80–81, 223n.54; black-white relations among, 75–76, 78; class-based world view of, 49–50, 52; classic problem of social history regarding, 214n.6; cold war's effect on, 50–51, 66–71; cold war's lack of appeal for, 183–84; industrial conflict during the war, 218n.61; internationalism of, 51, 66, 81–82, 83, 84, 225n.93; Irish workers in Britain, 77–78; miners' independence, 61–62; Nazi invasion of the USSR and, 57–58; pessimism about the UN, 68; postwar conditions at home and, 53; postwar distrust of U.S., 67, 68–71; postwar internationalism of, 53–56; postwar sympathy for the USSR, 68–71; pro-Soviet propaganda and, 61, 218–19n.65; racism toward Poles, 71–72; social constraints of, 52–53; Soviet invasion of Finland and, 56–57, 88; Soviet system esteemed by, 60–63, 67; Soviet women trade unionists and, 63–64; TUC as counter to radicalism of, 189; UN decisions supported by, 81; unrevolutionary stance of, 52; West Indian factory workers in Britain, 76; women workers during the war, 61
Browder, Earl, 124, 132
Brown, Irving, 34, 158
Bullock, Allan, 74
Bullock, H. L., 80, 107
Bureaucracy, and British internationalism, 81–82
Byrnes, James F., 165, 190, 263n.23

Cadogan, Alexander, 101
Cantril, Hadley, 241n.14
Carew, Anthony, 27, 33, 184
Carey, James: ACTU ties, 148–49; ALCIA radio discussions refused by, 156; alternatives to war seen by, 150, 151; ambivalence about Soviets, 148; anticolonialism of, 173–74; anticommunism of, 146, 148–49, 161; on breakup of the WFTU, 10; complaints to Russians in WFTU, 163; on cooperation with Soviet trade unions, 31; foreign policy speeches of, 149–50; irritation at State Department hard-liners, 172; postwar optimism of, 144; pro-Soviet sympathies of, 126; warned against Communists by Acheson, 171; WFTU championed by, 148; WTUC troubles of, 159
Catholics, American: aid to Britain and, 129, 241 nn.14–15; anticommunism of, 128, 129–31; Association of Catholic Trade Unionists (ACTU), 128, 130–31; influence in CIO, 128–29; pro-Soviet sympathies among, 129, 241n.15; religion as predictor of opinion, 128, 240n.7; Spanish Civil War sympathies of, 128, 240n.5; union membership of, 129
Celler, Emanuel, 126
Centre Syndical Français en Grande Bretagne (CSF), 37–39
CGT. *See* Confédération Générale du Travail
CGT-FO. *See* Confédération Générale du Travail–Force Ouvrière
CGTU. *See* Confédération Générale du Travail Unitaire
Challoner, Louis, 79
Chaplin, Charlie, 125
Chen, T. W., 45
Chinese Association of Labor, 170
Chinese Seamen's Union (CSU): Anglo-Chinese Agreement of 1940 and, 43; Anglo-Saxon Petroleum strike of 1942 and, 44; Bombay deportees, 44; Catch 22 of, 44–45; formation of, 42; Liverpool strike of 1940 and, 44; racism toward, 43; shift from Hong Kong to England, 43; traditional difficulties of, 42–43
Christoffel, Harold, 132
Churchill, Winston: Conservative doctrine of, 221n.28; on Nazi invasion of the USSR, 57; Reuther's denouncement of, 154
CIO. *See* Congress of Industrial Organizations
Citrine, Walter: AFL-TUC committee created by, 157; ambitions of, 90–91, 107, 109; anti-Soviet stance of, 88, 96; ASC exclusion of left-

ists and, 96; ASC headed by, 157; attempts to protect British interests, 106; basic principles pursued by, 90; Bevin contrasted with, 86; character of, 86; conflicts with Bevin, 90–92, 102, 108, 227n.22; cooperation with Foreign Office over WTUC, 103; on cooperation with Soviet trade unions, 30; on gravity of 1945 trade union problems, 17; on internationalization due to WWII, 54; meeting with AUCCTU leaders, 97; Nazi invasion of the USSR and, 57, 58, 88–89; Popular Front opposed by, 87; Potts's trip to USSR disapproved by, 229n.43; prestige of, 90–91; relations with Vichy France, 37; rise to power, 52; on Roosevelt's view of Anglo-Soviet-American Trade Committee, 166; on Soviet demand for second front endorsement, 98; Soviets excluded from power by, 27–28; Soviets invited to Britain by, 97; Soviet trade unionism approved by, 70; struggle against government control, 92–93; on TUC inconsistency toward communism, 60; on UN dependence on the WFTU, 2; U.S. culture disapproved of by, 69–70; on WFTU innovation, 1; WFTU misgivings of, 105, 191; WFTU's exclusion from ECOSOC protested by, 108; world federation favored by (1943), 27

Class: distinctions, and U.S. foreign policy, 135–36; hatred, vs. internationalism, 183; middle-class attitudes, British, 51, 69, 214–15n.9, 220n.13; middle class vs. working class, American, 118, 124–25, 237n.7, 239n.45; working-class culture, American, 118–20; world view of British workers based on, 49–50, 52. *See also* American workers; British workers

Clay, Lucius, 254n.4

Cohen, Benjamin, 165

Cold war: AFL instigation of, in European labor, 158; American immigrants and public support for, 131, 242–43n.28; American public opinion and, 134–38; beginning of, 168; Bevin's influence on British policy, 231n.6; bipolarization of conflicts during, 11; British role in development of, 213n.3; Eurocentrism ended by, 184–85; failure of internationalism after, 192–94; lack of appeal for American and British workers, 183–84; lasting union opposition to, 8; mass manipulation on both sides of, 188–89, 262n.17; revisionism during, 3, 191–92; shrinking of human expectations during, 183; U.S. policies accepted in Britain, 50, 189; WFTU as battleground of, 169, 170–71; WFTU failure and, 179, 184. *See also* Cold war liberalism

—effect of: on British trade union leaders, 109–10; on British workers, 50–51, 66–71; on U.S. labor movement, 144–46

Cold war liberalism, 149, 153–54, 190, 251n.44

Colonized peoples: African American workers' identification with, 141–42; and anticolonialism, 78, 140, 173–75; British workers' attitudes toward, 75, 78–79; CIO's stance on, 173–75; as delegates to the WTUC, 104–5; French Communists and African labor, 175; Indian nationalism, 79, 80, 140, 225n.88; TUC's involvement with, 11, 79, 224n.82; U.S. conflicts with colonial powers, 7; WFTU Colonial Department, 174–75. *See also* British imperialism; People of color; Racism; Third World

Comintern (Communist International), 23

Communist Party of Great Britain: bureaucratism critiqued by, 82; growth after Grand Alliance, 58–59; influence on TUC politics, 86–87; insurgency in ASW, 95; Polish resentment fomented by, 73, 74; postwar internationalism of, 55, 215n.24; postwar popularity of, 82–83, 225–26n.101; Soviets asked to counteract effects of, 97; union power gains during the war, 93–94

Communist Party of the United States of America: Nazi-Soviet pact and, 123–24; "red decade" gains of, 123; Taft-Hartley Act and, 138; unionists in, 122, 124, 238n.34

Communists: American antilabor sentiment and, 159–60; "boring from within" policy, 24; breakaway groups in U.S. and European unions, 24; CIO factional conflicts, 159–64, 253n.81; as CIO leaders, 122, 162, 238n.34; CIO purge of, 179; CIO's tolerance for, 145, 160; ethnicity in America and, 131–32; French, and African labor, 175; impact on IFTU of, 21–29; independent trade unions in U.S. and Europe, 24; issues about separation of labor and government, 23, 25, 29; Marshall Plan's effect on, 34–35; pro-Soviet propaganda in Britain by, 218–19n.65; Socialists unite against fascism with, 13, 24–25; volunteerism in WFTU questioned by, 28–29. *See also* Anticommunism; Communist Party of Great Britain; Communist Party of the United States of

America; Union of Soviet Socialist Republics (USSR)
Confederación de Trabajadores de América Latina (CTAL), 28, 175–77, 202n.3
Confederación de Trabajadores de México (CTM), 177
Confédération Générale du Travail (CGT): African colonial labor defended by, 175; antimilitarism in IFTU called for, 22; CGTU joint strike with, 24–25; CSF exile union and, 37; representation of colonial countries by, 11
Confédération Générale du Travail–Force Ouvrière (CGT-FO), 40
Confédération Générale du Travail Unitaire (CGTU), 24
Congress of Industrial Organizations (CIO): ACTU support in, 130; AFLCIA resignation, 156–57; AFL-CIO unity, 155–59, 252n.63; anticolonialism of, 173–75; Catholic influence in, 128–29; commitment to cooperative world order, 144–46; Communist factional conflicts in, 123, 159–64, 239n.40, 253n.78; Communist leaders in unions of, 122, 162, 238n.34; Communists purged by, 179; Communists' role in WFTU defended by, 171; Communists tolerated in, 145, 163–64; cooperation vs. ideology in, 30; diplomacy in WFTU backed by State Department, 167; economic concerns and internationalism of, 118, 236n.4; envoy to Soviets regarding the European Recovery Program, 172–73; exclusion from AFL-TUC committee, 157; ICFTU founded by, 34–35; IFTU exclusion of, 4; "industrial peace" proposal, 250n.36; internationalism of, 144–46, 149–55; Latin labor policy of, 157, 175–78; Marshall Plan controversy, 161, 171–73; national loyalty and union factionalism in, 162–63; no-strike pledge during wartime, 156; plans for national economy, 152, 250n.36; Popular Front embraced by, 155; pro-Soviet thinkers in, 125–26; purge of Grand Alliance vestiges in, 179; Rooseveltian vision of, 145, 152–53, 164, 172, 174, 178–79, 180; Soviet relations as anti-Communist strategy in, 160–61; State Department suspicions after Murphy report, 170, 256n.29; Taft-Hartley Act opposed by, 137–38, 246n.67; U.S. intervention in Greece and, 154; WFTU jettisoned by, 179; WFTU political structure and, 14; WFTU walkout, 34; "Win the War Rally" of, 125–26. *See also* AFL-CIO unity
—foreign policy: and African American workers, 132; Communist influence on, 159; contradictory bases of, 149–50, 151–52; makers of, 146–49; weakness of, 117–18
Congress of Irish Unions, 105
Connally, Tom, 190
Conservative Party, nationalism of, 55
Cooper, Duff, 88, 96
Cope, Elmer, 171
Cronin, James, 52
CSF (Centre Syndical Français en Grande Bretagne), 37–39
CSU. *See* Chinese Seamen's Union
CTAL. *See* Confederación de Trabajadores de América Latina
CTM. *See* Confederación de Trabajadores de México
Curran, Joseph, 125, 129
Curran, Murray, 119–20

Davis, Mike, 242n.28
Deakin, Arthur, 108–9
"Declaration of Peace Settlement," 105
Democracy: Carey on necessity of, 150; as minority dogma among British workers, 82; need for belief in possibility of, 194; Reuther's championing of, 180
Deproletarianization of the left, 206n.29
Donahue, George, 130
Dryden, John, 223n.70
Dubinsky, David: ALCIA maneuverings against the CIO and, 156; anticommunism of, 33; internationalism of, 25
Dulles, Allen, 173
Dunn, Robert, 186

Economic and Social Council of the UN (ECOSOC), 107–9
Eden, Anthony, 103, 158, 168, 252n.72
Edwards, Harry J., 79–80
Egyptians, British racism toward, 79
Ehrlich, Henry K., 26, 147, 148
Eisenhower, Dwight, 165
EITUC. *See* Emergency International Trade Union Council
Electrical Trades Union, 38
Emergency International Trade Union Council (EITUC), 26–27, 208n.32
Engels, Friedrich, 12, 205n.28
Engineering apprentices' strike of 1944, 61

ERP-TUAC. *See* European Recovery Program–Trade Union Advisory Committee
Essential Work Order, 61
Ethnicity: Americanism of ethnic American workers, 132–33; communism in America and, 131–32; and Irish workers' difficulties, 77–78; pluralism of American workers, 133. *See also* Colonized peoples; People of color; Racism
Eurocentrism, cold war as the end of, 184–85
European Recovery Program: American workers' disfavor toward, 135; CIO pressured to push in WFTU, 171–73; CIO split over, 161; European Recovery Program–Trade Union Advisory Committee, 171–73; exclusion of USSR by, 7; non-Communist split with Communists over, 34–35
European Recovery Program–Trade Union Advisory Committee (ERP-TUAC), 171–73
Executive Committee on Economic Foreign Policy, 150
Exile union groups: average wage of workers, 210n.1; as challenge to internationalism, 45–46; dependence on the TUC, 37–38; dual purposes of, 37; exile politics of, 37; IFTU and, 36, 39; postwar problems of, 39–40; relationship with European underground, 39, 211n.22; resistance to refugee workers, 38; size of memberships, 39; weak syndical presence of, 36–37. *See also* Refugee sailors; Refugee workers

Falin, Mikhail, 98
Fascism: communism equated with in pre-war years, 29–30; Socialists and Communists united against, 13, 24–25
Fenster, Leo, 132
Fimmen, Edo, 22
Finland, Soviet invasion of, 56–57, 88
First International, WFTU compared to, 19
Fishburn, John, 168–69
Fitzgerald, Albert, 129, 159
Fitzpatrick, Mike, 129
Fitzpatrick, Tom, 129
Foreign unions in Britain. *See* Exile union groups
Foster, William Z., 122
Franklin, H. W., 59
Fraser, Steve, 147
Freeman, Joshua, 129
Free Trade Union Committee, 34, 180, 209n.52
Free trade unionism: before the WFTU, 23–29; in cold war, 170–80; evolving definitions of, 29–32; Leninism vs., 29; transformation of, in the WFTU, 29–35
Friedlander, Peter, 131–32
Fry, Varian, 156
Fyrth, Patrick, 56, 77

Gandhi, Mahatma, 80
German-Soviet Nonaggression Pact, 26, 88, 123, 160
Germany: American attitudes toward, 139; friction over TUC involvement in, 106–7, 233–34n.43; and Nazi invasion of the USSR, 57–58, 88–89, 93–94; U.S. government help for WFTU in, 167; WTUC and, 105
Germer, Adolph, 175
Gerstle, Gary, 242n.28
Golden, Clinton, 154
Gompers, Samuel, 22
Grand Alliance: ACTU activities and, 130–31; British anticommunism and, 57–65, 84, 89, 101; CIO purge of vestiges of, 179; Communist Party growth after, 58–59; TUC/government opposition regarding, 101; utopianism kindled by, 183
Great Britain: Anglo-Soviet trade union cooperation during the war, 92–99; anti-Polish sentiment in, 71–75; exile union groups in, 36–40, 45–46; government conflicts over the WTUC, 102–4; Grand Alliance and anticommunism in, 57–65, 84, 89, 101; Polish army refugees in, 72–75; traditional foreign policy of, 48, 213n.3; U.S. policies accepted in, 50. *See also* British workers
Greece, 134, 154, 244n.46
Green, William: on AFL affiliation with IFTU, 25; at AFL-CIO hatchet-burying ceremony, 155; antagonism with Murray, 180; pure free trade unionism championed by, 32–33; TUC criticized indirectly by, 33; as WFTU trustee, 34
Gregory, James, 132
Grindon, L. S., 49, 56

Haessler, Carl, 162
Harriman, Averell, 101
Harris, Lou, 150
Harrison, Martin, 226n.107, 229–30n.51
Harrisson, Tom, 68, 83
Hate strikes of 1942–43, 243n.38
Haywood, Allan, 31

Herling, John, 178
Hickerson, John, 169, 170, 171
Hill, Ken, 10, 104
Hillman, Sidney: anticommunism of, 146–47; battle with Communist factions, 24; CIO frictions at WTUC mediated by, 159; at CIO "Win the War Rally," 125; commitment to institutionalized cooperation, 151; on cooperation with Soviet trade unions, 31–32; idealistic internationalism of, 147, 150–51, 193; as mediator and diplomat, 147; vision of political economy, 152, 249n.32; on WFTU as helpful to U.S. foreign policy, 165; on WFTU's significance, 1–2; work with Communists during the war, 147
History and Class Consciousness (Lukács), 187–88
Hobsbawm, E. J., 5
Hong, Wong Kwok, 45
Hoover, J. Edgar, 148, 248n.12
Horkheimer, Max, 194
Hull, Cordell, 193, 249n.27

ICFTU. *See* International Confederation of Free Trade Unions
IFTU. *See* International Federation of Trade Unions
ILGWU. *See* International Ladies' Garment Workers' Union
India, nationalism of, 79, 80, 140, 225n.88
Indians: American racism toward, 140; British racism toward, 79
Institutions, as active subjects, 202–3n.8
International Confederation of Free Trade Unions (ICFTU): anticommunism of, 34–35; founding of, 34–35, 179–80; Schevenels's career with, 20; split with WFTU, 6
Internationale (song), 59, 65
International Federation of Trade Unions (IFTU): AFL affiliation (1937), 25–26; AFL's refusal to participate in (1920), 22; AUCCTU demands refused by, 23–24; CIO exclusion from, 4; communism's impact on, 21–29; dependence on the TUC, 37–38; failure of antiwar program, 5; free trade unionism advocated by, 23; ideology before WWII, 21–22; intervention in exile union conflicts, 39; liberalism of, 22–23; Popular Front's benefit to, 25; postwar anticommunism of, 40; *Project for the Reconstruction of the International Trade Union Movement* (manifesto), 19, 26–27; RILU attack on, 2, 23; Schevenels's reinterpretation of, 30–31; separation of labor and government advocated by, 23; significance of, 2; Soviet exclusion from, 4; WWI's impact on, 22
Internationalism: American attitudes toward U.S. peacekeeping role, 119, 140–41; Americanism's coexistence with, 133; American workers' weak stance on, 142–43; of British middle class, 51, 214–15n.9; of British seamen, 56, 110–13; of British working class, 51, 66, 81–82, 83, 84, 225n.93; challenge of, by refugee sailors and exile unions, 45–46; of the CIO, 144–46, 149–55; Citrine's ambitions in, 91, 107, 109; failure of, for workers' movements, 192–94; ideology vs. practice in, 203n.9; importance of trade unions', 185–86; and labor, overview of, 4–7; of Labour Party, 55; meaning of, for rank-and-file union members, 18; meaning of, for trade union leaders, 18–19; postwar British attitudes toward, 53–56; present possibilities for, 193–94; relationship of national and labor diplomacy, 12–13; shortcomings of earlier treatments of, 7–9; sources of, 51–52, 90–96; of the TUC, 113–14; unions vs. political parties and, 205–6n.28; universalistic role of unions and, 9–10, 202–3n.8. *See also* World Trade Union Conference (WTUC)
International Ladies' Garment Workers' Union (ILGWU), 33, 122–23
International Trade Secretariats (ITS), 4, 34
International Transport Workers' Federation (ITF): Chinese sailors and, 44, 45; CSF rebuffed by, 39; intervention in exile union conflicts, 39; policies toward postwar Germany, 105; Seamen's section and refugee sailors, 41–42; subordination to International Federation opposed by, 29
International Workingmen's Association (IWA), 2, 13
Irish workers: conference on British trade union problems, 104–5; Congress of Irish Unions formed by, 105; ethnic difficulties in Britain, 77–78; Irish TUC, 104–5, 233n.31
Iriye, Akira, 203n.10
Irwin, M. W., 64
"Is the WFTU an Instrument of Russian Policy?" (Fishburn paper), 168–69
ITF. *See* International Transport Workers' Federation
ITS. *See* International Trade Secretariats
IWA. *See* International Workingmen's Association

Japan, WFTU delegation to, 167
Japanese, racism toward, 139
Jarman, Charles: anticommunism of, 111, 112; anti-German stance of, 105; internationalism of, 112–13; as NUS secretary, 110–13; refugee sailors and, 40, 42, 44; WFTU endorsed by, 112, 113
Johnson, Wallace, 104
Joint Anti-Fascist Refugee Committee, 162
Jouhaux, Leon, 25, 35, 37

Kautsky, Karl, 23
Kearney, Jim, 130
Keep Left group, 71
Kennan, George, 167, 174, 187, 190, 258n.58
Knight, Jack, 175–76, 177, 260n.72
Knight, O. A., 151
Kolko, Gabriel, 50, 188
Krane, Jay, 191
Kuznetsov, Vasili, 103, 173, 187

Labour Party: anti-Soviet propaganda by, 88; distrust of U.S. by Labour voters, 69; imperialism defended by, 79, 80; inconsistent views on communism, 59–60; miners' conflicts with, 61–62; postwar internationalism of, 55, 81, 225n.93; postwar popularity of, 82–83; pro-Soviet sympathies of, 56; Soviet invasion of Finland and, 56, 88; Soviet relations and, 101, 231n.7; struggle to control the TUC, 91–92; TUC affiliations, 29, 33; TUC internationalism frustrated by, 107–8; U.S. cold war politics accepted by, 50; as workers' vehicle for government opposition, 87; working-class support for, 52, 53, 55
Lademacher, Horst, 106, 203n.9
La Guardia, Fiorello, 125–26
Latin America: AFL intervention in, 157, 175, 177, 258n.50, 260n.74; labor policy of the CIO, 157, 175–78
Laurain, Jean, 175
Lawther, Will, 108
Leathers, Lord, 42
Leggett, Frederick, 98
Levering, Ralph, 124
Lewis, John L., 147, 159, 239n.40
Lichtenstein, Nelson, 242n.28
Lin, Patricia Yu, 53
Little, Kenneth, 78
Llanelly trade unionists, 55
Lombardo Toledano, Vicente, 13–14, 175, 176, 177, 202n.3, 259n.71
Lovestone, Jay: anticommunism of, 33, 158; cold war in European labor and, 158; Free Trade Union Committee of, 34, 209n.52
Lubin, Isador, 166
Lukács, George, 187–88, 192
Lunn, Kenneth, 75, 77
Lyon, Eugene, 123

Malkova, Anastasia, 64
Marshall, George, 172
Marshall Plan. *See* European Recovery Program
Martin, Long, 60
Marx, Karl, 2, 12, 205n.28
Mass-Observation surveys: on anti-Americanism, 69; on attitudes toward foreigners, 69, 196; on attitudes toward Russia, 68; on feelings about Poles, 72, 221n.31; on feelings about Russia, 56–57; on feelings about Russians and Americans, 60–61, 69, 195, 220n.13; importance of, 51, 214n.8; on nationalism and party affiliation, 81, 225n.93; omens for postwar world, 83; on opinions about separate peace between Russia and Germany, 197–98; on opinions of allies, 198; on religious differences in desire to help England, 199; report on foreign seamen's organizations, 77; on socioeconomic characteristics and attitude toward "tough" approach to Russia, 199; on world role of United States, 67, 69, 197, 220n.13
McCarthy, Joseph, 138
McKenna, Norman, 130
McKillen, Elizabeth, 236n.3
McShane, Denis, 8, 27, 28
Mead, James, 126
Meany, George, 180
Molotov, Vyacheslav, 108
Monroe Doctrine, 139
Morgan, Kenneth, 80
Mulliken, Otis, 170
Murphy, Ray, 169–70, 256n.23
Murphy Report. *See* "USSR and the World Federation of Trade Unions, The"
Murray, Philip: at AFL-CIO hatchet-burying ceremony, 155; AFL preferred over Communists by, 162; anger over AFL-TUC committee snub, 157; antagonism with Green, 180; anticommunism of, 146, 148; distrust of Soviets by, 148; Marshall Plan controversy and, 172; as

mediator, 147–48, 248n.10; plan for governing by industrial councils, 152; on requirements for peace, 9, 10; work in steel industry, 148; worries about Communist-led unions, 159; WTUC eschewed by, 148

National Council of Labor, 59
Nationalism: of American workers, 117, 127; of Conservative Party, 55; in India, 79, 80; of Labour Party, 81, 225n.93; postwar British attitudes toward, 53–54; sources of, 51–52; strength of class hatred and internationalism vs., 183. *See also* Americanism
National Labor Relations Board (NLRB), 137
National Minority Movement, 24
National Union of Agricultural Workers, 74
National Union of General and Municipal Workers (NUGMW), 38, 74
National Union of Miners, 74
National Union of Public Employees (NUPE), 230n.61
National Union of Seamen (NUS): anti-German stance of, 105; Chinese sailors and, 43, 44; internationalism of, 110–13; rank-and-file frictions after the war, 111–12
National Union of Tailoring and Garment Workers (NUTGW), 74
Nazi invasion of the USSR, 57–58, 88–89, 93–94
Nazi-Soviet pact, 26, 88, 123, 160
Nehru, Jawaharlal, 80
New Deal foreign policy: anticommunism and, 137; of the CIO, 145, 152–53, 178
"New World," postwar theme of, 54
Nicolson, Harold, 213n.3
Niethammer, Lutz, 209n.39
Nikolayeva, Klavdia, 63
Nitze, Paul, 171
NLRB. *See* National Labor Relations Board
Noel-Baker, Philip, 42
Nordahl, Konrad, 41
Norwegian Seafarers Union, 40–41
NUGMW. *See* National Union of General and Municipal Workers
NUPE. *See* National Union of Public Employees
NUS. *See* National Union of Seamen
NUTGW. *See* National Union of Tailoring and Garment Workers

O'Brien, Tim, 130
Office of Strategic Services (OSS), 167
Office of War Information, 51
Oldenbroek, J. H.: argument with Watt, 32; on Chinese refugee sailors, 44; as ICFTU general secretary, 35; refugee sailors and, 40, 41; resistance to IFTU control, 29
Operation Bilge, 44
Operation Overlord and WTUC postponement, 102–3
Orwell, George, 183
OSS. *See* Office of Strategic Services
Overcash, O. G., 118–19

Palestine problem and the WTUC, 104, 232–33n.29
Pavilchenka, Lyudmilla, 64
Pelling, Henry, 71
People of color: African American workers, 132, 141–42, 243–44n.38; British black-white relations, 75–76, 78; British Honduran lumberjacks in Scotland, 76–77, 223n.59; British seaport race relations, 77; English-Irish relations and, 78, 223n.70; French Communists and African labor, 175; in Great Britain in the 1940s, 75; hierarchy of races in Britain, 77–78; West Indian factory workers in Britain, 76. *See also* Colonized peoples; Ethnicity; Racism
Pepper, Claude, 126
Peyer, Karl, 40
Poland: Polish-Soviet conflict, 71–75, 126, 207n.18; Sikorsky-Maysky Accord of 1941, 72
Poles: anti-Soviet stance of, 73; army refugees in Britain, 72–75; British racism toward, 71–72, 78; unions banning, 74, 222n.42; WTUC exclusion of Lublin Poles, 103–4
Polish Resettlement Corps, 73, 74
Popular Front: ACTU and, 130; AFL-CIO relations and, 155; Communist influence in ethnic communities and, 130; Communist-Socialist split and, 13; disintegration of, 26; growth of, 24; IFTU benefits from, 25; Nazi invasion of USSR and, 159; Thomas's belief in principles of, 153
Potofsky, Jacob: on Hillman, 147; in Latin America, 157, 175, 176
Potts, John, 62, 96, 229n.43
Powell, Adam Clayton, Jr., 126
Prieto, Indalecio, 103
Profintern. *See* Red International of Labor Unions (RILU)
Project for the Reconstruction of the International Trade Union Movement (manifesto), 19, 26–27

Propaganda: anti-Soviet, by TUC and Labour Party, 88; by CSF, 38; pro-Soviet, and British workers, 61, 218–19n.65

Proudhoun, Pierre-Joseph, 2

Quill, Mike, 125, 129, 180

Racism: American anticolonialism in conflict with, 140; in the BDDFP, 42; in British seaports, 77; in the British military, 78; hierarchy of races in Britain, 77–78; Irish workers' ethnic difficulties, 77–78; toward Chinese sailors, 43; toward colonized peoples, 78–79; toward Indians, 79; toward Japanese, 139; toward Poles, 71–72, 78; toward West Indian factory workers, 76. *See also* Colonized peoples; Ethnicity; People of color

Railway Brotherhoods, 155, 157

Read, B., 58, 60

Red International of Labor Unions (RILU): collapse of, 25; formation of, 23; IFTU attacked by, 2, 23; problematic nature of IFTU relations, 21–22; size of membership, 24, 25; Social Democrats condemned by, 23. *See also* Soviet trade unions

Red scare: Americanism and, 133; CIO's vulnerability to, 145, 178–79, 247n.4. *See also* Cold war

Refugee Relief Trustees, Inc., 162

Refugee sailors, as challenge to internationalism, 45–46. *See also* Centre Syndical Française en Grande Bretagne (CSF); Chinese Seamen's Union (CSU); Exile union groups

Refugee unions. *See* Exile union groups

Refugee workers, difficulties of, 37–39, 211n.22. *See also* Exile union groups

Regulation IAA, 61

Religion: union membership and, 129. *See also* Catholics, American

Resistance coalition unions, 31, 209n.39, 255n.16

Reuther, Victor, 123, 163, 238n.36

Reuther, Walter: anticommunism of, 138, 146, 149, 154, 162, 238n.36; as CIO president, 147–48, 149; cold war liberalism of, 149, 153–54; conflicts with AFL over anticommunism, 179–80; on ICFTU anticommunist stance, 34–35; production plan for aircraft, 152; socialism of, 149; work in the USSR, 123, 149, 238n.36

Revolutionary Trade Union Opposition (Revolutionäre Gewerkschaftsopposition), 24

RILU. *See* Red International of Labor Unions

Rios, Los, 37

Roberts, Bryn: call for WTUC, 98–99; exclusion from WTUC, 99; internationalism of, 99; as pro–second front leader, 98; on Soviet invasion of Finland, 56; travels to U.S., 99, 230 n.59

Rollin, A. R., 63

Romualdi, Serafino, 178

Roosevelt, Franklin Delano: AFL-CIO unity promoted by, 155, 156; Anglo-American-Soviet labor cooperation favored by, 166; Hillman as advisor to, 147; labor attachés at U.S. missions endorsed by, 166; vision of world order, 152; working-class sympathy for, 120

Rooseveltian vision of the CIO, 145, 152–53, 164, 172, 174, 178–79, 180

Rosenblum, Frank, 147, 171

Ross, Michael: on anti-Communists in the WFTU, 163; Marshall Plan controversy and, 171, 172; on WFTU political structure, 14; on the WFTU's instability, 173

Rosswurm, Steve, 129

Rostow, Walt W., 10

Rous, René, 37, 38–39

Russia. *See* Union of Soviet Socialist Republics (USSR)

Ruttenberg, Stanley, 120, 160–61

Ryan, John A., 152

Sailors. *See* British seamen; Chinese Seamen's Union (CSU); Refugee sailors

Salert, Irving, 120

Sallach, David Louis, 236n.4

Salute to the Soviets (film), 61

Samuel, Raphael, 215n.24

Schatz, Ronald, 129

Schevenels, Denis, 19

Schevenels, Jules, 19

Schevenels, Walter: on cooperation with Soviet trade unions, 30–31, 32; as exemplary politician-bureaucrat, 19–20; on the exile unions' plight, 38, 39; on failings of prewar IFTU, 26; ICFTU's treatment of, 35; life story in brief, 19–20; on national autonomy in WFTU, 28; *Project for the Reconstruction of the International Trade Union Movement,* 19, 26–27; on rebuilding continental unions, 39–40; relations with Vichy France, 37; Soviets excluded from power by, 27–28; WTUC praised by, 27

Schwarz, Ernst, 176–77
Scotland: British Honduran lumberjacks in, 76–77, 223n.59; Polish army refugees in, 72–73
Scully, Edward, 130
Seamen. *See* British seamen; Chinese Seamen's Union (CSU); Refugee sailors
Second front: British miners' cynicism toward, 61–62; British workers' support for, 67; Soviet demand for TUC endorsement, 97–98
Second Socialist International, 5
Selly, Joseph, 175–76
Separation of labor and government: bonafide unions and, 29; Communist conflicts with, 23, 25; IFTU's advocacy of, 23
Sherif, D., 55
Shvernik, Nicolai, 64–65, 97, 98
Sikorsky-Maysky Accord of 1941, 72
Small, Melvin, 262n.17
Smith, Andrew, 238n.36
Smith, Howard W., 156
Smollet, H. P., 98
Social Democrats, Communists' condemnation of, 23
Socialism: American ethnic groups support for, 132; IFTU's affirmation of, 2; of TUC leadership, 113–14
Socialist Party of America, 122
Socialists: break with Communists at start of war, 26; Communists unite against fascism with, 13, 24–25; Spanish Socialists excluded from WTUC, 103
Sonsteby, Thor, 41
South America: AFL intervention in Latin America, 157, 175, 177, 258n.50, 260n.74; American workers' views of, 139; CIO's Latin labor policy, 175–78
Soviet trade unions: British cooperation with (1941), 30–31; corporatism and, 187, 261n.12; delegations to the United Kingdom (1942), 62–65; IFTU exclusion of, 4; in Nazi-Soviet pact years, 29–30; power struggles with the state, 186–88; relations with IFTU, 21–22; Social Democrats condemned by, 23; World War II and, 26–27. *See also* All-Union Central Council of Soviet Trade Unions (AUCCTU); Red International of Labor Unions (RILU)
Soviet Union. *See* Union of Soviet Socialist Republics (USSR)
Soviet Women (film), 61
Spanish Civil War, 128, 240n.5
Spanish Socialists, and the WTUC, 103
Spence, W. R. L., 110
Stalin, Joseph, 129
Star Spangled Banner, 132–33
State Department. *See* U.S. State Department
Stettinius, Edward R., 166, 168
Stilwell, Joseph W., 44
Stokes, W. H., 70
Strikes: British general strike of 1926, 52, 85, 86; CSU strike of 1940, 44; CSU strike of 1942, 44; during wartime, 61; engineering apprentices' strike of 1944, 61; forbidden by Regulation IAA, 61; hate strikes of 1942–43, 243n.38; Trinidad strike of 1937, 79
Sturmthal, Adolf, 8
Survey Research Center, 51

Taft-Hartley Act, 137–38, 157, 158, 191, 246n.67
Tanner, Jack, 99
Tarasov, Vasili, 28
Tewson, Vincent, 108–9
TGWU. *See* Transport and General Worker's Union
"Third Force," Great Britain as, 70, 71
Third world: AFL's manipulation of labor in, 174; American workers' attitudes toward, 138–39; CIO's anticolonialism, 173–75; CIO's Latin labor policy, 175–78; CIO's policy weakened by cold war, 173; defined, 205n.22; delegates to the WTUC, 104–5; international labor movement and, 10. *See also* Colonized peoples
Thomas, R. J., 153, 161
Thorne, Christopher, 203n.10
Tobin, Dan, 155
Tofahrn, Paul, 47, 90
Toledano, Vicente Lombardo. *See* Lombardo Toledano, Vicente
Tomas, Belarminon, 103
Tombs, Isabelle, 207n.18
Tomlinson, G. A. W., 55
Townsend, Willard, 136, 151
Trades Union Congress (TUC): AFL's poor relations with, 158, 252n.72; AFL-TUC committee, 157; Anglo-Soviet cooperation during the war, 92–99; anti-Communist stance of leadership, 88, 92–93, 95; anti-Soviet propaganda by, 88; ban on Communists in district councils, 95–96, 229n.41; Circular 16 of 1934, 95–96, 229n.39; after Citrine, 108–9; cold war's effect on leadership, 109–10; colonial affairs of, 11,

79, 224n.82; communism, inconsistent views on, 59–60, 89–90; Communist ties during the war, 89; Communist upsurge during the war, 93–94; cooperation vs. ideology in, 30; corporatist approaches to industrial conflict, 85, 109, 226n.1; as counter to workers' radicalism, 189; divisive forces within, 85; ECOSOC's exclusion of, 107–9; efforts to control opinion about the USSR, 59; exile unions' dependence on, 37–38; foreign policy inconsistencies, 47–48, 89–90; government cooperation by, 87; government friction over involvement in Germany, 106–7, 233–34n.43; ICFTU founded by, 34–35; internationalism of, 113–14; Irish TUC, 104–5, 233n.31; Labour Party affiliations, 29, 33; "leaders" and "leadership" defined, 213n.2; the left in, 86–87; leftists and WFTU involvement, 102; Nazi invasion of USSR and, 89, 93–94; Polish army refugees and, 74–75; Popular Front opposed by, 87; pre-war right-wing control of, 85–86; Soviet alliance issues, 100–101; Soviet demand for second front endorsement by, 97–98; Soviet invasion of Finland and, 88; Soviet relations and government opposition, 101–2; Soviet trade unions, cooperation with, 47–48; struggle against government control, 91–93; U.S. cold war politics accepted by leadership, 50; WFTU walkout, 34; world politics aspirations of, 107; WTUC agreed to, 99; WTUC political issues, 102–6. *See also* Anglo-Soviet Trade Union Committee (ASC); World Trade Union Conference (WTUC)

Trade Union Education League, 24

Trade Union Unity League, 24

Transport and General Worker's Union (TGWU): Communist upsurge in, 95–96; Polish refugees and, 74; self-rule for India favored by, 80

Trinidad strike of 1937, 79

Truman Doctrine, 136, 154, 191

Truman, Harry: call for aid to Greece and Turkey, 134, 154; CIO conflict over presidency campaign, 161; Fair Deal policy of, 158; Hillman respected by, 147; Taft-Hartley Act vetoed by, 137; WFTU position in UN denied by, 168

TUC. *See* Trades Union Congress

Turkey, 134, 154

UAW. *See* United Automobile Workers of America

UN. *See* United Nations

Un-American activities. *See* Anticommunism; Red scare

Union of Soviet Socialist Republics (USSR): American workers' attitudes toward, 117, 122–26, 135–36, 178, 236n.2, 245n.52; Anglo-Soviet trade union cooperation during the war, 92–99; British aid for, 59; British workers' postwar sympathy for, 68–71; Finland invaded by, 56–57, 88; German-Soviet Nonaggression Pact, 26, 88, 123, 160; Nazi invasion of, 57–58, 88–89, 93–94; Polish-Soviet conflict, 71–75, 126, 207n.18; Sikorsky-Maysky Accord of 1941, 72; system esteemed by British workers, 60–63, 67; trade union power struggles in, 186–88; U.S. culture contrasted with, 69–70; war effort and social system connections, 60–61, 125. *See also* All-Union Central Council of Soviet Trade Unions (AUCCTU); Red International of Labor Unions (RILU); Soviet trade unions

United Automobile Workers of America (UAW): factional battles and foreign policy in, 131, 153–54, 250–51n.42; Reuther's labor militance in, 162

United Nations: British workers' pessimism about, 68; British workers' support for decisions of, 81; ECOSOC's exclusion of the WFTU, 107–9; Harris' support for, 150; Hillman's belief in, 147; WFTU as support for, 2; WFTU exclusion from conference, 107, 168; WFTU parallels to, 10, 11, 185–86

United States: anticommunism as dominant ideology of, 190–91, 263n.25; British middle-class distrust of, 69, 220n.13; British workers' distrust of, 67, 68–71; Soviet culture contrasted with, 69–70; working-class culture in, 118–20. *See also* American workers; U.S. foreign policy; U.S. State Department

U.S. foreign policy: American workers' attitudes toward, 117, 119, 140–41, 235–36n.1; American workers' distrust of, 134–36; big business and, 134–35; class distinctions and, 135–36; cold war liberalism, 190; conflict with colonial powers, 7; in Greece and Turkey, 134, 154; link between domestic and world economies in, 150; right-wing resurgence in, 191; Truman Doctrine, 136, 154; unity at home and, 189–90; WFTU initially seen as helpful to, 165–66, 167. *See also* European Recovery Program; U.S. State Department

U.S. labor movement: cold war's effect on, 144–

46; Communists and American antilabor sentiment, 159–60; dissolution of, 181; as force for international peace, 151; internationalism of, 118–19; nineteenth-century liberalism of, 14; opulence of trade unions compared to British, 70; prewar antilabor legislation, 156. *See also* American Federation of Labor (AFL); Congress of Industrial Organizations (CIO)
USSR. *See* Union of Soviet Socialist Republics
"USSR and the World Federation of Trade Unions, The" (Murphy report), 169–70, 256 nn.23–24
U.S. State Department: anti-Soviet history of, 166–67; CIO's diplomacy in WFTU backed by, 167; CIO sympathizers suspected by, 170, 256n.28; good neighbor policy abandoned for interventionism, 177–78, 260n.76; labor attachés at U.S. missions created under FDR, 166; Marshall Plan pushed on CIO by, 171–72; WFTU initially seen as helpful by, 165–66, 167; WFTU investigation by Acheson, 170; WFTU opposed by, 2, 168–70. *See also* U.S. foreign policy
U.S. workers. *See* American workers

Vinson, Carl, 156
Volunteerism issues in the WFTU, 28–29

Wallace, Henry, 134, 147, 161
Warner, Geoffrey, 221n.28
Watt, Robert, 32
Weiler, Peter, 50, 106, 189, 224n.82
Welles, Sumner, 166
West Indian factory workers in Britain, 76
WFTU. *See* World Federation of Trade Unions
Wiesner, Louis, 171
Wilcock, H. D., 68
Willen, Paul, 126
Williams, William Appleman, 251n.44
Wilson, Hugh, 79
Wilson, J. Havelock, 110
Winter War of 1939–40, 56–57
"Win the War Rally" of the CIO, 126
Withey, Steven, 235n.1
Witte, J. H., 54
Wolf, Mortimer, 158
Woll, Matthew: on Citrine's ambitiousness, 91; internationalism of, 25; noncooperation with CIO over Latin American affairs, 157
Women: British workers during the war, 61; equal pay issues in Great Britain, 63–64; in Soviet trade unions' delegation to Great Britain, 63–64
Woodcock, George, 109
World Federation of Trade Unions (WFTU): Acheson's investigation of, 170; African politics in, 175; as cold war battleground, 170–71; Colonial Department of, 174–75; Communist and anti-Communist frictions within, 2, 106; Deakin's retreat from Citrine's goals, 109; delegation to Japan, 167; ECOSOC's exclusion of, 107–9; failure of, 2–3, 10, 168, 179, 184, 191; First International compared to, 19; Fishburn paper on, 168–69; formation of, 1, 4, 31, 48, 105–6; friction regarding Germany, 106–7, 233–34n.43; further information on, 203–4n.15; government friction over involvement in Germany, 106; historical importance of, 1–3, 8–9, 13, 184–86; ICFTU-WCTU split, 6; institutional history of, 4; leftists and TUC involvement in, 102; Marshall Plan controversy, 171–73; Murphy report on, 169, 256 nn.23–24; political structure of, 14–15; postwar optimism about, 1–2; realities of power expressed by, 11–12, 188; revisionism after failure of, 3, 191; southern countries, ineffectiveness in, 10–11; successes of, 11; transformation of free trade unionism in, 29–35; UN parallels to, 10, 11, 185–86; UN's dependence on, 2; U.S. government help in Germany, 167; U.S. government's initially positive view of, 165–66, 167; U.S. State Department's reversal of opinion about, 168–70; U.S. view as Soviet tool, 169–70; volunteerism issues in, 28–29
World Trade Union Conference (WTUC), 203–4n.15; African Americans' disappointment in, 141–42; Bevin's opposition to, 89, 100; Bevin's speech at, 100; "Declaration of Peace Settlement," 105; German policies of, 105; government conflicts regarding, 102–4; Lublin Poles excluded from, 103–4; Operation Overlord and postponement of, 102–3; Palestine problem and, 104, 232–33n.29; political issues for the TUC, 102–6; Roberts' call for, 98–99; Roberts' exclusion from, 99; Schevenels' enthusiasm about, 27; Spanish Socialists excluded from, 103; success of, 105–6; third-world delegates to, 104–5; WFTU formation and, 4, 31, 48, 105–6
World War I, impact on IFTU, 22
World War II: American blame of British for, 139–40; American workers' attitudes toward,

115, 119–22; break between Socialists and Communists with advent of, 26; conflicts in diplomacy leading to, 203n.10; governments established in aftermath of, 206n.31; internationalism advanced by, 53–56; nontraditional character of, 188

WTUC. *See* World Trade Union Conference

Zakharov, S. V., 104
Zizek, Slavoj, 192

VICTOR SILVERMAN is an associate professor of history at Pomona College and the author of children's books and films, including *Out of the Shadow* (Northwest Passage Productions), a dramatic treatment of the life of the immigrant writer Rose Gollup Cohen, and *Looking for Compton's: The Lost History of Transsexuals in San Francisco's Tenderloin* (TS/TL Productions).

The Working Class in American History

Worker City, Company Town: Iron and Cotton-Worker Protest in Troy and Cohoes, New York, 1855–84 *Daniel J. Walkowitz*

Life, Work, and Rebellion in the Coal Fields: The Southern West Virginia Miners, 1880–1922 *David Alan Corbin*

Women and American Socialism, 1870–1920 *Mari Jo Buhle*

Lives of Their Own: Blacks, Italians, and Poles in Pittsburgh, 1900–1960 *John Bodnar, Roger Simon, and Michael P. Weber*

Working-Class America: Essays on Labor, Community, and American Society *Edited by Michael H. Frisch and Daniel J. Walkowitz*

Eugene V. Debs: Citizen and Socialist *Nick Salvatore*

American Labor and Immigration History, 1877–1920s: Recent European Research *Edited by Dirk Hoerder*

Workingmen's Democracy: The Knights of Labor and American Politics *Leon Fink*

The Electrical Workers: A History of Labor at General Electric and Westinghouse, 1923–60 *Ronald W. Schatz*

The Mechanics of Baltimore: Workers and Politics in the Age of Revolution, 1763–1812 *Charles G. Steffen*

The Practice of Solidarity: American Hat Finishers in the Nineteenth Century *David Bensman*

The Labor History Reader *Edited by Daniel J. Leab*

Solidarity and Fragmentation: Working People and Class Consciousness in Detroit, 1875–1900 *Richard Oestreicher*

Counter Cultures: Saleswomen, Managers, and Customers in American Department Stores, 1890–1940 *Susan Porter Benson*

The New England Working Class and the New Labor History *Edited by Herbert G. Gutman and Donald H. Bell*

Labor Leaders in America *Edited by Melvyn Dubofsky and Warren Van Tine*

Barons of Labor: The San Francisco Building Trades and Union Power in the Progressive Era *Michael Kazin*

Gender at Work: The Dynamics of Job Segregation by Sex during World War II *Ruth Milkman*

Once a Cigar Maker: Men, Women, and Work Culture in American Cigar Factories, 1900–1919 *Patricia A. Cooper*

A Generation of Boomers: The Pattern of Railroad Labor Conflict in Nineteenth-Century America *Shelton Stromquist*

Work and Community in the Jungle: Chicago's Packinghouse Workers, 1894–1922 *James R. Barrett*

Workers, Managers, and Welfare Capitalism: The Shoeworkers and Tanners of Endicott Johnson, 1890–1950 *Gerald Zahavi*

Men, Women, and Work: Class, Gender, and Protest in the New England Shoe Industry, 1780–1910 *Mary Blewett*

Workers on the Waterfront: Seamen, Longshoremen, and Unionism in the 1930s *Bruce Nelson*

German Workers in Chicago: A Documentary History of Working-Class Culture from 1850 to World War I *Edited by Hartmut Keil and John B. Jentz*

On the Line: Essays in the History of Auto Work *Edited by Nelson Lichtenstein and Stephen Meyer III*

Upheaval in the Quiet Zone: A History of Hospital Workers' Union, Local 1199 *Leon Fink and Brian Greenberg*

Labor's Flaming Youth: Telephone Operators and Worker Militancy, 1878–1923 *Stephen H. Norwood*

Another Civil War: Labor, Capital, and the State in the Anthracite Regions of Pennsylvania, 1840–68 *Grace Palladino*

Coal, Class, and Color: Blacks in Southern West Virginia, 1915–32 *Joe William Trotter, Jr.*

For Democracy, Workers, and God: Labor Song-Poems and Labor Protest, 1865–95 *Clark D. Halker*

Dishing It Out: Waitresses and Their Unions in the Twentieth Century *Dorothy Sue Cobble*

The Spirit of 1848: German Immigrants, Labor Conflict, and the Coming of the Civil War *Bruce Levine*

Working Women of Collar City: Gender, Class, and Community in Troy, New York, 1864–86 *Carole Turbin*

Southern Labor and Black Civil Rights: Organizing Memphis Workers *Michael K. Honey*

Radicals of the Worst Sort: Laboring Women in Lawrence, Massachusetts, 1860–1912 *Ardis Cameron*

Producers, Proletarians, and Politicians: Workers and Party Politics in Evansville and New Albany, Indiana, 1850–87 *Lawrence M. Lipin*

The New Left and Labor in the 1960s *Peter B. Levy*

The Making of Western Labor Radicalism: Denver's Organized Workers, 1878–1905 *David Brundage*

In Search of the Working Class: Essays in American Labor History and Political Culture *Leon Fink*

Lawyers against Labor: From Individual Rights to Corporate Liberalism *Daniel R. Ernst*

"We Are All Leaders": The Alternative Unionism of the Early 1930s *Edited by Staughton Lynd*

The Female Economy: The Millinery and Dressmaking Trades, 1860–1930 *Wendy Gamber*

"Negro and White, Unite and Fight!": A Social History of Industrial Unionism in Meatpacking, 1930–90 *Roger Horowitz*

Power at Odds: The 1922 National Railroad Shopmen's Strike *Colin J. Davis*

The Common Ground of Womanhood: Class, Gender, and Working Girls' Clubs, 1884–1928 *Priscilla Murolo*

Marching Together: Women of the Brotherhood of Sleeping Car Porters *Melinda Chateauvert*

Down on the Killing Floor: Black and White Workers in Chicago's Packinghouses, 1904–54 *Rick Halpern*

Labor and Urban Politics: Class Conflict and the Origins of Modern Liberalism in Chicago, 1864–97 *Richard Schneirov*

All That Glitters: Class, Conflict, and Community in Cripple Creek *Elizabeth Jameson*

Waterfront Workers: New Perspectives on Race and Class *Edited by Calvin Winslow*

Labor Histories: Class, Politics, and the Working-Class Experience *Edited by Eric Arnesen, Julie Greene, and Bruce Laurie*

The Pullman Strike and the Crisis of the 1890s: Essays on Labor and Politics *Edited by Richard Schneirov, Shelton Stromquist, and Nick Salvatore*

AlabamaNorth: African-American Migrants, Community, and Working-Class Activism in Cleveland, 1914–45 *Kimberley L. Phillips*

Imagining Internationalism in American and British Labor, 1939–49 *Victor Silverman*

Typeset in 10.5/13 Adobe Garamond
with Futura Extra Bold display
Designed by Dennis Roberts
Composed by Jim Proefrock
at the University of Illinois Press
Manufactured by Versa Press, Inc.

University of Illinois Press
1325 South Oak Street
Champaign, IL 61820-6903
www.press.uillinois.edu